Paper Diver

Paper Diver

*How the World's Greatest
Underwater Treasure Hunter
Never Got Wet*

Gary L. Pinkerton

McFarland & Company, Inc., Publishers
Jefferson, North Carolina

Library of Congress Cataloging-in-Publication Data

Names: Pinkerton, Gary L., 1954– author.
Title: Paper diver : how the world's greatest underwater treasure hunter never got wet / Gary L. Pinkerton.
Description: Jefferson, North Carolina : McFarland & Company, Inc., Publishers, 2024 | Includes bibliographical references and index.
Identifiers: LCCN 2024012794 | ISBN 9781476694023 (paperback : acid free paper) ∞
ISBN 9781476652160 (ebook)
Subjects: LCSH: Rieseberg, Harry E. (Harry Earl) | Impostors and imposture—United States—Biography. | Treasure hunting. | Underwater exploration.
Classification: LCC HV6759 .P65 2024 | DDC 364.16/33092 [B]—dc23/eng/20240529
LC record available at https://lccn.loc.gov/2024012794

British Library cataloguing data are available

ISBN (print) 978-1-4766-9402-3
ISBN (ebook) 978-1-4766-5216-0

© 2024 Gary L. Pinkerton. All rights reserved

No part of this book may be reproduced or transmitted in any form or by any means, electronic or mechanical, including photocopying or recording, or by any information storage and retrieval system, without permission in writing from the publisher.

Front cover images: the back of a Mark V helmet (Mary Ryan, Naval Undersea Museum); man with fingers crossed © Andy Gin/Shutterstock.

Printed in the United States of America

*McFarland & Company, Inc., Publishers
Box 611, Jefferson, North Carolina 28640
www.mcfarlandpub.com*

*... the best liar is he who makes the
smallest amount of lying go the longest way.*
—*Samuel Butler*

Acknowledgments

In writing histories, I have always believed that the title of a book will ooze its way to the surface somewhere along the way, and that happened with this work as it neared completion. In his 1986 book *Les Chasseurs de Trésors du Gulf Stream (The Gulf Stream Treasure Hunters)*, the French author Jean-Yves Blot referred to Harry Rieseberg as a *scaphandrier de papier*—the paper diver. It is an ideal expression to describe a man who claimed to have made perilous dives in hard hat diving gear and inside a mechanical "diving robot" but who did so only on the pages of his books.

The list of people and places important to the research and completion of the book is gloriously lengthy. I continue to be amazed by the wealth of material. Major primary sources are listed in the Bibliographic Headnotes. I am humbled by the support for this effort by archivists across the country and from supportive colleagues in France and Québec. The advice and encouragement of my Canadian friend, Charles Daigneault, a true Renaissance man, has been brilliant and enthusiastic. Al Mikalow, the diver I met in Arizona, died shortly after our meeting. I am endlessly grateful for his invitation to visit his remarkable basement full of artifacts and ephemera to learn more about Harry Rieseberg from someone who knew him personally. Marilyn Morgan, the widow of one of Rieseberg's sons, has provided first-hand accounts of her limited time with Rieseberg. She and Mikalow both had in-person experiences to relate.

The tagline on an email stuffed with documents from Gina Bardi, Reference Librarian at the San Francisco Maritime National Historical Park Research Center, said, "History ... is not a re-creation of the past. It's an assessment of the past based on documents provided by people in archives and museums who will answer your letters." I hold up her sentiments and generous assistance as representative of dozens of other contacts I made with archivists worldwide.

As always, my wife, Mickey Hammond, has continued her loving patience, gentle editing, and tolerance for my messy desk.

Table of Contents

Acknowledgments — vi
Preface — 1
Introduction — 3

CHAPTER 1. May 17, 1935 — 5
CHAPTER 2. The Harry Before — 12
CHAPTER 3. The Treasure Game — 48
CHAPTER 4. The Great Fall — 60
CHAPTER 5. The Bottom — 85
CHAPTER 6. The Harry After — 98
CHAPTER 7. The Big Time — 116
CHAPTER 8. Target for the Fire of Rivals — 138
CHAPTER 9. The Business of Being Harry — 158
CHAPTER 10. Movie Time — 176
CHAPTER 11. Paradise — 193

Chapter Notes — 225
Bibliography — 245
Index — 253

Preface

This book started with the death of a giant octopus and my terminal case of curiosity.

While writing a history of Trammel's Trace, a nineteenth-century smuggler's trail into eastern Texas, I encountered a treasure legend that had lingered for 150 years. According to the legend, the pirate Jean Lafitte dumped six wagonloads of silver into Hendricks Lake, a small oxbow lake bordering the trail, to avoid its confiscation by Spanish troops pursuing his plunder. During my research on the legend, I discovered there were serious attempts to dredge, dynamite, and dive the lake in the late 1950s. To guide their efforts, the oil men who financed that project turned to someone considered an expert in the location of hidden treasure—Harry E. Rieseberg.

My search for some background about Rieseberg quickly turned up a story about how he killed a twenty-five-foot-long monster octopus using only a shark knife. At that point, I knew he was someone I wanted to learn more about. I did not realize that my initial curiosity would become a deep dive into the life of an intelligent, narcissistic fraud who sold himself as the world's greatest underwater treasure hunter. From 1935 until he died in 1970, Harry Rieseberg made a living telling first-person stories of undersea adventures that simply were not true. If he had labeled his fantastic tales as fiction, there might not have been any reason to continue this research. He did not, however, and vehemently maintained his stance his entire life.

A reviewer for one of Harry Rieseberg's manuscripts said of him, "Any man who can unselfconsciously refer to himself as the greatest living anything sounds like a good guy to stay away from." Instead, I was drawn deeper into knowing more. If my effort had at some point become a dead end with little more to learn, I probably would have set the project aside. Instead, it was quite the opposite. Every research thread I pulled exposed more of his story and poked more holes in his accounts. The point of no return in my initial curiosity was when my interest changed from wanting to know more about the adventures Harry Rieseberg claimed to have had to a sense of amazement about the person who built a career by pretending they were true for over thirty years.

As a federal employee from the 1920s through 1935, Rieseberg's personnel records revealed multiple investigations and terminations. As a writer, Rieseberg published numerous books and over a thousand articles about his supposed treasure ventures. He also disclosed bits and pieces of his personal life through his fabricated tales, early poetry, and incessant self-promotion. Correspondence with his publishers, agents, and magazine editors revealed his duplicity, bitterness, and rancor. Records from lawsuits shine the light of judicial truth on claims, agreements, and trusts broken by Rieseberg's repeated dishonesty. Time and time again, the facts located through research directly disputed Rieseberg's timeline of treasure ventures, as expressed in his first book, *I Dive for Treasure (1942)*.[1]

Archival documents are the foundation of this work, but personal experiences reinforced the story they told. In developing this work, I visited Maine to learn more about the four-masted schooner he claimed to have used for multiple treasure voyages. I drove across the Mojave Desert from San Diego to Lake Havasu, Arizona, to talk to an eighty-year-old hard hat diver, one of Harry's only trusted friends. With the *Uber* app and a list of addresses, I visited the former homes where Rieseberg and his parents lived in Washington, D.C., to understand his growing-up years.

From a researcher's perspective, the source material for this work has been an embarrassment of riches. The incredible volume of documents, letters, articles, and books has driven my interest in this project. With this work, I hope to interpret the fascinating story of Harry Rieseberg and provide insight into a time when writers like him could thrive in the world of men's magazines, adventure books, and post–Depression popular culture.

Introduction

Four tall masts towered above Harry Rieseberg as he lay on his back on the deck of a magnificent schooner. The mighty timbers tapered off into a blue sky strafed by clouds showing the promise of just enough breeze to put the vessel to sea. The taut, complex rigging that held the ship's heavy canvas sheets was ready to respond to the pop of the sails as they filled with wind. As he imagined heading out to sea, Rieseberg seemed to sense the sway of the deck when offshore swells caught the mighty vessel. Under sail, the ship would heave and then ease as it rode the near-silent surge of power and momentum toward a secret treasure trove that only he knew how to find.

Harry could still feel the bulky stiffness of a heavy canvas diving dress, wet outside from his dive and inside from his sweat after he escaped certain death yet again. Emerging from a dive and removing the heavy, brass diving helmet to breathe natural air again provided a sense of accomplishment and relief. Harry saw the diving robot secure on deck after it picked apart the hull of a rotting sunken galleon with its hydraulic claws. It had been freshly painted and was dripping with seawater. He hoped chests full of gold were safely secured below deck, ready to add to his riches and secure his fame.

Harry's quiet repose was interrupted by a blurry image of men running toward him with desperate looks. Some of them shook Harry and spoke to him in urgent tones. Before he could hear them, he could see them shouting and waving their arms around him. Were they congratulating him on his latest treasure haul?

"Harry, are you all right?"

Were they about to marvel at his escape from the giant octopus that held him in its tentacles as they hauled him on deck?

"Harry, Harry! My god, man, what happened?"

Judging from their excitement, Harry was sure he must have just accomplished some remarkable feat or beaten the odds in finding gold beneath the sea right where his charts said it would be.

"Find a doctor ... quickly."

Hearing the word *doctor* jarred Harry back to semi-consciousness. There were no doctors aboard ships at sea! Did they not realize there was no hospital on the open ocean? The shock of hearing that single word began to clear the heavy fog that clouded his thoughts.

"Harry don't move. We will get you some help very soon."

Help? What help could he possibly need? All he needed was a shot of brandy and a cigar to celebrate whatever impressive feat he must have just accomplished.

Harry Rieseberg began to see familiar faces appear around him and interrupt his moments of bewilderment and self-congratulation. Captain Alvin Loesche, the wizened master of the regal schooner, looked grave but disengaged. The treasure venture's business-savvy agent, Ralph Fleming, seemed somewhat faint and looked thoroughly incompetent in his jodhpurs and high leather boots. Harry wondered if it was a dream when he saw Sir William Phipps, the English sea captain and treasure hunter of the 1600s, who told him to get up and back into the diving gear. In the rigging above, Jean Lafitte shouted long-held secrets of where to find his hidden loot. The non-seafaring side of Harry's world appeared as well. Harry's father stood off to one side shaking his head disapprovingly, while his wife turned her back on him and walked away with their two children in tow.

Harry's hallucinations ended harshly and painfully. The cold compress applied to his forehead started to rouse him from his unconscious delusions, but searing pain finally forced an abrupt exit from his dream world. In May 1935, the most pivotal month of Harry Rieseberg's forty-two-year existence, he slipped and fell on the deck of the schooner *Constellation*. The man trying desperately to become a wealthy, world-renowned expert on underwater treasure badly broke his leg while docked at Water and L Streets in Washington, D.C. It was the day of Harry Rieseberg's Great Fall.

Chapter 1

May 17, 1935

*A couple of words is all it'll take
to make everything in my life Before and After.*
—Karen M. McManus

From the 1930s until he died in 1970, Harry Earl Rieseberg wrote stories about his life as a treasure hunter and expert on the final resting place of sunken ships bearing untold riches. By way of his many books translated into multiple languages, over a thousand newspaper and magazine articles, dozens of radio programs and newsreels, and one Hollywood movie publicity tour, Rieseberg became known as an international expert who had recovered hundreds of thousands of dollars in gold and silver from the bottom of the world's oceans. His tales of adventure enthralled the public and inspired more than a few young men to become divers.

Rieseberg supplied his readers with stories of a life filled with uncommon adventures, beginning with an extraordinary experience as a young man. Rieseberg told his readers how as a seventeen-year-old he accompanied President Theodore Roosevelt on a months-long safari to Africa after TR's presidential term ended. Roosevelt's well-documented stories captured the world's imagination, and his hunting supplied the Smithsonian Institution with thousands of specimens from the African continent. Before his twentieth birthday, Rieseberg's wanderlust carried him across the country from his home in Washington, D.C., to work on cargo ships off the coast of California. He suggested that perhaps adventure ran in the family's veins when he wrote that his father, a German immigrant who joined the U.S. Army, was once part of William "Buffalo Bill" Cody's Wild West shows.

During World War I, Harry's résumé showed him managing three hundred people in the War Risk Insurance Bureau, a precursor to the Veterans Administration. He was instrumental in using the Hollerith Tabulating Machine for a national emergency food survey during the war. Hollerith's company became the International Business Machines Corporation or IBM, and Harry was one of the earliest governmental experts in that technology.

While working for the Bureau of Navigation, a federal agency responsible for documenting all seagoing vessels, Harry developed an interest in the location of shipwrecks that could contain vast wealth. Purser's vaults filled with payroll and the jewels of passengers lost at sea were as much a part of his attention as Spanish galleons bearing golden plunder. He had access to historical archives, detailed ships' logs, and ancient maps through his job. After learning to be a hard-hat diver in the Potomac River, he described how a giant twenty-five-foot-long octopus attacked him on his first treasure dive. Harry barely managed to survive by cutting its sucker-covered tentacles off with his shark knife. Rieseberg boasted he was the only living person to see the sunken *Plata Flota* fleet at Silver Shoals and to walk among the coral-encrusted ruins of Port Royal, the Jamaican pirate port that sank beneath the waves following an earthquake and tsunami.

Harry Earl Rieseberg (*New York Journal American* Collection, Photographic Morgue; Harry Ransom Center, University of Texas at Austin).

In his diving robot, a steel sphere with nine-foot mechanical arms, Harry Rieseberg accidentally broke a record when the cable slowly lowering him toward a wreck spooled out to a depth of 1,404 feet, far deeper than any such vessel had been before. While undersea in the robot on one venture and accompanied by another man in a diving bell, Rieseberg filmed a giant octopus attacking the bell. He described how he freed the trapped man using his diving robot's crab-like pincers to cut the tentacles off the most enormous octopus ever filmed.

Disaster struck on a later voyage despite Rieseberg's uncanny ability to escape certain death time and time again. His ship was tossed on violent waves during a storm, and he was pitched down an open hatchway. Both legs were shattered, and he was unconscious at sea for hours. Even that physical limitation did not deter Harry from a life of adventure. He continued treasure-hunting expeditions aboard his four-masted schooner, *Carlotta*. He descended the depths to numerous wrecks in the undersea robot and found chests filled with gold coins guarded by the skeletons of long-dead sailors. Due to his careful research and mapping, Rieseberg often anchored directly over wrecks on the first diving attempt.

During World War II, Rieseberg patented "giant tongs" that could lift an ancient ship or a submerged submarine to the surface. Another invention, an underwater vehicle built like a military tank, could drive to wrecks along the bottom of the ocean and use one of its five cranes and mechanical arms to remove any treasure. After the war, Harry went on to film an underwater fight between a shark and an octopus, battle cobras and boa constrictors on an island in the Caribbean and survive another storm at sea that took the lives of his four native crewmen.

Rieseberg carried $60,000 in gold bars from city to city when touring the country in 1953 to promote a movie based on his expedition to the sunken city of Port Royal. He explained to the press that he did not need to sell the gold bars because he had made enough money on his books, articles, and other ventures. In his publicity tour for the movie, Rieseberg did 169 radio broadcasts, 74 television appearances, and 80 press conferences across 136 cities in only six weeks.

Harry Rieseberg told thousands of readers tales of a remarkable life for forty years through his books and articles.

If only they were true.

One would think learning that Harry Rieseberg's seafaring tales of adventure were not true would detract from the stories this book will tell. In truth, Rieseberg published more than two dozen poems about his early years in Arizona. He once led a large parade through the streets of Washington, D.C., dressed in cowboy regalia. Members of Congress, Senators, and a future Vice-President wrote letters of support to his federal employers. On the same Sunday in 1934, Harry published two full-page articles in the *Los Angeles Times* and the *Washington Post*. He was the technical adviser on a movie based on one of his stories, *City Beneath the Sea*, starring Anthony Quinn and Robert Ryan. The famous director, Cecil B. DeMille, briefly discussed getting Harry's help with a treasure expedition near Galveston, Texas. His public persona as Lieutenant Harry E. Rieseberg, international underwater salvage expert, did not begin coalescing until the mid–1930s after eighteen months in a Texas hospital to heal his broken leg. The Harry After emerged from the life he had led before.

Harry's truths include two failed marriages, federal investigations, dismissals from jobs with the government, and his leadership in a large chapter of the Ku Klux Klan. His story is of a complex man who could write romantic poems about places of beauty as easily as rancorous memos to his publisher and deliver speeches about the separation of the races.

The story of Harry Rieseberg reflects a time when war and the Great Depression led men to think about ways to strike it rich. Harry was confident he had found a way to do just that with his detailed research on shipwrecks. He never stopped promoting himself and his ideas to attract publicity and financiers. Though many curious people sought his knowledge and expertise, any who knew enough to ask the right questions quickly learned that Harry's claims were false fronts. Like the storefront sets for a movie western, his tales of adventures were facades behind which nothing of substance could be found.

Regardless of his fabrications, financial setbacks, obstacles, or accomplishments, Harry Rieseberg never once relented from the narrative he created for himself or the public persona he so actively promoted for forty years. Whether it was tenacity, stubbornness, financial necessity, or ego—or simply because he did not know what else to do—Harry Rieseberg held his secrets closely.

The Harry Before and the Harry After

May 17, 1935, was a Friday in Washington, D.C. The winds on Chesapeake Bay were moderate and northerly at eight to twelve miles per hour. The sky was cloudy, but there was no chance of rain, with temperatures near sixty degrees for the entire day. It was also the day that Harry Earl Rieseberg's life completely changed. It was the day of Harry's Great Fall.

Rarely does a single day in one's life become such a well-defined pivot point. However, for Harry Rieseberg, that day was his defining moment. It was the day that divided his life into the Harry Before and the Harry After. The Harry Before was a practiced writer who could stretch the truth in words and deeds. The Harry After used those traits to try and convince the public that he was the world's greatest underwater treasure hunter. To understand what happened on May 17, 1935, is to understand how he perpetuated his life-long effort to embellish and obscure the truth.

Big plans for that day originated in the ambitious mind of Harry Rieseberg. For years he had considered how to turn his research about vessels lost at sea into something that might make him rich. Rieseberg had been Chief of the Tonnage Division of the Bureau of Navigation, part of the Commerce Department. His role in the Bureau of Navigation was essentially tabulation—to track data about all registered merchant vessels. Harry and his workgroup, primarily female, tallied and tabulated the construction, naming, and sale of commercial boats and ships, capturing pertinent data, including size, gross weight, and tonnage. A straightforward sentence in Harry's job description defined his way forward. Harry Rieseberg was chief of the division responsible for "the care and custody of all original vessel documents for historical purposes and searching thereof." He had access to a vast archive of information and history about American ships. That archive, Harry realized some years later, included records about their cargo and their loss due to sinking. Harry's work group also documented a ship's demise.

It took a while, but Harry finally had an epiphany—he was the overseer for records documenting incredible wealth lost at the bottom of the sea. Using his writing skills and data he gathered through the Bureau of Navigation, Rieseberg promoted himself as an expert on the location and cargo of sunken vessels. Initially, he did so while never suggesting he was an accomplished diver. Harry took the initiative and looked for potential investors in a venture sparked by his charts, maps, and tables. He knew it would take more than that.

Rieseberg actively looked for ways to dive to the bottom of the ocean. The Patent Office was near the Bureau of Navigation in the Department of Commerce office building. In 1933, that was where Rieseberg first laid eyes on patent number 2,040,956. The schematics beautifully detailed a spherical diving bell with long, hydraulic arms and pincer-like grapples. Rieseberg said he recognized immediately that this was precisely what he had been trying to find—a way to recover treasure at greater depths than a diver could explore. Eugene Romano, the inventor, and Ralph Fleming, his son-in-law and business manager, demonstrated their "diving robot" in Seattle for the U.S. Navy, hoping to get a contract to provide them with a new tool for deep-sea rescues and salvage.

In late September 1934, another piece of Harry's treasure puzzle fell into place when the four-masted schooner *Constellation* sailed up the Potomac and anchored off Hains Point at the mouth of the Anacostia River. The ship's owner, Robert Royall, hoped to keep the ship and his dreams alive.[1] Royall was only twenty-nine years old but was pursuing a vision held by older seamen—to restore and operate a classic, wooden sailing vessel and to keep the sailing era alive. His ideas to turn that dream into a profitable venture were varied—a base for scientific pursuit, a club yacht, or a sailing school. His latest business idea for keeping the *Constellation* afloat was why he came to Washington—to open the vessel as a dockside restaurant and entertainment venue. Both sailors and cooks manned the vessel; both the sails and the tablecloths were white.

Harry Rieseberg claimed he was the impetus for bringing the Romano diving bell to Washington. He even said that he paid for the cross-country rail transport, but that is doubtful due to the expense and Harry's financial means. Ralph Fleming, the only real businessman among the partners, recognized he had a unique opportunity to show off the Romano robot on the deck of a magnificent ship amid his

The schooner *Constellation*, 1933 (courtesy Boothbay Harbor [ME] Historical Society).

Ralph Fleming, inside the Romano diving bell, shaking hands with Harry E. Rieseberg, at the Washington demonstration aboard the *Constellation*; May 11, 1935 (courtesy Rockwell Hammond, Jr., Romano Scrapbook).

would-be customers in the military. Eugene Romano died before the event, so Fleming and the vessel traveled by train from Seattle, Washington, to Washington, D.C. A struggling Robert Royall was more than happy to have his beloved *Constellation* be the platform for the demonstration. There is nothing in the record to help understand how Harry Rieseberg, Eugene Romano, Ralph Fleming, and Robert Royall cooperated to make their joint plans in early 1935. Still, Harry Rieseberg's passion, charm, and salesmanship were undoubtedly at work. With Harry's charts tempting any adventurous investor, a dramatic ship in which to go to sea, and a mechanical marvel in which to seek treasure at great depths, it seemed they had everything they needed—everything but money.

Rieseberg and his partners were ready for the biggest publicity event they could have imagined. In an engraved invitation, in a font almost too elegant to read, they extended a welcome to dignitaries and prospects in Washington and New York.

The Romano Submarine Engineering
and Salvage Corporation
takes pleasure in extending to you
an invitation to attend the
Initial Presentation to Official Washington
of the Romano Deep Sea Diving Sphere
on board the Ship Constellation.

Chapter 1. May 17, 1935

Water Street at L, S.W.
Friday, May 17th, 1935, 2 P.M.

American and foreign newsreel companies filmed the diving robot's claws clacking and arms moving, followed by a brief dunking off the side of the *Constellation*. One of the newsreels showed the diving bell emerging with a wriggling fish held in its pincers. Reporters gave away the secret that the newsreels cooperatively ignored. One of the promoters rowed out to the sphere suspended just out of the water and held up a fish for the operator to grab. The diving robot submerged, and the rowboat scooted out of view so the newsreels could get the dramatic shot of a mechanical claw holding the fish as if snagged while it swam by.[2]

In addition to the demonstration of the Romano diving bell, there was a parallel effort by Rieseberg and Fleming to raise money for a treasure expedition using Rieseberg's maps. When Harry Rieseberg slipped on the deck of the *Constellation* and broke his leg, his involvement in any venture ended. It did not end just because he was physically unable but because Rieseberg had made it clear that if he did not go on the treasure expedition, neither would his carefully protected maps.

The Harry Before thought he had a clear vision of his future. He would raise money from wealthy people who wanted to ride along for a month while he tried to use his maps and data to find treasure. Legitimate divers would go down to the bottom to retrieve it, and Harry would get his cut. The smiling Harry Rieseberg in the publicity photos was thinking about all those possibilities. His smile for the cameras belied that he had lost his job and his wife had given up on his crazy dreams and walked out. He did not know he was about to lose two years of his life to recover from a broken leg.

The Great Fall changed everything for Harry Rieseberg. To understand how The Harry After emerged from that desperate moment, it is necessary to understand The Harry Before.

Chapter 2

The Harry Before

*Lies are a little fortress;
inside them, you can feel safe and powerful.*
—William Paul Young

Harry Rieseberg's name is not one that many will recognize today. During the 1930s through the 1960s, however, he was widely touted as an international expert on the location of sunken riches. An imaginary persona he had been promoting since 1937 became codified in 1942 in his first book, *I Dive for Treasure.* His unrelenting efforts to promote his myth were so convincing that the obituary for his oldest son, Robert, identified Harry as a Navy Commander and "one of the Navy's first hard helmet deep sea divers."[1] Neither of these declarations was true. Robert W. Rieseberg was himself a Naval Captain who had a distinguished and exemplary career in the service during World War II. The son who never knew his father wanted to believe he was who he pretended to be. The power of repetition to change perceptions is indeed strong.

Through many printings of *I Dive for Treasure* in multiple languages, Rieseberg created and sustained an image as the world's greatest underwater treasure hunter, a title he assigned himself. Although he began promoting himself as an expert with knowledge of sunken ships as early as the mid–1920s, it was not until his writing career took off that he pretended to have been a diver. He spent forty years defending and extending those claims.

The man sprawled in pain on the deck of the *Constellation* that fateful day in May 1935 was a complex amalgamation of early life experiences, psychological complications, and passionate determination. He was a product of his upbringing as an only child with a tendency toward self-promotion and narcissism. He was charming, intelligent, and gifted with the ability and desire to communicate through the written word. He was also intent on becoming known as the source of information about where to find treasure beneath the world's oceans.

What can be known about Harry Rieseberg comes from four different categories of sources: contemporaneous records and newspaper articles; known events and the facts surrounding them; what others said about him; and what he said about himself. Any biographer will salivate when presented with primary sources to

Chapter 2. The Harry Before

document their subject's life. That has been the case with this project using a wide range of sources. When the subject's own words can be counter-balanced by independent facts, researchers can brush away the layers of deceptions that hide the patina of truth.

As a federal employee between 1909 and 1935, Rieseberg's employment records are preserved by the National Archives. Within those files are letters of recommendation, transfers, frequent disciplinary actions, and multiple investigations. Their chronological history is a dispassionate refutation of what Rieseberg claimed he was doing during those years. When dates from his employment records are matched against his claims of hunting for treasure in the Caribbean, Rieseberg's stories are exposed for their inattention to reality.

By the time Rieseberg was twenty-six years old, his employment records included theft from a venerable scientific institution, abandonment of a position after one week due to homesickness, dismissal due to poor attendance, and a full-blown federal investigation into false statements he made about a supervisor. Harry Rieseberg had an inauspicious start to his young adulthood.

Additional archival sources inspire a more comprehensive chronology of his life than the one he presented about himself. His letters to his agent and his publishers reveal much about his personality. Small slices of his life are found among seemingly insignificant newspaper articles. In the newspapers, we learn the names of the police officers who came to his door to arrest him for stealing a book from the Smithsonian and about a going-away party before he left to work at an Indian school in Oklahoma.

In 1935, when Rieseberg sought to raise money for a treasure expedition aboard the schooner *Constellation*, his name was not well known beyond Washington, D.C. Even within the capital city, he was primarily known for his avid participation in several fraternal organizations. In his elected positions in charge of publicity, he used his writing skills to present the organizations in a way that almost always included a few lines of self-promotion. The stories he told about himself after a significant event in May 1935 had an initial, broad outlet in *I Dive for Treasure* and his subsequent books and articles. Rieseberg's recipe for success as a treasure writer was to mix a largely factual story about lost wealth with a liberal helping of himself at the center of an effort to find it. He would then season the work with a healthy portion of outright bullshit. Without the ability of the readers of his day to easily confirm any of the facts of his stories, his concoction would satisfy the cravings of a populist audience. His stories of adventure lured one's imagination; his descriptions of himself as the centerpiece of those expeditions left his fabrications open to scrutiny.

Harry Rieseberg was no simple man. His intelligence was exceeded only by his self-centeredness. He made a living occupying the space between presumed expert and outright liar. To understand how that came to pass, it is important to understand aspects of his early life, the times during which he came of age, and the origins of the tales he spun about himself. His exaggerations were not confined to treasure tales, however. His stories about his younger years also failed to match the facts.

An Immigrant's Son

The myth-building effort Rieseberg undertook with *I Dive for Treasure* not only embellished his bio with imaginary events but also included exaggerated stories about his father, Henry. The eighteen-year-old Henry Robert Rieseberg, Heinrich in his native Germany, left his home in Goslar in June of 1881 and emigrated with two other young men to the United States. Not long after he arrived, Henry became a leather worker in Kansas City between 1881 and 1886.[2] He enlisted in the U.S. Army five years after arriving in the United States and was assigned to Troop C of the 5th Cavalry stationed at Fort Reno. Fort Reno was a somewhat neglected outpost in Indian Territory (Oklahoma).[3]

Skilled prevaricators use a common method: sprinkle half-truths and outright lies with the occasional speck of reality to pull people into the stories you want them to believe. In the context of setting the stage for his exploits, Harry tried to make a case for having adventurous genes with claims about his father. Rieseberg claimed his father engaged with tribes who might begin an attack at any time and that Henry was a sharpshooter who appeared in Buffalo Bill's wild west shows. Neither of those other claims was true.[4]

William F. Cody, later known as Buffalo Bill, scouted for the 5th Cavalry almost twenty years before Henry's enlistment. While Henry was in the Army between 1886 and 1891, Buffalo Bill's Wild West Show was in its prime, and Cody had been on tours to Europe at least twice by 1892. By the time Henry arrived in Indian Territory, the period of Indian wars had subsided mainly, and any hostilities were primarily between tribal groups. The military's primary role was to keep out the "boomers"—whites who moved illegally into Indian land to try to claim a share of the more than 40,000 square miles of unimproved land.

In 1891, Henry Rieseberg was honorably discharged five years to the day after his enlistment. Unable to leave even the most insignificant fact unmolested, Rieseberg expanded that to eight years.[5]

A Marriage, a Move, and a Son

At the end of his stint with the 5th Cavalry, Henry moved back to Kansas, where he married and became a U.S. citizen.[6] Henry's wife, Jennie Martin, was four years younger and grew up in Leavenworth, a city that would continue as part of the family's connections. Within a year after their marriage, the Riesebergs moved to Washington, D.C., where the Government Printing Office hired Henry as a helper in July 1892.[7] It was in Washington that their only son, Harry Earl Rieseberg, was born on September 27, 1892.

Chapter 2. The Harry Before

His parents were getting settled in Washington at a station in life where hard work and a government job meant something. His father kept that job for almost forty years, minus one furlough. There was no wage law at the time, no overtime pay requirement, so he scratched and scraped the best he could on wages of about twenty-five cents an hour.[8] Though hard work paid off, a little help from someone higher up never hurt. Another of Harry's claims about his father was that he was friends with Charles Curtis. Curtis was of American Indian descent and was later elected a U.S. Senator and Vice-President of the United States. The yarn Rieseberg wove was that Curtis was a hack driver in Leavenworth and would drive the courting couple around in a buggy.

Curtis spent part of his life working part-time as a hack driver as early as elementary school and later while attending law school. However, only six months after Henry Rieseberg arrived in the United States in 1881, a twenty-one-year-old Charles Curtis was already admitted to the bar from Topeka.[9] Curtis inherited a significant estate from his grandfather at age eighteen, so he was unlikely to have been taxiing Henry Rieseberg and Jennie Martin around the countryside.

The embellishment of his father's life history was not intended to benefit his father but to paint Harry as just another adventurer in the family. Rieseberg wanted his readers to believe that danger was in his DNA and that his affinity for a daring life was simply an extension of his father's examples. What was clear, however, in the other accounts and facts of Henry Rieseberg's life was that he was an honorable man well respected by others—a trait that his son, Harry, never seemed to acquire.

A Young Adventurer

As a youth, Harry Rieseberg stood out in many ways. His father was tallish for the time at 5 feet 10 inches, and Harry was over 6 feet tall by the time he was eighteen. His blue eyes and sharp features made a striking impression. Rieseberg said he was interested in baseball and football as a youth but was more bookish than he admitted. He stood out in his writing skills, even from a young age. Harry's educational history was perhaps typical of the time. He attended grammar school for eight years and then spent time at Washington Business High School, the Spencerian Business College, the Stenographic Academy, and the Columbian Correspondence College, honing his administrative talents. Growing up to work a desk job would be considered progress in his family, and being a supervisor or manager would be a source of pride for his immigrant father.

A First Job at the Smithsonian Institution

Harry's curiosity and ability to delve deeply into a subject showed itself early. He had a keen interest in birds, tracking their migration patterns through

Washington, and that hobby led to a part-time job with the Smithsonian's National Museum. He started work as a messenger on May 17, 1909, making thirty dollars a month.[10]

Another of Harry's interests was stamp collecting, and his enthusiasm for that hobby led to disciplinary action in December 1909. Harry used official Smithsonian Institution stationery to request some stamps be sent to him on approval. When the stamp company sent his manager at the Smithsonian a letter asking for a reference, they learned of Harry's misuse of the official stationery. Harry was required to write a letter explaining his misdeed to the library director and send a copy to his mother. Harry did not admit to using the museum's stationery in his typed statement, and his manager noted that omission. Not admitting any fault was an early trait of Harry's personality.[11]

Harry E. Rieseberg at age 18, c.1910. Smithsonian "Quarter Units" in the background (courtesy Marilyn Morgan).

A few months later, in August 1910, Harry's restlessness led him to apply for an appointment in the Consular Service, proceeding as far as getting a medical exam. Letters from two elected officials made their way into his file, recommending in one case "my friend, Harris [sic] Rieseberg."[12] Again, his father's Kansas roots were brought to bear with Congressman Charles F. Scott and Senator Charles Curtis writing the usual political requests for consideration for a constituent. In an apparent effort to make himself more Kansan, Harry sent a letter to the county judge in March 1909 asking to declare Leavenworth his legal residence. It was such an odd occurrence that the local newspaper called it a "strange request."[13] That job opportunity, nor the declaration, never materialized.

After almost two years as a messenger, Harry was promoted in February 1911 to a position as a Cataloguer in the Museum of Natural Science, reporting to the curator, Gerrit S. Miller. He would later describe his job as "one of an acrid nature," working in a shed behind the Smithsonian building, boiling the flesh from specimens of birds and animals to mount their skeletons.[14]

Harry to the West Coast

Knowing the background story for a particular milestone in young Harry's life would be interesting. In the summer of 1911, Harry took leave from the Smithsonian for a six-week-long trip to the West Coast. Society columns in two different newspapers called attention to the comings and goings of Washingtonians and mentioned young Harry's trip. The *Washington Post* reported on August 6, 1911, that Harry returned from a six-week trip.[15] The *Washington Sunday Star* provided additional details: "Harry E. Rieseberg of the National Museum has returned after a six-week trip to the Pacific coast, where he visited relatives in Los Angeles, San Francisco, and other cities."[16] What is interesting about this version of the notice is the much different narrative about this trip that Harry created when he published his first book. He began telling the tale differently as early as 1937.[17]

According to Harry, he set out on his own and headed for San Francisco. He was confident he would find a job quickly but became desperate and hungry when he did not. He rented a room on Market Street but ran out of money after only two weeks. A restaurant owner Rieseberg called "Greek George" fed him in kindness and sent him down to the docks to find work.[18] Harry presented himself to the hardened dock hands in his starched white collar, perhaps much like the one in his photo at the Smithsonian, looking for a job amongst the hardened stevedores and ship's crews. Harry said he was ultimately hired and made trips up and down the coast as an able-bodied seaman on the shipping vessel *Roanoke* with Captain Dorpen and later aboard *Admiral Farragut*.[19]

There are more than a few questions about the facts of his story. Harry said he worked the ships for six months when the newspaper articles both reported his entire trip was only six weeks. Given a week to travel each way, that would have left little time for shipping out while visiting his mother's relatives in Los Angeles and San Francisco. Regardless of the veracity of his claim, Harry used this as a pivotal event in explaining his interest and reported skills in going to sea. He would have only had time for a couple of boat rides.[20]

An item that adds intrigue to questions about what Harry did in the summer of 1911 comes from a return visit to San Francisco in 1937. The newspaper article noting Harry's visit to plan a treasure expedition said he wanted "to try and find the cheap waterfront joint where the proprietor took him in and fed him and found him a job on a sailing ship."[21] That this story appears five years before the publication of *I Dive for Treasure* may support some version of Harry's events.

One cannot help but wonder what his father's role was in either pushing his bookish son to leave the nest or simply supporting Harry's decision to do so on his own. His father had left his home in Germany at age eighteen to cross the Atlantic

Ocean, so he might have been predisposed to imagine that such a passage into adulthood was necessary.

Harry Rieseberg and Teddy Roosevelt

Harry Rieseberg went to great lengths to have us believe he had a minor role in a major story of the time. He wanted readers to think that he sailed out of New York in 1909, bound for an African safari at the personal invitation of a man whose likeness is carved into Mount Rushmore—Theodore Roosevelt. Before Roosevelt's term ended in January 1909, he planned a year-long hunting expedition in British East Africa. Early in the planning process, Roosevelt communicated with the Secretary of the Smithsonian, Charles D. Wolcott, about a significant role for the institution and having the Museum of Natural History receive and catalog the many specimens collected during a hunting trip expected to last over a year.

Harry wrote in *I Dive for Treasure* that he "was seventeen years old when we sailed from New York on the liner *Hamburg* on March 23, 1909."[22] Harry's story in *I Dive* takes on an even more dramatic tone through Rieseberg's assertion that Roosevelt sent a letter to Dr. Edmond Heller at the Smithsonian, specifically requesting that Harry go along on the trip to Africa.

> *My dear Doctor: I understand there's a young chap by the name of Harry Rieseberg working with you. I talked with him some months back and have an idea he might be a helpful assistant to you on the expedition.*
>
> *Yours, Theodore Roosevelt*[23]

Harry's tale of meeting President Roosevelt and accompanying him on his hunting expedition to British East Africa is just one example of how Rieseberg could deliver an engaging and exciting story where the facts were difficult to separate from the fiction. Simple facts help dismiss this claim rather quickly. The first is that Harry never mentioned the safari on any job application, and it never came up in letters from elected officials. There is no corroboration that Harry was a young celebrity in an event reported in detail for months. A news item mentioned that Harry went to California for six weeks to visit relatives, but there was no mention of him going to Africa. To omit the most incredible reference imaginable for a young boy from the newspapers or to fail to mention it on his many job applications would not have been an opportunity Rieseberg missed.

The second and much simpler fact is that Harry Rieseberg did not start work at the Smithsonian's National Museum until May 17, 1909. The Roosevelt expedition arrived in Mombasa by ship on April 21, 1909. He could not have been in Africa at the time. He was starting his first real job. The Smithsonian East Africa Expedition amassed a collection of 23,151 natural history specimens, and it took eight years to catalog all the material. Harry's only encounter with the expedition would have been to process the specimens by boiling bones in the shed behind the museum.

Harry Rieseberg could grow a seed of truth into a tree of deception. The reasons why he would attempt to stretch the truth so far remain intriguing and inaccessible. Since Harry did not publicly make this claim until *I Dive for Treasure* was published in 1942, perhaps the passage of time left a factual void he could fill to create an aura of legitimacy.

Harry at an Indian School … Briefly

In December 1910, while still at the Smithsonian, Harry looked into a transfer to the Bureau of Indian Affairs. His letter mentioned his interest in working for Indian reservations in Washington, Idaho, Montana, North Dakota, or Wyoming.[24] Young Harry seemed ready to start his own life of adventure, and what better method than to work in the Indian Territory as his father had done. Despite more letters of support from Kansas politicians, a job did not open.[25]

A year later, he renewed his effort. This time, there was an actual opening, but not in the Pacific Northwest as he had initially requested. The vacancy was near his father's old post, Fort Reno, at the Sac and Fox tribal school near Stroud, Oklahoma.[26] The letter notifying him of the transfer provided directions to the reservation to begin his service as an assistant commissary clerk working for sixty dollars a month.[27]

Harry worked as Messenger Boy and Cataloguer at the Smithsonian for almost three years. He was home every day for a dinner prepared by his mother and slept in his own bed. His one experience away from home was to head west for six weeks to visit relatives. Now Harry was nineteen years old and leaving home for an unknown period. There must have been a range of emotions stirring within Harry and his parents about this relocation. We can only imagine the look on his face on the train to Oklahoma as he arrived on May 11, 1912. He was probably as uncomfortable as the suit he was wearing.

It did not take Harry long to be overcome by the reality of his assignment in Oklahoma. Harry abandoned his position to return home five days after his arrival, stating he was "not at present in condition to stand the climate of this locality." In communication with the Commissioner of Indian Affairs, the school's superintendent provided additional details. "Mr. Rieseberg was not at all well during the short time he was here and in addition to his illness he had a very severe case of homesickness."[28] A telegram to the superintendent expressed some urgency in his father's concern for his son. Harry had already left the reservation by the time the wire arrived, but the superintendent calmly replied, "Rieseberg started for home last night … was to wire … no anxiety necessary." The tone of the telegram seems to indicate that the superintendent thought Harry's issues were being overly dramatized and that his father was overreacting.[29]

Despite Harry's early departure, the Bureau of Indian Affairs was not inclined to let him leave behind his assigned position. In multiple letters from the school, the Bureau was demanding he return to duty as soon as he was physically able. Four months after his departure and abuse of the granted leave, Harry asked for an extension of leave through October 5. The request was not for his health but because Harry did his best to avoid returning to Oklahoma by applying for a job with the U.S. Postal Savings Banks in Washington, D.C.[30]

Harry's predilection for stretching the facts started early. In a letter of August 24, 1912, applying for the position, Harry told the Director of the Postal Savings Banks that during his service to the Sac and Fox Indian Agency, he was "taken ill with malaria (and) was advised to return to Washington, D.C." His three years at the Smithsonian had also magically increased to "nearly four."[31] Harry finally resigned from the Bureau of Indian Affairs, ending his brief adventure in Indian Territory.

The Case of the Stolen Egg Book

Besides being unemployed, the twenty-year-old Harry Rieseberg was also in trouble with the law. In mid–October 1912, the Smithsonian Museum staff discovered two rare books were missing from the archives. They were a bound collection of 1875 issues of *The Oologist*, a serial much in demand due to being out of print for some time. Oology is the study of bird eggs, nests, and how birds breed. Their internal investigation led them to contact individuals who had written to the museum asking about copies to see if the books may have been offered to them for sale. An oologist named R. Magoon Barnes had indeed bought both books from young Harry Rieseberg, who had stolen them six months earlier.[32]

Ten days after discovering that the books were missing, Detectives Weedon and Fortney arrested Harry at his home on the evening of October 25, 1912. Luckily for Harry, the Assistant United States Attorney working the larceny case and the National Museum decided not to prosecute since the books were returned. An issue of *The Oologist* contemporaneous to the event bemoaned the fact that "a young man in the morning of life will blight his future."[33]

An action Harry took only two months after his arrest indicates his lack of remorse or guilt. Whether it was purely the request of a naïve, ambitious young man or an act of disregard for his situation, in December 1912, Harry wrote the Secretary of the Smithsonian Institution asking for a "statement of his services" (a reference letter) for his time at the National Museum. The Secretary knew about Harry's theft and added a handwritten note to Harry's letter when he passed it on to the person who would craft the reply. His caution was to remind the typist that Harry "was arrested for stealing a book after he left, so all we can say is that he exited the service on a certain date and left it voluntarily."[34] The pattern of Harry escaping the consequences of his transgressions would last his entire lifetime.

Maybe the Private Sector

After two stints with government agencies, Rieseberg had worked only a week at one position and stolen valuable property at the other. Harry's father knew that

Harry could ruin his chances of a career if that track record continued, so he tried employment in the private sector instead. On March 10, 1913, he went to work for Southern Railway Company in D.C. as an extra clerk. In short order, Harry was fired there as well after three months of poor attendance and barely average performance.[35] Harry Rieseberg was immature, self-centered, and unemployed. He needed a drastic change of scenery.

The Wandering Son

Writing later in life about how he became interested in treasure hunting, Rieseberg described "years of varied jobs and false starts" before enveloping himself fully in his character as the self-described world's greatest treasure diver.[36] His false starts had much to do with his behavior as an employee and would not end with his youth. In 1913, Harry Rieseberg was twenty-one years old, still living at home, and had failed in every job he had. It was time for him to take on the next stage of growing up by moving out of the house. Harry Rieseberg headed back to California.

Harry Out of the House

Harry had fallen into a disappointing pattern of failure in his earliest jobs. His father was a hard-working government employee who no doubt believed that type of work would have also been suitable for Harry. Henry Rieseberg used his connections with Senator Charles Curtis and other legislators from Kansas to try to help Harry settle down and work as a government employee, as he had done. With Harry's ignominious return from the Indian Agency, his arrest for theft, and his dismissal for poor attendance, he may have embarrassed his father enough for him to demand a change.

Whether Harry was kicked out of the house to go live with his relatives from his mother's side of the family is unknown, but that is where he went very shortly after his firing from Southern Railway in June 1913. Harry moved to Los Angeles to live with his mother's brother, Colin T. Martin, Martin's wife, Mary, and his mother's sister, Lillian. Colin was a salesman for Pacific Crockery and Tinware, and with Colin's help, Harry got a job within only a couple of months.[37] On August 8, 1913, Rieseberg went to work at Barker Brothers, a major household and furnishing retailer in Los Angeles, about a mile from where he lived with his uncle and aunt. Harry worked as a stock clerk in the hardware department but quit only a few months later, in February 1914.[38]

During this period, he also found an outlet for his collecting and writing skills in a magazine called Collector's World. For another journal in 1913, he offered an article with "Some Uses for Picture Post Cards" and placed classified ads looking for uncopyrighted photographs about travel. He offered to trade postmarks and pennants for Indian pottery and small blankets.[39]

While living with the Martins, Harry also placed some odd and inexplicable classified advertisements to sell kimonos and start a Vaudeville act. On October 10, 1913, a classified ad offered genuine Japanese kimonos imported from "the Flowery Kingdam (sic)" that were "neatly packed and delivered by parcel post for $1.75."[40] His ad in the *Los Angeles Times* the following day was different but still the stuff of a dreamer. Harry was looking for young ladies who would be part of a "Vaudeville sketch, which will eventually travel one of the big circuits."[41] In addition to his entrepreneurial spirit, young Harry may have also discovered the pleasures of keeping company with the opposite sex.

Harry the Arizonan

After leaving the Martins and California behind, Harry spent an undetermined amount of extended time in Arizona. In a later job application, Harry said he was in Los Angeles from 1914 to 1915 and Arizona in 1916. He described his jobs in California and Arizona as "reporter, cow-puncher, lumberjack, clerk, salesman, and store-keeper." On one application for employment, he said he worked for the United Verde Mining Company in Jerome, Arizona, in 1916 as a timekeeper. However, the company reported they could find no record of his employment only two years later.[42]

He was in Arizona long enough and at a time when the romance of the new forty-eighth state captured his emotions. Harry Rieseberg went to Arizona to pursue his version of an adventurous life. There are multiple indications that Harry not only lived in Arizona for a time but also connected with it personally. A significant list of poems and magazine articles professed his appreciation for the new state, and it was the setting for his coming of age.

Harry, the Author

One tangible result of Harry's trips to California was a literary-style article for *Every Where* magazine in 1912, published monthly by the well-known poet, Will Carleton. Although it is his earliest authored work yet found, it seems too polished to have been his first effort at writing. Harry's article, titled "Old Chinatown," was his account of a personal visit to that part of San Francisco. Visiting only five years after the Great Earthquake of 1906, Harry's story was an embellished account of a nineteen-year-old walking amid a forbidden zone of iniquity. Harry's descriptions of the sights, sounds, and smells were illustrative and meticulous. He even described in some detail a visit to an opium den filled with smokers who "were in grotesque attitudes, insensible, having the look of plague-stricken corpses." Harry either got a young man's tour of the other side of life on the west coast or made it up using the accounts of others. In either case, Rieseberg was actively working at publishing in more literate journals, a practice for which he would continue seeking outlets.[43]

Arizona inspired another of Harry's earliest published works, an article for a magazine titled *Arizona*. In 1912, a Constitutional Convention set in motion the final acts that led to Arizona's statehood. The magazine focused on the new state and was filled with articles describing the history and beauty of the region, along with ads by investors eager to sell pieces of it in land deals and development. Harry's contribution to the July 1913 issue was an article titled "Arizona, The Land of Mystery," calling his flowery work a "word picture of the Nation's Most Picturesque Plateau." One line of the article hinted at how his fascination with Arizona may have started when he said, "One never appreciates the full stride of American progress until he has traveled a Pullman car over such a vast territory." Harry had much to consider during his earlier rail trip from Washington, D.C., to California. Harry had the hand of a writer, even if the "word picture" he painted was gaudy and verbose.[44]

Harry the Poet

Harry's time alone in Arizona allowed him to mature and grow into a man. He professed to write a collection of poems about his months in the West. Between July 1913 and July 1920, Harry's poetic work about Arizona was published at least twenty-five times in various magazines and newspapers. In poems titled "Arizona" and "Flagstaff," he offered thoughts on the scenic beauty of the state and the people who had come before. His pondering in "The Old Santa Fe Trail" had him wonder "what tales of joys and sorrow that silent trail could relate."[45] His poem "The Lights of Clarkdale (as seen from Jerome AZ)" found him sitting alone atop one of the surrounding mountains, considering life from such a lofty vantage point. "Flagstaff Jim" is about a down-and-out prospector who visits a church, becomes rich, and gets a girl. In "Coconino Jim," Harry pondered life sitting outside a bunkhouse. He felt forgotten by friends and tempted by drink but resolved to maintain his "youthful thirst to rise, excel, and command."[46]

At least some of Rieseberg's words were not his own, and it leads one to wonder how much of his romanticism was plagiarized from the work of others. A researcher focused on literature about the Grand Canyon discovered that at least three of Harry's poems, "Grand Canyon of Arizona," "Sunset at El Tovar," and "The Old Santa Fe Trail" were snatched almost verbatim from earlier works by others.[47]

Harry exercised his muscles as a writer during these romanticized and youthful years away from home, but Harry, the social being, needed contact and reinforcement. Maybe that led him to submit his name and address to the *Boy's Life* magazine column previously called "The Lonely Corner," where boys could invite others to write them letters, a forum difficult to imagine in today's culture.[48] Harry seems to have achieved what his father had hoped by sending him West. He had worked on his own and separated from his parents and relatives. He had experienced hardships and seen how difficult life could be without the comforts and support of home. Now he was lonely, and it was time to head home to Washington and get on with life.

Adult Responsibilities

At some point during early 1916, Harry Rieseberg returned home to Washington, D.C., from his sojourn in Arizona.[49] Whether he had to ask to be allowed back home or returned triumphantly as one who had crossed the threshold of maturity is unknown. At age twenty-three, Harry finally seemed ready to grow toward maturity, but his first years of adulthood were rocked with more employment turmoil. Upon his return, Rieseberg quickly gravitated back to the family business—working for the federal government. The Fourth Assistant Postmaster General in charge of rural mail had an opening for an Assistant Messenger at the end of March 1916. The pay was only $720 yearly, but Harry was desperate and needed a job. In an early demonstration of his restlessness as an employee, Harry's position at the Post Office department lasted only a few months before he moved to the Postal Savings System in September 1916.

Harry the Husband

With a job secured, Harry continued to establish himself in the mold of his father. In July 1916, Harry petitioned Mount Pleasant Lodge No. 33 for membership in the Ancient and Honorable Fraternity of Free and Accepted Masons.[50] It seemed that Rieseberg was staged for success. He had a job, became a Mason, and had the written support of senators and congressmen whenever he asked. Harry then took another significant step in adulthood by getting married. Harry Rieseberg and Caroline Lowe were married at Christ Church in Alexandria, Virginia, on March 10, 1917.[51] Caroline was seven years older than Harry—he was twenty-five, and she was thirty-two when they married. One of Caroline's grandchildren described her as a strong, stoic, and rather buxom, fire and brimstone Presbyterian by the time he knew her.[52]

The week of Harry's marriage was also filled with other major life events. Only a few days after his wedding, Rieseberg was confirmed as a Master Mason. Two milestones like these in the same week would have been points of pride for Harry's parents. No matter the state of current happiness, it was soon to change. Harry and Caroline lived with his parents for four months after their marriage, creating significant disagreements. The living arrangement was temporary because Harry was headed west again.

Harry, the Draft Registrant

A war with Germany had the world in turmoil since 1914, but the United States stayed on the sidelines until early 1917. The U.S. severed diplomatic relations with Germany in early February and, on April 6, 1917, declared war, bringing the United States reluctantly into the world conflict. On June 5, 1917, all males between the ages of twenty-one and thirty-one were required to register for the draft. Harry was back living with his Martin relatives in Los Angeles, but this time with his less than enthusiastic wife, Caroline, along with him. He suggested on his registration form that having a dependent wife was a reason for an exemption, but draft exemptions had not yet been defined. Harry was never drafted into the war and said later that he was deferred due to a medical condition, but there is no other evidence of that claim.[53]

Soon after, Rieseberg started another job as Assistant Postmaster in El Centro, California, on July 26, 1917.[54] It is unclear whether the prospect of a job with the Post Office initiated his move back to California or he acted on his confidence in one of his political promoters to secure a spot. El Centro is two hundred miles southeast of Los Angeles and only a stone's throw from Calexico and the U.S./Mexico border in an agricultural region called the Imperial Valley. The post office in El Centro seemed to be growing at a rapid pace. A newspaper article soon after Postmaster C.W. Collins's arrival noted the addition of Harry to his staff, along with two other new clerks from San Francisco and Oklahoma City, giving him "the best clerical force in Imperial County."[55] There was barely time for the ink to dry on Collins' boasting before he drastically changed his opinion about his new employee.

Harry, the Investigated Employee

After only three months on the job, Harry Rieseberg was investigated by the Postal Inspector's office from Washington and removed from the El Centro Post Office. The investigation examined Harry's "loyalty, habits, fitness, ability, and nationality." A letter to investigators from a colleague and fellow Mason, John H. Kettner, offered the best summation of the trouble Harry caused. "In the year 1917 Mr. Rieseberg was an assistant postmaster, in El Centro Calif. Trying to be the "great I am" he endeavored to have Mr. Collins, the postmaster, removed from office by making false statements against him."[56] After Rieseberg attempted to prompt Collins's removal, the wily postmaster made accusations about Rieseberg's behavior and background. Unsurprisingly, Collins was more forthcoming about the reason for the dismissal. "He was removed for cause.... Later, this office was instructed by the Office of the First Assistant Postmaster General, to change the records of this office to show that he had resigned."[57] Harry Rieseberg was the focus of a serious investigation and was banned from working for the Postal Service in the future.[58] Harry managed to avoid any significant impact on his career, but for those who knew him personally, it confirmed Harry's willingness to do anything to promote himself. The "great I am" was building a bad reputation. His ability to somehow land on his feet and avoid the usual repercussions for such behavior steadily became the norm.

The War Effort

Two things are evident based on the timing of Harry's next appointment to a federal job back in Washington, D.C. The first is that he started looking for another position well before the final decision was made on his status in the El Centro Post Office investigation. Within a week, Harry's re-employment was supported by two U.S. Senators and three Congressmen.[59] The second clarifying fact is that the legislators writing his letters of reference and the new agencies receiving them had no clue about Harry's previous behavior or job history.

War Emergency Food Survey

Harry sent out multiple applications, one of which was to the War Risk Department, a new agency for insuring veterans. Any decision on his application there was pre-empted by his acceptance of a different position at the Bureau of Markets, part of the U.S. Department of Agriculture. The Bureau created a temporary position for Harry as a Typewriter at $1,000 per year, starting on January 2, 1918, and ending by April 1.[60] The additional position was due to the department's assignment to conduct a War Emergency Food Survey. The War Emergency Food Survey was a massive national effort to inventory national food supplies as the U.S. entered World War I. The intent was to ensure adequate food would be available and to plan the following year's production. Almost one million questionnaires were distributed by mail, and the department where Harry worked had the job of tabulating those results using Hollerith tabulating machines, equipment that led to the formation of the International Business Machines Corporation, or IBM.

Harry's job at the Bureau of Markets was to perform miscellaneous clerical work and typewriting, but he also helped operate the new tabulating machines processing data for the National Food Survey. In *I Dive for Treasure*, Harry enhanced this personal history by giving the impression that he was "in charge of the national food supply" during the war.[61] He was no more than an administrative worker who showed early technical promise. To hear him tell the story later, he was almost solely responsible for the entire effort and hundreds of people.

Instead of the valiant example of civilian leadership during wartime he promoted in his future narrative, Harry oversaw statistical tables showing the stocks of margarine, peanut butter, and grain for each region of the country.[62] What was a relatively mundane job at which Harry showed some aptitude became a nationally critical role when put through the Harry Rieseberg embellishment processor.

It was at this job at the Bureau of Markets where Rieseberg was introduced to compiling statistical tables. This skill would later transfer to other federal jobs and his yet unplanned career compiling data on possible locations for sunken treasure. Harry had been on the job for only two months when he started having other aspirations. He applied through the Civil Service for testing as a Statistical Machine Operator, a promotion from being a Clerk. The duties included operating the Hollerith tabulating systems and related punch card machines.[63] Harry's supervisor supported the change, saying that Harry was "especially well qualified to do the work on the punching machines, gang punches, sorting machines, and tabulating machines."[64]

War Risk Insurance Bureau

Harry restarted his application with the War Risk Insurance Bureau, with his temporary assignment at the Bureau of Markets finally expiring in July 1918.[65] In typical fashion, Harry was selective with the facts he provided on the application. He lied and said he had resigned from his last job at the post office in El Centro. He lied and said he had never been discharged from private employment. He lied again and said he had never been arrested on any charge.

Harry's connections may have been at work again as well. Handwritten at the top of his application was written "Mr. Batchelder, Start him right away. Macfarlane."[66] E.D. Batchelder was the Appointment Clerk, and William Macfarlane was the Actuary in charge of the group. Harry was hired the very next day in a temporary appointment as an Assistant Tabulating Expert.[67]

Harry did not take his oath of office for the new position until mid–July.[68] Though the wheels of the civil service appointments office could move slowly at times, this delay was likely due to the birth of a son to him and his wife, Caroline. Robert William Rieseberg was born on July 9, 1918, while Harry and Caroline lived with Harry's parents.[69]

Yet Another Investigation

Harry's comment to a co-worker or supervisor not long after starting work at the War Risk Insurance Bureau led to another months-long investigation into his background, work history, and character. It was wartime, and the War Risk Insurance Bureau handled records on hundreds of thousands of Americans. People were on alert to any possible subversive actions. When Harry reportedly commented on a world war that his uncle was in the German army and was very proud of that, it raised serious concerns since a war with Germany was underway. A memo on July 25, 1918, to C.W. King, an investigator with the department, outlined the action to be taken. King was to provide "all the information you can get" on Harry Rieseberg.[70]

King wasted no time in getting started. The very next day, at King's request, Harry submitted a form with five work references and five personal references, along with his employment history for the previous five years.[71] Congressman Charles Randall of California was one of Harry's references, and King's letter to the senator described the basis for his investigation.

> Because of the highly confidential character of the work [done by the War Risk Bureau], it is essential to exercise the greatest care in selecting its employees. The object of this communication is to obtain reliable information in regard to the individual named above, from the standpoint of:
>
> 1. Nationality and parentage;
> 2. Loyalty to our Government;
> 3. Habits, fitness or unfitness for a position in the Government Service;
> 4. Ability.[72]

Since the legislator's glowing, handwritten recommendation of Harry as "competent and trustworthy" only seven months earlier, Senator Randall had apparently received more information about the real story of Harry Rieseberg. King wrote Congressman Randall's reply at the top of the request letter, "Cannot recommend him, Randall."[73] Harry's second federal investigation within a year was not off to a great start.

Letters continued coming back to King. William Lowe, Harry's brother-in-law, attested to his loyalty and noted that his father had been in the U.S. Army but neglected to mention his German heritage. Harry's uncle and a frequent host for excursions to California, Colin T. Martin, focused on his Martin side of the family being U.S. citizens and said he had never met Harry's father, though they were brother Masons. A.A. Ormsby, an employee of the Office of Exhibits in the Department of Agriculture, said he had known Harry for ten years and found him to be "a young man of exemplary habits." A reference from the Bureau of Markets, where Harry worked on the Food Survey for only six months, avoided King's questions entirely, providing only the dates of his employment—a common sign that there was trouble that could not be reported.[74]

Two other employment references were not as favorable. The United Verde Copper Company in Clarkdale, Arizona, reported they could not find any record of Harry's employment at either the mine in Jerome or the smelter at Clarkdale.[75] Harry's 1916 poem "The Lights of Clarkdale," in which he described the nighttime view of the smelter from the hill above Jerome, makes it reasonably certain he was in that area for a time. His tenure with United Verde was either very short, unremarkable, or he was the beneficiary of shoddy record keeping. The second adverse letter came from the Southern Railway Company in Washington; the writer admitted knowing little about Harry but reported he was an average employee fired due to his poor attendance.[76]

Harry "Carefully Looked After"

An unidentified writer who signed simply as "ASH" sent a memo that identified both the problem with Harry and the success of his efforts in wooing congressmen and senators.

> Mr. Coler came in this morning about Harry Rieseberg. You may remember that he is being carefully "looked" after. Mr. Coler says they are not anxious to keep him and the War Department is asking that he be certified to them as a statistician. Mr. Coler thinks it will be well to let him go.[77]

Wendell P. Coler was an assistant actuary and head of the Insurance Section of the Bureau of War Risk Insurance and went on to become highly placed in the insurance industry. Harry being carefully looked after probably meant that generic letters were not the only support from elected officials.

Harry gave an excellent first impression to people in positions of authority. He was handsome, tall, energetic, and had strong verbal skills. He was intelligent and industrious. However, his excessive ambition and self-serving behavior started catching up with him. Coler wanted him out, but Coler did not have the final say. Rieseberg had maneuvered his way through the bureaucratic minefield once again.

THE INVESTIGATION CONTINUES

Responses to King's request for references continued to arrive.[78] Barker Brothers, the large household and furnishings company where Harry worked in Los Angeles, responded by only noting Harry's satisfactory tenure as a stock clerk.[79] The politely terse response came from the president of the company, and he made sure that King understood Harry was with them for such a short time that they did not have any other information. Barker was ducking the questions.[80]

The grand reveal of Harry's troubling behavior was a letter from C.W. Collins, the postmaster in El Centro whom Harry targeted with undeserved accusations. The restraint in Collins' tactful presentation of the facts covered a very unpleasant recollection of Harry's short tenure. Collins said he was "instructed by the Office of the First Assistant Postmaster General, to change the records of this office, to show that he had resigned."[81]

Collins directed King to the Post Office Inspector-in-Charge from San Francisco, who had done the investigation, if he wanted to know more. A week later, King sought information from that office, and Inspector Morse wrote back, apologetically explaining that the report was in Washington and contained confidential and privileged communications.[82] King was relentless in the matter and ultimately found the information he wanted. He confirmed that Harry Rieseberg was trouble.

> ... Mr. Rieseberg's removal was ordered for insubordination, inefficiency, and conduct unbecoming a postal employee.... The order for Mr. Rieseberg's removal was subsequently rescinded and the department accepted his resignation, November 22, 1917, with the understanding that he would not be eligible for reinstatement in the Postal Service.[83]

With the results of his investigation in hand, King approached both the head of the Appointments Division and Rieseberg's manager, William Macfarlane, with a litany of negative information on Rieseberg.[84] Despite the facts, King's handwritten note on a final memo affirmed that "Mr. Macfarlane approves this man and says he is doing fine."[85] Harry Rieseberg skated through yet again.

Wars Foreign and Domestic

The brutality of World War I ended with a victory by the allied forces, and an armistice was declared on November 11, 1918. Though the foreign war had ended, a heated domestic battle began less than two years into Harry's marriage to Caroline. For eight months following the completion of the second investigation and the end of the war, the twenty-six-year-old Harry Rieseberg continued his ambitious pursuit of better positions and higher pay. Harry's career may have progressed, but all was not well in the Rieseberg household.

An Unexpected Resignation

Harry Rieseberg's life was in turmoil in the second half of 1919. His personnel records with the War Risk Insurance Bureau indicate a sudden resignation and a request to transfer to a position with a different agency and an office in New Orleans. Harry had been successful at his work with tabulating machines and was promoted and supported by the director of the Actuarial Division, William Macfarlane. Why would he leave?

Even if Macfarlane was blind to Harry's shortcomings and failings, his co-workers were not. John H. Kettner spelled out the problems in an official letter. In addition to being a co-worker of Harry's, he was also Caroline's brother-in-law, a perspective that gave him an intimate, perhaps biased, look at Harry's shortcomings at work and home. Kettner believed Rieseberg resigned because he knew things would going badly for him.

> In July of 1918 Mr. Rieseberg's family was increased by the addition of a son, but instead of him assuming the responsibility of a father, he neglected his family shamefully, by his attentions toward some of his clerks in the War Risk Bureau, which resulted in the separation of him and his wife.[86]

Harry worked directly with a cadre of female keypunchers and had apparently become involved in a workplace dalliance. That was the opinion of more than just Mr. Kettner; Harry's wife also discovered something. She and their one-year-old son, Robert, moved out of the house where they lived with Harry's parents. The domestic war had been declared.

Tabulating Machine Company equipment from early 1920s. 10-key card punches. Library of Congress, Prints & Photographs Division, photograph by Harris & Ewing, LC-DIG-hec-20580 (digital file from original negative).

Chapter 2. The Harry Before

A Predictable Separation

The troubles between Harry and Caroline had been brewing for some time. In June 1919, just before Harry's resignation, Caroline confided to Harry's close friend, Fred Magruder, that she was unhappy with the living arrangement in the household with Harry's parents. Caroline wanted Harry to buy her a home or for them to move into her mother's home and operate it as a boarding house. She declared that she did not think they would ever get along. Magruder told others she simply had a "quarrelsome and dissatisfied disposition."[87]

In July 1919, Caroline moved out while Harry was at work, taking what little furniture and personal property they owned. She had enough of Harry Rieseberg. Caroline heard the stories about Harry's trysts and considered using that as leverage to get him to move out of his parents' home. She told Harry that if he did not move them to their own home, she would "run him out of town and ruin him."[88] Caroline was not shy about fighting back.

For his part, Harry later complained to a judge that Caroline spent money they did not have and accused her of "cruelty," causing him to have poor health. Harry said, "he came home to find her in terrible rages" and he felt "compelled to leave his home often at midnight in order to obtain peace of mind." If Harry was involved with other women at work, one must wonder what else he might have "obtained" during his midnight meanderings.[89]

An Odd Relocation

Amid all the turmoil, Rieseberg requested a transfer to the Federal Board for Vocational Education in New Orleans. As Kettner suggested, Harry was trying to get out of town before being fired. By the end of 1919, paperwork was flying back and forth between New Orleans and Washington. Wendell Coler, not one of Harry's supporters at War Risk, no doubt took some pleasure in his official response to the transfer request, writing that "the Bureau of War Risk Insurance will interpose no objection to the transfer of Mr. Harry E. Rieseberg to the Federal Board for Vocational Education."[90] Indeed.

Seeing an opportunity in Macfarlane's support, Harry secured a glowing letter of reference even as he left under a cloud. Macfarlane talked about how Harry had taken charge of the Tabulating section in delivering training and maintaining all the records. "In the trying days of the War when conditions as to work were not of the best you were able to adapt yourself to the circumstances and achieve exceptionable [sic] results."[91] A similar opportunity presented itself with a representative of the manufacturers of the Hollerith tabulating machine, who verified that he had been "in charge of the installation at the War Risk Insurance Department, Actuarial Department" for the last two years.[92] Either Coler and Macfarlane did not hear the rumors or get a call from Harry's wife, or simply believed, as many did at the time, that boys would be boys when it came to women in the workplace.

After Harry resigned from his position at War Risk on January 15, 1920, he received official notification that he should start work in New Orleans on January 20. However, in large, cursive handwriting across this correspondence in his personnel file was written a single word—DECLINED.[93] A telegram explained what happened: "Harry E. Rieseberg desires release for purpose of accepting position in Public Health Service under conditions which he feels would be to his advantage." Harry Rieseberg never went to New Orleans; he was headed back to Arizona.[94]

"Put the Manhood in You"

Harry Rieseberg's published poetry between 1915 and 1920 clarified his passion for the sunset state of Arizona. One of his poems said that men should come to the state because Arizona "will put the manhood in you." Harry was still looking for his. At the last minute, he turned down the job in New Orleans because he secured an assignment in his beloved Arizona. The letter from the interim Surgeon General appointing Harry as "Chief Clerk" at Fort Whipple had the air of another "watched over" arrangement for Harry.[95] Rieseberg wasted no time getting out of town. He left Washington by train on the evening of February 13, 1920, and arrived in Prescott four days later.[96] He left behind his wife, Caroline, his son, Robert, his parents, Henry and Jennie, and a bothersome list of encumbrances.

The U.S. Public Health Hospital in Prescott, also known as Fort Whipple, had been part of the federal government since the Civil War. From October through December 1918, there were 4,114,810 reported cases of influenza and pneumonia in the U.S., an epidemic resulting in more than 500,000 deaths that year.[97] This crisis and the sudden discharge of ill and injured soldiers led to a rapid expansion of public health facilities. Over thirty-six additional public hospitals were opened in the twelve months ending June 30, 1920.[98]

Despite the appointment made at his request, Rieseberg's restlessness was incessant. He started work on February 18, 1920, but after only six weeks in Prescott asked for a transfer out. At least he had the good sense to offer to make a move at his own expense. He wanted to go to a Public Health Service hospital opening during the coming months at Arrowhead Hot Springs in San Bernardino, California. Harry's explanation of an ill-defined ailment was odd for someone who had listed his health condition as "perfect" on one of his many applications. "My reasons for this request are that owning to the fact that the high altitude of this station being not very beneficial to my nervous system I consider that the locality in which Arrowhead Hot Springs is located more suitable."[99] Harry had previously spent enough time in Arizona to fuel his romanticized poems. Now that he was back, he wanted to claim his "nervous system" could not take any more. The Surgeon-in-Charge at Whipple said he would be sorry to lose Rieseberg and would not interfere with his request but reminded Harry of the sales job he had used to get the Prescott appointment. The surgeon told Harry, "The impression was given by you at the time of your employment, that you had formerly lived at Prescott and that assignment was specially desired."[100]

Rieseberg again secured letters supporting the move from an array of elected officials. None of the legislators knew anything about Harry's behavior in Washington or El Centro. One legislator was so confused by all the details that he called Harry "Doctor Rieseberg."[101] In this matter, however, simple circumstances provided an excuse for not making the transfer. There was no vacancy in Arrowhead Springs where Harry's services could be used. He would stay at Fort Whipple.

His "Arizona Girl"

Events with the objective authenticity of a verifiable timeline provide the certainty of a date when they occurred. A full complement of such records tells the story of Harry's divorce from his first wife and his marriage to his second. May seemed to be the month for momentous events in Harry Rieseberg's life. On the same day in May—May 6, 1920—Rieseberg filed for divorce from his wife, Caroline, and welcomed the woman who would become his second wife, Ellen Carver, to her new assignment at the Public Health Hospital in Prescott. His divorce filing was premature—he had to be separated for a year, and Ellen's arrival came with some questions. The big unknown is whether Harry knew Ellen already or met her only after she arrived at Fort Whipple as a twenty-three-year-old nurse from Ohio. Either way, her arrival in Prescott began a fast-paced chain of events.

Agnes Ellen Carver was born August 31, 1896, and lived in Cheviot, Ohio, just outside Cincinnati. After graduating from high school in 1913, she began her professional training as a nurse at Christ Hospital in Cincinnati and completed that training in May 1917.[102] She remained in Cincinnati after nursing school but worked in the Army Nursing Corps at Camp Lee, Virginia, for a few months at the beginning of 1919. Camp Lee had been a mobilization center for the 80th Division before it went to France.[103]

Ellen's stint at Camp Lee was during the time when Harry and his wife had their harshest disagreements and just before Caroline moved out of the house in July 1919. Camp Lee was about two hours from Washington, D.C. Harry could have met Ellen along the way since they both were involved in programs related to caring for veterans. Was Harry's active effort to relocate part of their plan to end up employed at the same federal health facility? With the timing of the court filing in Arizona, perhaps Ellen was not going to make a move until Harry finally took steps to end his marriage and file for divorce. At this point, there is no way to know with certainty, but indications that suggest a relationship beginning back in Washington are tempting to consider.

After leaving Camp Lee and Virginia, Ellen returned home to Cincinnati for private-duty nursing from May 1919 until May 1920, when she headed to Fort Whipple, Arizona. We can only guess whether Harry's two days of leave on June first and second were for them to be reacquainted, but it certainly seems plausible. It also seems likely that Ellen was whom he was writing about when he set one of his poems to music. Harry Rieseberg, the lyricist, was smitten when he composed a song titled "My Arizona Girl."[104]

What is known with certainty is that within a week of Ellen's arrival, Caroline filed formal charges against Harry for non-support. Ellen appearing in Arizona with Harry may have been the last straw for now vengeful Caroline. She began to pursue him through not only the civil courts but also with criminal charges.

Money Troubles

In addition to the legal issues caused by the abandonment of his family, Harry's money problems were compounding. In April 1920, Harry was arrested in Arizona on charges related to Caroline's accusations. By June 10, 1920, Harry had been indicted by a grand jury in Washington, D.C.[105] His request for an advance on his pay of one-hundred-fifty dollars on April 3 was the consequence of his bail.[106] He took other advances in July, two in September, and another in October 1920. The Saks department store in Washington also pursued Harry for non-payment of a $28.45 debt.[107]

Since he first arrived in Arizona, Harry had been trying to get away from Fort Whipple. In early August he submitted his application for a position as "Statistician, Assistant Statistician, or a statistical position of a supervisory nature in the Public Health Service in Washington D.C."[108] The position required a college degree, which Harry did not have, but he pled his case based on his experience. Harry's summary of his skills in 1920 is pertinent to his future career in trying to document treasure ships lost at sea. "I have had a number of years experience in the compilation and preparation of statistics and statistical reports of many classes having analized (sic) and classified statistical data for several Government institutions."[109] Harry was not qualified for the Statistician position but continued to press for a transfer. An August 26 letter to the Surgeon General repeated his request to go to Arrowhead Hot Springs in California. He also upped the ante by pointing out that the Surgeon General's office had previously given Senators and Congressmen assurances that Harry would be given every consideration possible. He had also enlisted a new politician who sent a letter of support for "a fine young man of his experience and qualifications."[110] If Arrowhead Springs was unavailable, Harry requested a transfer to several other named locations with public health hospitals, including Mount Alto in the District of Columbia; Waukesha, Wisconsin; and Fort Bayard, New Mexico.[111] Harry was ready to go almost anywhere.

Caroline Fights Back

To file formal divorce charges in the State of Arizona, Harry Rieseberg had to meet two criteria—he and Caroline had to be separated for one year, and Harry had to be a resident of Yavapai County for six months. Having finally met both requirements, he filed his official petition on July 23, 1920—one year and one day after

Caroline moved out of his parent's home. Caroline followed up on her promise to try to ruin him for abandoning her and their young son, Robert. She reported Harry's behavior and the abandonment of his family to his superiors at the Public Health Service. Their reaction was quite unfavorable for Rieseberg.

Hugh S. Cumming was the Surgeon General of the Public Health Service. Whether he initiated a request to Fort Whipple or the Medical Officer in Charge did so, something triggered a "Confidential Efficiency Report" on Harry Earl Rieseberg.[112] As a result, in late August, Surgeon General Cumming instructed the Medical Officer-in-Charge at Fort Whipple to request Harry's resignation. If he did not resign within forty-eight hours, the agency would "prefer charges against him complying in every particular way with Rule XII of the Civil Service."[113] Rule XII governed removal from an appointment. Those rules would allow Harry to file a rebuttal but left little room to escape an unfavorable decision.

Harry Forced Out Again?

Rieseberg must have seen this coming. He was trying everything he could think of to get out of Arizona. Rieseberg even tried to return to the War Risk Insurance Bureau, writing the director an urgent letter. Harry somewhat unnecessarily proclaimed that "this request is of my own accord and not caused by any differences with the administration."[114] It may have started that way, but Harry was in deep water again and would have to defend himself to keep his job, even if it was a job he was trying hard to abandon.

Harry did not surrender easily. The day after being presented with multiple charges, Harry denied them "seriatim and in toto," in order and completely. Harry said he welcomed the investigation, his third in three years.[115] On September 9, 1920, the Medical Officer in Charge sent a telegram to Cumming letting him know that Harry was answering the charges according to Rule XII, and asking if Rieseberg should be suspended while that continued. A telegram from Washington on September 17 confirmed that Harry would be suspended pending his answer to the charges.[116] On the 25th, after considering Harry's response, the Surgeon General informed him "that in view of the circumstances and conditions under which these charges were submitted and returned, they will be held in temporary abeyance."[117]

The fact that Caroline was out for his head was apparently taken into consideration. Harry was lectured for showing "poor judgment and indiscretion," likely meaning his relationship with Ellen. Caroline's complaints did not result in Harry's arrest, the outcome she would have preferred. The chief of military police at Whipple and the sheriff of Yavapai County joined in their effort to return the D.C. court's indictment unserved.[118]

Harry was not forced to resign, but that did not mean everything went back to whatever normal meant for him at the time. An official effort immediately began to get Harry out of Whipple and send him somewhere else—a recurring theme in his federal career. Those in charge at Whipple had to accept the reinstatement but sent

Washington a telegram on October 5 stating that "for the best interests of station request his immediate transfer to another station."[119] The response affirmed that it would occur as soon as Harry could travel. In the middle of everything else, Harry had a case of appendicitis. Like his homesickness at the Indian School in Oklahoma, Harry's constitution seemed to fail him in times of stress.

Rieseberg did not get a choice for his next assignment. On October 20, Harry was formally informed that he was relieved from duty at Fort Whipple and instructed to report to the Public Health Service hospital in Oteen, North Carolina.[120] Harry was dismissed yet again.

With the Ink Barely Dry

As Harry's departure from Prescott rapidly approached, he still had legal matters to address before the Superior Court in Arizona. On October 29, 1920, Harry withdrew his last bit of advance pay of $68.68 and pocketed the decree stipulating the finality of his divorce from Caroline Lowe Rieseberg. With his belongings packed, Harry departed for the Santa Fe rail station in Prescott, but he did not leave alone. Ellen Carver was on the train with him. On Halloween Day, two days after Harry's divorce was final and five hundred and fifty miles east of Prescott, they got off the train in El Paso, Texas, long enough to be married.[121]

The pace at which this happened, only four months since Ellen was transferred to Fort Whipple, adds credence to the likelihood that it may have been she with whom Harry was having a relationship while she was stationed in Virginia. Much like his inglorious exit from the Post Office in El Centro, Harry was married, between jobs, and tucking his tail following an investigation. And like before, he would somehow land on his feet. As for his family, Caroline never remarried, and his son, Robert, never knew his father. The family was not allowed to speak of Harry Rieseberg, and no one ever tested that unspoken rule.[122]

Mr. and Mrs. Rieseberg: To ~~North Carolina; Iowa;~~ Washington, D.C.

When they left Prescott, Arizona, Harry Rieseberg and Ellen Carver had plenty of baggage but little luggage. The Santa Fe railway conductor would not accept a box of quickly packed clothing because there were no handles. It took more than two weeks for Harry and Ellen to get some of their personal belongings delivered to them in North Carolina.[123] They had barely arrived before Harry's assignment changed again.

When arrangements were made for Harry's transfer to Oteen, North Carolina (now Asheville) he was a single man. When he arrived, he was a married employee for whom they had no quarters. Harry's reputation had preceded him and led to some grumbling and complaining by the medical officer in charge at Oteen. A Washington official wrote to the director there, noting that "it has come to the attention of the Bureau, unofficially, that you do not desire to retain Administrative

Assistant H.E. Rieseberg on duty at your station."[124] Before Harry settled in, he was asked to move along.

The Newlyweds Diverge

Though Harry had a position at Oteen, Ellen did not. Whether it was a conscious plan or simply a response to the stress of the past few months, Ellen resigned from the Public Health Service with no explanation only two weeks after marrying Harry. Not only that, but she went home to Ohio—perhaps to tell her family that she was now a married woman. After returning to Ohio, she remained for at least three months working private duty nursing again. Each time someone began a new job for the federal government, an updated personal information form was produced, so Harry Rieseberg had many of these in his personnel records. For the one he completed on January 8, 1921, he listed Ellen as his emergency contact at the same address where he lived, so it appears that Ellen and Harry were reunited.

On November 27, the wishes of the medical officer at Oteen were made official—Harry was removed from the new job and transferred to the public health hospital in Knoxville, Iowa, without his knowledge. Three days later, the surgeon in charge at Knoxville learned of the unsolicited addition. He stated clearly, "from what we have learned of Adm. Ass't. H.E. Rieseberg, we are positive that he would not be satisfied with his duty at this station."[125]

A Job, Then No Job, Then a Job

Harry was not at all interested in going to Iowa. While waiting for news of an assignment at his parents' home in Washington, D.C., he applied again for a position at the Bureau of Markets in the Department of Agriculture, saying he was available immediately and that a release from his current position could be arranged. His efforts paid off. On December 8, the Public Health Service confirmed they would not object to his transfer. Harry Rieseberg was again an employee of the Department of Agriculture. The bureaucracy had short-term memory loss.[126]

True to the Harry Rieseberg *modus operandi*, without providing any reason, Harry resigned from that new job at the Bureau of Markets only one month later. Rieseberg had no loyalties other than his ambition. When a $1,200 per year job as an accounting machine expert came up, he wasted no time making the change. On February 18, 1921, he went to work for the Internal Revenue Service, putting to use his previous experience with the Hollerith tabulating machines.[127] Rieseberg left his brand-new job with the Department of Treasury and the IRS so quickly that he forgot to submit his resignation. Before six months had passed in his job with the IRS, Harry was again looking to leave. He reapplied at former departments where he had not burned his bridges. One of those was at the restructured Bureau of War Risk Insurance, now part of the new Veterans' Bureau. After someone likely found the earlier reports of bad behavior, Harry's opportunity at the Veterans' Bureau died an undocumented death. The truth came out on many subjects.

Harry's ship might have been taking on water, but it was almost impossible to sink. Harry Rieseberg was again moving on.[128]

The Care and Custody of Documents

Harry Rieseberg's working life had been less than stellar. Even with the occasional letters of support by elected officials from three states, it is surprising that Harry had not been completely done in by his misdeeds. Large governmental bureaucracies did not have adequate tools for cross-department communication one-hundred years ago. Letters, telegrams, and memos took time and were filed away in distant folders and cabinets. The facts came out only when departmental investigators dug for references or a co-worker had first-hand knowledge, like Harry's official detractor, John H. Kettner. Harry's survival as a federal employee depended partly on his being a moving target with civil service credentials.

However, Harry Rieseberg finally showed signs of settling down at age twenty-nine. Like his father, he was active in several fraternal organizations, providing camaraderie and cover. He was finally living apart from his parents, a delay in separation resulting from his many humiliations and financial setbacks. He was married again, but this time to a professional working woman. Harry's focus was shifting. He was no less ambitious or self-centered, but his earlier bungling had become less self-defeating. His charm became more refined and focused, throttled by the lessons of the past. After all the bouncing around during his early years of employment and with all the lessons learned, Harry Rieseberg finally found a job where his intelligence and tabular talents could be focused.

An Archive of Sunken Ships

When Harry went to work for the Bureau of Navigation at the Department of Commerce in November 1921, the role and his skillset fit together nicely. Bits of experience from his previous jobs, particularly while working on the National Food Survey data, helped him assimilate into the department. His charm helped him climb up the ranks. Harry rose to a supervisory position as Chief of the Tonnage Division, tasked with tracking information about seagoing vessels in the United States. His job was tabulation. Not only were current vessels logged, but also ships out of commission, including those lost at sea. In the annual report published by the Bureau of Navigation in 1923, 29,600 vessels were listed with all the relevant statistics on each documented by Harry's department.[129]

The people tasked with maintaining the contents of Harry Rieseberg's federal personnel folder finally caught a break from the flurry of entries required by his moves and misbehavior. There were no scandals or investigations for a change, no sudden resignations. Harry progressed as a career man and had the interest, time, and energy to become involved in other areas where his sense of self-importance found expression. His increasing activity in social clubs and fraternal organizations was part of that change, but that was only one aspect of the rapidly expanding world of Harry Earl Rieseberg.

Adventure Enters

Harry's recognition of what was buried within the records he maintained and where it might lead him was not something he immediately understood. Initially, he was focused on doing his job, occasionally taking on public relations assignments, and becoming more engaged in fraternal activities and organizations outside of work. Harry's department was responsible for "the care and custody of all original vessel documents for historical purposes and searching thereof."[130] That meant he had detailed access to information about where they went down and the contents of their cargo. Harry's relentlessness, persistence, and intelligence kicked into full gear when he finally understood the magnitude and scope of what that information could mean. His income goals no longer included kimonos and burlesque shows; it was about millions in gold and silver.

By November 1921, the twenty-nine-year-old Harry Rieseberg had lived an unsettled existence between Washington, D.C., Arizona, and Los Angeles. When he was hired at the Bureau of Navigation, he quickly learned that given his writing skills and access to information in that role, he could become an "expert" in the eyes of others. Using his job knowledge as a platform, in 1923 Harry secured his first public acknowledgment as someone having expertise in sunken vessels. *Adventure Magazine* had been published in a pulp format since 1910 and became one of the genre's most successful and long-lived examples. The magazine began with fiction but moved toward adventure stories. It also became much like a fraternal group with offshoot "Adventurer's Clubs" formed across the country, gathering both real adventurers and those who wanted to live vicariously through them.

In the June 1923 issue, Rieseberg appeared on the magazine's pages as one of their experts, ready and willing to answer questions about any part of the seafaring world. Harry posted his expertise as one of the magazine's contributors.

> Historical records, tonnages, names and former names, dimensions, services, power, class, rig, builders, present and past ownerships, signals, etc., of all vessels of the American Merchant Marine and Government vessels in existence over five gross tons in the United States, Panama, and the Philippines, and the furnishing of information and records of vessels under American registry as far back as 1760.[131]

In his earliest connection to those who considered themselves adventurers, Harry presented himself as one with information rather than someone focused on treasure. Twenty years later, he said that he "was the expert on sunken treasure" for *Adventure*, embellishing his role as Harry was known to do. He told one of his future publishers he "received hundreds of letters from readers of that volume each month."[132] Experts like Harry were paid fifty cents for each response. Harry's knowledge, acquired through his job, was called upon in at least ten articles in the magazine between 1923 and 1925.

Tell Us About Yourself, Harry

By way of an introduction to the readership, in the February 20, 1924, issue of *Adventure*, the editors invited Harry to tell the readers more about himself.[133] This was a welcomed outlet for a young man already quite full of himself. With an opportunity for self-disclosure, he provided readers with a timeline of his life between 1914 and 1921. By comparing this with known events, there is an indication of Harry's ability to stretch the truth.

Rieseberg told readers he was "married to the best little girl in the world" without telling them that it was his second try. There was no mention of job terminations and investigations. He claimed to have dealt faro, a gambler's card game, at *The Owl*, a notorious bar and casino in Mexicali, Mexico, just across the border. No further mention of his cross-border adventures appears in any other source. He also admitted to a history of writing highlighted by rejection slips, including one from *Adventure* magazine. Harry's introduction to the readers in *Adventure* makes his life much more interesting than it was.

> I have wandered through every State of this great country of ours with the exception of those up in the far northeast corner; have been throughout southeast Alaska, punched cattle and rode line in Wyoming and Arizona, mucked in the U.V. Mine in Jerome, Arizona, signed on the West Coast boats from San Diego north to Wrangell (Alaska), once as purser and several times as an A.B. (able-bodied seaman). Swamped in the lumber camps of Omaha and Whitefish, Montana, and worked all the box factories of Flagstaff, Arizona.[134]

With the verification of much of his personal history during this period well documented by other sources, it is hard to understand when and how Harry Rieseberg could have done any of the travel he claimed. There is simply no time in between verified events and locations. In Harry's self-made life story full of intrigue, he tried to project an air of adventure that would have the manly Ernest Hemingway giving Rieseberg a thumbs up.

How to Become a Lieutenant

At thirty-two years of age in 1925, Rieseberg had many engagements and obligations. Being Harry Rieseberg was a full-time job. Harry continued to shine at the Bureau of Navigation as Chief of the Tonnage division. His pay increased to $2,500 annually, and he managed nine people in his workgroup. As a result of the transfer of some of the Bureau's work to the Census Department, he could focus on helping with press releases and public information, tasks which were right up his alley. Harry had been identified as a "publicity expert for various private organizations" and that skill played right into the changes to his role at work. Harry's extracurricular involvement in numerous fraternal clubs and social organizations seems impossible to balance with his full-time job managing a statistical division at the Department of Commerce. If his ambition fed his ego, it was exceptionally well-nourished for the next nine to ten years of his career.[135]

In June 1925, Harry was granted permission to accept a commission as a reserve officer in the U.S. Army Quartermaster's Corps, Water Transportation Division. After World War I, the Quartermaster Corps was re-established with an increased emphasis on civilian reserves. One of the branches of the Corps was the Transportation Service. With Congress' lack of support for a standing army and the loss of qualified service personnel to retirement or other roles, the Corps looked to hire civilians selected for their clerical skills in a reserve capacity to fill in the gaps.[136] For fifteen days a year, they would gather at one of the regional headquarters to receive training and prepare as if they may be called upon, and he got to be Lieutenant Harry E. Rieseberg.

In a letter approving his commission to the Corps, his manager said it would not impact his ability to perform his regular duties. Harry Rieseberg was appointed a Second Lieutenant, the entry point for an officer-level post. That explains his later self-serving reference to himself as Lieutenant Harry E. Rieseberg while building his persona as a treasure-hunting expert. For his last thirty years, he would play that title to his advantage every chance he could.[137]

Becoming a Writer

Harry had boundless energy for anything that brought him attention or might earn a few extra dollars. He had an after-hours business selling imitation Indian blankets for the Cayuse Indian Blanket Company. During that era, Pendleton Mills made colorful woolen blankets that were widely sold and labeled as Indian trade blankets.[138]

Harry also continued to regularly write poems and articles about Arizona. The January 1922 issue of *Arizona, The State Magazine*, listed Harry as the Associate Editor for a few issues. In May 1926, a similar tourist-oriented magazine named *Progressive Arizona* announced Harry as one of their regular contributors, noting he was "well known as a writer of ability, having contributed to various publications throughout the State and elsewhere." In that issue, his article titled "Into the Land of the Yavapai" was illustrated with photos calling attention to the "sumblimity [sic] in changing vistas of nature" for any motorist crossing the region. Four months later, in September 1926, another travel article by Harry appeared in *Progressive Arizona* magazine. "To the Highest Peaks in Arizona" offered a first-person account of a mule trip up a mountain for an overnight stay.[139]

Becoming a Parent.... Again

On June 30, 1927, Ellen resigned as Head Nurse at a Public Health Service dental clinic.[140] Her official paperwork said it was due to illness, but the "illness" was her pregnancy with her first child and Harry's second son. Henry Earl Rieseberg was born in Alexandria, Virginia, on September 13, 1927. Another sick leave in Ellen's personnel record was the birth of their daughter, Shirley Ellen, on January 16, 1931.

Harry's son, Robert, with his first wife, Caroline, was nine years old when

Henry was born. Even though they lived in the same city, Harry never spent time with Robert as the boy was growing up. It was as though Harry did not exist for his first-born son. Shirley and Henry never met their half-brother, Robert, and did not know he existed until only a few years before Harry died in 1970. Not once in any of his dozens of books and thousands of articles did Harry mention a wife, a marriage, or a family. They did not fit the narrative he wanted to create.

Harry the Joiner

Harry's membership in organizations of all kinds seemed to have been an obsession. For one who constantly sought the limelight, aligning himself with new groups kept him with a steady stream of fresh admirers. In today's terms, Harry was what would be called a "joiner." A *Washington Post* article in January 1933 cited his membership in a wide range of organizations.

> He is a member of Mount Pleasant Lodge, No 33, F.A.A.M., a thirty-second degree Mason, holding membership in Mithras Lodge of Perfection, No. 1, A.A. Scottish Rite; Evangelist Chapter, Rose Croix, No. 1, A.A. Scottish Rite; Robert de Bruce Council, Knights Kadosh, No. 1, A.A. Scottish Rite; Albert Pike Consistory, No. 1, A.A. Scottish Rite, Southern Jurisdiction; a member of Alma Temple, Ancient Order Nobles of the Mystic Shrine; charter and life member

Harry Rieseberg's son, Henry, and his wife, Ellen Carver Rieseberg, April 13, 1928 (photograph courtesy Marilyn Morgan).

of Capitol Forest, No. 104, Tall Cedars of Lebanon; Washington Chapter, No. 3, National Sojourners Club of Masons, and several other Masonic clubs; a member of the A.E. Talbot Camp, Modern Woodmen of America; Adventurers Club of New York City; Yavapai Club; Independent Order of Odd Fellows; American Statistical Society of America; Logan Tribe, No. 8, Improved Order of Red Men; Washington Council, No. 13, Junior Order of United American Mechanics; Knights of Nem Der; and honorary member of seven Mystic Shrine Temples.[141]

In only a year, Harry's participation in fraternal organizations and lodges, primarily Masonic or offshoots of Freemasonry, grew from seventeen to around thirty. He had even given up membership in several and, in an incalculable understatement, said he could not attend all the meetings but was interested in their work.[142]

The Tall Cedars of Lebanon

Records of Harry's increasingly active role in literally dozens of social clubs and fraternities far exceeded his father's lifelong participation as a member of a Masonic order. One of the civic groups in which Harry was most active was the Tall Cedars of Lebanon. The Tall Cedars was an offshoot of Freemasonry designed more for "Fun, Frolic, and Fellowship," and open only to master Masons. In July 1927, Harry was elected publicity chairman for the Capitol Forest No. 104 chapter of the Tall Cedars of Lebanon.[143]

A formal ball in 1928 at the Washington Auditorium was attended by several thousand members of the Tall Cedars, the Improved Order of Red Men, and the Maccabees. Harry also publicized an event the following year at the Willard Hotel for over 1,500 members of the Tall Cedars. Harry was also in charge of the publicity and program for the thirtieth annual Supreme Forest Session of the Tall Cedars of the United States of America to be held in Washington in May 1933.[144]

In late 1932 he was elected Junior Deputy Grand Tall Cedar for Capitol Forest No. 104. It may be meaningful that Harry's post was the only officer's position contested. The results were explained:

> "…after a spirited fraternal contest, Harry E. Rieseberg, charter and life member, chairman of the supreme forest convention publicity and program committee, and chief of the Tonnage Division of the Bureau of Navigation and Steamboat Inspection, Department of Commerce, was elected by a large plurality, which upon a motion made unanimous."[145]

Given how Harry was presented in the press release, it seems a foregone conclusion that he wrote those glowing words about himself.

A Different Kind of Social Club

Harry's personnel files had been comparatively bland for a few years, but true to his nature, they did not remain that way. On May 9, 1929, Malcolm Kerlin, Administrative Assistant to the Secretary of Commerce, sent a memo to William M. Lytle, Deputy Commissioner of the Bureau of Navigation that broke that trend. Attached to the note was a disturbing letter about Harry Rieseberg. The anonymous writer wondered if the Secretary of Commerce knew that Harry Rieseberg was the Grand Kleagle for the District of Columbia branch of the Ku Klux Klan.

During the KKK's reincarnation in the early 1920s, members of the Klan were, according to one historian, "if not the 'best people' at least the next best ... the good, solid middle-class citizens." Those good citizens just happened to be part of a brotherhood that believed "Catholics were stockpiling weapons to take over the country, that a cabal of Jewish bankers controlled world affairs, and that white people must prepare themselves for a race war with people of color."[146] The anonymous whistleblower was very specific in the accusations toward Harry and clear in his distaste for the organization.

> ... the nefarious activities of the so-called invisible empire—the Ku Klux Klan—of the relm (sic) of the District of Columbia, are being conducted by an employee of the Depar (sic) of Commerce; during the office hours of that department and with the use or help of other employees of that department in some instances not with their consent but through fear of losing their positions they are afraid to refuse.[147]

The letter went on to state that not only was Harry doing this almost daily, but also a member of the Navy Department was coming to Harry's office for such purposes. Incredulously, the writer said these circumstances were "almost unbelievable were it not an actual fact" and stated that all the information he provided could be easily verified.[148]

In the Klan hierarchy, Kleagles were organizers and recruiters paid on a commission basis for securing new members to the Klan—four dollars for each new convert. They were trained to find issues common with Klan goals among other fraternal groups, co-workers, or friends. Harry may have responded to a Klan recruiting ad like this one—the description certainly seemed to tap his skills and interests. "Wanted: Fraternal Organizers, men of ability between the ages of 25 and 40. Must be 100% American, Masons preferred."[149] Harry Earl Rieseberg fit the bill.

Yet Another Investigation

Deputy Commissioner Lytle said his investigation found no unnecessary talking about subjects other than work. He reported that a Navy employee working with Harry on the List of Merchant Vessels of the United States had been to the office often but solely on work-related matters. Lytle seems to have considered the complaint at only a surface level. He did not mention speaking with any of Harry's employees or even with Harry himself about the allegations.

Had Lytle dug more deeply, he would have learned the truth about Harry Earl Rieseberg and the Ku Klux Klan. Rieseberg was indeed a member of the Klan, just as the letter writer said. However, the accuser was wrong about one thing—Harry was not a Kleagle. He was the Imperial Representative of the KKK in Washington, D.C., the office that appointed Kleagles and was responsible for establishing a new realm. The Klan operated like a pyramid sales organization whose product was racism.

Rieseberg was appointed Imperial Representative on February 15, 1929, just three months before the anonymous letter. His certificate was signed by none other than Hiram W. Evans, the Imperial Wizard of the Ku Klux Klan.[150] Evans may have been impressed by the zeal Rieseberg expressed in an article he wrote for the January 1929 issue of *The Kourier*, the organization's member magazine.[151] His editorial comments answered "yes" to his own question, "Are There Slackers in the Ku Klux Klan?" Rieseberg complained that some members were not wholly invested in the Klan's mission and only paid their dues or passed through the levels without supporting their brothers in the Klavern. By then, the Klan was looking for dues-paying members who would also buy the regalia. They wanted customers as much as converts.

Money, Belief, and a Belief in Money

Harry's appointment was part of a last-ditch recruitment effort to revive the Klan. Membership in the hooded order declined steadily during the 1920s. There were almost nine million members in 1925, but by 1930 those numbers dropped to under 35,000. In the District of Columbia during that same period, Harry's group shrank from 15,000 to under 200. The high point of the Klan's revival may have been in August 1925 when an estimated 30–35,000 Klansmen marched down Pennsylvania Avenue in a hooded show of strength. Complaints about the financial shadiness of the leadership drove the exit rather than a disavowal of the skewed values and purpose of the organization.[152]

On July 6, 1929, only two months after the letter accusing Harry of recruiting for the Ku Klux Klan, the Imperial Wizard, Hiram Evans, spoke at a large gathering complete with a burning cross in nearby Forestville, Maryland. Harry Rieseberg introduced the Klan leader, and in his opening comments called attention to statements by the Speaker of the House calling the Klan "obnoxious" in their efforts. Rieseberg asked the crowd rhetorically why that may be true and then provided an answer that credited the Klan with the election of Herbert Hoover saying, "on November 6 the Klan passed a voice through the air that caused the downfall of the greatest destruction we would have ever had."[153]

In the "Club and Society Activity" column of the *Washington Post* the following morning, readers learned that Mr. and Mrs. Lee Farr spent the weekend in North Beach, the Georgiana Sewing Circle met, and over 2,000 people from Virginia, the District of Columbia, and Maryland were in a field listening to Harry Rieseberg and watching an eighty-foot cross burn in the night.[154] There was nothing secretive about Rieseberg's involvement with the Ku Klux Klan. The local newspaper still considered it as simply "club news."

Disagreements over finances between Harry and the Klan leadership grew to the point where he resigned from his post in March 1930. Since taking over the role of Imperial Representative in July 1929, Harry had increased membership by 4,000, but the Klan was still in trouble. Not only were there stories of fraud and embezzlement among the leadership, but it likely also meant that Imperial Representatives and their Kleagles were not getting paid for new memberships they garnered.

Though Harry left this group behind, it did not mean his worldview was changing. Harry was a socially connected minor star in Washington, D.C. He was tall, charming, intelligent, and able to express himself through his writing and speech. When the *Washington Post* called attention to a "patriotic body (being) formed by former members of the Invisible Empire" in April 1931, we can be certain that Harry Earl Rieseberg had been involved from the beginning. It would be expected that he wrote the press release announcing The National Order of Protestant Clubs with the stated purpose.[155]

> ... of uniting acceptable white male citizens of unrestricted but Protestant convictions and beliefs, into a strong, mutual, militant fraternal organization incorporated and mutually owned by its members as a whole, and not by any one individual or group of individuals, thereby eliminating all thought of patriotic commercialism.[156]

The new group would still promote an "undiluted" white race and oppose racial intermarriage between whites and blacks. They would still be anti-Catholic, like the KKK but without the financial shenanigans. A Jewish magazine of the time, *The Sentinel*, wondered if another era of hate was about to begin and why legitimate Protestant groups would not immediately denounce any organization with such a purpose.[157] In a move perhaps to soften its image, the group started calling itself the Harmony Club. Almost as quickly as it appeared, news and articles about the group disappeared after 1932. Rieseberg's involvement had fed his need for attention and notoriety, but there was no shortage of other outlets.

One Good Parade Calls for Another

The national convention for the Tall Cedars of Lebanon was to be held in the capital city for the first time in May 1933. Over 50,000 Trees, the group's name for its members, were expected to attend with their families. Harry crowed they would take up the two large ballrooms on top of the Willard Hotel. The plans for the event took on an epic tone.

> There will be parades each day of the meeting, composed of gayly colored marchers from the Ellipse to the Capitol composed of about 30 bands of the various unites [sic] of the order, and the many uniformed drill teams and other elaborately dressed bodies such as Arabs, Zouaves, the 800 steel-helmeted marching unit of Baltimore's unit, &c.—in all there will be about 20,000 members in each parade.[158]

Harry's press releases said the parade during their convention would be ten miles long, including one hundred drill teams and a hundred bands.[159] That seems an exaggeration, but that was Harry's style.

Not long after Harry was appointed publicity chairman for the Tall Cedars event, another article called the parade "American's Homecoming Week" stated that over 100,000 would attend. Harry's plans extended that claim even further. He said the purpose of the committee planning the event was to:

> ... produce from the assemblage of Americans of the Masonic fraternity a patriotic rally more impressive than any ever before witnessed by the members of the order—one whose beneficent (*sic*) effects will be felt in every nook and corner of the country—a thrill of hope, of

courage, of good fellowship and cheer and inspiration to carry on, with full confidence in the government of a free people, a panorama of whose birth and development will be spread before the masses.[160]

The excitement conveyed about his event is exceeded only by the breathless, single sentence Rieseberg used to describe it.

Harry was on a roll during the summer of 1932. He could not contain his enthusiasm or his self-promotion. His grandiosity in promoting the Tall Cedars parade in 1933 was probably based on a parade that had just occurred in the capital that summer. Harry Rieseberg wanted a repeat performance. An estimated 100,000 people viewed the George Washington Birthday Bicentennial celebration in June 1932. Each state brought a separate group to celebrate its role in the union. Harry's unit, sponsored by the Arizona State Society, was one of 150 entries. State societies were social groups organized by federal employees and elected officials from each of the forty-eight states, with Arizona being the most recent to enter the union in 1912. Even though Harry was born in the District of Columbia, he still chose to identify with Arizona because of his previous residence in the state.

On June 23, 1932, Harry Earl Rieseberg led the Arizona contingent down Pennsylvania Avenue dressed in full cowboy gear, including leather chaps and spurs, past a waving President Hoover. Behind him were Indians, Spanish girls, prospectors, frontiersmen, and stagecoaches pulled by teams of horses. And Harry Rieseberg somehow managed to lead them all.[161]

Chapter 3

The Treasure Game

*Men are so constituted that every one
undertakes what he sees another successful in,
whether he has aptitude for it or not.*
—Johann Von Goethe

In psychology and treasure hunting, understanding the concept of intermittent reinforcement is important. Reinforcement theory examines how behaviors change when rewards are delivered in different ways. One type of reinforcement, intermittent reinforcement, is provided on an entirely unpredictable schedule where the reward is expected or hoped for, but when it might come is unpredictable and uncertain. It turns out that reinforcement of behaviors using this approach has a very high response rate. If the payoff or reward cannot be predicted, it increases the likelihood that someone will continue their behavior in hopes that the next instance will deliver the reward despite no assurances. Lottery tickets would be an example—or treasure hunting.

The financial impact of the Great Depression during the early 1930s is well documented for its widespread loss of employment and the resulting governmental programs and projects designed to regain economic stability. Less well-known is how it contributed to risk-taking that would not otherwise have been considered. When a story of the success of a get-rich-quick scheme hit the papers, it created a flurry of people trying to make a buck the same way. Some of those were people who wanted to manufacture an income, but others wanted to prey on those desires. From 1927 to 1932, one journalist noted over seven hundred stories about found wealth published in newspapers and said, "The fact is that we are now entering upon a new era of treasure hunting. The depression has whetted the common desire for an easy acquisition of wealth."[1]

Whether they were one-person efforts, an accidental discovery in a scoop of dirt from an excavation, or a well-funded underwater expedition, all types of treasure ventures increased after the Depression. There were just enough successes to reinforce the idea that almost anyone could wildly succeed. Just the thought of plucking millions of dollars from the sea floor was enough to generate interest. When there were stories of even one success, it could obscure any doubts the next fifty failed ventures should have reasonably considered.

The story of the 1922 wreck of *Egypt* captured the public's attention. The cargo of silver bullion and gold sovereigns worth millions was the lure for would-be salvors. The wreck of *Egypt* was found in August 1930, and the first gold recovered in June 1932 was valued at over $3,700,000. In 1933 another $1,250,000 was raised, and in 1934 an additional $800,000 was brought to the surface.[2] Everyone who read the stories wished it had been them.

Science, Adventure, and the Gambling Instinct

In 1933, multiple and varied sources of news and information were not widely available. Stories by the Associated Press and other wire services became the standard, primary news sources nationwide. More prominent newspapers like the *Washington Post*, Harry Rieseberg's hometown paper, had the resources to gather news independently. Still, wire services distributed general stories of note nationally. The year 1933 was filled with detailed newspaper accounts of the successes and failures of treasure ventures being read nationwide.

Underwater expeditions developed at a quickening pace during the post–Depression years. A *New York Times* article in August 1931 did an excellent job of dissecting some of the questions about what drove men to make such incredible efforts in the face of often irrational possibilities for success. The headline proclaimed, "Science, Adventure, and the Gambling Instinct All Play a Role," and acknowledged

Cover art typical of the dramatization of underwater treasure hunting. The interior article, "The Treasure Hunters," mentioned Rieseberg and the Romano diving sphere. *Popular Mechanics*, August 1934 (used by permission of Hearst Magazine Media, Inc).

that desperation was lurking in the background.³ One article noted that springtime seemed "when most treasure hunts are launched, chiefly from armchairs." Nothing seemed to stop men from fantasizing and imagining they could be the ones to find some lost wealth. That audience was generally not the few able to fund and carry out an expedition but those who could only afford to dream. Treasure articles were for those who would "locate and loot them (treasure sites) while still enjoying the comforts of one's home," an act the writer described as one of the "pleasantest exercises of a robust imagination."⁴

There were, in fact, some logical drivers for the attention being given to underwater treasure hunting. One was the salvageable contents of vessels lost during World War I to German torpedoes. Additionally, stories of Spanish galleons full of gold captured the imagination. However, it was the development of equipment that allowed deeper dives that reignited the interest and publicity. Zoologist William Beebe set a 1930 depth record of 1,300 feet in his spherical bathysphere and broke that record in 1934 by descending to 3,000 feet. Even though he could only observe undersea life through a tiny window in his steel ball, such a device might allow its occupants to direct hooks or cranes from the surface to secure and raise a vessel from the bottom.

In the world of treasure hunting, there are three ingredients required to undertake a venture: an expert with the technical means to make the dive; someone with enough money to invest in the effort; and finally, a compelling story about the riches to be gained to attract the talent and money. Rieseberg had the perspective of a poet, the gall of a traveling salesman, and access to information about sunken ships. He began to imagine how that might make him a wealthy man.

Harry Enters the Treasure Game

An article about the Bureau of Navigation in the *Washington Post* on December 31, 1931, had director Arthur J. Tyrer's name in the byline and his stern photo affixed in two column inches squarely atop the article. The copy style was strikingly similar to Rieseberg's writing, however, and was likely his submission.⁵ The report noted that more ships of 100 gross tons or larger were lost at sea or abandoned in the prior year than those built. Ships were sinking, and Harry Rieseberg was keeping count.⁶

Harry described his interest in locating sunken treasure as a transformational series of events that were natural offshoots of his job compiling statistics on ships and sailing vessels. By his telling, a woman came to see him at the Bureau one day asking about information on sunken treasure ships. After she could not locate anything at the Library of Congress, Harry went there himself and discovered "musty old records of shipwrecks, mutinies, and ship disappearances."⁷ Harry said he was overwhelmed by his discoveries and dove into them so profoundly that he lost track of time. When forced to leave the archive, he headed home in the dark, his head spinning with ideas of a career that could make him rich and provide real adventure.

Harry said that everything about him changed after looking at those old records and charts. Harry the Joiner became Harry the Insatiable Researcher, spending "every free hour for many months—indeed years—running down new material." In addition to the information on wrecks, he said he researched the history of the sixteenth, seventeenth, and eighteenth centuries. As with any research of this type, one scrap of data led to other references to track down and leads to follow. Lawsuits, admiralty charts, and hydro-graphics became his new areas of expertise. Given his job history working with tabular, statistical data, he already knew how to manage data. Harry seemed to be made for this passion, and he says he took it up for years, hoping and dreaming. Harry became a man on fire, believing he had access to valuable knowledge available to no one else. In modern-day terms, Rieseberg thought he could monetize the knowledge he had gathered.

Contrary to his later recasting of his personal history, Harry Rieseberg was not diving or treasure hunting in 1932 and 1933. Instead, he did something else that was the beginning of his career as an author of adventure stories that were more fiction than fact—he wrote a newspaper article about ships. Harry began promoting and publishing stories about the ships he encountered in the records through a series of newspaper articles beginning in 1933. What appears to be Harry's first major publication was a full two-page spread in the *Washington Post* in October 1933. The article was about the decline of windjammers, speedy and elegant sailing ships whose era was coming to an end.[8] Harry's research had him on the edges of treasure tales, but he had not yet claimed he was directly involved. In this article, he focused on the romance and glamor of the sailing era. Harry's article previewed his later writing style with the facts dramatically exaggerated. At this early stage, however, his work did not stray into the factual discrepancies and self-serving focus that evolved later in his career. This article was about the lovely ships with no claims about himself. Harry was just a technician with access to exciting and valuable records who could charm readers with his words. He was not yet all about treasure, but events soon changed that perspective.

First Treasure Articles

Only three weeks after his first significant newspaper article on windjammers, Harry's name appeared again in the byline of a two-page article for the *Washington Post* in October 1933, in what would be his first article related to treasure. In the *Post*, a full two pages of dramatic phrasing and headlines suggested that great riches were just out of reach.[9]

Wealth Beyond Croesus' Wildest Dreams
Beckons from Hulks of Foundered Treasure Ships

Modern Salvagers May
Retrieve Hoards That
Lured Adventurers to Doom

Harry wasted no time in unleashing the youthful poet and his inner Hemingway. The second paragraph of the article got right to the hooks by fantastically describing the possible treasure. "Hidden gold! Dripping, slimy gold ingots and silver plate, and jewels galore! Blood-stained romances and glorious woven legends, stiffened with the rich brocades of old Castile."[10] In the article, Rieseberg listed the names of wrecks he would write about for the next thirty-five years—the *Merida*, the *De Braak*, the *Brother Jonathan*, the *Islander*, and the *Hussar*. The article contained indications of Harry's extensive research into shipping records and worked hard to make the case that the wealth on the bottom of the sea was readily accessible. It is notable that nowhere in the article was there the slightest mention that Harry himself had anything to do with treasure salvage. However, there were signs he was starting to think about it. "Today large capital and unlimited patience are all that are required to place these fortunes within the reach of those treasure hunters who in their dreams hear the call of John Silver's shrill parrot cry: 'Stand by to go about! Pieces of eight! Yo ho! Pieces of eight!'"[11] He acknowledged that other men had succumbed to the lure but did not yet pretend it was his adventure. There were none of the first-person twists to the story that he mastered years later—not even a representation of himself as a treasure expert. He was not yet "Lieutenant Rieseberg," a title that would later add an air of credibility to his bylines.

On the same date as the *Post* story, what was essentially the same article also appeared in the *Sunday Oregonian* in Portland. However, the article in the Sunday Oregonian had a slight change of tone. For the first time, Rieseberg stated he possessed information about sunken vessels containing treasure waiting to be salvaged. In particular, Harry said he had a letter from a man whose father saw exactly where a west coast wreck, *Brother Jonathan*, sank.

> My father saw the Brother Jonathan when it sank. It ran up on a rock, balanced and pitched forward, sinking almost at once.... He offered at the time to tell searching parties, but they were not willing to compensate him for his knowledge. I would be willing to show the proper persons the exact spot of the sinking of this vessel.[12]

He teased others with the information he purported to have by saying that "the resting place of the rotting hulk of the steamer, with its unsalvaged cargo of immense treasure, remains a secret"—a secret Harry Rieseberg wanted others to believe he now held.

For the closing in the *Sunday Oregonian* article, his conclusion was much more definitive, and perhaps personal, in saying that "engineers are turning to the salvaging of these undersea monuments of disaster and misfortune as a profession and a new means of acquiring wealth." Harry desperately wanted to be part of that trend by pitching himself as the man with knowledge of the wrecks' locations.[13]

Hidden Treasure Waters

Within a week, another of Rieseberg's treasure articles appeared in the magazine section of the *Cleveland Plain Dealer* in November 1933. "Hidden Treasure Waters of the Americas" focused on the western hemisphere from the Great Lakes to South America. As would be his future pattern, much of the article was a re-use of the one a few weeks prior. Harry repeated his teaser, saying, "riches lie waiting for resourceful men who have the money to buy the latest equipment for diving and who know just where to look." He ensured readers understood he was the man who claimed to know just where to look.[14]

The byline for this article is the first instance of Rieseberg using "Lieutenant" before his name, adding a layer of credibility. Interestingly, in his first paragraph, he may have written what could easily be the definitive summary of his career to come. "Fiction writers have not been slow to seize upon such fragments of truth as there may have been in many of these tales [of treasure] to work them into a form of romance which will never lose its appeal to the public." There are no better words than his own to describe the business plan for Harry Rieseberg. The only catch was that the fiction he later wrote was pitched as reality.

Two Articles on the Same Day

One must wonder how Harry went from working publicity for fraternal groups to multi-page articles in major newspapers so quickly. It may be that this author's research has not yet found earlier or shorter pieces leading up to these. His ability to be a self-promotor and his writing skills came together at the right time with his newfound passion for treasure. No matter what method he used to get there, on January 7, 1934, Lieutenant Harry E. Rieseberg of the Quartermaster Reserve Corps, now self-reported as a "treasure expert," had two articles published in major newspapers on the same day. The *Los Angeles Times* published "Go Down to the Sea…. FOR GOLD!" and the *Washington Post* ran "Mystery Ships Add Exciting Chapter to Lore of the Sea."[15] The article in the *Post* told stories of phantom ships mysteriously lost at sea. In the *Times*, he upped the linguistic wattage of his overly dramatic phrasing.

It is important to note that Rieseberg did not insert himself into any of the treasure stories he told at this point in his career. Harry was still finding his voice and testing the waters with an indirect search for potential investors who might pay for his purported knowledge. He was a researcher with a knack for telling stories and did that in rapid succession. From February through June 1934, article after article appeared in nationally known newspapers under Rieseberg's byline.

> "Six Nations Compete for Sea Supremacy," (Portland Oregonian, *March 4, 1934*)
> "Seek Ghost Mines—Find Death," (Milwaukee Journal, *May 20, 1934*)
> "Tales of Buried Pirate Gold Hold Lure," (Portland Oregonian, *June 10, 1934*)

Harry desperately wanted to connect with real adventurers and treasure seekers who had money and equipment. In October 1934, an article appeared in *Popular Mechanics* magazine that did not have Harry's byline but was clearly his based on the writing and content style. "The Treasure Hunters" opened by suggesting that people interested in an adventure could contact "Lieut. Harry E. Riesenberg (*sic*) of Washington, D.C., to start you off on a jaunt that would give you a thrill of a lifetime."[16]

Harry Rieseberg was sure he was onto something big, and he wanted to find people with enough money to pay him for what he claimed to know.

Aspirations and a Role Model

Rieseberg was also learning from the success of actual divers who were getting publicity and attention, noting their approach and methods. One of those men was John Craig, a Hollywood-level filmmaker who became a diver. While Harry was building his résumé of major newspaper articles between March 1933 and late 1934, Craig began touring movie theaters around the country to show his documentary-style movie titled "Sea Killers." The film was a series of short underwater clips tied together with music and a story delivered in person from the front of the theater.

> In my own [film] morgue, I had a lot of film from various expeditions—cutouts and odds and ends the studios hadn't bought. I went into retirement and fitted these together. Then I wrote a sound track, and titled the result Sea Killers. With this I decided to tour the country, barnstorming, to get audience reaction. In that way, I could find out what the people wanted ...[17]

Craig described their crude audience research methods when showing the movie in theaters. "I made a short speech of introduction. Then, with pencils and pads, we checked the ohs, ahs, uhs, gasps, and hand-clapping at the various points, until we had settled pretty well just what parts of the picture the audience liked, or was frightened or impressed by."[18] The publicity-minded Rieseberg most certainly noticed the attention Craig paid to polishing his persona. He also saw that making movies of an expedition could be a revenue stream, a concept he would later promote as a hedge against not finding any treasure. Images of a staged fight between divers and a faked battle with an octopus that Craig produced were also mentally filed away for Rieseberg's later use. Perhaps it was Craig calling himself Captain without the benefit of a military commission that led Harry to put his Lieutenant title in front of his byline.

An Eighth of the World's Gold

Just because Harry was not diving for treasure does not mean that some of his claims about his research were not true. In fact, his claim about collecting wreck data may have been all that was true regarding Harry's involvement in the treasure-hunting frenzy that seemed to capture everyone's imagination. With his research coming out through his newspaper articles, Harry was beginning to convince others that he might be more than just a self-proclaimed expert. Evidence of that success lies in a phrase he would repeat for the next thirty years; it appeared in print for the first time in June 1934. Harry repeatedly said that one-eighth of the world's gold was "at the bottom of the ocean in rotting ships." The article went on about Harry's work saying that "Lieut. Rieseberg also has charted the location of all treasure ships that have been sunk since 1588. Salvage companies, adventurers and sportsmen have applied to his office for data in organizing treasure-retrieving expeditions."[19] Harry was convinced he had found a way to make money by selling

John Craig flyer. 1939, Redpath Chautauqua Collection. https://digital.lib.uiowa.edu/islandora/object/ui%3Atc_52382_52379.

information to others but needed to happen faster to be wealthy and famous. While others were already putting together expeditions seeking riches, Harry Rieseberg was actively beginning to assemble records, and misinformation, about old wrecks and their possible treasure.

If that focus and expertise had remained his only point of contact with the world of underwater treasure hunting, there would be far less interest in the life of Harry Earl Rieseberg. Instead, Harry made a career by telling the world about his fabricated diving adventures. Though the wrecks, legends, and stories were based on actual events, the tales of his role in their discovery or dives to reach them were all fantasy. Among those seven hundred stories of found wealth in the late '20s and early '30s, not one was about Harry Rieseberg.

What Harry Said He Did

After being Chief of the Tonnage Division of the Bureau of Navigation for a few years, Rieseberg grew comfortable with the duties and workload. Outside of work, he was busy organizing galas and balls and attending meetings for dozens of fraternal organizations. News stories about the fortunes of others through treasure hunting continued to proliferate and create interest among people who had no practical or logical ability to act on the reports ... people like Harry Rieseberg.

As with most invented narratives, it was often difficult for Rieseberg to maintain consistency in the alternative facts he offered. During these years, when Rieseberg was a federal employee and gathering resources for his personal gain, he later claimed it was when he began diving for treasure. When telling his tales, he most often pointed to 1931–1932 as when that occurred. Over the years and in different published accounts, Rieseberg had several versions of when he said he made his first dive. The previous sentence was carefully worded to say when Harry *said* he made his first dive because the research raises doubt about whether he ever did that at all.

In a newspaper article he wrote in 1935, Harry said he began compiling his research into a manuscript for a book he titled "Cracking Davy Jones' Treasure Vaults." He said the book focused on what he was making his stock-in-trade, information about the location of these wrecks. By his telling, when word got out about what information he possessed, he was "besieged by engineers, financiers and adventurers in a flood of correspondence from all over the world." It took seven more years for his first book to appear.[20]

A Navy Diving Tank

Shortly after losing forty sailors in a tragic submarine accident in 1929, the Naval Deep-Sea Diving School in Washington, D.C., became the focus of the Navy's research and training to improve the means and methods for underwater rescue. A tank at the Washington Navy Yard was used for training divers and practicing underwater rescue. To test equipment at pressure like those at depth, Navy engineers modified the tanks to simulate dives of 150 to 200 feet in a vessel only twelve feet deep and eight feet in diameter. Harry's later stories about his introduction to diving included an assertion that he used that facility himself.[21]

Rieseberg said he was deeply into his research on sunken treasure when a Naval

Diving exhibition. Navy Day was celebrated at the Washington Navy Yard by various exhibitions including the diving show put on here by 2nd Class Gunners Mate Emerson Burie. A diving school is maintained at the yard. October 28, 1935. Library of Congress, Prints & Photographs Division, photograph by Harris & Ewing, LC-DIG-hec-39513.

officer named Thompson came by the Bureau of Navigation office to ask if Harry would like to watch divers training at the Navy school. Harry said he accepted that offer and then returned day after day to watch the divers. After a week, he claimed the Naval instructors allowed him to suit up in hard hat diving gear and enter the tank. This claim loses credibility since it is doubtful that the Navy would let a civilian suit up and dive, much less without the preliminary training required to don the heavy suit and learn to breathe correctly.[22]

To stretch his story even further, Harry said, almost in passing, that "the day after my first dive, I enrolled for a course in deep-sea diving." Commercial diving was limited then, and Navy training was the primary path for hard-hat diving instruction. Harry's single sentence of explanation for how he became a diver does not explain how a diving course was ready and waiting for his enrollment. Even if Harry may have maneuvered an unauthorized dunk in the Navy tank using his charm and his fraternal network, there is little reason to believe his diving went past that point.[23]

It is not easy to know whether this single event that in Rieseberg's invented history is accurate. Given his regular contact with Naval personnel, his fraternal affiliations, and his job in a maritime-related role, one can certainly imagine he got the invitation to watch. That he somehow ended up in a full-dress diving suit without training is a stretch. The odds do not favor any belief that Harry Rieseberg, the self-proclaimed world's greatest underwater treasure hunter, ever got wet.

Early Dives?

In his 1942 book, *I Dive for Treasure*, and a lead-up article published in 1940, Harry went to some lengths to establish his version of an invented treasure diving history. Harry's approach in these stories was to be vague about the dates. However, without naming a date, he boxed himself into a timeline around 1932. Based on events that he reported independently, Rieseberg placed many of his claims in context with verifiable events. It is then that his half-truths and outright fabrications are exposed.

In *I Dive for Treasure*, Harry provided a story in which his dates do not add up. Harry recounts a story where he and a friend named George Wright had $6,000 each and big dreams of using Harry's research to find treasure while Harry was still a federal employee. Where Harry came up with $6,000 with his small federal salary would be interesting to know since that amount was over three times his annual income. They reportedly found a boat for rent in Miami, bought diving equipment and supplies, and took a three-month leave of absence from work. At least the notion that they "were sailing around haphazardly" adds some believability. The idea that Harry had the money to squander after the Depression or the time to take that much leave from work, is beyond belief.[24]

Credibility by Association

It has been rare during the research for this work to find even partial confirmation of statements Harry Rieseberg made about his invented diving career. His use of half-truths is part of what allowed him to maneuver around the facts. However, the timing of one of his assertions in his book can be directly disputed by the accounts of a credible person and dates established as fact. That association also refutes much of what Harry Rieseberg wanted the public to believe years later about his purported exploits as an undersea treasure salvor.

In Harry's capacity at the Bureau of Navigation and because of his published articles, Harry met a young M.I.T. student named Max Eugene Nohl. Max Nohl became a true pioneer of deep-sea diving. He set a depth record in 1933 by mixing helium with breathing air and built a deep-diving sphere he called "Hell Below." From January 14, 1934, until June 1 of that year, Nohl suspended his studies at M.I.T. and worked as Assistant Engineer and Superintendent of Diving aboard the ship *Seth Parker* for an expedition organized by a radio star of the time named Phillips Lord.[25]

Rieseberg said in his book that he met with Nohl both before and after that expedition in the first half of 1934. This is very important to note. Harry said, "I was envious of Nohl, going off like that to hunt for treasure, but I knew *I wasn't ready yet* and was reasonably content to follow the accounts of the expedition in the newspapers."[26] So in late 1933, Harry said he "was not ready" to hunt for treasure. By saying he was not ready to conduct his expedition and was content to keep up with Nohl's expedition in the newspapers, Rieseberg made clear he had no opportunity to do the earlier underwater work he claimed. Subsequent statements Rieseberg made at different times and in other articles over the years claimed he started treasure dives in 1931, 1933, and 1934.[27] The weight of evidence on Harry's diving history was that he never made any of the treasure dives he wrote about.

There is no evidence that Harry Rieseberg ever dove for treasure other than his own stories. There is not a single remaining photo of him in diving gear. Not one. The only photos said to be him in diving gear are either faked or taken with a diving helmet already in place and provide no identifying facial characteristics. There are no pictures, no contemporaneous newspaper articles, and no artifacts. Nothing found then or now has proven even a fraction of what Harry claimed to have done. Even so, it is what Harry would like us to believe about him that makes the rest of his story so intriguing.

Chapter 4

The Great Fall

*The hardest tumble a man can make
is to fall over his own bluff.*
—Ambrose Bierce

Harry Rieseberg described himself as a man on fire after his epiphany regarding his access to the archival records of sunken ships. He believed he was on to something big. He was convinced that his access to records and his feverish research put him in the unique position of knowing more about the details of lost ships—and their potential wealth—than any other person in the treasure game. All he had to do was find someone with the money and equipment to pay for that knowledge. In 1934, it appeared that Rieseberg's stars were about to align. To go after any of the treasures he believed he knew how to find, he would need a ship to get there, a means to get to the bottom, and the money to bring the supposed treasure to the surface. Harry Rieseberg's intelligence, will, and tenacity were primed for success.

An Inventor and His Diving Robot

Between 1932 and 1934, when he was building his research, Rieseberg monitored patents coming into the U.S. Patent Office. The patent office was in the same building where he worked, making the viewing of incoming designs much more accessible. Harry wanted to find equipment that could operate in water deeper than a hard hat diver could descend and to connect with inventors and treasure seekers. He wanted to be inside a diving bell, not a hard hat. Though many adventurers in the early 1930s used mechanical devices to seek treasure at greater depths or convince financiers they might be able to, one inventor from Seattle became a major part of Harry Rieseberg's story.

On Saturday, November 4, 1933, an article in the *Washington Post* and that evening's *Washington Evening Star* told readers how the U.S. Navy was testing a diving robot with mechanical arms in Seattle.[1] The inventor claimed he had already taken the sphere down to 850 feet and could go to 1,500 feet if needed. Hard hat divers could only work with any duration at 100 feet, so the ability to perform work at that depth was a tremendous breakthrough. When the Patent Office opened the following Monday, it is easy to imagine that Rieseberg was waiting at the door.

Chapter 4. The Great Fall

When Harry first laid eyes on patent number 2,040,956, he must have been buzzing with excitement.[2] The schematics beautifully detailed a spherical diving bell with long, hydraulic arms and pincer-like grapples. Rieseberg said he recognized immediately that this was precisely what he had been trying to find—a way to recover treasure at depths greater than a diver could explore. Harry obsessively examined every detail of the drawings all afternoon and evening, imagining all the possibilities.

Many inventors in the early 1930s, legitimate and otherwise, developed mechanical devices to probe for treasure amidst rotting wood or twisted steel. Investors were looking for inventors and could just as likely connect with shysters out for a quick buck or luck into a fortune. In March of 1932, three men based in Seattle were crafting underwater diving apparatus that could dive deeper than helmeted divers. More than one of them would cross paths with Harry Rieseberg.

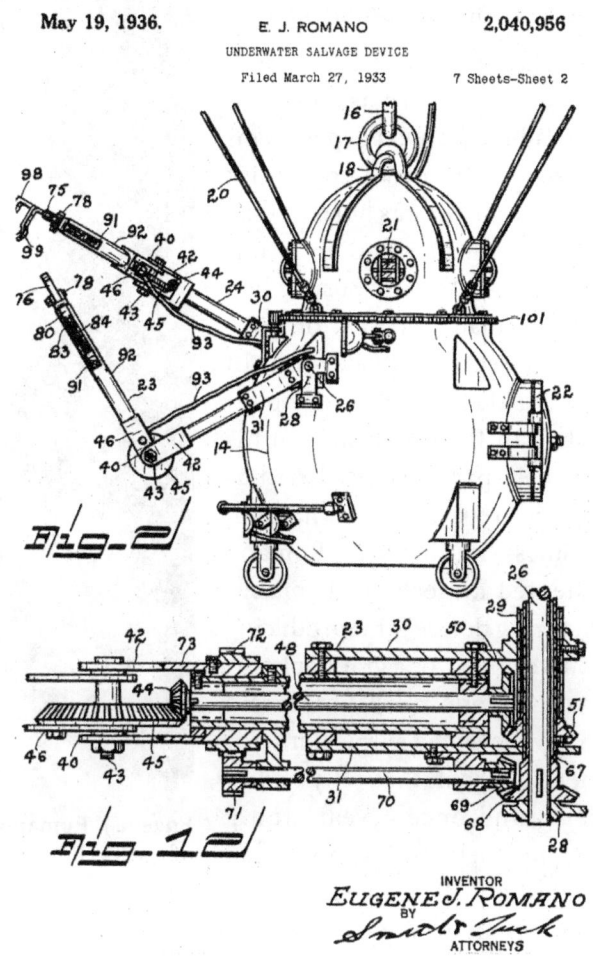

1936, "Underwater Salvage Device," United States. Patent number 2,040,956, filed (March 27, 1933) and issued (May 19, 1936).

Carl Wiley was one of the three from the western Washington area. He and his diving bell were often mentioned in connection with the wreck of the *Islander* in southeastern Alaska, using a diving bell of his design and patent.[3] A man named P.E. Peterson was reported to have sketches for a diving bell that could direct cutting with acetylene torches that he was pitching to an Italian salvage company trying to recover treasure from the *Egypt*. Little can be found about Peterson or his sketches, but if all he had were sketches, he was far behind already.

The third Seattle man mentioned among those planning treasure salvage was Eugene J. Romano. Eugene Romano was different—he liked to build things.

Inventor Extraordinaire

Eugene J. Romano of Seattle had a track record as an inventor and mechanical expert combined with the make-up of a risk taker. Romano was born in California in 1870 to Italian immigrants. By his early 30s, he had already made a name for himself in Seattle and beyond. In the Seattle City Directory published in June 1901, he and his business partner were listed as "expert repairers" in the auto business. In June 1903, Romano patented a mechanical manufacturing device for reproducing sound tablets for a graphophone. During World War I, he was said to have invented surgical instruments, a clock that only had to be wound once a year, and a rowing shell that won a speed contest at Lake Geneva. He was educated in Italy and spent several years working for *Scientific American* magazine, traveling in Europe in search of novel inventions.

Eugene J. Romano (photograph used with permission of Rockwell Hammond, Jr.)

Romano's mechanical interests were not limited to strictly legal endeavors. In January 1910, Eugene Romano (sometimes seen as Jean in Seattle papers) was facing trial as one of the primary promoters of slot machines in King County, where it was a felony to possess them. He had shown mechanical prowess with the machines for some time. In 1903, while an employee of the Star Novelty Company, he testified in a trial about how the machines work. The defendant was found guilty and fined ten dollars for having a machine on the counter of his cigar stand.[4] By 1905, Romano founded his own gaming company, American Novelty Machines of Seattle.

The Romanoplane

Although Boeing put Seattle on the aerospace landscape, it was Eugene J. Romano who was one of the earliest to build an airplane and have it fly over Puget Sound—doing business as the Romano Aerial Navigation Company. On July 4, 1911, the first flight of the *Romanoplane* took place as part of a huge Independence Day celebration, and it was also the date of the first crash.[5] To call it an aircraft was a bit of a stretch—its nickname was the "flying bedpost" due to the frame and size of the structure. Though admired for many of its technical innovations, the *Romanoplane* was never more than a novel dream.[6]

A personal description of the inventor helps explain the pace and expanse with which he undertook ventures.

> When Romano, always an interested student of intricate and puzzling mechanics, first decided to follow out in actual construction several novel ideas concerning aeroplanes that had come to him in the study of already existing types, he had a few thousand dollars, and was so comfortably fixed that he gave little thought to the financial end of his new venture.[7]

The Romano Special

Romano's interest in setting speed records was not only in the clouds; the *Romano Special* automobile made a splash on the racing circuit in the Northwest. Romano shifted his focus to auto repair and machine work for his business and setting auto racing records for his enjoyment. The *Romano Special* was quite a spectacle in the growing sport of automobile racing. His racer was believed to be the first eight-cylinder motorcar to enter a race sanctioned by the American Automobile Association in June 1913. Not surprisingly, the engine was from one of his former aircraft. At the time, mostly six- and four-cylinder models slugged it out to find a design mix that worked. Experts expected that the *Romano Special's* transmission would not be able to endure the increased power and would break down before the twenty-fifth lap.

Romanoplane test flight, c. 1911 (photograph used with permission of Rockwell Hammond, Jr.)

Romano Special, Eugene Romano at the wheel, Ray Lentz in passenger seat, others not known (photograph used with permission of Rockwell Hammond, Jr.)

It did not break, and in fact, the *Romano Special* excelled. In a race on July 12, 1914, Romano Special driver, Perry Barnes, set a new world speed record in a 25-mile race of 22 minutes and 7 seconds … a blazing sixty-plus miles per hour. Even more notoriety came Romano's way. The first annual race to the top of Pikes Peak in 1916 was won by twenty-two-year-old driver, Rea Lentz, driving a *Romano Special*. The press described the car as nondescript, small, and powered by an aircraft engine. The prize of $3,000 and the Penrose trophy went back with them to Seattle.

The Romano Diving Robot

Using patents for a diving bell and salvage buoys filed in 1931, Eugene Romano formed yet another venture, the Romano Marine Salvage Co. Their articles of incorporation and subsequent stock offering said they planned to "manufacture sufficient salvage buoys, apparatus, and accessories to salvage sunken vessels and to purchase sufficient ships and barges to carry on salvage operations."[8] Romano's "diving robot" quickly became widely discussed in the press. An early mention in the newspaper during October 1932 said Romano "is building a diving bell and will test it on ships now lying at the bottom of Elliott Bay."[9]

The Romano diving bell had all the structural qualities of similar diving bells of the era. It was constructed of a ⅞" steel plate to withstand high pressures at extreme depths. The Romano bell was pear-shaped owing to the armored headroom at the top. Four port holes at the top were for viewing and entry was through a hatch in the middle of the sphere. The nine-foot-long arms had mechanical and hydraulic components strong enough to clamp down on objects but sensitive enough to maintain a light touch. A hose delivered breathable air from above, and a filter inside the sphere removed carbon dioxide.

An Unapproved Secret Mission

To fulfill the business plan and prove the capabilities of the diving robot, the next order of business for Romano Marine was to secure some salvage expertise to support their demonstrations. Romano engaged one of the most widely publicized salvors and treasure seekers of the time to help them in their cause—Carl Wiley. Wiley and his brother, Elbert, started as Seattle house movers but built and patented their own underwater diving bell.[10] Romano was aware of Wiley's experience and notoriety in salvage effort for the *Islander* and seemed the right man to help connect them to the real mission of Romano Marine Salvage—to raise or pick apart a treasure ship. Wiley was prominently featured in the center of the Romano Marine letterhead as "General Salvage Expert Captain Carl H. Wiley, Submarine Engineer."[11]

That was just one of many things that Romano and Wiley were up to. Carl Wiley had already flown to the east coast months earlier on a different mission for the company—to try to locate the wreck of the *S.S. Merida* and salvage her treasure. In mid-February 1932, an article in the *New York Times* reported that a wizened old treasure hunter named Harry Bowdoin would use his iron diving suit to make an attempt on the *Merida* at the end of April.[12] That announcement may have lent some urgency to Wiley's mission for Romano Marine. After reading that, Romano flew Wiley across the country to Washington, D.C., to insert themselves into that search and to grab headlines with the announcement that Romano Marine would also be going after the *Merida*. A telegram from Ralph Fleming to Wiley gave him direct instructions to tell the press that they knew where to find the *Merida* and that the equipment required for the salvage would be headed east very soon.[13] Fleming's instruction may have been less about announcing an actual venture and more for publicity to stir further investors. On March 30, 1932, the *Washington Post* and the *New York Times* ran a story that confirmed Wiley had been in the area since March 9. However, he said his diving bell would be used in the salvage operation, not Romano's.

After a disagreement with the state over the unauthorized use of investor funds to pay Wiley and a dispute between Wiley and Romano Marine, Wiley was discharged from the project in April 1932.[14] Fleming and Romano also began to wonder exactly what Wiley had accomplished at their expense on Capt. Olaf Larson's boat off the coast from Norfolk looking for the *Merida*. Fleming sent two letters to Captain Larson via general delivery. "We would greatly appreciate it if you would tell us what you did for Mr. Wiley and for us as we are quite anxious to check up on this work and also see what will be necessary for any further operations."[15] Fleming and Romano wondered if Wiley was withholding information for his own use later. Despite the lack of a reply from Capt. Larson, Romano Marine was not letting anything slow them down. In late November 1932, Romano Marine printed a four-page sales brochure about the diving robot—they needed investors to keep them afloat.

A Target Is Found

Romano was anxious to demonstrate the capabilities of his diving bell with underwater recovery. When they found the wreck of a barge that sank in 825 feet of water, a sense of anticipation and excitement engaged the crew. They had already lifted a ten-ton set of railcar wheels from the bottom using Romano-designed salvage buoys and the Romano diving bell.

When Romano's payment for the dredger used in the recovery was not completed in full, the owner refused to allow Romano to operate the crane and prevented any further work. He essentially held the equipment hostage until Romano paid in full. To make matters even worse, the dredger owner and Carl Wiley each filed maritime lawsuits against Romano on July 2, 1932, resulting in all the Romano equipment being seized and impounded by U.S. Marshals from July 1932 until the case was decided in federal district court in January 1933.

Diving Bell Held Hostage

A Notice of Seizure appeared in the *Daily Journal of Commerce* in Seattle on July 7, 1932.[16] The U.S. Marshal seized the equipment where it lay aboard the barge, *Patterson*. Months passed before the case could be resolved. On October 14, 1932, Fleming complained to the judge about the condition of their valuable equipment.[17] Fleming said the bell and other equipment was exposed to the harsh saltwater and weather, which would rust the bell in no time. After his request to protect the equipment was denied by the U.S. Marshal's office, Fleming pleaded with the judge to shelter it from the elements. In addition to the diving bell and salvage buoy, there were 6,600 feet of wire cable, four rented anchors, and 800 feet of electrical and telephone wire also confiscated due to the lawsuit.

The barge owner assured Romano, and the judge, that the diving bell was out of the water and "covered with several coats of red lead, which constitutes a preservative commonly and ordinarily used on such equipment to protect against rust." The buoy was more challenging to secure. At thirty feet long, eight feet in diameter, and a gross weight of five tons, it remained in the water. When the suit was settled and the Romano diving bell freed from impoundment, Romano wasted no time returning to their business plan.[18]

Raising the *Bahada*

To demonstrate the capabilities of his diving bell and salvage buoys, Romano's initial securities filing named the tug boat *Bahada* one of their stated objectives.[19] Lying on the bottom in 260 feet of water near Anacortes, Washington, the *Bahada* sunk on November 21, 1926, following an explosion. Fragments of the 85-foot steel-hulled craft were all that remained afloat. Only one of the nine men aboard was found when his body washed ashore.[20]

During the summer of 1933, Romano Marine's crew had been on the site for a month, preparing their work and doing their best to ensure the demonstration's success. Each of the buoys were filled with water and lowered to the bottom, where they were attached to the vessel by a diver inside the Romano diving bell, a significant accomplishment. By July 23, 1933, six of Romano's salvage buoys were attached to the *Bahada* in their preparations to raise the hulk.[21]

An Interest from the Navy

The time had come for Romano Marine to prove the diving bell's value or not. The primary customer Romano Marine sought was the U.S. Navy. Navy Commander H.E. Saunders was invited to observe the operation of the diving bell and buoys. "Savvy" Saunders was no junior officer sent out for public relations purposes. Harold Eugene Saunders was a brilliant Naval architect and submarine builder who had received the Navy Distinguished Service Medal as the salvage officer in charge of raising the submarine S-4 (SS 109), which had sunk in December 1927 off Cape Cod. Saunders' visit was only a preliminary inspection and expression of interest by the Navy but led to a favorable recommendation. It also led to a second demonstration for a contingent of higher-ranking officers.[22]

Characteristically, when Harry told the story about the capabilities of the Romano diving sphere in his 1942 book, he embellished it with an unnecessary and indefensible exaggeration. Harry said the Romano test dive for the Navy was 5,000 feet in Puget Sound when the water there is only 900 feet at its deepest.[23]

Saunders expressed his doubts that the fittings on the *Bahada* around which the buoys' cables were looped would hold. As the pumps pushed water out of the buoys and they began to rise, about eighteen tons of steel was torn from the hull and raised to the surface, clearly demonstrating the assessment of Commander Saunders upon his earlier inspection. Two anchors, four-hundred feet of anchor chain, and the anchor winch were hauled out, still hooked to the towing tee from the bow of the *Bahada*.

Compressors began pumping air into the six buoys a second time. After five hours, the *Bahada* started to give way on the bottom of Puget Sound, and the water above the tug suddenly rose three feet above the surface in a 100-foot circle. Light green water filled with bubbles rose high off the surface like a plateau of water. Pressure gauges indicated that the *Bahada* was rising but was coming up stern first. The uneven load stressed the harnesses beyond their capacity. Halfway to the surface, one of the forty-ton buoys broke loose and shot to the surface. The *Bahada* fell back down to the bottom. The weak point in the lift was a specially cast manganese steel shackle with a breaking point of 245 tons. A trip to the bottom in the diving robot found the vessel sitting upright and that the specially designed shackles had broken under stress.

The officers viewing the demonstration concluded that "the diving chamber should be of particular interest to the Navy as it has been demonstrated to be practicable for use in salvage operations to a known depth of 800 feet." Saunders found that the diving chamber could "do everything a diver can do, many times more efficiently and with arms that have tremendous strength." He believed it to be a "tremendous stride forward in deep-sea salvage operations" and that "an officer with special qualifications should be assigned for observation of the operations in the interest of the Navy."[24]

Demonstrations Don't Create Income

Eugene Romano's invention was getting the recognition he had always hoped for, giving investors some optimism. Nevertheless, the salvage attempt did not impress crewmen who had undoubtedly seen it all at sea. One expressed a particularly crusty opinion of the diving robot's claws, saying, "You can't raise a wreck by picking at it like a crow."[25]

Romano's pitchman and son-in-law, Ralph Fleming, was more inclined to keep promoting the diving bell to recover treasure, and continued investments pointed toward that kind of mission. Romano Marine purchased a four-masted barkentine, the *Conqueror*, in May 1933 and leaked to the press that it would be used as a base for treasure recovery. When the Romano Marine purchase was announced in May of 1933, the newspaper said the vessel would "spread her canvas soon under sealed orders to seek treasure long lost in Davy Jones' locker."[26] The romantic tone quickly gave way to an explanation that the *Conqueror* would be ingloriously towed to the Straits, where it would anchor above an unnamed wreck while the diving bell was used to salvage the treasure.

The purchase of the *Conqueror* and the treasure venture for which it was to be central turned out to be a boondoggle. Romano Marine Salvage's fourth-quarter financial report to the state Securities Division in 1933 did not show an entry for any income, and cash on hand was down to $778.07.[27] Even amidst the financial difficulties, Romano Marine received positive signs that the U.S. Navy and other world navies were interested. The indications of that were abundant and glowing. Rear Admiral Ernest J. King, Chief of the Bureau of Aeronautics, communicated directly with Ralph Fleming after receiving additional details.

> Your diving sphere most certainly opens new fields in salvage operations, making possible work that we could not have considered heretofore with ordinary salvage gear. You can be assured the Navy Department will appreciate fully the merits of the Romano equipment and give the matter its thorough consideration.[28]

Losing Momentum

Despite the optimism around the possible adoption of the diving bell by the Navy, the reality was that Romano Marine Salvage had a lot of equipment but no income. Romano investors had financed costly demonstrations and attracted the attention of the highest levels of the Navy, but there was no movement on a contract. They were looking for options and running out of money.

One attempt to use the diving bell for commercial purposes arose as part of the construction of the Golden Gate Bridge in San Francisco. Construction began in January 1933, and by January 1934, there was much speculation about the stability of a rock bed one hundred and ten feet below the surface where a critical supporting structure was to be placed. Romano Marine Salvage made an offer—a plea, really—to assist. Romano went through the San Francisco Chamber of Commerce and offered the diving bell to go down and illuminate the bottom for inspection amid concern that there could be a vacated space—a "mermaid's cavern"—beneath the bedrock. The diving bell was to be inspected by the bridge directors, but there is no indication that this project ever materialized. Their best publicity still could not generate income, and public attention did not result in private investment.[29]

The state securities commission would not allow Romano Marine to sell more stock. The *Merida* was off the east coast, and the diving bell was in Seattle. Any possible treasure venture seemed a dream. Romano Marine was struggling, and their financial statements demonstrated that the end could be near.

A Four-Masted Opportunity

The four-masted schooner *Constellation* was a beautiful reincarnation of an old-world seagoing vessel and an embodiment of the romance of the sea. Its arrival in Washington, D.C., in late September 1934, was intended to be a way to keep its owner's dream alive. Instead, it turned out to be the beginning of the end for the old ship.[30]

The *Constellation* began life in Harrington, Maine, in 1918 as a cargo ship named the *Sally Persis Noyes*. She was 204 feet long, almost nineteen feet abeam, and had a draft of fourteen and a half feet. Following the shipping boom of World War I, there was a drop off in commercial shipping leading up to the Depression. The *Sally Persis Noyes* sat idle for three years, and in 1931 business conditions forced its sale. The fate of many of the old schooners was most often to turn them into barges. Without masts, they looked as lifeless and powerless as they were. The *Noyes* was rescued from that fate by Robert Royall. On August 28, 1931, he purchased the vessel for around $3,000. A newspaper reported that Royall's rather romantic notion was to "test whether or not a schooner of another day can be made to fill some useful purpose and find a place in the modern world."[31]

After the purchase, craftsmen transformed the cargo ship into a magnificent pleasure craft with the finest touches and details. The hold that once held coal and lumber was graced with beautiful paneling and rows of staterooms with red upholstered furniture. A newspaper article in 1932 called Royall's project a "mysterious renovation of a vessel from an era when four-masters ruled commercial shipping."[32] Rumors said that Royall spent $70,000 on the renovation. As the completion of the project neared, there was discussion among the family for an appropriate name for the vessel. The *Polynesia* was Royall's first choice, while his father liked *Southern Cross*, but they ultimately settled on *Constellation*.[33] Once it was renamed, Royall decided to open it as the New England Nautical Schoolship *Constellation*. A retired

Navy officer was engaged as commander, brochures were prepared, and publicity was widespread. Unfortunately, nobody else thought much of Royall's business plan, and the venture was dead in the water.[34]

Disappointment only led to more ideas to save the ship. Though Royall purchased an ad in *Yachting Magazine* in October 1933 to sell the *Constellation*, his approach would hardly be described as letting go. He offered to captain it for any buyer, help them with profitable ideas for its use, and even suggested he and his Maine craftsman could restore other equally magnificent vessels. When no offer was made, Royall made an interesting business decision—he spent even more money on upgrading the *Constellation* to the level of a private yacht to make it a floating nightclub and restaurant. With the latest renovations, Royall was ready to test the public's interest in boarding the ship for dinner and tours. The old ship was towed from Linekin Bay to Boothbay Harbor, Maine, where it was opened for dinner and dancing.[35]

The *Constellation* had not sailed for almost four years, so people across the region took note in mid–August 1934 when it hoisted sails. Royall's love for what he was doing extended to the people who worked for him, especially to Alvin Loesche, a German who would be captaining the vessel. He had settled in Boothbay Harbor, Maine, and there met Royall. Loesche and his wife, Johanna, had sailed his entire life and commanded similar schooners.

The *Constellation* was anchored at Boothbay for about a month, offering lunch, dinner, or merely a visit. The shrimp cocktail cost sixty-five cents, and the boiled lobster was only $1.50. A ferry to the vessel for a visit was fifty cents, but only if his customers did not have food. Some days Royall made three hundred dollars, boosting his confidence in his new business plan.

On September 14, 1934, Royall, Loesche, and their crew set sail for Washington, D.C.[36] They planned to head south, stop at Washington, and proceed further south to spend the winter in Florida. As an unpowered sailing vessel, the captain and crew were swiftly reminded of their dependence on favorable winds in the sail. Their trip from Maine to Washington took sixteen days.

Constellation, the Club Ship

By October 1934, *Constellation* was tied up at the Harbormaster's Dock at Water and M Streets S.W. following a slow sail down from Boothbay Harbor. Royall was joined by his sister, Alwyn Inness-Brown from Long Island, to live aboard. They landed on the social calendar in the capital by hosting a dinner dance aboard the magnificent ship.[37] It was not a reporter covering commerce or navigation but the society writer who attended the affair. The writer told who attended, what they wore, and how their hair was done. She also glowingly described the vessel and her crew.

> The *Constellation* presented a beautiful sight, its black hull with white trimmings silhouetted against the dark water and the four tall masts towering into the sky, losing themselves in the stars. Dapper ship's officers in dark blue uniforms, snowy white caps, assisted the guests from the gangplank to the decks.[38]

Constellation was a spectacular attraction for a few months at the end of 1934. When the crew hosted a banquet for a group of ship modelers in February 1935, Loesche and Royall regaled the group with stories of tall ships from the past and with a meal that included fare named for the sea. Their Moby Dick cocktail was paired with Broiled Sea Cow, Sargasso Seaweed, Tarred Hemp, and Greased Green Horn.[39]

The ship was a hit—until it was not.

A Change of Plans

The Club Ship ran its course as a dining venue and the novelty *of Constellation* as a dining venue wore thin. It was expensive to keep a big schooner, even at the dock. The cost of a planned relocation to Miami could not be sustained by the limited income. None of Robert Royall's business plans for the *Constellation* were working out. The School Ship failed quickly for lack of interest. Royall still had to look for ways to remain financially afloat. Display ads in a yachting magazine in March and April 1935 confirm that Royall forced himself to reconsider what was undoubtedly a last resort—he again put his beloved *Constellation* up for sale. The *Constellation* had run out of options, but Royall was not the only one in trouble. While dinner guests dined to the music of George Gaul, an influential orchestral leader, on the deck of the *Constellation*, Harry Rieseberg was having serious troubles at the Bureau of Navigation.[40]

Retention Is Impossible

There are signs and signals of one's personality which are indicators of how their life may evolve. People's choices for the future are generally very similar to those they have made in the past. After a rough start to his career as a government employee, Harry seemed to have found some stability at the Bureau of Navigation. In 1934, he was forty-two years old and had stuck with his second marriage for fourteen years. Robert, his son by his first wife, Caroline, was by that time sixteen and growing to be an exceptional young man despite no contact with his father. Harry's children with his second wife, Ellen, were very young. Henry was six years old, and Shirley was only three. It did not matter much because Harry's job as Chief of the Tonnage Division of the Bureau of Navigation and Steamboat Inspection was coming to a self-inflicted end.

Rieseberg's director wrote to the Secretary of Commerce in October 1934 recommending that he be transferred to a position in Mobile, Alabama, effective October 31, 1934.[41] The message being sent to Harry by cutting his pay in half and transferring him to the Deep South was clear—he was no longer wanted in the employ of the United States government.

> Mr. Rieseberg is Chief of our Tonnage Division and has under his supervision, six female clerks. This recommendation is made because of the actions of Mr. Rieseberg, inconsistent with those of a gentleman, and for the good of the service. I consider that under the circumstances the retention of Mr. Rieseberg in his present position is impossible.

Though couched in bureaucratically veiled terms, Harry Rieseberg was accused of philandering—again. While supervising female employees at the War Risk Bureau, he was moved out of that job resulting in a separation from his first wife. Given that he appeared to be a serial harasser, there may have been other circumstances unknown to his employers or his wives.

A family story about Harry losing his job at the Bureau of Navigation was that when the Democrats won an election, he lost his job to patronage. As he was a Civil Service employee, that would not have been the case. In a decision that would forever alter his life and those of his wife, children, and even his parents, Harry Rieseberg resigned from his position at the Bureau of Navigation rather than accepting the demotion and transfer. Five weeks later, effective November 23, 1934, the Department accepted his resignation with prejudice. A resignation accepted with prejudice may not be withdrawn or retracted, and that person may not be rehired.[42] Harry Rieseberg's career as a federal employee was over.

Who knows what Harry told his wife and parents, particularly his father, about why he was forced to leave his civil service job. His father's experience would have held a government position in high regard. There is no way to know how the conversation went when he first broke the news or if he even told them the truth about why it happened. We can only wonder what life at home was like during the five weeks he suspended until the day he formally resigned. His tenure at the Bureau of Navigation, his prominence in the Washington fraternal organizations, and even his new-found fame as a national figure in the growing field of underwater treasure hunting all seemed to suggest that the immature, wandering Harry had become part of the past. His ego, however, was always in the lead. He was held captive by the pull toward self-centeredness; he was driven by it and often at the expense of the truth.

Few people would have the gall to ask an employer for help in this situation, but Harry Rieseberg asked for a letter of reference. He was keeping his options open about finding other employment. A generic, two-paragraph letter reporting his employment gave the dates and an acknowledgment that "under his administration, our Statistical Division reached its highest degree of efficiency and accuracy."[43] He must have had a friend on the inside to grant such a generous, yet scant, reference.

Socially, Harry was forced to limit his many fraternal affiliations. As a result of losing his job, he requested and was granted a remission of his annual membership dues in Masonic Lodge #33 beginning in October 1934. It is unclear whether his fraternal brothers knew or cared about his resignation and its reasons. As if all was normal, Harry was nominated to become the Grand Tall Cedar for Capitol Forest #104 in December 1934. Harry may have had the support of his fraternal brothers, but he was otherwise on his own. It was not just his job coming apart; his family was as well.

A Job and a Marriage Come to an End

Only a few weeks after his resignation under duress from the Bureau of Navigation, Harry's wife, Ellen, left Washington. She packed up their two children during the height of the Christmas season in 1934 and moved to Leavenworth, Kansas, where she went to work for the Public Health Service as a mental health nurse at the federal penitentiary. Prisons at that time were only beginning to escape a reputation as brutal institutions. Death by hanging was still in practice for executions, and Leavenworth was a notoriously dangerous place. Her desperation to leave overrode any concerns about her working conditions. She wanted to be far away from Harry. She wanted to protect her children.

Leavenworth, Kansas, was a curious location for her escape from Harry since it was where Harry's mother had family. In the past, Ellen had always retreated to her own family's home near Cincinnati. Whether the Kansas location was chosen with help from Harry's parents or simply the only job available as far from Harry as possible is unknown. She reported for work there on January 7, 1935. Ellen offered at least a minimal explanation for their split in a later divorce petition. The language was appropriate for the court but only partially explained the family dynamics at the time.

> ... the defendant [Harry] was guilty of excesses, cruel treatment and outrages. That particularly on or about the 1st day of January A.D. 1935, the defendant quarreled with this plaintiff [handwritten addition, abandoned this plaintiff] and nagged this plaintiff to such an extent that a further living together of the parties as husband and wife is impossible and insupportable.[44]

After his firing, Harry Rieseberg made a choice that Ellen could not tolerate. He saw losing his job as the opportunity of a lifetime. He decided to not only leave his career but also to invest any money they had in a treasure-hunting scheme. Harry believed in his dream of wealth. He thought he was on the brink of a fortune, and the way to achieve it became crystal clear. He did not give up his visions of wealth at the bottom of the sea; he gave up his family to seek it.

A Bold and Desperate Partnership

There is nothing in the record to help understand how Harry Rieseberg, Eugene Romano, Ralph Fleming, and Robert Royall came together to make their joint plans in early 1935. The passion, energy, and salesmanship of Harry Rieseberg were undoubtedly at work. Once Rieseberg saw the *Constellation* and her mighty white canvas sheets raised high above the decks, Harry had no turning back. All the necessary parts of the formula for him to be "wealthy beyond Croesus' dreams" seemed to be falling into place. The opportunities seemed brilliantly obvious. Harry Rieseberg would help bring the Romano diving bell to Washington, where it would be on display aboard the *Constellation* while they attracted investors for a treasure expedition using Harry's research.

A sequence of events between December 1934 and May 1935 appears to have been entirely orchestrated by Harry Rieseberg—Harry the publicity chairman, Harry the statistician, Harry the fraternal brother, Harry the passionate pitchman.

After discovering Romano's patent application and newspaper coverage of their promotion and testing of the diving bell, Harry recognized it as a possible breakthrough in man's ability to dive for deeper wrecks. As Rieseberg said, he could be "like the mine owner who suddenly taps a great new ore-body at levels below his former workings."[45] Harry was utterly energized by his discovery of the Romano diving bell in Seattle. He knew he already had part of the treasure puzzle with his research because of the interest it had stirred up and the attention his newspaper articles brought. Now he could envision a way to put that research to use. It did not take much to kick Harry's ego into overdrive. Every element of his dream appeared to come together with him at the center of it all.

A Diving Robot Comes to Washington

Rieseberg questioned all his Washington contacts about what they knew about Romano's diving robot. Harry said in his book that he learned that Romano had a business agent in Washington at the time, and Harry quickly tracked him down. He excitedly promoted the idea of testing the bell on some treasure dives and described how the robot arms could help bring up treasure from the bottom of the sea. Romano's business representative in Washington was J.W. Carpenter, whom Fleming referred to as Commander Carpenter, likely a former Navy man. During November and early December 1934, Carpenter pitched the Romano equipment to potential military buyers.

Carpenter wrote a two-page letter to Fleming and the other Romano Marine shareholders describing his activities on their behalf.[46] He did not mention hearing from Harry Rieseberg, but that, too, bears toward truth in Harry's version. Rieseberg said that despite his efforts, Carpenter "wasn't at all keen about having the invention used by an individual" and was intently focused on "selling the robot to the government at some enormous figure."[47] Carpenter's business focus was to sell the diving robot to the military, domestic or foreign.

Despite Carpenter's discouragement, Rieseberg was already promoting the Romano robot for publicity. Harry fed information about the diving bell to Ray Coll, Jr., a syndicated columnist. Coll's column at the end of January 1935 not only touted the details of the diving bell but also noted that Rieseberg told him he was receiving three hundred inquiries a week inquiring about sunken treasure because of his many newspaper articles.[48]

Even if the Washington agent was not listening to Harry's wild ideas, Ralph Fleming was thinking about treasure. When Carpenter brushed Rieseberg off, Harry said he sent a long letter to Eugene Romano, and Romano agreed to allow Harry to test the robot. Having already invested thousands of dollars in building the diving bell, Harry said Romano told him "he had used ... every cent he could borrow from his friends."[49] The agreement between Harry Rieseberg and Romano Submarine Engineering required that Rieseberg pay for a cross-country rail shipment of the Romano diving robot.

Chapter 4. The Great Fall

Harry said the diving bell arrived in Washington five weeks after contacting Eugene Romano, but the inventor himself would not be part of the project. Eugene Romano died "comparatively poor" in Seattle on February 10, 1935, after a six-week illness and hospital stay.[50] An article in the *Seattle Times* identified May 1, 1935, as the day the Romano diving bell left Seattle for shipment to Washington to be placed aboard the *Constellation*, with arrival expected ten days later.[51] The savvy Fleming may have taken advantage of Harry's enthusiasm and lack of business acumen. Rieseberg said his agreement with Romano Marine was to pay the freight cost to get the diving bell to Washington. Harry said he was so excited that he had not fully considered what it would cost before agreeing to pay the total amount, so the $1,600 bill from the freight company may have been his first surprise.[52]

However, Fleming had Harry on the hook for far more than shipping costs. The agreement Rieseberg signed with Romano Submarine Engineering and Salvage Corporation on April 15, 1935, had terms shockingly favorable to Fleming. Harry agreed to lease the Romano diving bell for up to one year for "the purposes of conducting an expedition for the search and salvage of treasure lost at sea." Harry agreed to pay $10,000 on delivery of the diving bell and $5,000 each month until $50,000 had been paid. In addition, he would pay Romano Submarine ten percent of "the gross value of any and everything recovered or salvaged."[53] Harry's only acknowledgment of that arrangement was his saying he was paying a "whopping monthly rent for the iron critter."[54] The financial impossibility of Harry keeping this agreement is certain.

Ralph Fleming, Commander Carpenter, and the other Romano Marine investors must have looked at each other in disbelief at their good fortune. They would have an opportunity to demonstrate their diving bell firsthand to a large audience, and the crazy treasure guy, Harry Rieseberg, would pay for the cost of getting it shipped across the country. It was indeed a win-win for both Harry and Romano Marine. Harry would have access to an attention-getting piece of equipment that could attract investors for a treasure venture. Romano Marine would provide hands-on access to their invention to generate hoped-for sales. Royall and his *Constellation* would be the platform for the demonstration and a base for the proposed treasure venture.

But where would Harry have gotten the money? Did he ever actually pay this amount? He would have had to find moneyed investors. Unfortunately, there is no corresponding financial statement for the business to indicate any payment by Rieseberg to Romano Submarine, so the contract may have been a sham document for the benefit of their investors and the securities division in the State of Washington. In newspaper articles as early as March 1935, Rieseberg and Fleming explained Harry's role in the venture as guiding the group. On one version of the letterhead for the company, Harry Rieseberg was the only name listed, and he was titled Research Engineer.

Displaying the Romano diving bell on the deck of the *Constellation* as a technical curiosity would not only attract attention, but it would also provide a readily available platform at the dock capable of supporting the equipment to lower the heavy bell into the water next to the ship while demonstrating its capabilities for the military. Royall received income from having the bell on deck and charging people to come aboard to view it. Harry Rieseberg got to see his hopes of untold wealth begin to materialize. He hoped the diving robot could attract investors who wanted a piece of the treasure-hunting action based on his closely guarded charts and research. It is one thing to track down the history of a sunken vessel and something entirely different to know enough to anchor a salvage ship over the top of it in a vast ocean and drop down a diving bell or a diver in a hard hat suit. The next question for Harry was how to get to that opportunity.

Like a prophet having visions, Rieseberg saw confirmation that his dreams of great wealth could be realized everywhere he looked. He was the man with the information and had found partners with the equipment and expertise to use it. It seemed only a matter of time—and money—before his name would be in the newspapers heading up a deep-sea expedition. One downfall of such zealotry is the inability to understand why others do not see the world the same way. What Harry was working out during those five weeks of contemplation before he resigned under duress from his position with the Bureau of Navigation was audacious.

Changing Business Plans

Commander Carpenter's sales efforts in Washington helped keep up optimism that Romano Marine might still make a sale to a military customer. He met with the Swedish, Argentine, Italian, and French embassies to gauge their interest in an attachment to the diving bell that would allow it to be used for submarine rescues. That feature was far more critical to the world's navies than the equipment's ability to help salvage a disabled submarine after all inside had been lost. In Carpenter's review of their prospects, it appeared there was enough high-level interest to keep the hope of a large sale dangling like a carrot at the end of a stick.

However, Carpenter also exposed some key concerns and obstacles and acknowledged the beginning of the end for the prospects of Romano Marine Salvage to sell their invention to the United States Navy. It was not completely clear to the military if the Romano bell, as designed, could quickly connect to a submarine hatch, and Carpenter pointed that out in his letter. The Navy appeared to confirm they were not a customer at the time but seemed to ask Romano to keep the bell ready at his own expense should there be a need for another rescue.[55] Carpenter's summation of the hesitance not only of the U.S. Navy but also of the Argentine, French, and Italian maritime branches drew the line between success and failure. His hope was hinged on the need to demonstrate "that the Romano Equipment can handle bolts and nuts under water more advantageously than a diver in a suit."

All the multi-ton lifting capacity of the buoys, the ability to dive to greater depths, and a drill attachment to secure cables to the vessel were impressive but missed the target for the military. If someone inside the Romano bell could not safely unscrew a hatch and attach a rescue bell to a disabled sub before all inside drowned or suffocated, then the mechanical robot was going nowhere with the Navy.

It was probably not just a whim that led Romano Submarine Engineering to change its focus from selling to the military to seek other uses for the diving bell. The Navy had moved on to equipment better suited to submarine rescue. A new diving bell tested off southern California could rescue up to eighty-eight submariners in about four hours at three hundred feet. Commander Carpenter was right. The Navy needed something that could unscrew bolts like a diver. The hopes for a big sale to the U.S. Navy were withering away.

Romano tried to regroup by quickly resubmitting his patent for the diving bell with a new name to catch the attention of their potential customers again. The original patent #2,040,956 for his Underwater Salvage Device had been filed in March of 1933. Still, in January 1935, during Carpenter's sales trip to Washington, Romano filed a new application for the diving bell, renaming the patent as a Submarine Salvage Apparatus.[56]

Publicity Time

Harry could not wait to announce the venture to the world. The first public indication of the most significant event in his life was an article in the *Washington Evening Star* on March 7, 1935. Harry was the source for the article, expressing his standing as "an international authority on sunken treasure who will be treasurer and research engineer of the corporation."[57] The article also confirmed that Harry's focus was research on the location of vessels and not diving for them himself. Readers were told that "For the past several years Rieseberg has made studies of the history and location of a great number of sunken ships bearing treasures of jewels, gold, and silver bullion."[58]

In his 1942 book, Harry said he was the one who reached out to Romano, which seems most likely based on other evidence. However, in this article, published in the heat of the moment at the event, Harry said that Romano read about him and initiated the contact, a less likely and more self-centered approach magnifying his fame.

In an April 28, 1935, press release picked up by the Associated Press, Harry decided it was time to press the issue further. He went out on a limb and announced that the *Constellation* would be leaving soon to salvage treasure from the *Golden Hind*, a ship sunk in 1502 off the coast of Haiti.[59] On Friday, May 3, he contacted a reporter with *Science News Digest* to give them the story before the diving bell's arrival. The reporter's notes on the back of the photo explain his perspective.

> A Lt. Riesburg? called at the request of an NEA man to tell us about a story. He has a diving bell which the Navy calls as important as the invention of the airplane. It will be here Monday or Tuesday, and he is willing to give us stuff for release now. He is at Dist. 2123, on board the Constellation where the tests will be held. He is there day and night.[60]

Besides explaining how the story about the venture began circulating, the information also acknowledged where Harry lived after his wife left him. Harry's living arrangement aboard the *Constellation* likely reflected both his focus on this project and that he had no other place to live.

Romano Submarine Engineering

On Romano's side of the United States, a news story in Seattle confirmed Harry's press release and added more detail to the business arrangement. Ralph Fleming announced that the company would soon begin to search for sunken treasure and said the key person guiding operations would be "Lieut. Harry E. Rieseberg, U.S.N., retired, expert salvager of treasure hidden in ocean graves."[61] Whether it was Rieseberg who tried to pass himself off as a former military man to the Romano group or an embellishment made by Fleming is unknown. The other stretch of the truth was to describe Harry as an expert salvager, not just a man with research since he had done nothing of the sort.

Even though Fleming was no longer required to update the Securities Division of the State of Washington on the state of the business, he still did so in acknowledgment of their "courteous treatment" and "business-like manner" used to handle all the details regarding Romano Marine Salvage.[62] Fleming shared the newspaper articles from the *Washington Evening Star* and the *Seattle Times* with Eugene Sisson, the director of the license division, and communicated his optimism about this turn of events saying, "by this time next year our company should be paying real dividends."[63]

Fleming told Sisson he would head to Washington and New York for business within a week. A re-formed corporation, Romano Submarine Engineering & Salvage, was organized in Delaware on April 9, 1935, just before the diving bell was on its way to Washington. Their articles of incorporation clearly stated their purpose to, "search for, explore, conduct expeditions, and engage generally in the locating, raising and salvaging of sunken ships and vessels, cargoes and materials of the sea."[64]

An Observer Adds Perspective

The recollections of a young sailor hired to work on the *Constellation* during this crossroads of interests add immensely to an understanding of the fast-paced events taking place in April and May 1935. Though his recollections were some fifty years later, they add astonishing detail to the history of the *Constellation*.[65]

A young man named Bill Carey was hired by Robert Royall in April 1935, about the same time Royall was making his business arrangements with Rieseberg and Fleming. Evidence from correspondence between Carey and Royall indicates part of their financial arrangements. Carey had limited skills but was interested in sailing on one of the big schooners after a stint in the Coast Guard. The treasure venture was already on the table since Carey reported he was prohibited from taking pictures or speaking to the press about his work on the ship. Royall, Carey, and Captain Alvin Loesche made the vessel spic-and-span for visitors.

Chapter 4. The Great Fall

The way Harry Rieseberg tells the story of what happens next is, of course, focused on himself. He says it was his idea to sell admission tickets to allow the public to come aboard the *Constellation* to tour the ship and see the diving robot up close while they also sought investors. Bill Carey's version of the events matched that narrative but was limited to his point of view as a crewman for Robert Royall. Carey noted that crowds suddenly gathered after raising the huge sails to dry them out on a sunny spring day. Royall painted a big sign offering tours for twenty-five cents, inviting them aboard for "Romance and Adventure."

Rieseberg claimed he was in charge of publicity to bring people in to tour the ship and get a sales pitch about investing in the treasure.[66] A four-page brochure offered tours of the "Gold Ship" for visitors to see the "strange and startling ROBOT which will reveal to the world the long-sought secrets of Davy Jones' locker!"[67] Though the brochure glamorized the hunt for gold nuggets, silver bars, and precious jewels, it was also designed to get people aboard the vessel to tour the ship and see the diving bell. In addition to the ship being in top-notch condition, the diving bell had been updated with fresh paint and large letters, noting it could achieve a depth of 5,000 feet. Carey said Rieseberg and Fleming were "selling stock in the treasure hunt like real estate developers."[68]

Despite what seemed to be an ideal match among the partners, differences in the agendas of each of the parties were soon exposed. With so much at stake, the pressure mounted. Money and time became scarce commodities, and each participant had their timetable and vested interests despite the common opportunity. While the tours drew attention, they attracted little revenue. In three months of public tours, ticket sales were only $256.40—hardly enough for anyone's purposes. Fleming and Royall were splitting that small amount.[69] Interest in the treasure expedition stirred up activity, but little came of it. It was time for a different approach. Fleming arranged for J. Howard Lawler to take over the publicity, research, and other promotional activities on behalf of Romano Submarine Engineering.[70] Harry focused on treasure, not on recouping the Romano investment in their equipment and sales demonstrations. Lawler not only assisted with the project in Washington but tried to secure other sales of the diving bell for which he could earn as much as a twenty-percent commission.

A Hoped-for Investor?

The group thought they had an investor with salvage expertise, but it was a false lead with a disturbing history. Fleming stated in the *Seattle Times* article that Leo C. Pyne of the New England Salvage Company of Brookline, Massachusetts, would oversee the treasure diving. Reportedly, Pyne was about to start the salvage of the *Sagamore*, a freighter of the Eastern Steamship Line, which sank in January 1930 in less than fifty feet of water only about one hundred fifty yards offshore of Portland, Maine.[71]

The addition of Pyne to the project is interesting because he had a well-documented history of swindling people over salvage projects that never took place. As recently as November 1934, just months before Fleming mentioned his involvement, Pyne was charged with larceny in Massachusetts for a scam business named the International Chartering and Shipping Company.[72] It was not the first time he had been in trouble. A similar case with the same business name found Pyne charged in January 1933 with stealing $3,000 from a Worcester widow. Pyne also filed for bankruptcy in July 1931 for a salvaging business.[73] In a *Seattle Times* article on March 16, 1935, Ralph Fleming reported that the venture, including Pyne, would have paid seven hundred dollars monthly for using the Romano diving bell, plus a thirty-five percent royalty on any treasure salvaged from the *Sagamore*.[74]

Harry Rieseberg also mentioned Pyne in *I Dive for Treasure*. He said that in response to their search for funding, Pyne and Cecil Conrad came to Washington to talk about investing. Harry's version of the story in his book was that Pyne and Conrad invested in a fictional treasure cruise to Silver Shoals, one of Harry's long-time tales, and took their wives along. Rieseberg's story about two investors he named "Smith and Jones" in the book were the resumes of Leonard C. Pyne and another man. Harry explained how in talking to "Jones" as an investor, it came to light that he had indictments and that "investors all over New England wanted their money back from him."[75] Consequently, Jones/Pyne and his hoped-for financing were removed from the venture.

The Big Show

After all the painting and varnishing were done, after the diving bell and the crane were secured and adjusted on the deck of the *Constellation*, and after shirts were pressed and shoes were shined, the crew was ready. A demonstration of the Romano diving bell aboard the *Constellation* was set for May 17, 1935.

In a letter to Eugene Sisson at the Securities Division back in Washington, Fleming supplied a three-page list of the dignitaries and businessmen who attended. Pennsylvania, New York, Ohio, Texas, Wisconsin, Florida, and many other states and countries were noted. The group's significance and potential to invest in the salvage operation or the treasure expedition was notable.[76] Fleming also passed out newspaper clippings and copies of the press releases and brochures at the event. Fleming was confident this was finally the opportunity they needed to make a much-needed sale to government buyers.

American and foreign newsreel companies filmed the claws clacking and the arms moving, followed by a brief dunking in the Potomac off the side of the *Constellation*. One of the newsreels showed the diving bell emerging from the water with a wriggling fish snared in its pincers as if snagged while swimming by, but another gave away the secret that the newsreels cooperatively ignored. A "publicity-minded promoter" rowed out to the diving bell suspended just out of the water, held up a fish for the bell operator to grab, and then the diving bell submerged. Ralph Fleming himself

Romano diving bell, demonstration on deck of the *Constellation*, Washington, D.C., May 17, 1935 (Acme Photographs).

was inside the bell this time. After Fleming slowly cranked in the robot's pincers, the rowboat scooted out of view so that the newsreels could get the dramatic shot of the diving bell coming out of the water holding the fish in its mechanical claw.[77]

For over a week, newspaper stories about the demonstration appeared across the country, most of them a re-publication of a United Press (UP) story. Harry continued to point out that with this equipment and his treasure maps, there was now a way to recover that one-eighth of the world's gold still at the bottom of the sea.

Staying Focused on Business

Following the demonstration, Fleming wasted no time giving instructions to the crew and business representatives aboard the ship. He was off to New York and Chicago seeking investors. In a memo to an employee named Johnny O'Neal just four days after the demonstration, Fleming was particular in his assignments.[78] Every morning O'Neal was to inspect all the equipment to keep it in first-class condition and to keep a close eye on the equipment inventory in the event anything else was needed from Seattle. Fleming referred to a "submarine model," the scale model of how the diving bell would support a submarine rescue, their primary business target. O'Neal was also instructed to paint over the "Patent Applied For" notation on the diving bell and replace it with "Patented." Most importantly, Fleming emphasized the importance of ongoing publicity and communication with anyone who came aboard who might be considered a prospect. He counted on the crew to put a sales pamphlet in each visitor's hands and to "be on your toes at all times."[79]

J. Howard Lawler also assisted Fleming in business activities, including publicity, research, and other promotional events.[80] Besides living aboard the Constellation along with Harry, Royall, Loesche, and the crew, Lawler received no compensation. A letter he wrote to Fleming indicated that he had "treasure fever." He foresaw "untold success for us lying ahead," and "untold wealth ahead enough to make us all financially independent."[81]

Though no one wanted to admit it, those untold riches were well beyond anyone's reach. The core purpose of Lawler's letter was to plead for fifteen dollars to take care of personal needs, including "the problem of getting some clothes soon." Even after the big show of mid-May, Lawler had concerns about the ongoing publicity for the venture, suggesting that interest had died out quickly. He told Fleming that "the matter of publicity for the ship and diving bell exhibitions is at present acute" and that something must be done. Publicity for the Romano diving robot was not the only problem. The entire treasure venture was about to fall apart.

The Great Fall

Amid the loss of his marriage to his ambitions of a treasure expedition using the Romano diving robot, Harry Rieseberg experienced another major life-changing event. For many people, what happened to Harry would have wholly devastated them. What followed was his most desperate emotional state and the lowest point of his life. However, he was confident and optimistic to a fault. It was that drive that allowed him to overcome his situation.

A newspaper photo taken during the demonstration of the Romano diving bell aboard the *Constellation* on May 17, 1935, is a prescient forecast of a change in the

Chapter 4. The Great Fall 83

direction of Rieseberg's dreams.[82] On the image he saved in his personal collection, Harry drew an "X" to mark his place on the deck. The photo appears to have been taken some twenty feet above the deck, perhaps in the rigging. To the left, on a platform extended beyond the ship, the Romano diving bell was held by cables ready to be lowered into the Potomac. On the platform was Ralph Fleming, wearing a coat and tie, and an unnamed man wearing white overalls. On the deck in front of the diving bell, one can see fifteen men in coats, ties, and hats. The entire group looks off the photo's frame as if listening to another person speak. The photo is likely an earlier demonstration for a select group rather than a later demonstration for the public with a crowded deck showing in the newsreels. To the rear of the group, wearing a white shirt with his sleeves rolled up above his elbows and leaning against some rigging is Harry Rieseberg.

Several interesting aspects of the scene are evident, but knowing the story of what has taken place before this event crystallizes its interpretation. In Rieseberg's telling, he was the one who paid for the bell to come east, and the pivotal "research engineer" on whom the entire treasure venture depended. Rieseberg's dress and body language make clear that he is not important to the demonstration taking place. For an event where not only the Romano businessmen wore suits but every man in the crowd was as well, to see Harry with no jacket and tie and his shirt sleeves rolled up is a curious difference. Clearly, he was not a focal point of the demonstration, and his body language suggests that perturbs him. Rieseberg looks to be marginally engaged in the big unveiling. Harry Rieseberg was not used to standing at the back of the crowd. He was used to being out front. This photo, however, seems to place him closer to a job as a deckhand rather than a research engineer and international salvage expert.

Shortly after the demonstration, Harry Rieseberg broke his leg. He broke his leg badly when he slipped and fell on the deck of the *Constellation* while docked on the Potomac River. Knowing that fact is the key to understanding the falsehoods he peddled for the next thirty-five years. Breaking his leg altered the course of his personal history and his pursuit of dreams of riches at the time and for the remainder of his life. In many ways, it dictated his career options. Harry would not be able to participate in any planned treasure venture because, by his stipulation if he did not go, neither would his charts. Harry himself reiterated many times in books and articles that any agreement he made about using his charts was that he would be the only one handling them. Ralph Fleming and Romano Submarine Salvage and all the other people working for nothing hoping for shares of a treasure find would have to find another expert and another wreck to pursue.

Early in the research that led to this book, it was clear that the facts surrounding this singular event were central to determining the overall credibility of Harry Rieseberg's grand descriptions of his underwater adventures. It would have been physically impossible for him to be a hard-hat diver at any point after such a severe break. Harry was forty-two years old in 1935, beyond the typical age for starting a

What Really Happened to Harry?

In *I Dive for Treasure*, Rieseberg goes to great lengths to explain his broken leg. Anyone who knew him after the Great Fall would have easily seen that he had a severe injury because of the visible stiffness and limp. Harry made it a part of his reinvented narrative in his fictional autobiography. By his telling, after unexpectedly descending to a record depth of 1,404 feet in the Romano diving bell, a total fabrication, he was caught in a storm at sea.

> At the top of the companionway, I glanced up at the sails. Perhaps I was a bit dazed from my extraordinary experience. Anyhow, the vessel heeled sharply, my feet slid from under, my hand was jerked loose from its grip on the rail. For a wild moment I grabbed thin air—then was hurdled down the companionway. I felt a tremendous blow on my leg, a terrific pain; I heard a loud snap as a bone gave way. Unbearable pain shot through me. I passed out. My leg had been shattered in three places; just above the ankle, and just above and below the knee.[83]

Harry said he spent two days unconscious and strapped in a bunk while the ship—according to him, the *Constellation*—tossed through the hurricane. He said Captain Alvin Loesche treated his compound fractures with splints.

None of the story is true and is verified by Rieseberg's inadvertent admission before he decided to promote his persona as a treasure diver. Nevertheless, Harry made it part of his legend. Before he identified the need to make up this hurricane story seven years after his fall to create his myths about himself, Harry told the truth two times about how he broke his leg on the deck of the *Constellation*. Ironically, his exposure of the truth resulted from interviews he did with newspapers in Texas touting another expedition he would be "starting soon," even though he could not walk at the time.[84] In a moment of self-disclosure, Harry's own words correctly relay his dilemma around his accident. "I was devilishly uncomfortable, and it seemed humiliating, after everything I had faced, to fall while on board my own ship and ruin a shining success by breaking a leg."[85] Harry was right about the humiliation. There was no way the self-described international treasure expert could admit that he fell on the deck of a docked ship visited by Girl Scouts and matronly brunch groups. Harry Rieseberg had lost his job, lost his wife and his children, and had no money. His entire life before the Great Fall was gone, and now his dream of untold riches was as shattered as the bones in his leg.

Chapter 5

The Bottom

*Pride goeth before destruction,
and a haughty spirit before a fall.*
—Proverbs 16:18

Desperation is a powerful anesthetic. For an injury as severe as Harry Rieseberg's, the ordinary course of treatment would have been to perform surgery, followed by a period of immobilization and rehabilitation. Instead, Rieseberg did little more than strap on a brace and grab some crutches to hobble back to the *Constellation*.[1] His pain would have been considerable. Harry's complete refusal to accept his medical condition reflected the fact that he had no other options. Even though ignoring the severity of his injury caused his leg to heal poorly and worsen his condition, he pushed himself to hang on to what was left of his hopes for a treasure expedition. His dreams of underwater riches were as badly shattered as his leg, but he was not ready to admit to either of those facts.

Rieseberg could no longer be part of the treasure venture with Romano Submarine Salvage. The entire business venture died when the fragile co-mingling of Rieseberg's showmanship, Fleming's financial desperation, and Royall's emotional desire to keep his ship afloat failed to attract investors for a questionable treasure expedition. Even after his injury Rieseberg persisted in trying to seize the moment. As a last resort, he ran classified ads in the *New York Times* and the *Washington Post* in June 1935 to try to turn nothing into something.

> INTERNATIONALLY KNOWN AUTHORITY on locations and cargoes of sunken treasure ships has option on the world's more practical deep-sea diving equipment, and has chartered the only known sailing passenger ship, quarters of which were recently renovated at cost of $60,000; will consider forty passengers on cruise with participation in treasure recovered. Lieutenant Harry E. Rieseberg, P.O. Box 238, Benjamin Franklin Station, Washington, D.C.[2]

The wording of Harry's ad is fascinating, coming from the "internationally known authority" himself. Rieseberg mentions that he knows the location of treasure ships and boasts that he has access to diving equipment. However, the ad is directed toward people who would pay to go on an extended cruise on a newly renovated schooner without the Romano diving bell. Harry recognized his limitations and was trying to cut his losses by organizing little more than an adventure vacation, likely against all medical advice. Then almost as a postscript, he suggested there might be "participation in treasure recovered." His address is also no longer "aboard the Constellation" as before the demonstration. He had been evicted from the ship. Harry was also clearly going out on a limb by making this *his* expedition with the responses coming to him personally, no longer as part of the grand plan with Romano, Fleming, and Royall.

In *I Dive for Treasure,* Harry said his ad in the *Washington Post* got zero responses … they knew him already in the capital … but his *New York Times* classified generated about thirty inquiries.[3] The trip never materialized, and Harry would soon learn that his leg was in worse shape than he allowed himself to believe. It may have been his insistence that he could tough it out, which led to the serious medical issues he was about to face.

The Fate of the Constellation

As far as Robert Royall and Alvin Loesche knew, they were to keep the *Constellation* and its crew prepared for a yet-to-be-scheduled treasure venture. Since Rieseberg and Fleming quickly parted ways on their initial plan, Royall's path forward was in concert with Ralph Fleming and the Romano diving bell. After Fleming and his business partners had time to regroup, the *Constellation* departed from its months-long berth on the Potomac in mid–July 1935.[4] The beautiful four-master did not sail from its berth; it left under tow to Colonna's Shipyard in Norfolk, Virginia, to be hauled out for maintenance. The *Constellation* moved to New York, where again the public was invited to tour the "Gold Ship." After arriving at the Playland dock on Rockaway Beach on August 2, 1935, the ship attracted much attention but little income. Royall and Fleming duplicated their marketing methods from Washington but altered their ticket pricing. Ticket prices were upped from twenty-five cents to one dollar, but now each ticket teased the bearer with 1/200,000th of the net profits from any future treasure venture.[5] Signs went up inviting visitors "See the Robot Diving Bell," which the crew had nicknamed Oscar. They would lower the diving bell into Jamaica Bay waters several times daily.

By the end of October 1935, the promoters brought a group of Sea Scouts aboard to see the Romano diving bell and hear stories of treasure ventures never pursued.[6] After that somewhat humiliating publicity for the once proud vessel, nothing more about the *Constellation* appeared in the newspaper or any records researched for over a year. Romano Submarine Engineering disappeared into a silence that history magnifies over time. The harbors of New York and New Jersey had become the horse latitudes for the *Constellation* and the Romano diving bell—there was no monetary wind to fill their sails, and they were becalmed in place.

Romano Marine was still actively trying to salvage their company from disappointment and financial dissolution. In 1935 the wreck of the *General Grant* was getting much attention. A claim on it had already been made when Romano Marine inquired about the possibilities of using the diving bell on the wreck in November

1935.[7] It is probably fortunate that Fleming could not squander anymore of the investor's funds on ventures that were doomed to fail. All they ever had, even when they had Rieseberg's charts to show, was a false front with impressive optics. All they ever had was a ship that could not anchor precisely, a diving bell that did not maneuver easily, and an "expert" with charts full of stories but offering little detail.

A Winter at Rockaway

Despite their alliance with Romano Marine, Robert Royall and Alvin Loesche fought to keep their dream alive. Royall and Loesche drastically changed their plans when the Big Show of 1935 failed to provide income. In January 1936, he tried to organize a 3,000-mile cruise of the Caribbean for fifty passengers.[8] Royall warned that "This cruise is not for ordinary 'Landlubbers' or easy-chair sailors." Only "dyed-in-the-wool Sailors and discriminating Sportsmen" would be able to manage a working cruise like that he had planned.[9]

But it was not to be. There was no winter rescue for the *Constellation*. Instead, Royall, Loesche, and his wife, Johanna, lived aboard the *Constellation* docked at Rockaway Beach, New York, during the winter of 1936.[10] A first-hand observer of that state of affairs who deeply respected the vessel, and the captain said it was "sad to see the highly experienced mariner and the sound sea-ready schooner in what was practically a sideshow."[11] Like someone with a terminal illness able to enjoy a perspective on the richness of their life rather than the calamity to come, the owner and crew of the *Constellation* were determined to enjoy their last days. They could see their life aboard ship would not last long—they were running out of ways to keep the *Constellation* afloat.

The Constellation Is Sold

The demise of the *Constellation* seemed inevitable. It might be delayed but would not be avoided. The only way out was the transfer of ownership of the *Constellation* from the man who rescued her and lovingly restored her to a businessman hoping to succeed where others had failed. On July 25, 1936, Robert Royall sold his ship and his heart to the Empire Marine Salvage and Engineering Corporation for $15,000. Four thousand dollars was paid upfront, and the balance with interest over time as a mortgage to Loesche and Royall. A caption beneath a photo of the *Constellation* with all it sails raised to the winds referred to it as the vessel "formerly owned by Robert Royall of Boothbay Harbor."[12]

The agreement allowed Royall and Loesche to stay aboard and required the buyer to pay for all food and supplies, plus a salary for the crew for the duration of the mortgage.[13] Empire Marine had the same goals as the Romano Marine venture but significantly more financial backing. They also wanted to find treasure and attract investors to support using a deep-sea diving suit invented by Empire's president, Thomas P. Connelly. By July 29, 1936, the *Constellation* was towed from Rockaway Beach to the dock at Grand Street in Jersey City, New Jersey. There the new owners began outfitting and supplying the ship for another treasure voyage. Royall's letters to his family showed his amazement at the amount of money Empire was spending, in his opinion, by foolhardy and inexperienced investors. Royall wrote: "People buy these things that know nothing whatever about boats or ships. They are spending a tremendous amount—it goes out like water."[14] After so many years of enduring ongoing hardship to keep the *Constellation* afloat, it was difficult for Royall to wonder where all this money had been when he needed it the most.

The Dynamite Anchorage

On August 20, 1936, the *Constellation* sailed from the Toothpick Dock at Grand Street in Jersey City with a crew of twenty-one in search of treasure. Empire Marine kept the destination of the ship's quest for treasure a closely guarded secret as the date to set sail approached. Finally, they made the announcement. The *Merida* would again become a target with its reported riches and relative proximity. The nearness and potential wealth of that wreck were hard to resist. Newspaper accounts said that Connelly and his investors spent $250,000 on their venture and were prepared to spend up to two months at sea. Loesche was aboard as Captain and his wife as the only woman in a crew of twenty-two. Royall was there as well.[15] Word of a hurricane in the Atlantic delayed their departure for a day, leading to an anchorage off Sandy Hook to wait for a better forecast.[16] More dangerous than any hurricane or superstition about a woman being aboard was the 3,000 pounds of nitroglycerine in the hold; no one happened to mention this to the press or likely to the harbormaster.

What happened in the two weeks following the start of the expedition was told only when the *Constellation* returned to the Jersey docks on Thursday, September 3, after a harrowing experience at sea.[17] The *Constellation* and her crew were caught in a gale that broke one of the anchor chains, leaving the ship unable to maintain its position. Captain Loesche quickly decided to put up the big sheets and sail before the wind, allowing it to drive the schooner back to New Jersey.[18] In a September 9, 1936, letter to his parents, after it was all over, Royall reported on the situation once at the harbor. He told them "the big boys are coming tomorrow to discuss what's next." They seemed foolish enough to give the *Merida* another try that fall, and Royall knew "they have to learn as we did—through experience—it is the only teacher."[19]

After an explosives expert joined the ship to stabilize and remove the dangerous cargo, the *Constellation* was towed back into the harbor, a beautiful failure. When the *Constellation* set sail on its final treasure voyage, an editorial noted the bittersweet reality so easily ignored by treasure hunters hoping to hit it big. "Good luck to the treasure-hunters and the men financing it! They could doubtless make more money in breakfast cereal or soap or pig iron, but there is no romance in them, and this mechanized and regimented world needs romance."[20] After returning from the failed *Merida* venture, the big ship was moved from dock to dock over the fall and winter months. Royall told his family he could do better in Maine by being a lobsterman. On what must have been an unbearably emotional day for him, Royall left the

Constellation behind. He returned to his home in Maine and spent the remainder of his years managing fine dining establishments and engaged in civic activities. As Jim Hunt so richly described in his history of the *Constellation*, "Robert Royall went home to Boothbay, leaving behind his beautiful schooner, most of his money, and a piece of his heart."[21]

A Reprieve and an Ending

As a benefit of a new fourteen-mile road that allowed access to Brooklyn's shoreline, New York residents in July 1940 could see the rotting hulks of once-grand tall ships, including Royall's magnificent *Constellation*.[22] The Marine Basin at Sheepshead Bay in Brooklyn in 1940 was where Frederick Kaiser found the *Constellation*.[23] In 1941 Kaiser was aboard again on the City Pier at 69th Street, where he saw the *Constellation*'s anchor chain sadly heavy with ice. Later that year, her masts were pulled. The ship was on its way to support the war effort.

The Intercontinental Steamship Company owned the *Constellation* in 1943. The *Constellation*'s cabins and staterooms, so meticulously crafted by Robert Royall, were gutted and removed for the bulk storage of coal once again. When World War II broke out, every merchant vessel that could float was called into use at high prices for transport or shipping. Captain R.J. Peterson was the Master of the *Constellation* while it was docked in New York.[24] On July 19, 1943, when the *Constellation* left New York bound with cargo for Venezuela, the seventy-one-year-old Captain Howard Neaves was in command, but he had been brought on only two weeks before. He was primarily responsible for the end of the once-grand sailing vessel. Its sinking was not the result of a submarine attack but a Bermudan reef on July 30, which took it to the bottom.

The vessel was a total loss. The cargo included a wide variety of goods: tennis rackets, bags of cement still hardened in place, barrels of crockery, crucifixes, and hundreds of thousands of ampules of adrenaline, iodine, penicillin, and morphine which would surface for years after. The cargo also included seven hundred cases of whiskey; a cargo that dedicated sailors of the U.S. Navy rescued from the bottom.[25] The *Constellation* of Royall, Loesche, and Rieseberg was no more. The ship, which was to be used as a base for adventurers to seek treasure on the bottom of the ocean, was on the bottom itself.[26]

The Fate of the Romano Bell

Just as the *Constellation* faded from the foreground, so did the Romano diving robot and the companies formed to promote it. The *Conqueror*, a proud barkentine of the Northwest, which Romano Marine had acquired and considered for their treasure venture, also languished. For a ship considered lucky, the once grand tall ship did what unloved boats do; its condition got worse while deterioration and rot took over. At least the *Constellation* went down fighting.

About the Money

After all the glowing letters and newspaper clippings that Ralph Fleming sent to the Washington state Securities Division in May 1935 about their demonstration in the nation's capital, there had been no follow-up or response to the state's questions. Harry Huse, the department director, sent Fleming an end-of-year letter on December 27, 1935, stating the corporation's shortcomings. A terse note highlighted the fact that "we have not received an up-to-date statement of the affairs of your company and we insist that you immediately have a copy sent to us."[27] Fleming wrote back within days to let Huse know that the Romano accountant, E.J. Miner, would get back to them soon. Miner did that the following day but told the state he was behind because Romano Marine had yet to promptly deliver their records to him. Fleming confirmed that all the patents had been assigned to the corporation.[28] Their appeasement of the state did not last long.

Ralph Fleming probably did not know he was the object of intense scrutiny by auditors at the Securities Division. The constant need to remind him of the company's obligations, apparent violations of securities laws, and the lack of basic business practices compounded the lingering suspicions that he was not legally conducting the company's business. An auditor's report explained that his thorough review of their books "confirms the charges I made against Ralph S. Fleming" that investor money had been misspent. He urged them to put the company in "receivership and have the receiver prefer charges which can easily be substantiated against Fleming."[29]

Romano shareholders were told about the potential wrongdoing and that an investigation was underway. The state suggested that "the party whose name was mentioned" [Fleming] should be the focal point of their concerns since there appeared to be evidence of fraudulent activity. Fleming's accounting records were later transferred to the Postal Inspector's office, where their auditors reviewed them for the potential of a federal crime.[30] Despite all the flurry of activity about possible illegalities, the investigations died down, and no further action was taken.

A Final Resting Place?

The Romano robot remained aboard the *Constellation* throughout the winter and spring of 1936 in its various New York and New Jersey anchorages. The metal sphere had been aboard Royall's "Gold Ship," taking on tour customers, but no reports of it ever descending again exist. Royall filed a lawsuit in the courts of Queens County, New York to recover monies owed him by Romano Submarine Engineering and Salvage. In June 1936, a month before the *Constellation* was sold, Royall settled the lawsuit by agreeing to store the Romano gear aboard ship until August 10, 1936. If Fleming and the Romano investors had not removed it by then, he would place it in "recognized public storage."[31] That deadline was just before the *Constellation* was outfitted for the Empire Marine expedition with "Iron Mike."

In 1939 the diving bell, its machinery, tools, and even its records had been stored in the Jersey City Storehouse at 14th Street and Provost in Jersey City by Ralph

Harborside Terminal, c 1931. Photo Image # 1988231_070_06_006. Hagley Museum & Library, Wilmington, DE. Pennsylvania Railroad Photographs 231, Box 70, Folder 6.

Fleming.[32] At some point, they were sold due to the lack of payment for storage and ended up a few miles away at the Harborside Warehouse Company in Jersey City, New Jersey.[33] From there, the fate of the Romano diving bell is lost in court records long destroyed. It is difficult for this author to accept that all evidence of the Romano diving robot is gone, but that is the state of its known history. Perhaps it was just too much iron to sit around after World War II began.

A Leg to Salvage

In the weeks and months after Harry Rieseberg broke his leg on the deck of the *Constellation,* we are left to wonder what he was doing. His trail of records from his federal employment and his writing suddenly stopped. However, a few verifiable events help tie down where he was between 1935 and 1936.

Harry's unreliable self-reporting through his books and articles years later leaves a raft of questions as we look back at what happened. He had no job and was unable to work due to his injury. He had never worked anywhere outside the federal government, and he had burned his bridges there. Any money he withheld from his wife, Ellen, when she left with their two children for Kansas was spent on his grand scheme. He might have even had anyone who handed over money for the failed venture looking for him. Harry could only rely on his parents or friends. His temporary residence aboard the *Constellation* and his dreams of treasure had sailed away. What was becoming more apparent to Harry was that his broken leg was not healing well at all.

Not Giving Up

Rieseberg's circumstances and medical condition did not stop him from trying to cash in on his only asset—his research on sunken vessels. In September 1935, Harry wrote Simon Lake about a wreck named the *Earl of Abergavenny*, an 1805 English ship lost with reported treasure. Lake was a well-known, well-funded inventor of a mini submarine he had used on a few attempted treasure recoveries. Their communication offers a hint to Rieseberg's plans months after his accident.[34]

Lake wrote to Harry in Sudley, Maryland, a small unincorporated area of the state east of the capital. Harry said that after his initial treatment, he had gone to stay with his parents on the Chesapeake Bay, where they had a retirement home. After being renters their entire lives, they managed to buy some property at Back Bay Beach in 1921.[35] By recognizing Harry might have some helpful information, Lake encouraged the ever-hopeful Rieseberg. "We apparently have a mutual interest in old ships, and I have had a thought that perhaps an association might be made that would be mutually profitable to us."[36] Lake also referenced something Rieseberg must have said in his letter to Lake: that Harry would soon be "heading south." Harry was indeed doing that, and plans were already being made at the time of their communication in October 1935, five months after Harry broke his leg. His leg had not improved and in fact, had gotten worse. Harry's parents were about to abandon their hoped-for retirement and travel across the country looking for a way to save their son's leg.

Heading South

Immediately after the accident, when Harry was still trying to keep the treasure venture from being a complete failure, he exacerbated the break by ignoring it to the point where the bones reset themselves improperly. Harry said his leg was "like a dead stick" with "no movable joints below the hip." A doctor's only suggestion was to amputate because the leg would be not only useless but also dangerous to his health if unhealed.[37]

On hearing that, Harry said he unleashed "a wild kind of anger and blind resentment" on the physician, losing "every scrap of restraint." One can only imagine the impact of this information on Rieseberg. Not only was his life as a federal employee and married father of three children over because of his choices, but the life he *wanted* to lead was as crushed as his leg. Harry was not only in severe physical difficulty, he was depressed as well, saying the "years ahead held nothing but blackness." Harry credited Fred Magruder, a friend for life, with supporting him in a way only those kinds of friends can. Magruder and his wife offered to let Harry live with them, but he went to his parents' home in Maryland instead. With his parents' and Magruder's support and resilience, Harry found enough energy to look for other medical options.

What Harry described happening next was a remarkable act of self-sacrifice on the part of his parents. Henry and Jennie Rieseberg gave up their retirement to travel the country with Harry on crutches, wearing a steel brace, and looking for medical treatment. He says they got medical consultations in "some of the largest hospitals in the East," followed by travels to Chicago and all over the Middle West. The truth of that statement cannot be verified. Given that he had no money or insurance, his rejections may have resulted from having no ability to pay for anything more complicated than an amputation to prevent further issues with infection in his "dead" leg. What is known for sure is that the family wound up in Fort Worth, Texas, living temporarily with relatives from his mother's side of the family.

What Was Harry Doing in Fort Worth?

Harry was indeed headed south in late 1935, and his need for self-promotion verified his whereabouts. "Visitor Here Is Planning Hunt for Sunken Treasure" was the headline of the *Fort Worth Press* article signaling Harry's arrival in North Texas in November 1935.[38] The article was a repeat performance of the publicity he propagated in Washington. It was a working model for the core outline of his articles which consistently included four themes.

> One-eighth of the world's gold is under the sea;
> Only he knows where it is;
> He has a schooner and a diving bell to retrieve it;
> He is planning a treasure expedition very shortly.

This was Harry Rieseberg's mantra, his editorial touchstone. A key difference between the Fort Worth article and those yet to come was that he had still not begun claiming he had dived on sunken treasure. He had not conjured up that fabrication just yet. The photo accompanying the article showed a smiling forty-two-year-old Harry Rieseberg, who appeared to be on top of the world. The image portrayed in the story is difficult to reconcile with Harry's accounts of his pain and suffering.

With Harry broadcasting his expertise as much and as often as possible, it did not take long after he got to Texas to hear about a long-standing treasure myth involving Jean Lafitte and a smuggler's road called Trammel's Trace.[39] Lafitte treasure legends existed all over Texas. This version of the legend said that Lafitte stole Spanish treasure from a ship named the *Santa Rosa* that was plundered on the shores of the Texas Gulf of Mexico. Pursued by Spanish soldiers up Trammel's Trace toward the Red River, Lafitte supposedly dumped six wagon loads of silver in Hendricks Lake in East Texas. In September and October of 1935, an uncredited, full-page article about Hendricks Lake appeared in papers across the country.[40] The prose had the verbal seasoning of Harry Rieseberg but was without a byline. However, as part of this research, an illustration from the article was found among artwork Rieseberg donated to an archive in the 1960s.[41] This was confirmation that in 1935 Harry was already networking among Texas treasure hunters and learning to take advantage of his new residence. Harry again mentioned Hendricks Lake in an interview for a newspaper article in January 1936.[42]

A Family Reunited

In *I Dive for Treasure*, Harry specifically said he stayed in Fort Worth while receiving some medical evaluation or treatment. He claimed that he heard about a doctor in Houston while there, but trying that lead only resulted in the same prognosis. Six months after his injury, all the medical opinions were that his leg had to be amputated. Hard medical choices were overtaking his tenacity. After leaving the Houston doctor's office, he said a nurse followed him and suggested he contact a famous orthopedic surgeon named George Eggers, an internationally recognized orthopedist at John Sealy Hospital. Eggers became the first full professor of orthopedics for the University of Texas Medical Branch in Galveston, and his research led to a design of an internal brace called the Eggers plate (or Eggers splint) in 1948. Harry moved to Galveston with his parents and became a patient of Dr. Eggers, where he began months of grueling medical treatment for his broken leg.

In Galveston, Harry Rieseberg was also reunited with his wife and children. In early August 1935, Ellen Rieseberg was transferred from the Leavenworth penitentiary to the U.S. Public Health Service Hospital in Galveston, Texas.[43] The reason for the transfer is not reflected in her personnel records, but her brother, Bernard Ralph Carver, was an oil worker in nearby Houston. Her pay was the same as in Leavenworth, but the opportunity to leave the federal prison system would have been desirable.[44] Ellen had just been transferred to Galveston only a few months before Harry's relocation to Fort Worth, so it is far more likely that she was the nurse who provided him with the information about Dr. Eggers rather than someone in Houston.

Ellen struggled as a single mother of two children, and her efforts were apparent to her employer. In a performance evaluation, the chief nurse noted that she was a little slow and only an average nurse but was acknowledged as helpful and conscientious. According to her supervisor, she seemed a little self-conscious, but perhaps it was because of her older uniforms, something he noted in her report. She was a woman whose life was turned upside down by her husband's misdeeds and dreams of treasure.[45] Her supervisor acknowledged her in the report in a way that she probably appreciated hearing when he admitted, "Mrs. Rieseberg is putting up a brave fight to make a home for her two children."[46]

When Harry first came to Galveston, he lived with his parents. Within a few months, Harry, his parents, Ellen, and their two children, Henry and Shirley, lived together in a three-room furnished apartment less than a mile away.[47] Ellen must have had a high level of patience and sympathy to forgive Harry enough to have him come to Galveston, much less to share her home. Her performance appraisals consistently described her as exceptionally caring and well-liked, and she had become dedicated to her religious beliefs through active membership in the Seventh-Day Adventist Church. To have Harry back nearby must have been a significant emotional strain on her, but also on their two children, Henry at age seven and Shirley just turning five.

Harry Still Being Harry

Regardless of his medical condition and irrespective of Ellen's feelings about his failed treasure dreams, Harry Rieseberg was up to his usual self-serving publicity. He contacted the local Galveston press to talk about himself within only a few weeks of his arrival. Harry continued his self-promotion around his research and his always-in-the-future plans for a treasure expedition. The article said an "odd robot diving suit was used in former expeditions" without mentioning that there had been no expedition. In Galveston, he began trying to promote himself as having been on multiple underwater treasure adventures. He bragged about appearing in four newsreel movies when the newsreels were about the Romano diving sphere and the *Constellation*. He said he had just completed a book titled "Cracking Davy Jones Treasure Vaults!" hoping that would inspire the kinds of letters and phone calls he received before the accident. Also, Rieseberg said he was abandoning his use of the robot in favor of some unnamed invention that could find gold at the bottom of the ocean.

The *Galveston Tribune* article was the first instance where Harry attempted to craft a story through tone and tense to create the perception that he had done things he had not. That was a significant change from directly promoting himself as the source of information. Rieseberg was not one to ever let the facts slow him down. Now that he was away from Washington, he was unencumbered by his messy reputation back east.[48]

Harry's Hospitalization

Somewhere between the details of the injury that Rieseberg described in *I Dive for Treasure* and the scant few blurred pages of medical records from his hospital stay are the facts of Harry's medical condition and treatment.[49] Harry said he spent eighteen months in the hospital at Galveston, but there is documentation that he spent much less. After moving to Galveston in December 1935 or January 1936, Harry entered the hospital in February 1936.

His initial examination tells the story—doctors found an old fracture of the left tibia just below the knee, entering the joint and affecting the cartilage. Harry's use of crutches and a brace to get around before obtaining complete medical treatment left him with *traumatic genu valgus*—commonly called knock-knee. Harry's left knee angled abnormally inward, and his range of motion was limited to about ten degrees. The *fibrous ankylosis* of his knee was an abnormal stiffening and immobility of the joint due to the fusion of his untreated broken bones.[50]

Dr. Eggers' surgical plan was to perform an *osteotomy* on Rieseberg's knee. During this procedure, the bone is cut to make corrections and adjustments to relieve the abnormal pressures caused by the misalignment. Harry's left knee had deformities and fractures where the bone was splintered into more than two fragments. The injury was severe, and his ability to endure it for nine months after the accident before being hospitalized was a testament to his determination to continue his efforts to organize a treasure venture.

A wedge of the bone removed on the outside of the knee was surgically inserted on the inside to adjust the alignment. The medical notes do not reveal the day-to-day treatment, but Harry would not have been able to bear weight for quite some time. Even today, patients would expect to use crutches for several weeks after discharge and follow that with months of physical therapy. Even with modern treatment, walking unaided would take up to twelve weeks.

Beyond just the medical procedures, Rieseberg would have also had some pain during his recovery. Harry described the pain as so extreme at first that all he could do was "lie in bed and stare dumbly at blank walls and ceiling." The drugs to treat the severe pain led to restless dreams where he awoke "in a cold sweat, brought to full consciousness by the touch of the nurse's hand or the sound of her quiet voice, calming me." Though he said he got used to the pain, the sense of utter confinement brought him down.[51] Hanni Loesche was a letter writer, so Rieseberg was kept informed of events regarding the *Constellation* docked in New York. In a March 20, 1936, Hanni told Mrs. Royall she "wrote a letter this morning to Galveston," where Harry Rieseberg lay rehabilitating his leg.[52]

After the cast came off, he made slow progress over the following months. A brace finally led to his standing erect but stationary and walking with crutches inside the hospital room. It took a few weeks before he could go outside on the hospital grounds. One crutch was discarded, then another, replaced by a heavy cane. Following his discharge on May 12, 1936, after almost three months in the hospital, Harry was released as "improved." When rechecked in July, the doctor noted that he could bear weight on the leg but commented that he may always have a slight deformity. In later life, Harry would be seen using a cane from time to time, and into his sixties and seventies, his family noted that his leg would stiffen and need to be elevated. The injury never left him, and Harry found ways to make his noticeable difficulty feed into the narrative he invented about how it happened.

The different accounts of his injury and treatment that Rieseberg offered over the years, and their conflict with the facts, leave room for questions. Though the emotions he reported during that time ring true. His physical recovery was just part of the process. There was also the downtime and his inability to be mobile. As his physical health improved, he said his optimism and demeanor also improved. Medical records showed Rieseberg's discharge from the hospital in May 1936, but Harry said it was not until a year later.[53] The months needed for physical therapy and follow-up could account for that difference.

The likely answer to the question of what he was doing in the months after his discharge from the hospital is that he was recovering in the same home as his estranged wife, their children, and his parents. While he provided a hospitalization timeline that does not match the facts, Harry may have inadvertently provided an accurate picture of what he was doing during those ten months. Harry Rieseberg was re-inventing himself.

Rehab for More Than a Broken Leg

One indicator of Rieseberg's hiatus in the hospital and the severity of his condition was his journalistic silence. This research has cataloged almost 2,000 stories and articles Harry Rieseberg published during his career. The period between June 1934, just before his firing at the Bureau of Navigation, and December 1937 is absent of authored publications.

Adventure Magazine enabled Rieseberg's attempt to create a mythology about his broken leg. After he fell on the *Constellation*, the magazine explained he would be on hiatus "due to the pressure of other activities."[54] When Harry again joined their team of experts replying to reader questions in 1943, the explanation for his absence was that "he left us in 1935 … to engage in expedition and salvage operations in remote waters where, away for months at a time, he could no longer devote attention to *Adventure* inquiries." What happened during those years was far from being in "remote waters."[55]

As Harry regained his strength, he resumed his attempts to use his research as a bargaining chip to join the surge of interest in recovering underwater treasure. While in the hospital, Harry realized that all the research he had gathered over the years had never been organized. He said he refocused on his only assets—the information he had collected: "… I had trunks full. In half a dozen different places I had one of the greatest collections of factual information on treasure ships that had ever been compiled."[56] The trunks of material Harry stashed may have included original documents stolen from the National Archives and other repositories connected with his work at the Bureau of Navigation. Harry seemed to admit as much over thirty years later in a letter saying that when at the Bureau of Navigation "the files from the beginning came under my supervision, from which authentic records were taken."[57]

Harry said his friend and fellow Mason, Fred Magruder, back in Washington, and a long-time friend, J. William Karbe, gathered all the books and papers for him. Harry claimed he filled his days in the hospital by transcribing all his handwritten notes. Given that he had talked about finishing a book and selling his knowledge, one would think his research would have been more organized. Nevertheless, his mission was to pull it all together during his rehabilitation. The recovery from his injury gave him the time and opportunity to re-focus on his collection of maps, manifests, and documents as he never had before.

Harry Rieseberg emerged from his long recovery as Lieutenant Harry E. Rieseberg, treasure salvor and international expert on treasure from the deep. There is no faster way to become the world's greatest anything than to declare it yourself.

Chapter 6

The Harry After

*What we call the beginning is often the end.
And to make an end is to make a beginning.
The end is where we start from.*
—T.S. Eliot

At age forty-four, Harry Rieseberg fabricated a new persona and reintroduced himself to the public as someone he was not. His time recovering from his broken leg was the genesis of the false narrative he promoted to the public for the remainder of his life. What is generally known about Harry Rieseberg is the person he invented during his rehabilitation in the hospital in Galveston. His summation of that transition sounds like it should be spoken in a dramatic voice-over with heroic background music. "I wasn't any longer just a hospital case with a monotonous routine of medical care; I was Lieutenant Harry Rieseberg, treasure salvor."[1] Though it was intended to read as if he had risen from adversity to reclaim his lost status, it was, in fact, the formulation of a character he would present to the public. Lieutenant Harry Rieseberg emerged from the hospital like a comic book hero transforming from a secret identity to one with superpowers of underwater discovery and survival. He started with the data he had collected on treasure ships and then added the made-up adventures and half-truths on which he based the next thirty-five years of his life. His new persona was based on remarkable exaggerations and outright lies.

Although bits and pieces of the apocryphal story he used to explain his transformation dribbled out in magazine articles as early as 1938, it was only presented fully when he published, *I Dive for Treasure* in 1942. Harry began his story of reemergence in Galveston, where he was living at the time. What he said happened next is beyond believability. Rieseberg said that while pondering a future along the Galveston seawall one day, broke and injured, he accidentally encountered George Wright, a diver friend from Washington, D.C. Harry said Wright just happened to have a ship docked in Galveston loaded and ready to leave at that very moment for a treasure expedition in the waters off southern California. Supposedly, Wright had "chartered a tight little schooner and signed on a crew of Guatemala natives" and invited Harry aboard that night to join in the search.[2]

As was usually the case in Harry's stories, the circumstances are difficult to accept as reality. Expecting his readers to believe that someone from Washington,

D.C., would charter a ship in Galveston for treasure hunting in far-off southern California extends the disbelief required to accept another of Harry's tall tales. It simply was not practical or sensible to travel over 5,000 nautical miles just to get to California. Harry invented a scenario where George Wright rescued him at his lowest moment. If the reader swallowed that story, he would also have them believe that he killed a giant octopus on that trip while diving for treasure in a hard hat diving dress. Harry Rieseberg, barely able to walk unaided, without income or support, became super-human when his freshly reinvented-self dove for treasure.

At times, parts of Rieseberg's story can appear a bit closer to the truth. Harry said that after his discharge from the hospital he "stayed around Galveston during the spring of 1937, trying to line myself up" for a treasure venture.[3] He had no other options. It must have been more manly to assert that he lived only with "enough money for a cheap room and meals at one-arm joints" rather than with his wife, children, and parents. He admitted that "twinges of fear would override my confidence." Rieseberg said he reached out to all his contacts looking for any way to be part of a treasure-hunting expedition or to finance the use of his research. To Harry, "It looked like the last throw of the dice."[4] The emotions he shared in *I Dive for Treasure* were more authentic than his versions of events.

"Yarns of Fabulous Riches"

Harry probably did not read the headline in the October 11, 1936, edition of his hometown paper, the *Washington Post*. If he had, he would have zeroed in on a significant truth about treasure hunting. The headline read, "Yarns of Fabulous Riches on Ocean Floor Fill Treasury Files, but 100% Record of Salvage Failures Dims U.S. Reward Hope." The article was a run-through of what Harry knew all too well but refused to accept. It even pointed in Harry's direction by repeating his claims without calling him by name.

> … your heart would leap into something akin to St. Vitus dance as you pore over the positive claims of gold-hunters that they know just where the stuff is buried. They've got maps—and charts. They've got statements from direct descendants of pirates. They've got incontrovertible records. But they got no dough.[5]

The failures of other treasure hunters were also becoming well known—Simon Lake and the *Hussar*; the *Constellation* and Connelly in search of the *Merida*; the *DeBraak* off Cape Henlopen, Delaware; and the *Brother Jonathan*. All had stories and multiple failed attempts to recover any reported treasure.

Promoting Himself

By the end of 1936, Rieseberg's physical progress meant he could walk with a cane, an assistance he would use off and on for the remainder of his life. It added to his cachet and was something he could make up a good story to explain. While in Texas, Harry began making new connections and promising that his next new venture was just around the corner. In the *Galveston Daily News,* there was a weekly column of local news from Texas City, a community on the mainland to the north. Harry communicated with a local columnist to ask if he knew anyone in Texas City interested in buried treasure. Rieseberg told the writer he was planning to edit a new magazine to be called "Treasure Trove" beginning around the first of January 1937. That magazine never materialized.[6]

The best sign that Harry was trying to hobble back into the treasure game was a December 1936 ad in a San Antonio newspaper where he used his same formula again to look for investors.

> TREASURE! Internationally known writer-salvor, recognized by nation's press, scientific magazines, newsreels, etc., as the world's foremost authority on authentic locations of salvageable treasure-laden ships containing vast wealth, is interested in several individuals desirous of forming legitimate organization promoting actual expeditions for retrievements (*sic*) of such treasure from authentic wrecks; possession authentic locations invaluable; statements cited guaranteed; national publicity assured by reputation; opportunity rarely submitted public; legitimate and legitimately interested only answer.[7]

There are several interesting aspects to this advertisement. One of the most basic questions is who was paying for the ad. Harry had not been employed since October 1934. For two years, he had no income. His only support would have been from his parents. His father had a small pension and could pay part of the expenses, but the prospect of Harry having any money was virtually nonexistent.

The second item is even more personal and pivotal to his family. Though not apparent to others, the return address in the ad is the Galveston home of his estranged wife, Ellen. One might imagine that the living arrangements with Ellen had some positive aspects, with young Henry and Shirley benefiting from the care of their grandparents and their father's attention. Given the apparent generosity of the wife he had cheated on and abandoned to pursue his crazy treasure dream, placing an advertisement to do the same thing again *and* have the inquiries mailed to her home address seems inexcusable for its lack of judgment and empathy. Harry's ability to emotionally disconnect from his family and the personal and family dynamics at work is as mysterious as the locations of the buried treasure Harry sought.

When Harry's rehabilitation ended, so did his welcome in Galveston. Harry and his parents left Galveston to live in Los Angeles with his mother's Martin relatives. Harry Rieseberg sacrificed his relationship with his wife and two young children for the second time. By 1937 Harry Rieseberg was in Hollywood pumping the press for attention. He finally arrived in a place where he fit in—a land of fantasy where everyone had a made-up story to tell.

Hollywood Harry

Indications of Harry Rieseberg's relocation to California with his parents appeared by early May 1937. Following his arrival, he wasted no time contacting the press, securing copyright protections for potential movie scripts, looking for investors, and boasting publicly about treasure-hunting trips just ahead. Harry's life in the center of the entertainment industry in southern California was off to a difficult start—he lived at three addresses in Los Angeles between May and December 1937.[8]

His earliest known address in Hollywood, the Brevoort Hotel, was a hard-luck destination for "the actor between pictures" where a room could rent for ten dollars a week.[9] Harry had made it back to California with little more than boxes of files, a limp that needed a back story, and a hopeful business plan built on the gullibility of people looking to get rich quickly. His most prevalent skill at the time was being a pitchman for himself, and even in Hollywood, he managed to stand out in his effort.

The Usual Formula

The Associated Press published a short article from Rieseberg with a byline of Los Angeles on May 18, 1937.[10] Harry used the same sales pitch he had been using since before the Great Fall in 1935. Harry said he was the world's greatest salvage expert and vaguely referenced diving gear he did not have. He claimed a ship was currently being outfitted for a trip, and there were wrecks close by with millions of dollars just waiting for someone with money who could pay Harry to tell them where they could be found. That was his formula.

Within a week of the press release, he wrote a letter to Capt. G. Allan Hancock of Hancock Pacific Expeditions, a legitimate researcher and explorer. Upon learning they did photographic exploration Harry wrote to ask about doing business together. Hancock's polite reply, including an enclosed flyer, pointed out that their type of expedition was "wholly scientific, done in the interest of science for the benefit of the more prominent universities and scientific institutions in this country." Harry retained their turndown letter for his personal files because Hancock said he had read about Harry and "admired the manner in which you planned your expeditions." Given that George Allan Hancock was a wealthy pillar of Southern California education, oil, and philanthropy, a letter like that certainly could not hurt Harry's credibility when pitching himself to others. If George Hancock swallowed the tales, who else might?[11]

By September 1937, Harry was in San Francisco touting an expedition backed by "two wealthy San Francisco sportsmen."[12] The article about his visit there also provided some interesting and surprising details. This article is Rieseberg's first mention of a story he later related in *I Dive for Treasure*. Harry told a story about being broke during his visit to California as a seventeen-year-old and getting help from "Greek George," a restaurant owner on the waterfront who helped him get a job on a ship. Harry retold that story in a newspaper article five years before his book, adding some credibility to at least some part of his story.

While in San Francisco, Harry also upped the ante on his potential involvement with financial backers and began telling half-truths that would continue to be part of his repertoire for years. This time, his narrative involved the *Constellation* and the Romano diving robot, both back in New Jersey following their repeated failures. Harry said he would undertake an expedition using "the only sailing four-masted schooner afloat." Harry neglected to mention how he might get the equipment and the grand vessel from the Atlantic coast to the Pacific.[13]

Additionally, Harry made two claims of previous treasure salvage which have no basis in fact. Harry Rieseberg did not have the means or the opportunity to pursue his treasure interests on his own, either before The Great Fall or after. The timeline established by his personnel records and other documentary evidence point toward the venture with the Romano bell and the *Constellation* as his first and only brush with an actual treasure voyage. In the article, Harry gave himself credit for recovering significant wealth from two Florida wrecks. He said he brought up $52,000 from a shipwreck near Amelia Island and $27,000 from one near Soldier's Key. The only Amelia Island wrecks gaining any press were the *San Miguel*, which was never found, and an unnamed British ship that sank near Soldier's Key. That he did not name the wrecks himself was probably his way of avoiding getting cornered on his fabrication. Those were not the only false claims of successful salvage. He also claimed to have been paid a commission for two treasure recoveries. For one of them off Cape Hatteras, NC, Harry said he recovered over $250,000 in silver.[14]

Me, Myself, and I

The fact that Harry Rieseberg was able to find some measure of success as a writer can be attributed to the likelihood that he was an accomplished narcissist. The repeated and pervasive misrepresentation of the facts of his life, his participation in fraternal organizations to the extreme, and his difficulties in interpersonal relationships define Harry Rieseberg's existence. An internet meme described narcissist as a polite term for a self-serving, manipulative, evil asshole with no soul. From that perspective alone, Rieseberg certainly seemed to fit the pattern.

The Mayo Clinic and other authorities on personality disorders provide a more specific overview of the traits related to narcissism, lending toward a reasonable armchair identification of Harry Rieseberg's tendencies. Those with narcissistic traits tend to exaggerate their accomplishments and importance and require excessive and regular admiration. They go out of their way to tout their achievements and abilities as more significant than they actually are. Their need for praise and acknowledgment never seems to be satisfied. In search of that validation from others, they will oversell their abilities and exaggerate their accomplishments. In their relationships, narcissists take advantage of other people when it helps them achieve what they want. Their inability or unwillingness to sense the needs and feelings of others often leaves the limited number of people who might have relationships with them feeling hurt or disabused.[15]

Narcissists can be charming and charismatic, but only to gain admiration for themselves. They often do not reveal negative behavior right away, especially in relationships. Another common trait of narcissism is manipulative or controlling behavior. A narcissist will initially try to please and impress, but eventually their needs will come first. Narcissists like Harry Rieseberg already see themselves as superior to others, so they may become angry or abusive when they don't receive the response they think they deserve.

Harry Rieseberg repeatedly demonstrated these traits from his early youth until the months before he died in 1970. Example after example appears in the pages of his own words and the descriptions of others. Examples of grandiose ideas are the rich fantasy world of his creation and his angry reactions when things do not go his way appear repeatedly. The Narcissus of Greek mythology fell in love with his own reflection. Harry Rieseberg fell in love with his fabricated accomplishments and self-importance.

Harry Rieseberg, Writer

Harry's living arrangements in Hollywood put him in the middle of actors, writers, producers, and technicians connected to the entertainment business. One of his neighbors was a minor actor named Arthur Van Slyke. Van Slyke worked in radio and appeared in eight movies between 1936 and 1938, four in uncredited roles. *Variety* magazine maintained a Protected Materials Department where authors and other copyright holders could submit sealed works to ensure any future claim. Harry wrote to *Variety* in September 1937 to say he was about to produce a series of radio programs titled "Neptune's Treasure." The connection between Van Slyke and Rieseberg resulted in an effort by Harry to secure copyright protection for stories he had prepared. It was Van Slyke who helped Harry learn about the process.[16]

In December 1937, Harry again sought copyright protection through their Protected Materials Department in New York. That was what you did if you were a Hollywood writer. This time Harry said it was for "a scenario script which has originated from my activities in the field of undersea work, and whom you no doubt, have read of."[17] Harry did not copyright an actual work, but rather used the process to reserve titles like "Salvage," "Conqueror of the Unconquerable," and "Phipps (*sic*) and Phipps Company."[18]

Newspapers around the country picked up one of Rieseberg's stories that appeared in the *Los Angeles Times* on October 31, 1937, with the headline "Robots Will Aid Search for Lost Sea Treasures." A headshot of Harry and a separate photo of Captain Alvin Loesche with the "Iron Mike" robot from Empire Marine aboard the *Constellation* ran with the article.[19] In the article Harry continued to raise the stakes and abandon the truth in his attempts to garner attention and investors. He tossed out the possibility of millions of dollars to be recovered, more to impress readers with the potential magnitude than to value the potential recovery. Harry claimed five billion dollars lay beneath the sea, and said he knew the location of $600,000 of that bounty. Harry touted that he was "now in Hollywood completing organization plans for an expedition that will utilize every modern diving method." Upon reading that article, one would not know whether to be impressed with the potential financial windfall, attracted to the opportunity of partnering with a man of Rieseberg's stature or amazed by his audacity.

Harry went on in the article to mention how the hazards of depth and pressure, sharks, and octopuses, would be overcome using the Romano diving bell. Harry even went so far this time to say that the "diving bell has already been placed aboard the schooner *Constellation*, commanded by Capt. Alvin Loesche," a complete and utter fabrication.[20] That the *Constellation* had a new owner, was in New York, and had not sailed anywhere for over a year were omitted from Harry's assemblage of facts.

Hooked a Big One

Harry's Hollywood network and self-promotion finally seemed to pay off in a connection to Cecil B. DeMille, the famous film director. It may have been Van Slyke who helped with the introduction since he had appeared in one of DeMille's Lux Radio Theatre presentations. DeMille's interest in treasure blossomed during the research and filming for his 1938 movie, *The Buccaneer*, about Jean Lafitte and the Battle of New Orleans. While making the movie, De Mille's researchers believed they had unearthed previously unknown information about the treasure's whereabouts. One newspaper report in November 1937 said DeMille had "instructed intermediaries to deal with Lieutenant Harry Riesenberg (*sic*), former Federal Marine expert, to organize a syndicate to search for $5,000,000,000 in sunken treasure."[21]

The article said Rieseberg would be "heavily financed and with iron robots capable of descending a mile and picking up a dime." Nothing ever came of this planned expedition. This venture was a dream, just like all the others. In Hollywood, it seemed reasonable to expect that there was always a catch.

Romano Robot Rescue

There are indications that Rieseberg's belief that he might once again have access to the Romano diving bell was not entirely without basis. Harry's old friend, J. William (Bill) Karbe, had attended the demonstration in Washington and heard Rieseberg's stories of how it could be used to find investors for a treasure expedition. Karbe wanted Romano's diving robot, and his tenacity in that effort began in earnest in 1938.

After the failure of the venture with the *Constellation* and Connelly, Romano Marine Salvage and Romano Submarine Engineering both faded away. An attorney from a Seattle law firm, Edward R. Taylor, wrote the Securities Division for the State of Washington in February 1938, saying he had been "acting as president of the corporation for some time" and that there had been no activity in Romano Marine Salvage for three and a half years. His lack of familiarity with the company led to his misstatement of the name as Romano Machinery Salvage Company.[22] The attorney asked for the State's approval to consider Karbe's proposal to purchase a controlling interest in the company. Karbe had made an offer to Mrs. Romano to pay $25,000 for controlling interest in the company, and control of its assets. Though an offer was made, he said Karbe had "paid no money, and we can only speculate on his good faith."[23] Based on his proposal, Karbe wanted two things. He wanted to make sure there were still shares remaining that could be sold, and he wanted possession of the Romano diving robot. The language in the agreement he offered Romano Marine ensured the shares' status was clear and that he would not get stuck with any existing debts. At the time of Karbe's offer there was less than four-hundred dollars of debt.

Lula Romano had no money to finance any use of the equipment. The Romano diving bell was still stashed away and impounded in a warehouse, and without this offer, it would sit idle. Romano and the attorney did not know Karbe's history and suggested it was a good plan to accept.[24] The state ultimately okayed the sale, but it went nowhere. Lula Romano died later that year on December 19, 1938. The assets of Romano Marine Salvage remained in limbo, and the Romano diving robot was locked up securely in New York, rusting away in a dockside warehouse. Karbe's passionate interest in the Romano diving bell begs the question of his motivation. Who was this mysterious J. William Karbe other than Harry's friend and the man trying to buy the Romano diving bell?

Karbe's History

This was not Karbe's first involvement with salvage operations. Like Harry, he sought to raise money through somewhat questionable means for expeditions that never seemed to materialize. In an August 1920 classified ad, he said there was "big money for all" who invested in a venture by his International Deep-Sea Salvage Company to recover "fabulous fortunes in gold, silver, imperishable cargoes, precious stones, jewelry, pearls, coral, and sponges."[25]

In early 1921, Karbe resigned as president of the Leavitt Deep Sea Salvage Company when he was found to have misappropriated $1,000 of the company's bonds. Benjamin Franklin Leavitt invented and patented a hard metal diving suit but seemed more interested in fundraising than diving. By 1922, Karbe and Leavitt made amends and were selling stock in the Leavitt Lusitania Salvage Company to finance a proposed salvage of the most famous shipwreck of the time.[26] When the *Lusitania* scheme failed, Karbe moved on to more tangible salvage, the recovery of coal from sunken ships, claiming he knew of more than seven hundred ships loaded with a salvageable cargo of coal.[27] Within a year, in February 1924, Karbe was again charged with taking money in exchange for a promise to deliver coal at a low cost after the salvage and never coming through with the delivery. When a judge dismissed the charges four months later, he said the business dealings were "more the schemes of dreamers than of swindlers."[28]

The next mention of Karbe in connection with Rieseberg was Harry's reference to him personally helping out after Harry broke his leg while he was still living Washington. The relationships between the two are not fully understood, but they were obviously interested in working together. In 1939, J. William Karbe knew where to find the Romano diving robot. Whether he had rehabilitated himself from a life of fraudulent schemes remained to be determined.

A Scent of Credibility

J. William Karbe continued to work on new salvage schemes and joined Harry Rieseberg to try and acquire the Romano Diving bell. As part of their plan, Karbe incorporated a business name for an organization in Washington, D.C., in April 1939. He chose a business name that sounded credible—the Federal Board of Trade. There is little information available about any other activities of this group besides Karbe's association with the name. To further add to a tone of authority, Karbe registered the name in Washington, D.C. He also created an official-looking letterhead for the Federal Board of Trade's "New York Council" using an address on Wall Street.

Karbe badly wanted to acquire the assets of Romano Marine Salvage and the diving robot. After getting nowhere with his letter to Lula Romano before her death, Karbe made another appeal to one of Romano's long-standing allies and a partner in all his mechanical ventures, Chester Latta. Chet Latta had been one of the primary drivers for the Romano racer and was involved with mechanical work on the Romanoplane. He had been on the salvage crew in Puget Sound with Romano and stuck with him through all his ventures. Under the Federal Board of Trade name and on stationery featuring a large photo of a hard hat diver, Karbe wrote Latta with a plea for help on May 25, 1939, saying that without his agreement "the entire equipment and assets, here in storage and in which matter, numerous claims and obligations have been piling up these few years, might be lost."[29]

During research like this, the optimistic belief that physical remains of the Romano diving sphere might still be found is never eliminated from possibility. The thought of discovering it rusting away somewhere has remained, with the reality that one may never know what came of it dimming that hope. In his 2005 book about William Beebe's record-setting dives in his bathysphere, *Descent*, Brad Matsen opened with a story that any researcher would relish. Matsen describes how with help from a friend, he avoided security to sneak into a storage yard on Coney Island to discover the rusting remains of Beebe's diving bathysphere used during his famous descents between 1930 and 1934. Matsen described his discovery by saying that "finding the Bathysphere in an outdoor scrap yard under the Cyclone in Coney Island was like coming across a Mercury space capsule among rusting tools and nicked furniture at a flea market." A discovery of Romano's diving bell and equipment would inspire the same kind of excitement.[30] Karbe found the entire inventory of Romano equipment in the Harborside Warehouse in New Jersey. His suggestion that Latta help rescue the equipment urgently communicated that the diving bell was about to be scrapped or sold to pay off storage fees. Chet Latta was one of several people to receive a similar letter from Karbe about the diving bell.

Only two weeks later, another part of Karbe's plan became evident when he formalized an ongoing plan with Harry E. Rieseberg. On June 15, 1939, again using Federal Board of Trade letterhead, Karbe wrote Rieseberg in Los Angeles to add some formality to their discussions. Karbe very formally and in glowing terms welcomed Harry Rieseberg as President of the Federal Board of Trade, Inc.[31] Further evidence of their collaboration can be seen in the means Karbe used to raise money from potential investors. Karbe's letter to Latta not only used the Federal Board of Trade as the vehicle for the request, but also he sent it styled as the "Undersea Explorers Legion, a unit of the Federal Board of Trade Inc., Washington, D.C."[32] The only evidence of the existence of such an entity is an "Application for Advisory Board and Membership Privileges" created by Karbe.[33] Rather than shares of stock, the Undersea Explorers Legion sold memberships with some unusual characteristics. The basis of the membership arrangement was that Karbe wanted to sell 1,000 memberships at $100.00 each. What the applicant got in return was 1/1000 of a share of 25 percent of any profits from future salvage ventures.

In the fine print on the agreement, buyers gave up rights to see any financial data used to establish gains on their investment. They had to agree that "no member shall be entitled to an accounting and the right for an accounting is hereby expressly waived."[34] Karbe did not come up with that approach on his own. The membership application for the Undersea Explorers Legion laid out by Karbe was virtually

"Membership." Application for Undersea Explorers Legion. From Karbe Letter to Latta, May 25, 1939 (photograph used with permission of Rockwell Hammond, Jr.)

verbatim of the Undersea Explorers and Engineers Syndicate form used by Romano Submarine Engineering, Ralph Fleming, and Harry Rieseberg only a few years prior.

In another juxtaposition with the Romano scheme, Karbe and his Legion featured a powerless, four-masted schooner from Maine as the base of the proposed operations. Instead of the *Constellation,* this time it was the *Doris Hamlin,* a vessel with its own curious history connected with a widely regarded fraud. In 1931, L. Ron Hubbard, who later founded the Church of Scientology, used a similar approach to recruit students to pay their way on a cruise aboard the *Doris Hamlin* for purposes seemingly related to research and history but ultimately became part of Hubbard's quasi-religion.[35] Hubbard ran out of money, and the scheme was a disastrous failure. Given the earlier timing of the L. Ron Hubbard approach to raising funds, it may be that the first Royall/Romano/Rieseberg venture used Hubbard's venture as their model.

Potential investors probably did not know that the *Doris Hamlin,* proposed for use in Harry's latest romantic venture, had been hauling coal and goat manure only a year before. By 1939 she was wasting away in a Baltimore anchorage.[36]

Do Depositions Add Credibility?

Perhaps Bill Karbe learned something from his mistakes of the past. Questions from investors needed answers, and the answers better be good. Karbe proposed using rusting undersea equipment to look for treasure, but what proof did he have to offer that it worked as described? To address that concern, Karbe sought depositions from at least two people directly involved with the Romano equipment between 1933 and 1936 when it was last used: John O'Neal, who was part of Romano's Seattle-based crew, and Harry E. Rieseberg.

Both depositions, dated from April 1939, are similar in content, indicating they were written for the purpose Karbe required.[37] They attest to the deponent's involvement to "supervise, demonstrate, and test the efficiency of the 'Romano' devices." Both testified that the Romano diving bell was an absolute success despite never being used for treasure recovery. Both said they were present and in charge of the tests made with the U.S. Navy, which could not have been true for Rieseberg.

To cover any questions about Karbe's use of the equipment for underwater photography, the statements also attested to each of the men being present when Gerald Dwyer of the *Seattle Times* dove to four hundred feet and used the diving bell's powerful lights. Dwyer provided his own reference letter for Romano marketing material back in 1935. They both asserted that the equipment "possesses unlimited possibilities for successful and profitable underwater operations."[38]

O'Neal played a key role for Romano and was at least in Seattle and involved with Romano then, so his statements had a bit more credibility. His deposition said he was "capable and willing to handle the proposed diving, broadcasting, motion picture photography, and general salvage operations now being formulated by J. William Karbe."[39] Harry's statements were, of course, false. Harry was nowhere near

Seattle for the Navy tests and was not there when the *Seattle Times* reporter went down. Harry said he was "endorsing this equipment" for Karbe's purposes, not that he would be directly involved in the venture. Harry also used the deposition to further his claim of a depth record inside the diving bell. O'Neal's deposition said he was a diver and operator of the bell and tested the equipment at 900 feet. Harry said he did the same but at 1,404 feet, the depth he always used in his false claim of a record descent connected during one of his concocted treasure dives.

O'Neal's deposition was dated April 17, 1939, squarely in the middle of Karbe's effort to rescue the Romano equipment and raise money via the Undersea Explorers Legion. Harry's deposition, typed on the letterhead of the Romano Submarine Engineering and Salvage Corporation, seemed to offer even further support for the credibility of the claims, particularly with six signatures at the bottom attesting to Harry's affidavit. In harkening back to his misuse of the official stationery of the Smithsonian Institution, Harry used letterhead from the defunct Romano Submarine Engineering and Salvage Corporation that listed him as "Lieut. Harry E. Rieseberg, Research Engineer."

Questions about when Harry created this affidavit are raised based on his chosen dates. Harry's deposition is dated June 25, 1935, only a month after he broke his leg on the *Constellation*. In the letter, however, he says he worked with the Romano equipment in 1935 and 1936. How he could attest in 1935 to something he did in 1936 was a detail Harry overlooked. Further, Harry compounded that issue by referencing the operations "now being formulated by J. William Karbe and his associates," a project that did not take place until 1939. Even if one were to assume that the 1935 date was a typo, used when 1939 was intended, Harry's claims are still unsupported by fact.

Harry also added a list of signatures at the bottom of his affidavit, but it is uncertain to what they were attesting. Identities of the signatories have not been fully confirmed, but two of them had the same names as Masonic brothers back in Washington, D.C. Since Harry was in California at the time, it seems unlikely that he sent the letter back east to gather signatures. It is more likely that he misappropriated the names and had someone in Hollywood sign the document. Harry retained the original deposition in his files for thirty years and relied on it to support his stories.

No Response to Karbe's Offer

Despite Karbe's offers and fervent pleas to help save the Romano diving bell in 1939, it languished in a waterfront warehouse in Rockaway, New Jersey. When he received no replies, he warned the stockholders that "the Diving Bell, Machinery, Tools, Records, and other property, previously stored with the Jersey City Storehouse, by Mr. R.S. Fleming, for the 'Romano' account, were sold for non-payment of accumulated storage costs."[40]

In 1943, after the nation had settled into the fact that they were engaged in another world war, Karbe renewed his attempts to access the equipment. Taylor, the attorney and acting president of Romano Marine Salvage, sent a letter in January

1943 authorizing Karbe as "agent for the recovery of certain apparel, equipment, records and property" owned by the company and found in the Harborside Warehouse in Jersey City.[41] Later in September 1943, Karbe made another appeal to former Romano shareholders. This time Karbe used the letterhead of the "American Defense Assembly, Unit of the Federal Board of Trade." The letterhead included an image of the diving bell used in the 1935 flyer for the demonstration aboard the *Constellation* and a note that Karbe's business was "building and employing 'Romano' world-patented submarine equipment."

Karbe explained that since being granted the authorization in January, "after many months of effort," he could recover the Romano stockpile if he immediately came up with 2,500 dollars. It is clear from the silence that followed that the Romano diving bell was never recovered.

Harry Looking for Money in Hollywood

At the same time Karbe was trying to acquire the Romano diving robot, Harry was in Hollywood trying to drum up financial backers. Harry claimed he would use the Romano bell for a venture to the Caribbean where he claimed eleven Spanish ships loaded with silver went down during the same storm. Harry added two new fabrications to the narrative in this wave of publicity. Harry began to say he had already dived into the *Merida* when he had not. Even more impressively false, Rieseberg started to repeat a statement that would help him explain away questions about why there was no evidence of his claims regarding past expeditions. Harry said that "treasure from about twenty ships has been salvaged (by him) ... without knowledge of the rest of the world because the expeditions usually work in secret," a very convenient explanation for why nothing was found in the newspapers.[42]

The idea of Harry Rieseberg keeping quiet about anything beneficial to his persona seems laughable. The timeline of Harry's well-documented life events does not allow time and opportunity for him to have done *any* treasure dives, much less twenty. Being in California raised the stakes on Harry's made-up stories, but he still needed someone to make a bet.

Dead Men Hoist No Sails

In early 1938, Alvin Loesche began a year-long descent toward his death due to illness. For a man whose forty-five years at sea included being shipwrecked seven times and losing a vessel to a German submarine, the circumstances of Loesche's last voyage almost seem fitting. In a final effort to go home to Germany during the last year of his life, Loesche and his wife were part of the 592 passengers and 400 crew members aboard a German liner, *Deutschland*, which was disabled because of a fire at sea.

During his illness, Loesche lived with Captain Earnest G. Lundt in Bloomfield, New Jersey. Whether it was an illness exacerbated by his life as a live-aboard or the inevitable accumulation of years at sea that finally took his life, his death at age sixty-four dragged out over the previous year. He died at the Marine Hospital on Staten Island in April 1939.[43]

In seeking to judge Harry's statements and stories against fact, one of his claims connected to Loesche had a significant role in confirming that Harry Earl Rieseberg did none of the things he claimed to do. Not only was Harry promoting an expedition with a rotting ship and a rusting diving bell, but in October 1940, Harry also said that Alvin Loesche would navigate a proposed expedition.[44] Dead men may tell no tales, but their obituaries do. Loesche had been dead for eighteen months when Harry made his claim, and Rieseberg was apparently not invited to the funeral.

A Family Forgotten

Harry Rieseberg's trips to the western United States always seemed to involve an escape or a separation. As a young man, he separated from his parents and escaped the obligations of a wife and son when he moved to Prescott, Arizona. After his discharge from John Sealy Hospital in Galveston, as soon as he was well enough to move around freely, he moved to California and abandoned his second wife, Ellen, and their two children. Based on how he presented his life to the public, it gave the appearance that only time or money prevented him from going on his next diving adventure, never something as mundane as family obligations. Real adventurers did not bow to such limitations on their manliness.

Fine People, All

Since both his father, Henry, and his second wife, Ellen, were federal employees, there is some insight into their personalities and behavior through their performance reviews at work. At Henry's retirement from the Government Printing Office in 1930, his supervisor said he would "deem it an honor to be able to state that in his retirement this office loses one of its most faithful and trusted employees."[45] Harry's father was also a lifelong Mason and rose to leadership positions in the local council.

Harry's second wife, Ellen, was a hard-working nurse and mother raising two children in Galveston. Her performance evaluations consistently noted she was a "fine woman," an "excellent nurse," and was "well-liked by patients and staff." She was "very kind to the patients and cooperative with the doctors." One year the reviews even mentioned that "a patient told me that 'Mrs. Rieseberg is too nice to be a nurse.' whatever that might mean." It seems to be a compliment. She was acknowledged for her "high standards for living and nursing" and as one who "never gossips nor is over critical of others."[46] Ellen was a faithful and active member of the Seventh-Day Adventist Church. Her daughter, Shirley, was a member of Miss Elizabeth Newton's dancing and expression classes and part of the Girl Scouts.[47] Her son, Henry, was the scribe for his Boy Scout troop, an honors student, and became an Adventist missionary.[48] By all accounts, the Rieseberg family was steadfast and honorable—and then there was Harry.

Enough Is Enough

Even someone "too nice to be a nurse" could not tolerate her husband's second abandonment. Ellen filed for divorce in Galveston County, Texas, on September 4, 1940.[49] In her petition, she said they had initially separated around the first of January 1935. She claimed that Harry had quarreled with her and nagged her to "such an extent that further living together of the parties as husband and wife is impossible and insupportable."[50] Ellen had also penciled in that Harry abandoned her and their two children. The judge quickly ruled on the case, granting her custody of the children. Ellen was finished with Harry Rieseberg.

There is no indication that Harry was ever a part of his young children's lives after he got out of the hospital in 1937 and moved to Hollywood. He missed the fact that Ellen did the best she could for his children. He missed their accomplishment and advancement. Harry missed a lot, but he was a busy and important man. He had a false life to live.

"A Phlegmatic Disposition and a Long Neck"

Harry Rieseberg relied on a story-telling approach where he would lay out past events without providing a time frame. When he felt constrained by facts, he presented only limited details so readers could draw their conclusions and fill in the spaces between events as they saw fit. In the place of factual data, he often included dialog between persons in the story, even though it was impossible to know anything about such banter. His fictional stories were never offered as fiction, however. Instead, they were used to set the stage for the part of the story where he located a well-known treasure ship. To cover for the lack of silver and gold to show for his efforts, Harry's diving tales often ended with an octopus, a shark, bad weather, or a foreign country's gunboats preventing him from any recovery. Despite having said he saw the treasure firsthand, he never seemed to return to recover it.

When Rieseberg moved to Hollywood, he changed the narrative of his previous life to include a dozen or more dives that he repeatedly made in a full diving dress and hard hat. By examining what it meant to be a hard-hat diver in the 1930s, holes develop in Rieseberg's narrative. Understanding the diving profession and equipment at that time helps establish a basis in truth for comparison to his tales.[51]

Who Became a Diver?

In 1938, when Harry first began making his claims about being a hard-hat treasure diver, about four-hundred diving suits were sold to all military and commercial buyers. Only about 1,000 qualified divers were in the United States at that time, most of them trained by the Navy. If a diver did not come up through the Navy or learn from a former Navy diver, their training could have been through labor unions or commercial enterprises. The Navy selected divers who "must be under 30, wiry and resilient, with fine hearts and lungs, of phlegmatic disposition, with long necks rather than short and not too florid complexions."[52] Navy divers were disqualified by the age of forty for the master and first-class ratings but could continue as second-class divers. The diving suit restricted divers to heights between 5'6" inches and around 6'. At 6'2" tall, Rieseberg was just above the upper limit.

Diver Training

The 1943 Navy Diving Manual begins the section on training by saying, "Diving is arduous and hazardous work, and the art can be mastered only by training."[53] Before training, candidates in the Naval Diving School had to pass a rigorous physical examination. Divers selected for Naval training attended a twenty-six-week course directed by Lieutenant W.A. New at the Deep-Sea Diving School and Experimental Diving Unit in the Washington Navy Yard on the Potomac. Twelve men at a time completed twenty-six weeks of training, so only twenty-four recruits a year could graduate from the school.[54] The diving tank there allowed simulated dives at pressure matching a five-hundred-foot descent. They also dove into the murky Potomac. Students learned principles of science, submarine mechanics, and rescue work. A course designed for officers in charge of divers but who did not dive themselves was an additional twelve weeks.

In 1938 the Navy had only sixteen master divers qualified to go down to three-hundred feet and supervise diving operations. First-class divers, 116 of them, could go to that depth but not supervise. A group of 361 second-class divers could go only to ninety feet. Navy divers were elite sailors who were well-trained, skillful, and physically fit for difficult and dangerous conditions.

Diving Dress

A fully equipped hard hat diver wore two hundred pounds of clothing and ballast. The weighted belt alone weighed 112 pounds, and the lead-soled boots weighed eighteen pounds each. Warm long johns and one or two woolen sweaters went on to combat the cold at depth. A wool watch cap was pulled down over the ears. The diving dress was a thin rubber sheet between layers of heavy canvas. It took two people plus the diver to get the gear fully in place. The feet were enclosed like a child's footie pajamas. The sleeve ended with cuffs around the wrist tight enough to keep the air inside and required a cuff expander to remove at the end of the dive. Ordinary work gloves might have been worn in warmer waters, but in colder conditions, rubber mittens provided more warmth but less tactile control.

The copper and brass helmet assembly included the helmet and the full breastplate covering the shoulders and upper chest. It attached to a rubber seal around the neck of the diving suit. Inside the helmet was an air escape valve the diver could open with his chin to allow air out. An over-inflation of the suit could lead to the rapid rise of the diver to the surface like a balloon. A rope lifeline to the surface was wrapped around the diver's waist. The airline hooked under his arm and was tied to the breastplate, so there was no tension on the air intake at the back of his helmet.

Working at depth was made difficult not only by the suit and the pressure but also by the resistance of the water. Every movement is slowed by a fluid that weighs eight pounds per gallon. Even a simple hammer for underwater work weighed four to four and a half pounds.

Diver Limitations

At two hundred feet, a diver would typically stay down for only twelve minutes. The total time working underwater was short due to the staged decompression needed to avoid the bends, a painful and potentially deadly formation of bubbles in the tissue of a diver who ascended too quickly. The diver would have to stop at sixty feet and stay there for two minutes. Two more minutes at fifty feet, three minutes at forty feet, five minutes at thirty feet, seven minutes at twenty feet, and ten minutes only ten feet from the surface added thirty-two minutes to a twelve-minute dive. If a diver had to stay at two-hundred feet for an hour, perhaps due to some emergency, the ascent time required to allow the nitrogen in his bloodstream to dissipate went up to four hours.

Why We Know Harry Was Not a Diver

When Rieseberg's narrative is held against even the most basic facts about the diving profession of the 1930s, his stories fail in credibility. The facts stacked against Harry Rieseberg being a hard hat diver are overwhelming and primarily fall on two key points. The first point of failure is in Harry's own words. In *I Dive for Treasure*, he wrote that he was not yet ready to dive on his own when Max Nohl was aboard the *Seth Parker*. Harry said, "I was envious of Nohl, going off like that to hunt for treasure, but I knew *I wasn't ready yet* and was reasonably content to follow the accounts of the expedition in the newspapers."[55] So in late 1933, Harry said he "was not ready" to hunt for treasure. Then in 1934, he lost his job at the Bureau of Navigation and set the stage for the Washington demonstration of the Romano diving bell aboard the *Constellation* in 1935. That short window during which he *might* have gone underwater leaves no room in the actual events of his life to conduct the type of months-long expeditions he later described.

A second shortcoming is Harry's physical ability to dive. When *I Dive for Treasure* debuted in 1942, Harry Rieseberg was already fifty years old. Even allowing some flexibility in Harry's later story that he began diving around 1930, he would have been at the age where divers began to slow down, not starting the extensive training required to become a diver. Harry treated diving like a simple process, quickly learned and managed by anyone. He even described diving solo in hard hat gear; an impossible feat since it required the manual operation of air pumps from the surface. The *Constellation* had a crew of twenty-two on one trip, but Harry would have readers believe that he and a fraternal brother managed a dive just fine all on their own.

After Rieseberg broke his leg, he was physically unable to dive, and he walked with a limp or carried a cane for the remainder of his life. After his broken leg, Harry would not have been physically able to don the gear, much less carry out a dive below the surface. Harry did not have the stamina, the training, or the opportunity to be a hard-hat diver in search of treasure. He did not own a ship or have a place to store equipment. He had no artifacts, and his financial difficulties indicated no paydays with hundreds of thousands of dollars of silver and gold. Beyond the remote possibility that Harry suited up and descended briefly at the Navy facility, it seems evident that Harry Rieseberg, international treasure expert, never got wet.

Though that fact may lead some to question much of his published work, it also leads to an appreciation of the energy required to maintain that charade for the remainder of his life. Rather than run from this deficiency in his résumé, Harry magnified it by educating himself about the science of diving. At public appearances, he proudly displayed charts showing the water pressure at various depths. He could describe the decompression process and how the bends could result from an ascent that did not follow that process. Harry was the master of the primary rule of obfuscation—if you can't baffle them with brilliance, dazzle them with bullshit. He learned nautical terms, read travel brochures to learn about foreign locales, and carefully studied maps so he could describe the geography of remote places. The list of lost ships that he cited as his finds—*Merida, Brother Jonathan, DeBraak,* and others—were real treasure hoards, but the way Rieseberg inserted himself in the stories was entirely made up.

The inescapable truths about him being utterly incapable of living the life he assigned himself as Lieutenant Harry Rieseberg, treasure salvor, were no deterrent to his claims. From the time he emerged from his rehabilitation in Galveston in 1937 until he died in 1970, the Harry After never once relented in promoting that reputation. If you are going to build a career on lies, you might as well start with a big one.

Chapter 7

The Big Time

*A lie is often the mirror image of the truth;
by examining it carefully, you can reconstruct
the fact that lie was designed to conceal.*
—K.J. Parker

An editor commenting on the grand plans for an expedition Rieseberg touted in one of his articles noted that it was being conducted from Hollywood "where many strange events are reliably reported to have their beginning."[1] Finally, someone got it right.

By 1940, Rieseberg and his parents had lived in Hollywood for three years.[2] For the two years immediately after he broke his leg, he was in Galveston for treatment and recovery. His last permanent job had been with the Bureau of Navigation, which ended in 1934. Harry said later he found a way to eke out a living in Hollywood by doing some writing for the studios. The only verifiable income from 1937 through about 1940 was from fifty or more magazine articles. A friend said he had noticed Harry's financial difficulties and even loaned him money.

Living amid screenwriters, radio personalities, authors, and actors of all grades, Harry quickly caught the fever and connected with people in the entertainment industry. In that setting, everyone who could type wanted to write a movie script, and anyone who could dramatically lift an eyebrow wanted to make the next casting call. Rieseberg began submitting magazine articles to all kinds of outlets while continuing attempts to attract willing investors to bite on his pitch for a treasure expedition.[3]

One of the intriguing aspects of Harry Rieseberg's personal life is how little of it he lived apart from his parents. There were probably years when his father's $1,000 per month pension was all they lived on while Harry recovered from his broken leg. Between 1935 and when his parents died—his mother in 1942, and his father in 1944—their only child, Harry, lived with them almost continually. One cannot help but wonder about the family dynamic. Who was dependent on whom? It seemed that Harry could not support himself fully for years at a time, so the assumption is that Harry could not have pursued these aspirations or been able to build his persona without the financial grounding of his parents.

In the land of outsized self-promoters, Harry Rieseberg still stood out. He was experienced in selling himself but needed a way to break through the din of Hollywood publicity machines to claim a niche where he could be famous. To accomplish that, he invented and refined his adventurous résumé as an expedition leader, treasure hunter, expert on the location of wrecks, octopus killer, and idea man for the movies. By his account, after every magazine article, newspaper feature, and radio appearance, he received hundreds of letters from people who wanted to know where to locate the treasure themselves. They were generally not from the people Harry wished to attract.

A Lack of Attention

Since his encounter with Cecil B. DeMille and the famous director's passing interest in one of Harry's treasure ideas in December 1937, Harry had trouble gathering even a hint of legitimate financial interest. Any investor who took more than a passing notice of Rieseberg's schemes could quickly detect that Harry had high enthusiasm and charm but wreck location information that was too general for use in an expensive expedition.

In early 1938 all the news and attention for underwater adventures went to John Craig and Max Nohl, men with legitimate diving credentials. Max Nohl, an MIT graduate and inventor, was on a national speaking tour promoted by a major public relations firm. Nohl was young, photogenic, a true scientist, and had legitimacy in all his ventures. Photos of Nohl in various places around the world wearing different types of diving equipment were all over the news. There were no questions about his abilities. In January 1938, Craig and Nohl dove the *John Dwight*, a Prohibition-era wreck that went down with hundreds of thousands of dollars of scotch and an expected $225,000 in cash. Their well-publicized salvage found pinholes in the metal caps of the bottles had ruined the hoped-for recovery of alcohol, and the money was nowhere to be found. They dove into the wreck, there were pictures, and the facts of their venture were unassailable.[4] In March, *Modern Mechanix* magazine ran a cover story on Nohl's record-setting dive in an article titled "Helium Method Raises Sunken Treasure."[5] Compared to Craig and Nohl, Harry was just a pretender.

Harry Took to the Airwaves

With the help and advice of his new Hollywood contacts, Harry took advantage of any form of media to get his message out. One United Press International (UPI) article about Rieseberg appeared in dozens of papers nationwide for two to three months, spouting the usual formula. Harry's "thrill of seeking sunken treasure in the sea" was also the subject of the radio show, *Thrills* on March 23, 1938.

Harry repeated one of his regular assertions in that radio show that he had set a depth record inside the Romano diving bell. An article about the broadcast noted, "Rieseberg and William Beebe, the explorer, are said to have gone deeper into the sea than any other living person."[6] There is no mention of Harry setting a record other than the claim he made himself and repeated for thirty years.

Harry seemed to be everywhere and in every medium. In December 1940, he appeared on the national Columbia Network radio show *We the People*.[7] A telegram indicated he had only a week's notice of the invitation to appear. The producers wired Harry on December 9 to arrive in New York on the 15th for a show on December 17, 1940, all expenses paid. It is unlikely that Harry was told in advance that he would share this time with a man who dislocated his jaw trying to eat a large sandwich and three men who were wrongfully convicted and released from prison after seven years. His ego would not have allowed it.

Octopus No. 1

Harry pulled out all the stops in embellishing his personal history even with no immediate prospects for a venture. He had no investors, expeditions, equipment, or wealth. Harry had to do something different to stand apart from actual divers like John Craig and Max Nohl. With the help of inventive Hollywood types all around him, he jumped in front of the publicity parade with the most audacious and indefensible claim possible.

In a full-page photo spread in the *St. Louis Post Dispatch* on Sunday, August 14, 1938, Harry Rieseberg told the public that he killed a twenty-four-foot octopus while diving for underwater treasure.[8] The article reported that Harry had encountered such a creature and photographed a battle with the beast in the Silver Shoals off Haiti. Dramatic photographs show an octopus attacking a metal diving bell. Rieseberg claimed that the diver inside the bell summoned the surface for help and that Harry was swiftly lowered to the bottom inside the Romano bell.

Movie publicity photograph. *Below the Sea*, © 1933, renewed 1960. Columbia Pictures Corporation. All Rights Reserved (courtesy Columbia Pictures).

Images from film *Below the Sea* (1930) in a February 1939 article in *Mechanix Illustrated*. Rieseberg claimed this was him in the diving dress, and that he owned the copyright to the image. Used with permission of John Schroeter.

When a reader of another of Harry's octopus stories challenged the tale and asked how he killed the monstrous beast, the editor replied on Rieseberg's behalf. The answer the editor wished to be swallowed was that "The octopus was killed by the use of the nine-foot arms of the robot by pinching or severing five of its eight tentacles and mutilating the other three."[9] Upon examining the details of Rieseberg's claim and the photos attached to them in his publications, it becomes clear that Harry Rieseberg made up one of his grandest and most persistent deceptions to make this statement. The photos Rieseberg used were stills from a Hollywood movie showing the exact scene. Harry appropriated the photos and claimed they were his own.

In March 1933, Fay Wray and Ralph Bellamy starred in *Below the Sea*, a movie about recovering an underwater treasure. Wray received attention for her role in *King Kong* just a few months before. In the film, a hard hat diver is attacked by a giant octopus, a diving bell is in peril, and the heroine inside is saved. In a remarkably bold and blatant falsification, Harry used still photos from this movie and claimed they were his own. He even cited images lifted from the film with his copyright. Rieseberg said he was the diver shown in the photo instead of an actor from the motion picture.

Harry repeatedly published these photos over many years and made his outlandish claim with only slight adjustments to the story over time. In a November 1938 modification to the story, Harry explained that the diving robot was not seen in the picture because the camera was housed inside it. He was also questioned about the quality of the light at the reported 120-foot depth, and countered by saying three 5,000-watt lights were attached to the arms of the robot, giving the scene movie-quality illumination.[10]

The story Rieseberg told in *Mechanix Illustrated* in 1939 was a shortened version of what became chapter twenty-one in his book *I Dive for Treasure*.[11] The difference was in the circumstances of the octopus' attack. Harry began making up stories about himself to get into print at any opportunity. He reached a brief pinnacle of bogus credibility when a one-page article with these fake photos was published in *Newsweek* in October 1938.[12] Various versions of the octopus story appeared between August 1938 and November 1939 and continued to pop up every few years. Somehow Rieseberg got by with this whopper of a tale, even when it could easily be disputed but it was Hollywood, after all. What gets sold is what people will buy.

The Sunken City of Port Royal

A lifelong focal point for much of Rieseberg's publicity-seeking was an idea he pitched to Hollywood producers—Jamaica's Port Royal. Port Royal was his setting for a treasure story involving a 1692 earthquake and tsunami which sent the old city below sea level. Harry circulated a story to the newspapers that in 1932 he had walked that sunken city after discovering it by accident on one of his world cruises in search of treasure. The location was the theme for a full-page feature article titled "He Walks with Davy Jones," published in hundreds of newspapers nationwide from December 1941 through early summer 1942. The heavily illustrated article went out nationwide through the NEA, the Newspaper Enterprise Association, a syndicated news reporting service. Reading this article is like reading a summary of *I Dive for Treasure* and is much like reading the core of virtually every other work Harry produced for the next thirty years. The article established his narrative, and Rieseberg stuck to it unflinchingly.

> He has battled sharks and octopi in the ocean's fastness (*sic*); he has encountered feasting cannibals in the South Seas; he was the first man to explore the sunken city of Port Royal, Jamaica—once known as the "Pirate's Babylon"; he has captured on film the largest octopus ever recorded and has had a ringside seat at a battle between a shark and an octopus; he has examined and disproved the legend of treasure on Cocos Island; he holds the world's record for a depth dive in a workable robot [1404 feet].[13]

Harry's entire fake résumé was thrown at the publishing wall—and was starting to stick.

Cocos Island

An opportunity to add credibility and dispute the treasure claims of others involved a treasure myth called the Loot of Lima. Cocos Island, a small island off the coast of Costa Rica, had been the source of this legend for centuries. The legend was founded on a report that the golden riches of a cathedral in Lima, Peru, had been stolen and buried on Cocos Island.[14] The Loot of Lima was big news in 1931 when famed adventurer, Sir Malcolm Campbell, organized an expedition that was more theater than treasure hunt.[15]

A subsequent attempt for the treasure, and the one that inspired Rieseberg's rebuttal, originated in California with news of treasure hunters with more time and money than good sense going after the buried treasure on Cocos Island. In November 1939, a group sponsored by the California Society for Archaeological Investigations prematurely announced they had found the treasure worth a reported $60,000,000. The group planned to return with excavating equipment in January 1940.

It took only a couple of months before the true nature of the discovery was admitted—they had found only a piece of cedar, the wood reportedly used to encase the treasure. The group was ill-equipped and had only fourteen days on the island. They had gelignite material for blasting, but only three men were assigned to dig holes in the sand. Heat, humidity, insects, and the jungle seemed to catch the amateur prospectors off-guard. Their story was the same as dozens of others—they based their efforts on suspect reports and legends without any idea of the facts or conditions.

With this renewed focus on Cocos Island, Harry took advantage of it in a revealing and opportunistic manner. In a full-page article for the *Los Angeles Times*, he sought to discredit both the current attempt to find it and the myth itself.[16] Harry suggested that he had recently renewed his research on the Cocos Island legend in preparation for promoting his own expedition. He said, almost in an oh-by-the-way manner, that when he just happened to be in the southern hemisphere looking for a galleon off Ecuador at Manta Bay, he decided to stop in at Lima, Peru, another eight hundred miles to the south. Upon arriving, he said he visited the cathedral mentioned in the legend only to find the supposedly buried Golden Virgin still in its rightful place in the cathedral.

Harry's persistence in promoting himself in the article led to two different outcomes. The first was around his fabricated credibility. The piece opens with a summary of Rieseberg's credentials. "Lieutenant Harry E. Rieseberg, who wrote this article for The Magazine, is indisputably the outstanding American authority on deep-sea salvage and treasure search."[17] That was true not because Harry Rieseberg earned that distinction but because he rigorously promoted it himself. The second outcome was not nearly as positive. Harry Rieseberg did not write this article. A neighbor and friend of his who was a real writer, Eric Strutt, was the author. They had initially agreed that Strutt would be credited, and he was not. That was not a result of an oversight by the editor, but because Rieseberg reneged on a promise to his friend.

A Neighbor in the Business

As far back as 1935, Harry said he had begun compiling his research into a manuscript for a book about the possible locations of ships lost at sea. The working title he claimed was "Cracking Davy Jones' Treasure Vaults." At that point, he had not decided to create his persona as a treasure salvor and was only looking to cash in on his knowledge about submerged wrecks and their purported locations.[18] After moving to Hollywood, where there were hundreds of others with big ideas to pitch, Harry had the opportunity to meet people who would more readily buy into his stories. If the stories were entertaining, Hollywood values cared less about the differences between fact and fiction. Reality was something created in the back lot of a movie studio.

Harry was good at making up stories but needed help with his literary expression. Though Harry had written—and plagiarized—poetry and travel articles, he realized his skills needed to be improved to publish works for books, radio, or film. That is when he met Eric Strutt. Eric Strutt was an experienced writer who produced advertising copy and radio scripts for the Raymond R. Morgan advertising company. After moving to California from his native Canada, Strutt worked for a small newspaper in Huntington Park, California, where he wrote articles using five different bylines to make it look like there was an entire staff.[19] He worked freelance for five years and wrote humorous columns for four newspapers. CBS and NBC used over two hundred of his scripts for radio productions.[20] Strutt had paid his dues and had credibility as a writer. He also lived just around the corner from Harry Rieseberg, and over time they became friends. Strutt was also interested in collecting writing credits wherever possible, so he teamed with Rieseberg to submit articles for newspapers and magazines.

Strutt described his first meeting with Rieseberg in July 1939 in the preface of the first draft of their book manuscript, "I Walk With Davy Jones." He said Harry was "tall and lean, about six-foot-two, straight and broad-shouldered." Strutt was struck by Harry's lean figure and face, with high cheekbones and a sharp jawline. What stood out the most, however, were his eyes of a "brilliant blue." Harry's lingering physical limitations due to his broken leg were still evidenced by the cane he carried to support his weight. When Rieseberg sat down in Strutt's small apartment, his "long, tweed-wrapped leg projected stiffly in front of him," leading Stutt to notice that Harry was also wearing a light steel brace.[21]

Rieseberg and Strutt agreed to equally share profits in "a joint venture to exploit commercially and profitably the subject of the search for and recovery of treasure from sunken ships."[22] Rieseberg was to provide factual data, and Strutt would turn them into a literary work that could be published in books and magazines, produced for radio, or even become a movie. After a series of conversations, the book Harry said he had begun to hack out back in 1935 became a collaborative project with Strutt doing the writing and Harry feeding him treasure tales. Publishers wanted adventure stories, so Harry did his best to provide them, even if it required him to make them up. It is unclear if Strutt knew at the time that none of the adventures Rieseberg related had happened or if he was duped like everyone else. Over time, however, Strutt came to understand that Harry's stories were complete fiction.

Strutt's Contributions

Strutt wasted no time taking on a long list of story ideas from Harry, turning them into articles, and creating a proposal for a grand series of radio programs. In 1939, two radio scripts were completed for a series called "Sunken Treasure." Strutt and Rieseberg were relentless in their pursuit of outlets. Strutt made notes on the material he received so he could go back and question Rieseberg's inconsistencies and exaggerations. Sometimes the articles appeared under Rieseberg's byline with "as told to Eric Strutt." Strutt's papers also retain both Rieseberg's writing and Strutt's revisions to an early story about Port Royal for a magazine article. Rieseberg's version was called "How We'll Seek the Sunken City of Port Royal," but it was Strutt who inserted the title "City Beneath the Sea" into the final work. Strutt said that anyone who compared the two manuscripts could clearly see that he "did more than dot a few I's and cross a few T's."

A series of 240 radio script ideas were proposed for a series they were calling "Neptune's Treasure, A New, Different, and Original Radio Program for Sponsorship."[23] In one of the scripts, Harry claimed he walked the "slime-covered decks" of the *Merida*. Another 1939 manuscript was Harry's oft-repeated story about diving at the Silver Shoals. Harry was throwing out ideas and expecting Strutt to clean them up. From 1940 to early 1942 Harry Rieseberg and Eric Strutt published dozens of articles in magazines and newspapers, perhaps as many as 750 of them according to a number Rieseberg liked to promote. It was Eric Strutt who wrote Rieseberg's full-page articles in the *Los Angeles Times* and ghostwrote the "X Marks Nothing on Cocos" article about Cocos Island under Harry Rieseberg's byline.[24] The *Los Angeles Times*, *Grit Weekly*, the *Boston Herald*, the *Kansas City Star*, and even the Spanish-language newspaper, *Prensa*, ran similar newspaper stories. Magazine stories in *Pic*, *Blue Book*, *Sea*, *True*, *Catholic Digest*, *Grail*, *Sport*, *Boy's Life*, *Travel*, *Teens*, and *Pioneer* carried the same story. Some of them had the byline "by Eric Strutt as told by Lt. Harry Rieseberg," but many did not mention Strutt at all. Rieseberg made it clear that he saw Strutt as just a hired gun, not by his words but by his actions. Giving him byline credit was seen as a gift, not a right.[25] The most extensive and successful of all of Rieseberg's deceptions was that he wrote *I Dive for Treasure* when it was Eric Strutt who did the work.

Harry Gets an Agent

In early 1941, Harry Rieseberg was in search of an agent. Most of Rieseberg's efforts to find an outlet for his tales were directed toward one of his stories becoming a movie, and he believed the way to get to that goal was by producing a compelling radio series. Radio was also where Eric Strutt had the most experience.

Strutt and Rieseberg had submitted the manuscript on their own to publishers over a period of two years. Rejections came from Ziff-Davis in October 1939; Little Brown & Co in January 1940; J.B. Lippincott Company in October 1940, and Viking Press in November 1940. A rejection from Doubleday, Doran, and Company arrived in March 1941.[26]

In July 1941, Rieseberg wrote a letter to the Edmond Pauker agency in New York with four single-spaced pages of sales pitch, hype, and name-dropping. Pauker was born in Hungary in 1888 and came to the U.S. in 1922. His business focused primarily on the theater, but he was also taking on literary work. Much of his business was with agencies in Germany, Hungary, and Austria trying to get into U.S. markets.[27] Full-page ads in *Writer's Digest*, Harry's go-to source for outlets for his material, put Pauker at the top of Harry's list of possible agents.

Harry's letter to Dr. Pauker was verbose in explaining that he was not a writer, and in fact, he would not be "interested in writing as a means of livelihood or otherwise." Rieseberg went to some length in his self-promotion by listing publications where his articles appeared and made sure Pauker knew he was "internationally recognized as the foremost world authority on sunken treasure ships." Rieseberg's hard sell was not primarily about his writing, but in promoting his stories as movie ideas. "Man of Destiny," a storyline Rieseberg would promote for years, was a movie idea he thought could eclipse *Mutiny on the Bounty (1935)*.[28]

The reply from John Gainfort, a vice president at Edmond Pauker Inc., simply asked that Harry submit some manuscripts for their review. Rieseberg noted in a reply that Pauker also handled radio work and spent another two pages in a letter on July 8 telling Gainfort about his "500 complete half-hour dramatizations of true factual treasure stories" that he had available for radio. Gainfort's polite reply was to say that they needed to see the material to make any decision.[29] Rieseberg met that request a week later by sending three examples of his work. Two of them were radio scripts and the third was a "brief brochure of 21 pages" explaining his broad plan for marketing himself and his programs and suggesting that Gainfort take the time to "read from the beginning through to its end."[30]

Reluctantly, a Book Manuscript

There is no clearer example that publishing a book was not at the top of Harry's wish list than his letter to Gainfort in late July. Rieseberg's assumption was that he would not overload the Pauker agency with material all at once. However, in a conversation with Eric Strutt about that, Strutt convinced him to submit all he had to his prospective agent. The letter accompanying the partial manuscript provides some insight into the earliest iteration of what would become *I Dive for Treasure*. The proposed chapter titles reflect the themes of Rieseberg's articles repeatedly published for the next thirty years. The sunken city of Port Royal, underwater battles with a giant octopus, Cocos Island, Silver Shoals, and Manta Bay are all there from the beginning. Also, there was an acknowledgment of the work put in by Strutt, with the work to be styled "written by Lieut. Harry E. Rieseberg, as told to Eric Strutt."[31]

A Relationship Begins

Based on the scripts Rieseberg submitted, the Pauker agency sent Harry a contract allowing them to represent him on radio—a simple letter of agreement which he quickly signed and returned. In the agent's agreement dated August 8, 1941, Pauker was tasked with finding an outlet for "radio programs now bearing the general title 'CARGOES OF GOLD,'" a collection they felt was worthy of the New York-based radio networks.[32] Based on some initial interest from publishers, Gainfort pressed for the rest of the book manuscript for "I Walk with Davy Jones" so Rieseberg and Strutt got to work on completing the final five chapters. They were on their way to the Pauker agency by express delivery on October 28, 1941.[33]

A Book Not Well Written

Only two publishers expressed an interest following their brief review of the book manuscript. Both said the work was poorly written. Even Gainfort admitted that had been the Pauker agency's initial opinion as well. While one publisher rejected it outright, the second one, Robert M. McBride & Company, was interested but said "certain difficulties present themselves." The conditions required some substantial changes.[34]

The manuscript as written was unacceptable and only justified an "expression of interest." The language in Strutt and Rieseberg's manuscript that was "material of a general travel character" would have to come out and other "adventure material" would have to be added to maintain the book's length. Gainfort also had three questions for Harry. First, could he provide "additional adventure material." Secondly, Gainfort asked if Rieseberg would be willing to accept a "professional collaborator who will be satisfactory to the publisher" and share 50 percent of his royalties. If so, then Gainfort wanted Harry to come to New York to work with a writer on the manuscript for as long as three weeks, so the new ghostwriter "might familiarize himself with your personality and point of view."[35] Harry's reply spent over a full page ducking the question and asking "why."

> Were I, myself, a writer of note I would have interjected such talent which perhaps the manuscript now lacks, and therefore it would need not further revision—but not being such my presence would add little to a writer's powers toward revision of some of the chapters as you say require same.[36]

Harry knew he could not pretend to understand how to write if sitting in a room with someone of genuine talent. Even his letter was written badly. Harry told his agent that the book could proceed without his further involvement. He had relied too heavily on travel brochures and libraries when he needed background and color for his made-up diving adventures.

Just in case Harry had his feelings hurt about the rejection of the manuscript in its current form, Gainfort closed the door in advance to any thoughts that Harry might find acceptance somewhere else. "You probably consider that it is well enough written to be saleable. The fact is that it is not. This was our opinion in the first place and the only two publishers who expressed any interest in the book said exactly the same thing."[37] Harry's problem with moving on as Gainfort proposed was what to tell Eric Strutt. Rieseberg had been upfront with his agent by telling him that Strutt helped write the manuscript for the book. He also admitted to Gainfort that he had not yet told Strutt there would be another ghostwriter and that Strutt's work would not be what would be published, at least not in its present form.

While Rieseberg acknowledged Strutt's work, he also minimized it. Strutt, however, saw his role as central to Harry's book—he saw himself as the real author. In the January 1942 issue of *Swank* magazine, Strutt published an unrelated article, "In Wolf's Clothing." In the bio for the article, Strutt said he "just completed a non-fiction book called 'I Walk with Davy Jones,' which concerns the adventures of Lieut. Harry Rieseberg, treasure salvor."[38] Strutt's approach to the book was that it was his book written *about* Harry Rieseberg. That may have been true since no original manuscript is extant. In Strutt's 1997 obituary, the family said he "wrote a best-selling novel called 'I Dive for Treasure' under the pen name Lt. Harry E. Rieseberg."[39] That point of contention continued for Strutt's entire life and resulted in future litigation between Strutt and Rieseberg.

A Ghostwriter for the Ghostwriter

The requirement that Rieseberg travel to New York to work with another ghostwriter was eventually sidestepped. In a telegram on November 24, 1941, Gainfort told Harry he had "found a collaborator acceptable to publisher and familiar with region you write about STOP therefore possible without you coming New York."[40] Harry wrote back immediately with a notation at the top of his letter, the tone of which would become a source of both irritation and entertainment on the part of Harry's agents for many years to come. He typed, <u>IMMEDIATE ATTENTION REQUIRED</u> ... **Bold**. CAPITALIZED. <u>Underlined</u>.

Harry agreed to the terms of the contract but pointed out that it appeared he would be the last to have any financial gain from the project. With the agent getting his percentage and Stutt and the new ghostwriter receiving a cut, Harry lamented "there'll be only left my name on the book." Harry explained that he was not doing this to see his name in print because "I've had it there millions of times." He proclaimed that having his name on a book "doesn't bring up exalted egotistical feelings in my being" but was "a means to a certain end." Harry saw his books as a pathway to his real interest—Hollywood movies.[41]

Vast Potential Possibilities

With a book contract underway and a rework of the book continuing without any further contributions from Harry, he wasted no time dusting his hands together in a "now that is done, what about this" manner. Harry brought up a subject with his agent that would become a recurring theme in his communications with Gainfort and the Pauker Agency. Rieseberg had already mentioned a second manuscript, either in the works or solely in his head, titled "Man of Destiny," which focused on Harry's treasure-hunting idol, Sir William Phipps.

Harry, the idea man, had already tried the Phipps topic out on some of his Hollywood contacts and was sure it would be a successful as a movie, but getting it published in book form first was the way to get there. To add credibility to his assessment of "Man of Destiny," Harry told Gainfort that Grace Hayes, a former actress, told Harry it would be an excellent movie and asked him to let her send it to her industry friends. Though she no longer had a movie career, Hayes most certainly had many Hollywood friends. At the time, she was the proprietress of the famous Grace Hayes Lodge, a local nightclub that claimed Howard Hughes and Bugsy Siegel among its patrons.

If the opinion of Hayes, the professional hobnobber, was not enough, Harry dropped the names of others who had gotten his hopes up. Leo McCarey wrote, directed, and produced remarkable and timeless movies, including the Marx Brothers' *Duck Soup* (1933) and *Make Way for Tomorrow* (1937). McCarey won the first of three Academy Awards for *The Awful Truth* (1937), starring Cary Grant. McCarey was also Rieseberg's relative on his mother's side somehow and likely the facilitator of any gainful employment Harry had during his early days in Hollywood.[42] Though Harry contended that McCarey told him "Man of Destiny" had potential if re-written by actual scriptwriters, McCarey's primary recommendation was that the story should come out as a book first.[43] Rieseberg's obsession with Phipps's story would continue, and his focus on transferring his fame to the movie industry would soon become a point of contention with his new agents.

Even while getting *I Dive for Treasure* underway, Harry persistently asked about his "Man of Destiny" manuscript. Gainfort played it down by saying he recalled getting a synopsis from Harry sometime prior, but the entire work had not been submitted. However, from what bit of the outline version he had read, Gainfort recalled that "it sounded somewhat contrived."[44]

Ghostwriter #2

Things were moving quickly on the book. A 1942 spring launch was the goal, but as of December 1941, the book still needed to be written. Gainfort responded quickly to Harry's acceptance of the terms with Strutt's replacement—a second ghostwriter. He assured his author that even though the details were yet to be worked out, he would seek "the best possible terms" on his behalf. Oddly, Harry's agent immediately began to downplay any short-term financial benefit of publishing and emphasized the importance of getting "a major publication for you even if you receive no royalties at all" because it would have an "important bearing on radio and other possibilities."[45]

Denis Plimmer, an employee of the Pauker Agency, was chosen as the second ghostwriter. According to Gainfort, Plimmer was "a writer of wide experience and proven ability who has been chosen to make the revised version of your book."[46] The agency had identified a new collaborator, but the final decision for the selection would not be made until Plimmer submitted one or two chapters of his work to assess his ability to match the vision for the book.

Plimmer was pleased with the opportunity and was passionate and energetic about the result. He envisioned twenty-one chapters (there were eventually twenty-six) and about 80,000 words. Plimmer had already sent Harry a list of questions and was waiting for his reply. With answers, Plimmer believed he would not need much additional input from Rieseberg to complete a "damned fine book." Plimmer quickly forwarded his first draft of chapter one to Allen Churchill, the editor at McBride.[47]

Though Plimmer was touted as a "writer of wide experience and proven ability," it took Allen Churchill at McBride only four days with Plimmer's re-write of chapter one to dismiss him as an acceptable ghostwriter for Harry's book. Churchill was an editor whose job was to write letters like the one he wrote to Plimmer in response. A critique moderated by professional politeness resulted in a letter quickly coming to the point. He opened by reminding Plimmer that when his name first came up for this task, they all agreed to go "right back to our former working arrangement and that there would be no hard feelings" if it did not work out.[48] Churchill felt "something lacking" in the book, and he was not the only one at the publishing house who felt that way about his draft. While giving Plimmer credit for his technical skills, Churchill dismissed the spirit of the book.

> Such a book as this we feel should be written in a very relaxed, informal style which makes the author out to be a nice, easy going and likeable fellow. The style in which this chapter is written is tense, somewhat strained, and altogether gives the impression that this is a piece of literary work and not informal story telling.[49]

Churchill suggested that Plimmer find another collaborator among their clientele—in other words, that he finds his replacement. The young Plimmer's hopes to earn some royalties for himself were not to be.

Fame Won't Pay the Bills

Amid Harry's fast-paced, back-and-forth communications with his agent about his book, on December 7, 1941, the world changed forever with the attack at Pearl Harbor. Harry Rieseberg restrained himself for only nine days after that tragedy before he could no longer resist the urge to change the subject back to his favorite topic—Harry Rieseberg. He wrote a blistering letter to his publisher with his standard default heading—**IMMEDIATE ATTENTION—AIR MAIL**—at the top. Rieseberg wanted to know why there was a delay in getting his book contract. "What happened? Did the Japanese blitzkrieg scare the publisher of the book out, cause them to suddenly change their mind on the proposed contract?"[50] There may not be any other comment or act by Harry Rieseberg that better illustrates his extreme self-centeredness. While a publisher was considering his book, 2,403 Americans died, and another 1,178 were wounded when Japanese planes sunk eighteen U.S. ships at Pearl Harbor. The Congress of the United States declared a state of war, and all Harry wondered about was himself and his book. Harry Rieseberg, the "great I am," was angry that world events had upstaged his interests.

Harry's approach was also typical according to Eric Strutt. In the Preface to the manuscript in Gainfort's hands, Strutt's cautionary words were part of his description of the author. When Strutt and Rieseberg first began talking, Strutt noticed Harry's tendency to come right to the point, a trait with which he quickly became familiar. "In his speech, he is the most blunt person I have ever known. There is no suavity, no indirect approach such as is so often advocated by experts in the art of conversation."[51] Gainfort failed to recognize the warning.

Not Counting on the Movie

Looming financial necessity forced Harry to look for a job while waiting to hear from Gainfort about the book's status. Harry's friend and collaborator, Eric Strutt, had noticed his financial condition deteriorating, saying, "Rieseberg's suits were getting a bit fuzzy around the cuffs." Strutt had loaned Rieseberg money on two occasions.[52]

Rieseberg wrote the Veterans' Bureau on December 18, 1941, to reapply for "appointment to an administrative official capacity in which such qualifications and experience of World War I may be used."[53] Harry's standard header for his letters was irrespective of standing. The director of the Veterans' Bureau got the same treatment as his editor, with **IMMEDIATE ATTENTION—AIR MAIL** at the top. His detailed, two-page letter reviewed his experience with the War Risk Insurance Bureau, the War Emergency Food Survey, and his work at Fort Whipple for the Public Health Service. The letter would have remained within a tone more proper for a qualified job seeker had Harry stopped with his résumé of government experience. Instead, he spent most of the second page talking about his current treasure exploits and his made-up career as a salvor. "I have been internationally recognized as the foremost authority on sunken treasure-laden craft and hold the world-record for depth-penetration in an all-metal ultra-modern deep-sea diving robot."[54] The length of Harry's "elevator pitch" required a ride to the top of a very tall skyscraper. He explained that "more than 750 leading newspapers and magazines, with a combined circulation over 700,000,000," had published his work. He mentioned rotogravures and double-page layouts about himself, radio programs, and newsreels in such an over-the-top way that it would make one wonder why he needed a job if he was so damned famous.

Two weeks later, Harry got his answer from the Veterans' Bureau Director of Personnel—thanks, but no thanks. Their practice was to fill higher-grade positions through promotions or by reassigning active employees, so they only hired into the lower-grade positions.[55] Harry would have to continue trying to make a living while his book was being considered.

Ghostwriter #3

After Gainfort received Harry's letter complaining about the delay after Pearl Harbor, he returned a brief but affirmative letter to Harry. He assured Harry that the book was still on track and contracts were being completed.[56] Harry's book, which was Strutt's book, which was briefly Plimmer's book, was becoming a reality. What Harry did not know, however, is that it was also about to be assigned to a third ghostwriter.

In addition to the onset of U.S. participation in the world war with Japan, another less significant action took place in a brief period of letter-writing silence—hiring ghostwriter number three. The publisher did not believe Plimmer's style would appeal to book club readers, and McBride suggested that perhaps an experienced newspaperman could fit the bill. That is precisely whom they found.

James M. Kieran, Jr., picked up where Plimmer left off just before Christmas in 1941. Kieran worked for the *New York Times* for many years, but more notably, was press secretary for New York Mayor Fiorello LaGuardia. Kieran and LaGuardia had a falling out, so Kieran was freelancing in public relations. He had done work for McBride before and had already submitted a sample chapter. Besides Kieran receiving fifty percent of Harry's royalties, McBride also requested the entire $500 advance go to Kieran so that he could dig in and work exclusively on this book. Any financial benefit of the book to Harry Rieseberg was quickly dribbling away.[57]

Reading the Not-So-Fine Print

A contract was finally prepared by Harry's agent, Edmond Pauker, who wrote to Harry about it on Saturday, December 20, 1941. Pauker's letter explained that he signed the contract with Robert M. McBride & Company on Harry's behalf. Pauker thought the sales prospects were strong. The book would not mention Eric Strutt, Denis Plimmer, or James Kieran. Pauker reassured Harry that the "book will be out in early spring, and it will appear under your name only."[58]

Over Christmas, Harry finally had a few days to consider the McBride contract and wrote back to Gainfort with questions on December 26th. The agreement was standard contract language with only a few variables written in blanks, but Harry had a few uncharacteristically polite questions.[59] Despite the common language that the author pays for corrections to the final proof, Harry wanted to ensure they understood that the final book might be far removed from his and Strutt's original words.

"As a matter of curiosity," he asked about the provision that allowed twenty percent to McBride for movie rights. Harry rightly understood that this work was not the type of book that led to a movie script. However, he believed that his second work, the "Man of Destiny" manuscript about Sir William Phipps and the Plata Flota, could be adapted for the screen. That outcome was essentially his primary motivation for writing it. This contract clause concerned him more for his next project than this one.

Harry also reminded Pauker that his last name was misspelled in the contract, without the middle E, five times. Even literary agents make spelling errors.

Future Literary Compositions

Harry's earlier, short-term agreement with Pauker to be his agent for radio programs had expired. So, when John Gainfort wrote Harry on New Year's Eve, 1941, about executing a three-year general contract with Pauker, it did not immediately raise any questions or concerns with Harry.[60]

Then he took the time to read it.

Two weeks later, Harry wrote Gainfort another letter asking for Immediate Attention. Harry explained that his mother, Jennie Martin Rieseberg, had "a paralysis stroke" a few weeks prior, and his preoccupation with his family's needs led to a delay in questioning the contract further. She would never recover from that stroke, and the challenges for him and his father must have been overwhelming. Harry's new questions about the provisions of his agreement with Pauker were only a tiny hint of the disputes to come. The contentious phrasing—confusing in Harry's view—was where the agreement gave Pauker control over Harry's future "literary compositions."[61]

Rieseberg's initial concern was what he could or could not do with his bread-and-butter magazine articles. Harry wrote, "many short articles such as I dispose of to religious and other half-cent and cent rates for their pages and whose sums range from ten to fifteen dollars per article." Harry's livelihood depended on quickly pushing out dozens of articles, repetitious adaptations of the same themes, to as many publications as possible. Quantity over quality was his business plan, and it made sense for him to ask the question.

Before Gainfort saw the additional questions from Rieseberg, he put another letter into the steady stream between him and his troublesome author asking for the agent's agreement to be returned. Gainfort was concerned that the contract with Pauker he had sent two weeks before had not yet been returned. "We should now have a contract covering everything you write or have written and … all matters involving publication or similar rights should be referred to us."[62] Harry had acted on the book contract but had not yet returned the agent's agreement. The words in the contract about giving Pauker "all rights to my literary compositions" were a sticking point.

What Part of All Do You Not Understand?

In early January 1942, deep disagreement between Gainfort and Rieseberg emerged from their letters about the agency's contractual agreement. It is clear from

Harry's complaints and questions that he had segmented his work into categorizations around the outlets for his ideas. He slotted Pauker as the agency that would help him get this first book published. The agents were also on his list to help with radio programs since they were based in New York, where most national radio programs originated. Where Harry started to have conflict was their role in movie rights and with his regular mass production of small articles for various magazines. He did not consider Pauker to have access or control in those areas. Harry wanted Pauker to stay in those businesses where he had mentally slotted them. The small magazine articles were his primary income. The agreement's language concerning "all literary compositions" flew in the face of the paradigm Harry had in his mind.

From the agency's perspective, Harry was not fulfilling the entire arrangement. All his work meant all his work, and Gainfort sought to clarify by answering Harry's earlier questions. "The small matters you refer to—religious publications, etc.,—should pass through this office also…. It is impossible to work successfully without having complete and absolute authority…. The agreement covers all rights of every kind."[63] Harry Rieseberg's life was built around his ego. *He* was the one with complete and absolute authority, and the notion that he was being asked to sign that away was a shock that would reverberate in their correspondence.

I Know It Says All, But….

The copy of the Pauker Agency agreement that Gainfort sent to Rieseberg does not remain in the records. Only a copy of the retyped version that Harry submitted to Gainfort for discussion in a letter on January 27, 1942, has been found. Harry said all he changed was to add some items in the last paragraph, which he told Gainfort he believed "there will be no question on your part to their reasonableness."[64] What Harry added was language that said any article, such as those which Pauker is unable to "sell or dispose of within a reasonable period, shall be returned intact and that such manuscripts then disposed of by myself shall not be subject to any salary or fees." This is where Harry's business plan and the agency agreement began to diverge. Harry's experience was that he could find an outlet for everything he wrote. "I can dispose of practically everything I write, good or bad, and believe if I cannot get a good rate for it first and it is rejected, to dispose of it elsewhere."[65] Harry essentially asked Gainfort why he should wait on his agent to do something he could do better himself. He even fed Gainfort some of his own words from a letter in August. Harry pointed out that he sent Pauker three manuscripts in the previous July for sale as magazine articles, and nothing had happened since then. In August, Gainfort told Harry, "We now have enough of your material, and we will not ask you to send any more manuscripts." The Pauker agency could not keep pace with Harry's prolific cycle of flooding articles into small outlets.

I Repeat ….

Harry initially appeared to make a sincere effort toward updating Gainfort on all his pending projects. Rieseberg explained a potential radio deal in some detail out in Los Angeles, and Harry said, "I have hesitated from bringing this matter to your attention due to the fact that the party who brought it to mine has and still does, think she can handle it, and that there is something in it. However, she's a woman, and I'm a little skeptical of those she was dealing with."[66] Harry's report of this effort resulted in a rather sharp rebuke by Gainfort, warning Harry that he should avoid such contacts and send everyone through Pauker. "In other words—to repeat—whenever you are approached on any matter involving your writings you should refer the inquiry to us by telling the inquirer to communicate with us."[67] Harry's silence in responding to such a sharp reprimand was the best result for Gainfort, as he soon learned. Both men would quickly unleash a fusillade of words expressing their mutual dissatisfaction and disagreement.

Ghostwriter #4

Harry was not the only one who was difficult to manage. It took only a couple of weeks with James Kieran on the project to rewrite Harry's book before he was jettisoned, and ghostwriter number four was brought on board. A letter from Allen Churchill at McBride in early February 1942 noted that Kieran had become "obstreperous." A new collaborator was already "working day and night to finish the Rieseberg manuscript in the three weeks."[68]

The new collaborator was Henry Wysham Lanier. Lanier was a writer of some note who had published a wide variety of more literary work than the former newspaperman, Kieran. More importantly, given the timetable, Lanier was readily available. Lanier had also worked before as a collaborator in another underwater adventure-themed book by Victor Berge titled *Pearl Diver*. For that 1930 work, Lanier said he sat with the Swedish diver and adventurer for weeks with a stenographer taking down his exact words. He would have no such luxury on this project. We cannot know the condition of the manuscript Lanier was given and whose words he was altering. Harry Rieseberg, Eric Strutt, Denis Plimmer, James M. Kieran, and now Henry W. Lanier all had a hand in the book, with Rieseberg being the only one acknowledged as the author. It was a race with the calendar to meet the deadline.

About That Thing with Roosevelt

In the closing sentence of one of his many letters to his agent, almost as an afterthought, Rieseberg asked a question that had clear importance to him. "Roosevelt's frontispiece stays in doesn't it? I believe this will help sales and also give it some additional prestige."[69] The book manuscript already contained Rieseberg's fabricated story about accompanying President Roosevelt to Africa as a seventeen-year-old in 1909, but that was not the focus of Rieseberg's question. With his initial submission of the Strutt manuscript, "I Walk With Davy Jones," there had been a placeholder for an opening to the book by Teddy Roosevelt—not the long-dead former president, but his son Theodore Roosevelt, Jr.

A Sunday School Teacher

In *I Dive for Treasure (1942)*, Rieseberg stated that the son of the President of the United States had been his Sunday school teacher at the Church of the Good Shepherd in Washington, D.C.[70] Unlike most of Rieseberg's claims, this one has more than a few grains of truth. The president's oldest son, Theodore Jr., did indeed teach Sunday school at the small Episcopal mission church. The Church of the Good Shepherd was formed in 1893 as an outreach of members of the Brotherhood of St. Andrew in St. Mark's Episcopal Church. By locating in that part of town, the mission was "realizing the need of a definite religious work in the community lying along H street northeast and the railroad track." Located on Sixth Street NE and I Street in Washington, D.C., the church was only a mile and a half from Harry's home with his parents.[71]

Teddy Jr.'s mother, Edith Kermit Carow Roosevelt, was a devout Episcopalian and most often attended St. John's Church at Lafayette Square. St. John's was dubbed "the church of the Presidents" since it was located across from the White House. Mrs. Roosevelt had likely heard about Good Shepherd church, its campaign for a new building, and its ongoing mission to the community. A newspaper account in April 1905 reported that "Mrs. Roosevelt has made a habit of attending the services once or twice a month," and that the president himself had been making "quiet visits" to Good Shepherd.[72] Their visits to the church had not been reported publicly and it seems the congregation has enlisted their support for Roosevelt's privacy in attending. The article also reported that Teddy Jr. had been quietly leading a Sunday school class for young boys at Good Shepherd since September 1904. Teddy had been in Boston at Groton School, an Episcopal boarding school, and was studying with a private tutor in Washington during this period. He would enter Harvard as an eighteen-year-old freshman in September 1905.

In describing his own experience with Teddy Jr., Rieseberg said that "almost every boy picks out somebody a little older than himself to worship," and that Teddy Jr. was his "particular hero."[73] Harry would have been twelve years old at the time so that admiration is an understandable response. Teddy Jr. had also taught a class during the summer of 1904 at Christ Church in Oyster Bay, New York, the church near their home of Sagamore Hill. The boys there had a similar excitement.

> He had been teaching his class for several weeks, and the fact came out through the refusal of the son of a fireman on the Long Island Railroad to earn a quarter by carrying a message. "I'd be late for Sunday School," he explained, "and the teacher's a good storyteller even if he is the President's son." Theodore was found seated in a corner of the Sunday school, and about him was a semi-circle of boys, ranging in age from eight to ten years.[74]

His mother was certainly making sure young Teddy was fully involved in his Episcopalian upbringing. Without an independent verification that Rieseberg actually attended Good Shepherd, the information available certainly suggests that this part of Rieseberg's story could be true.

Boy Meets Teddy

Where Rieseberg's story in *I Dive for Treasure* begins to lose credibility is his claim that young Teddy took Rieseberg and some of the other boys to the White House where they met President Roosevelt. Harry claimed that he was working at the Smithsonian Institution at the time. He began that job as a seventeen-year-old in 1909, working as a messenger in the library. President Roosevelt's term in office ended in March 1909. The alignment of verifiable dates with Rieseberg's narrative do not support his tale of Roosevelt requesting Harry go to Africa in support of his safari. Could young Harry have met TR as a twelve-year-old while Teddy Jr. was teaching his Sunday school class? At least that is certainly possible. What Harry did next with that connection is the background to the "frontispiece" so important to the opening of Rieseberg's first book manuscript.

The Frontispiece

In his letter to Gainfort on July 29, 1941, with his first manuscript submittal, Rieseberg listed a "Frontispiece by Theodore Roosevelt" as the opening for the book. Before the submission, Teddy Jr. had completed a refresher training for former soldiers in 1940 and returned to active military duty in 1941, ultimately becoming the only brigadier general to take the beach at Normandy with his troops. Just prior he had worked in corporate roles with Doubleday and American Express.

Rieseberg produced a letter from Roosevelt Jr. describing how he remembered Rieseberg as a "gangling sort of kid with a great interest in natural life."[75] There is no mention of taking Harry to meet his father, no mention of a trip to Africa; there is no letterhead, title, address, or date. A signature that appears similar to other verifiable handwriting by Teddy Jr. is the only indication of the letter's possible authenticity. Other than a passing acknowledgment that TR Jr. is "credited with helping him indirectly to discover that which has become his life work," there is nothing in the letter to connect Harry's life to the Roosevelts.

Harry's half-truths fail the test of fact, but his ability to link himself to people and events beyond his reach continues. The frontispiece Harry wanted to make sure was in the book never made it to print. Perhaps the publisher and his agent had similar questions about its authenticity.

Your Passport, Mr. Rieseberg?

Rieseberg's claims about finding treasure had him all over the world. Locations around South America, the Caribbean, and Southeast Asia were only a few of those added to his stories. He said he dined with cannibals and was chased by pirates. Jungles, islands, multiple oceans, and both hemispheres were his domain.

Layered across all those stories is one simple, demonstrable element that questions every one of them.

It appears that Harry Earl Rieseberg never had a U.S. Passport.

At least that is the report received from the U.S. Department of State, Office of Legal Affairs, Law Enforcement Liaison Division. A search of their records from 1925 to 1970 failed to locate any relevant documents.[76] Harry never addressed how to travel to all the locations he would later say he visited. He would just be there, leaving the messiness of logistics, distances, and cost out of his beautiful fabrications. Departing from and returning to U.S. ports with a vessel suitable for treasure hunting was an expensive and time-consuming undertaking, a messy detail Rieseberg avoided. In Harry's world, he would appear at sea or in a foreign land like a time traveler unencumbered by the physical laws of nature.

One of the other topics Harry avoided was simple and basic—where is the money it took to undertake such ventures, and where is the supposed treasure he recovered? He would explain away the lack of funds by saying he just put anything recovered into the next venture. He downplayed the nonexistence of any artifacts by expressing a complete disinterest in anything other than gold or silver. He claimed to have sold any retained artifacts before returning to the U.S. to avoid taxes. His lack of a passport is another brick removed from the wall of deception he erected to control his narrative.

Readers Will Want to Know

There was still much work remaining to get a book out the door in only a few weeks. Miss Arabel Jaquette, the Publicity Director for Robert M. McBride and Co., led the effort to collect information to help market the book. Harry had loaded up Gainfort with three boxes of material early in January: two with photos of various subjects, some pretending to be Harry underwater, and many photos of the diving robot, including close-ups of the claws, along with a treasure map Rieseberg produced. Harry also sent a copy of an article already in the pipeline for *Popular Mechanics* titled "Billions Waiting to be Taken."[77]

Jaquette also asked Harry an obvious question for a man claiming to be a treasure hunter. She wondered what relics, treasure chests, or gold coins Harry might have that could be used in publicity. Harry had also told the agency he had a list of 750 publications that had used his articles, so she asked for that list as well. Harry did not immediately respond because he did not yet have a good answer for Miss Jacquette.

"I Never Do Anything I Am Not Interested In"

Kenneth Meeker, McBride's Sales Manager and Western Representative, wanted to meet Harry in Los Angeles to learn how best to sell Harry's book. Jaquette said Meeker would be there from February 18 to the 24th.[78] They had a short meeting to discuss his sales plans for the book and show Harry a mock-up of its cover. Harry was not impressed and told Gainfort he "could have, had I been advised beforehand, had a damn-sight better one prepared out here."[79]

One of the more interesting aspects of this type of research is an insight into the personalities reflected by one's written words. Meeker wanted Rieseberg to do book signings in April at some of the more prominent outlets, but Harry resisted that idea, saying he did not have "the time to spend going about doing that sort of thing." Meeker was a professional persuader, and Harry reluctantly relented but made sure that he expressed himself for the record and Gainfort's future reference. Harry wrote, "He (Meeker) is quite a convincing and persuasive gentleman, I must admit, to get me to do something which I do not want to do; I never do anything I am not interested in, nor care to put myself out for, as a rule."[80] One of the primary terms and conditions of being Harry Rieseberg emerged in this letter. It was Harry Rieseberg's rule number one; there would be others. This rule made clear that Rieseberg never did anything he did not want to do. Harry's rules were in stark display as the correspondence between him and his agent continued to degrade.

Understanding His Audience

The more Gainfort cornered Harry with the parameters of their agreement to handle all his work, the more Harry seemed exasperated by his agent's lack of acceptance of Harry's self-promotion. When the Spring 1942 book catalog came out from McBride, Harry noticed what he considered a glaring omission in the catalog's marketing of his upcoming book.

The book's appendix listed detailed information about hundreds of lost ships that were straight out of Harry's research work. That list was where Harry started down this path before the Great Fall. The charts were not mentioned in the marketing piece, and Harry considered that an oversight by Miss Jacquette and the publicity team. He pointed out, perhaps rightly, that people in those days during the war were looking for any opportunity to be better off, no matter how far-fetched. He explained it somewhat cynically to Gainfort. "… with such a list many would find an untold incentive to buy the book, even though they hadn't the means to equip any expedition capable of going after it or had the exact latitude and longitude."[81] His perspective somewhat mocked his audience but failed to recognize that the description also fit him. He had no clear idea where to go, he was not a diver, and he had no money, and yet he continued to chase the lure of treasure as blindly as he suggested his readers would.

Chapter 8

Target for the Fire of Rivals

... the guy who related this story was described as getting more mileage out of the inner tube of reality than anyone he'd ever met.
—Letter to Harry from Vaughn Greene[1]

The problem with fabricating a persona using a false and misleading history is that it must be consistent and complete to be swallowed as fact. While getting his manuscript to print, Rieseberg kept bumping into suspicions about his stories expressed by his collaborators, agent, editors, and the publicity department at McBride. Their circumspect doubtfulness is found in the pages of correspondence that remain in archival collections.

Harry's version of the truth was being systematically scrutinized and probed for its validity. His agent and publisher were not necessarily interested in the truth; they were publishing for profit and entertainment value. However, as his agent, Gainfort, pointed out to Harry, "a book once published can be a target for the fire of rivals, competitors, [and] critics."[2] Their editorial warning was based on their discovery that Harry's stories failed to meet a relatively low factual threshold required to publish such work, and some of his stories were simply beyond belief. One of those imminently fishy tales was that Harry Rieseberg walked the underwater pirate city of Port Royal, Jamaica.

In an article written by Eric Strutt but not credited to him, the *Los Angeles Times* published a two-page story titled "City Beneath the Sea" in their *Sunday Magazine* on October 13, 1940. The article began with a single sentence bursting with deceit. "It was eight years ago, in the course of hunting the sea depths for the treasure-filled hulk of an ancient galleon, that I came upon the enchanted city of Port Royal, 30 fathoms under the surface ripples of Kingston Harbor in Jamaica."[3] Eight years prior would have been in 1932. Harry was an active social and fraternity group member that year, leading Washington parades dressed in cowboy regalia, not diving for treasure in Jamaica. Even more astonishing was for him to say that Port Royal was 180 feet deep, when it was only forty to sixty feet. Anyone with knowledge of Port Royal would know that basic information, but Harry counted on such facts not being common knowledge.

For the first one and a half pages of the article, Rieseberg and Strutt did nothing but tell a dramatic history of the pirate stronghold that anyone could have described. However, by inserting himself in the story in the first paragraph, Rieseberg hooked the reader into connecting him to the treasure. Rieseberg used this literary sleight-of-hand consistently in his articles and books. For the balance of the article, he created a fictional account of him walking amidst the sunken city and through the doors of the former cathedral, whose church bell still hung dramatically in the tower. Something about that account did not ring true with his agent and publisher.

Tell Me About Port Royal

Harry's second of the four ghostwriters, Denis Plimmer, asked Rieseberg directly about his reported dive to the sunken city of Port Royal. It was not described fully in the manuscript then, so Plimmer asked for more detail in a letter to Rieseberg. Plimmer gave Harry the benefit of the doubt in saying that he understood Rieseberg did not see everything, but "speaking imaginatively, what must be there and what does it look like?"[4]

Harry's letter in response on December 2, 1941, was interesting on many levels. His three-page, single-spaced letter back to Plimmer deserves attention, both for what it says and does not say. Harry began the letter with an elaborate, wordy attempt to beg off answering. He tried a dismissive wave of the hand and a reference to what he had already submitted in Strutt's manuscript. Those seemed insufficient, so he fell back on his "I am a salvor, not a writer" explanation. "I have no imagination; just cold facts as I see them, and even then possibly lose all sense of description by leaving out many things which you writers make much over and which I see little in."[5] Harry's reply to Plimmer essentially told him to make something up. In his clumsy and convoluted attempt to explain the nature of coral growth, Harry provided data without providing information. He did not avoid Plimmer's question entirely, however. Rieseberg mustered a description as an offering to Plimmer. Despite the letter's blizzard of words, there was little to help verify whether Harry was describing something he saw or how he envisioned a movie producer staging his scene.

The remainder of Harry's three-page letter reverted to the literary diversions he later perfected. He went back to his stories about the history of Port Royal, what kind of treasure might have been lost, and the pirates who ruled the island two hundred and fifty years prior. He said nothing else to answer Plimmer's question about his presence there. Instead, Harry substituted filler that he hoped would add credibility. After a final apology to Plimmer to "excuse the writing as I do this on my lap and am not a typist any more than I am a polished writer," Harry ended his reply.

Robert Marx and Port Royal

If Rieseberg's own words were not enough to question his veracity, the observations of a diver and underwater archaeologist may be. Bob Marx was an underwater archaeologist for fifty years or more and was knighted for his re-creation of the voyages of the *Kon Tiki* and Columbus' *Nina*. In 1973 Marx published *Port Royal: The Sunken City* as his account of his discovery and salvage of the remains of Port Royal. His facts are indisputable and verifiable. Marx methodically excavated relics at Port Royal for four years, from 1964 to 1968. Before his work began, he made two scuba expeditions to reconnoiter the site. At that time, he could not locate the ruins because all he could see was "coral head and thousands of spiny sea urchins."[6]

Marx could occasionally embellish a story—it seems to be in the DNA of the adventurous—but would not falsify information for his own gain. He had no need. Marx cites and then refutes Rieseberg's 1941 article about finding the great cathedral in one-hundred-eighty feet of water. Marx even disputed Harry's claims about the need for greater depths to find treasure generally by saying that "more than 99 percent of all old shipwreck losses in the Western Hemisphere occurred at depths between ten and forty feet of water."[7]

When Marx was ten years old, he read *I Dive for Treasure,* and Harry's claims of visiting Port Royal captured his childhood imagination. Marx loved the stories but said that he did not necessarily swallow the entire yarn even then. Despite crediting his reading of *I Dive for Treasure* with inspiring his interest in diving as a young boy, Marx unabashedly called bullshit to Harry's accounts of Port Royal. "Only when I visited Port Royal did I discover that the book catalogued under non-fiction in the library should have been catalogued under fantasy. I hold no grudge against the author, even though he was an out and out liar."[8] A French author said that Marx came to Port Royal "with his Rieseberg under his arm and a scuba tank strapped to his back," but after seeing what was there, he "put his Rieseberg away in the attic."[9]

Harry Rieseberg did not walk the streets of Port Royal. His descriptions of the city beneath the sea were pure fantasy and lacked even basic facts of what lay beneath the surface. He learned what little he knew from travelogues and the accounts of others and then made up the rest. Plimmer, and others, had difficulty getting facts out of Harry Rieseberg because he had so few to offer.

"Pictorial Youthfulness"

Among the material Harry submitted to his publisher was a headshot photograph for the book jacket. The photo he submitted was one he had used for earlier newspaper articles. Rieseberg was fifty years old when his first book was published in 1942. The photograph was of a quite obviously younger Rieseberg, too young for someone born in 1892. Harry's agent sent it to the publicity department but said, "if pictorial youthfulness seems contradictory to the tone of the book, please let me know, and I'll get a more mature one."[10] Miss Jaquette agreed that the photograph Harry sent appeared too young and suggested Gainfort ask him for a more recent one like "a more informal photograph—possibly one of him emerging from his diving robot, or something of the kind."[11]

Unfortunately for Miss Jacquette, a credible photo of Harry Rieseberg in diving gear is nowhere to be found. There are a few fakes, but they are very obviously and clumsily altered. In all the books, magazine articles, newspaper photo spreads, and publicity pieces over Harry's entire career, there is no single photo of him that would verify any of his claims of diving. Not one. A photo reportedly of Harry entering the diving bell has the face hidden by the subject's arm. Images submitted for his book, allegedly of Harry in a hard-hat diving suit, show the helmet already attached and obscure any facial identification. Even a magazine photo with Harry's expressionless face peering out of a diving helmet is such a poor paste-up job as to be laughable.

Readers are asked to believe that in all his years of adventure and diving, in all the weeks and months Harry Rieseberg reportedly spent at sea, with all the loot he says he hauled up from the bottom, there is not one single photo to establish that any of it ever occurred. Nothing.

This faked photograph of Rieseberg wearing a hard hat dive helmet appeared in the December 18, 1941, issue of *Popular Mechanics*. A similar paste-up was seen in other publications. Rieseberg created the image for submission. (courtesy Hearst Magazine Media, Inc.)

You Were a Lieutenant?

Another question about Rieseberg's credibility asked by his publisher was regarding his self-titled rank of Lieutenant. Gainfort asked for more information in an almost taunting tone. "The suggestion was made in conversation that there would probably be much opportunity for the use of your skilled knowledge about diving in connection with the recovery of sunken ships," Gainfort wrote. He was probably certain by that time that Harry was a fraud, but one worth publishing nevertheless.[12]

When Harry began using "lieutenant" in his bylines after his hospitalization in 1937, he was not the only writer to add an air of credibility with a military title. Frank Gruber, one of the most successful and prolific writers of the pulp era, recounted a similar trend in 1934.[13] Arthur J. Burks, a writer who had been an actual lieutenant during World War I, began using the title, and other writers took note. Writers with no military background suddenly became captains, majors, and even a general. Gruber said one writer used that method to the extreme. The man claimed he had been a Marine for seven years, an Amazon explorer for four years, an African hunter for three years, and a civil engineer for six years; he also had spent four years in Brazil and barnstormed in his flying circus for six years. The twenty-six-year-old prevaricator, and successful writer, was indignant when Gruber said that in doing the math on his exploits, he must be around eighty-four years old.

When Rieseberg wrote to the Veterans' Bureau about a job, he felt it necessary to qualify his use of the "Lieutenant" title. Harry refrained from using Lieutenant on the signature line, but it was used on the articles and publicity he attached to his letter. Rieseberg let the Bureau know he "held a 'Commission' in the Officer's Reserve Corps for ten years, therefore, the explanation of the title on the enclosure [a newspaper article] still sticks when writing about my activities."[14]

Frank Gruber's observation of those writers who deemed themselves explorers is telling, and it certainly applied to Harry Rieseberg. He noted that when writers who invented adventurous personas for themselves could "sometimes confuse fiction and fact," and begin "to think that he himself has lived some of the adventures of which he has written."[15]

Show Us Some Treasure, Lieutenant Rieseberg?

It was a simple and obvious request by the publicity department at Robert M. McBride and Co. One can imagine that when they learned they would be promoting the book of a treasure hunter, they thought of gold doubloons and silver bars used to promote the book. Gainfort wrote to tell him that "McBride's publicity department telephoned me today to ask if you have available any treasure that may be exhibited in connection with plans they have for publicity for your book."[16]

Who would not have at least one item that, when someone asks about treasure, got pulled out from a secret place, wrapped in velour, to show off to anyone who could be trusted with knowledge? One account of a more recent treasure hunter found his home stuffed with relics, including roughly five million dollars' worth of silver pieces of eight from the seventeenth century kept in plastic bags in the old seaman's bathtub.[17]

Harry Rieseberg had no such artifacts. Whether it was the wordiness, the shifty-eyed offering of an implausible explanation, or how quickly he attempted to change the subject, his reply reveals a conscious tactic to evade. He worked as hard to escape such questions as he did to repeatedly avoid the tentacled clutches of any giant octopus he encountered.

> Unfortunately, I do not possess these relics any more, as the gold and silver coins are salvaged on the various expeditions were usually turned in for their "content" value, and the few which I have retained have, as time went on, been given away to various individuals for pocket pieces, etc.

Rieseberg went on to say that the metal pieces had all rusted away, and besides, as a man who seemed to be always in other parts of the world, he did not want to pay for storage, "therefore, I disposed of it."[18]

Harry moved from place to place, but not because of treasure ventures. He was fired from multiple jobs, left his wife, broke his leg, and was hospitalized for two years. Harry's tales as a world traveler and adventurer defied the calendar and his checkbook. Harry had no answers for anyone interested in the cold, hard facts of his adventures because there were none.

Gee, This SOUNDS Familiar

Harry's assertions in his treasure articles had never gotten any real scrutiny. His outlets were not the top magazines and were not necessarily concerned about the facts of their author's work. Harry told a decent story of around 2,000 words or less and that was usually good enough. Other than the minor likelihood of a letter to the editor disputing his claims, there was no real forum for feedback. No harm, no foul.

It was different with the publication of a book, however. Violations of copyright laws put not only the author at risk but the publisher as well. Harry's work had already passed through the hands of four ghostwriters and been read by agents and editors. It got scrutiny only when it got closer to deadlines and proofs. When John Gainfort of the Pauker agency sent Harry a letter on January 30, 1942, just weeks before the deadline date to publish, it was unexpected but not surprising. Gainfort gingerly let Harry know they had found plagiarism in his submission. The person who likely tipped them off was none other than Harry's 4th ghostwriter, Henry Wysham Lanier. "Some of the editors, going over the material for your book, have observed a marked similarity in certain scenes to similar scenes in a book called 'Pearl Diver' by Victor Berge. I refer specifically to the fight with the octopus and the fight with the shark."[19] Victor Berge's 1930 book, *Pearl Diver*, was an account of his adventurous life at sea and underwater. Though it was written in the first person, Berge had a co-author credited with him for the work—Henry Lanier. Lanier was working furiously on a complete rewrite of *I Dive for Treasure* and discovered the obvious similarities with *Pearl Diver*. Gainfort asked specifically about a battle between a shark and an octopus which appears in both books.

> Then that powerful, sudden hydraulic drive of his explodes into action; he shoots himself at his enemy so fast that the eye cannot see [*Pearl Diver*, p. 203].

> Suddenly the powerful hydraulic drive of the octopus exploded into action. It threw itself at the shark so fast I could hardly follow the motion [*I Dive for Treasure*, p. 128].

Both works continue to describe the attack.

> There's a flash, a blur—and the octopus is locked fast to the shark's neck, those thug's arms wound about and holding on by their leechlike suckers. That's when you get the water flying! [*Pearl Diver*, p. 203]

> The shark had been too slow. His neck was bound by two tentacles; others darted forward to lay their leech-hold on the rest of his long gray body. The water began to fly [*I Dive for Treasure*, p. 128].

Oddly, Gainfort went out of his way to try and make sure Harry did not see the question about *Pearl Diver* as a criticism, and he probably did not want to jeopardize the publication at that point in the process. He even gave Harry an out by suggesting part of the answer his agent wanted to hear. "We all realize, of course, that such episodes might naturally be much alike, inasmuch as an octopus, for instance, probably acts in a fairly routine manner."[20]

Though one might wonder if Lanier was getting double duty out of his earlier work on *Pearl Diver* by reusing his earlier material, that is not the case. These scenes as published in *I Dive for Treasure* were found verbatim in the first manuscript delivered by Strutt and Rieseberg. Harry denied having read *Pearl Diver* and quickly accepted the offering by Gainfort. Rieseberg passed it off as similar creatures behaving in the same way due to the tendencies of their species.[21] Even though all such encounters between these underwater enemies may appear the same, as Harry suggested, and their apparent tactics part of their nature, neither the shark nor the octopus composed the words describing their battle. The words and sequencing were unashamedly alike, even after editing. Rather than continue his denial, Harry punted. He pointed out that the words were now in the hands of McBride and the chain of ghostwriters who had the work.

Harry "I never apologize" Rieseberg made clear he thought it was the problem of Robert M. McBride and Company, since they had a long list of collaborators pounding away. At that point in the process, with a deadline date only weeks away, Gainfort did not want to know any more. Even though it seemed apparent that Harry lifted Lanier's words from *Pearl Diver*, Gainfort accepted Harry's answer and replied, "with regard to the incident of the shark and the octopus, we, of course, accept your assurance without any reservation at all." He even pointed out tersely that "the material will have to be edited to avoid any unnecessary similarity."[22] He was letting Harry know they would be cleaning up his mess.

And Others They Missed

Another scene in Harry's manuscript also matched the wording and sequence of an almost identical one in Berge's 1930 *Pearl Diver*. The comparison that follows is by no means the extent of it. The scene follows Harry's description of being attacked by a giant octopus below the sea's surface.

> That's the last thing a diver resorts to in an emergency—four pulls, meaning, "Pull until the line breaks" [*Pearl Diver*, p. 174].

> Now I began to wonder if it wouldn't be better for me right then to give the danger signal—the diver's last resort, four sharp jerks of the line. That would mean… "Pull until the line breaks" [*I Dive*, p. 64].

By Harry's account, it seemed like he was unconscious in the depths whenever he was attacked by one of his invented monsters.

> Just before the wave of fear-freighted unconsciousness swept over me I threw up my arms, caught both lines, gave four frantic pulls [*Pearl Diver*, p. 176].

> The blackout feeling began to creep over me again. I blinked, raised my arm, and gave four sharp jerks on the line [*I Dive*, p 66].

Despite the obvious reuse of previously published material, each about an event that did not happen to Rieseberg, nothing more was said to question Harry's story.

At least now, Rieseberg's publisher and agent fully understood what they had on their hands—fiction being passed off as fact.

And this LOOKS Familiar

Not only had Rieseberg used Lanier's words to produce content in the book, but he also used someone else's film of a fight between a shark and an octopus and described it as his own. Stock footage of a shark and octopus battle appeared in several productions and magazine articles then and may have been filmed by Victor Berge.[23] One of the earliest appearances of the clip was in a documentary-style movie with minimal dialogue, a 1933 United Artists release called *Samarang*.[24] An article in *Modern Mechanix* magazine revealed how the footage was filmed.[25] The same stock footage appeared again in the movie serial *Flash Gordon: Space Soldiers (1936)*. In chapter three of that serial, "Captured by Shark Men," Buster Crabbe, playing Flash Gordon, is captured. On the way to the Shark Kingdom, they witness the same footage between a shark and the creature they called the "Octo-Sac."[26] In 1941 Universal Pictures released a twelve-part serial titled *Sea Raiders* starring The Dead-End Kids. In episode ten, "Periled by a Panther," the very same shark and octopus fight was poorly edited into a scene where it was made to appear one of the boys was in a battle with the octopus when the shark showed up to distract and kill the octopus. Amazingly, the footage repeatedly appeared until at least 1957 in the low-budget sci-fi film *The Incredible Petrified World*.[27] Reusing stock film footage was not unusual in the movie industry at the time. What was surprising, however, was that Rieseberg claimed as early as 1941 that he shot the video himself and was never called to task on that statement.

The earliest use of his misappropriated tale before its appearance in *I Dive for Treasure*, was in the November 1941 issue of *Sport* magazine. In an authored article titled "Octopus Battles Shark to Death in Undersea Duel," Harry combined two photos of an octopus ejecting ink with some screen grabs from the stock footage. He made a series of claims in only three paragraphs, not one of which was true. Rieseberg said he descended to 180 feet in the Romano diving bell, at the same time it was scuttled in a New Jersey warehouse. He said the tiger shark was eighteen feet long and the octopus twelve feet when experts could tell from the photos that the octopus was likely a dead sample released from a jar. The photographs were supposedly taken with an Eyemo camera, a waterproof device, while lit in the darkness by lights on the diving bell, when the angle of the shadow disputed that claim.[28] At least five other examples of the same claims and photos have been found published by Rieseberg in 1942, 1943, 1947, 1951, and 1959, all with the same explanation.[29]

Harry was relentless in his reuse of material over his entire writing career. In our current era, with the ability to research decades' worth of video and print publications, search digital archives, and do basic fact-checking, it is hard to imagine how he could get away with such blatantly false assertions. In his era, the manual effort that would have been required to disprove his claims was a solid deterrent.

Sequence of images of faked "Battle Under Sea," appearing in U.S. *Camera* magazine, for an article in March 1943.

Pushing Man of Destiny

It was common for literary agents to ask for a second book before the first one was complete. Rieseberg wanted *Man of Destiny* to be that book and desperately hoped it might lead to a movie deal. He continued to mention it in nearly every letter he wrote his agent. Even though *I Dive for Treasure* was not yet published, from Harry's perspective, he had already checked it off his mental list. He wanted to get to his real treasure—a Hollywood movie.

What Do You Mean Contrived?

Harry kept saying he was not a writer, and generally proving it with his wordiness. At the same time, he was thoroughly convinced that his *Man of Destiny* book about Sir William Phipps would be a surefire hit because it had material he was certain no one else had. Gainfort's early feedback, however, was that it "seemed contrived." Harry's answer to Gainfort's questions about *Man of Destiny* dripped with a feigned humility to gain favor with his agent, saying, "Maybe this impression was entirely due to my meager efforts and lack of knowledge in properly writing up a hurried synopsis."[30]

Even with Rieseberg's celebrity review of the movie's potential by his cousin, the director Leo McCarey, Gainfort was unimpressed by *Man of Destiny*. From Gainfort's brief acknowledgment of the manuscript at the end of 1941, it sounded more like he had not had the time to focus on a second project before the first one was fully underway. Gainfort tried to support Rieseberg and, on January 12, 1942, told Harry, "Now that your first book is disposed of, we are offering MAN OF DESTINY to the same publishers."[31] Sending Harry's manuscript to publishers only resulted in further confirmation of its poor first impressions.

Allen Churchill, the senior editor at Robert M. McBride & Co., looked at the manuscript, as did several others. Miss Morrow at McBride even considered it an adventure book for teens, and her review was not favorable. Churchill assessed it as a book for adults and felt the same way. If Harry needed to publish a book to make it fodder for a film, Robert McBride and Company said, "we feel that this is not possible."[32] McBride had a contractual option on future books by Rieseberg but after seeing Harry's badly written manuscript for *Man of Destiny,* they lost interest. Harry's publisher offered a possible way out by saying, "inasmuch as this volume was written previous to our signing with Lieutenant Rieseberg that our rejection of it does not alter the existing arrangement"[33] In other words, the publisher did not want this book but would still require Harry's next "second" work to meet his contractual obligation.

Gainfort neglected to tell Rieseberg that "Man of Destiny" did not pass muster. After a month, Harry brought it up again and Gainfort let him know that *Man of Destiny* was not going to be published. "MAN OF DESTINY has been given a lot of thought and consideration by MacBrides (*sic*) but they haven't found a satisfactory way to handle it. It is something of a problem and we haven't yet found the answer."[34] Whether that reply would keep Harry's questioning contained was yet to be seen.

Let's Get Things Straight

The process of educating Harry Rieseberg on the expected behavior of a writer under contract to the Pauker agency continued in every communication from Gainfort. Harry regularly sent his agent letters with ideas but doing so often revealed that he had ignored the terms of the agreement. Gainfort would then nudge Rieseberg toward compliance by explaining their concerns with each aberration. Initially, Gainfort was patient with Harry since he was new to such agreements and did not know all the ins and outs. Over time, however, Gainfort learned that it was not just Rieseberg's lack of knowledge but his downright stubbornness that led to violations of the agreement.

Gainfort slowly began to make clear to Harry that their contract covered *everything* he did. Gainfort said they would release any material they returned to Harry as unsaleable, but that did not mean he could revise or rewrite it and then sell it himself. Pauker *owned* Harry's work, and Harry was slow to accept and understand that.[35]

A Book to Publish

While all the back and forth between Rieseberg and his agent continued, Henry Lanier worked on finishing the book. On February 23, 1942, he reported to Gainfort that he was getting close. "I practically finished the job last night—though there seem to be one or two small points for discussion with the publishers."[36] The debut of Rieseberg's first book was getting close—that is the first book of Rieseberg, Stutt, Plimmer, Kieran, and Lanier.

Harry begged off plans for a lecture tour to support the book, pointing to his mother's paralysis due to a stroke. However, if there were a movie to promote, he would somehow make himself available. It seemed her health per se was not the problem, but the extent to which it excused what he did really not want to do.[37] Harry continued to flood Gainfort with material and ideas, hoping for encouragement. Earlier in February, Gainfort received six articles from Rieseberg for placement.[38] Harry sent him treasure charts and told him about a *Science and Mechanics* magazine prospect with "great enthusiasm at the boiling point" over interest in one of his articles.[39]

Harry was not the only one who needed some adjustment in their thinking to make this business relationship work. Harry's approach to publishing was not without some success but was far different than Gainfort's experience. Harry told his agent, "I can write them (articles) so damn fast that the rates of compensation have meant little to me; I write them quick and want quick returns, and am willing in so doing to accept the difference."[40] If Gainfort's message to Harry was to make clear that when we say send us everything, we mean *everything*, then Harry's message was to say okay, but you had better work on it pronto. Harry wanted results in quantity, not quality.

In Reading Over the Recent Agreement....

Even as the book approached printing, Harry became uncomfortable with parts of his contract with the Pauker agency. On January 27, 1942, Harry sent Gainfort a retyped version of the proposed three-year agreement. He explained his modifications about returning unused work so it could be disposed of quickly.[41] After a couple of weeks of back-and-forth correspondence, a letter of agreement was signed and fully executed by Harry, Edmond Pauker, and John Gainfort.[42] Another two weeks passed before Harry began a line of questioning that would quickly escalate into a bitter postal dialog between the new business partners. Rieseberg had signed the agreement but was now questioning a change. Rieseberg noted that Pauker had removed language Harry inserted to remove any movie deal from Pauker's involvement.[43]

The re-typed agreement Harry signed and submitted did not have any language qualifying a different arrangement for movies. Even though he was working on a book and other printed works, his laser focus was on the future benefits of those toward his goal of having a movie produced in Hollywood. Not only that, but Harry also planned to "handle it at this end," meaning in Los Angeles. Harry lived in Hollywood, had a relative in the business, and knew of an "agency that handles motion picture material for their own stars only."[44] Harry was convinced he did not need any help from Pauker. It made no sense in Harry's view for an agency in New York to handle work he could do himself with studios right around the corner from his home in Los Angeles. He assured Gainfort they would get their percentage but was somewhat disturbed that language clarifying that approach was not a part of the agreement he had signed two weeks earlier. Harry wanted Pauker to stay out of his movie contacts.

Rieseberg's mind was racing with the regret of being a signatory to a major commitment. He sensed he had made a mistake in signing the agreement and would be forced to change plans he had made to his benefit. Before Gainfort could respond to Rieseberg's initial letter, Harry wrote another two days later with demands disguised as suggestions for changes in the already signed agreement.

Harry's interpretation of the contract covering his "literary compositions" included only his written works. He wanted specific language clarifying his plans for movie rights, admitting that "having had previous experiences with contracts in my business of salvage, I want things clear and not so they may be later brought up as 'intent.'"[45] Harry was straightforward in his instruction to Gainfort about what he expected. "Therefore, kindly submit to me a statement to the effect that our agreement signed on February 12th, 1942, does not, in any manner cover motion picture rights…. Please submit this statement by return airmail, for which I enclose stamped return envelope."[46] Harry must have been quite satisfied with himself on that matter. He was forceful and clear, removing any excuse for a slow response by providing an already addressed and stamped envelope. He ended his mandate with a "so much for that phase of the matter" as if he was verbally dusting his hands together in a demonstration of completion before moving on to other topics in the same letter. Gainfort wasted no time in sending back a polite yet terse reply.

In his letters to Rieseberg, Gainfort did his best to diagram how their agency worked and to address Harry's concern, but Gainfort's patience was starting to wear thin. He explained to Harry that it would be impossible for the contract to cover every contingency or define methods for addressing them in advance. He said, "the essential meaning of our contract is that we handle the affairs of the writer in whatever manner may be most advantageous to him."[47] To exclude bits and pieces of work, particularly before their being presented, was not a practice that Pauker's years of experience as agents would suggest were sound business for them. Gainfort attempted to address Harry's concerns and close the door on further dissent.[48]

Just as Harry had transitioned and closed with a "so much for that matter," Gainfort's response can be paraphrased as "thanks for your suggestions, but we've got this." Gainfort had a signed agreement and was not about to start renegotiating it after only two weeks.

My Problem Is Rieseberg

Eric Strutt was a decent guy. He was a neighbor of Harry's and lived just around the corner. Strutt had been a friend to Harry Rieseberg, at least until he realized Harry was cheating him behind his back. When Pauker and McBride finally entered into agreements with Harry Rieseberg, his partnership with Eric Strutt was cast aside, but Strutt refused to step away quietly. On February 27, 1942, Eric Strutt wrote John Gainfort at the Pauker agency a four-page, single-spaced letter detailing his dilemma. He began his letter by explaining, "My problem is Lieut. Harry E. Rieseberg, and because you and I have a mutual interest in Rieseberg, I felt this letter must be written."[49]

Strutt's letter sought to explain to Gainfort how his writing relationship with Rieseberg was soured by Harry's double-dealing. Strutt began to understand that Harry was not being entirely truthful about when their collaborative articles were published and under whose byline they appeared. Harry told Strutt an article had been rejected when in fact it had not, and Harry simply kept the payment for himself.

Strutt "considered Rieseberg a friend (and) never doubted his word on these (rejections)" because, despite a few questions, Strutt never thought Harry "might double-cross someone who had played as square with him as I had."[50] Strutt's doubt came to the forefront when a *Los Angeles Times* article about the myth of Cocos Island was published in February 1940.[51] The article was to appear with the byline "by Lieut. Harry E. Rieseberg as told to Eric Strutt." However, when the article appeared, it had only Rieseberg's name. When Strutt asked Harry about it, he claimed that he sent the article in with both of their names and did not know why it would have come out with only Harry's name on the byline. Strutt doubted his word enough to call up the editor of the *Times Magazine* where the story appeared and learned that Strutt's name was nowhere on the article the magazine received from Rieseberg. When Strutt told Harry what he had learned, all Strutt got back was a "scathing denunciation" of the editor, Bob White, whom Harry said was "just covering up his own error." Strutt said he grudgingly accepted that. He was Harry's friend, after all.[52]

Then it happened again. The week before his letter to Gainfort, Strutt discovered Rieseberg had distilled a series of articles from the book and submitted them to *Grit* magazine without telling him. Strutt took mental note of Harry's behavior but said nothing to him. The magazine only paid ten dollars or so for each, but Strutt had loaned Harry money before, so he knew Rieseberg's finances were tight.

Then it happened again. A friend in Long Beach sent Strutt a tear sheet with the full-page "He Walks with Davy Jones" article in the *Los Angeles Times*. This time Eric Strutt's name was in the byline, but Harry had not told Strutt that he sent the article for syndication by NEA. The same article had also appeared in *St. Joseph Magazine*. Strutt waited for Harry to tell him about it and pay his share, but it did not happen.

Strutt and Rieseberg lived near each other, and Strutt said, "there was a time when it was difficult to avoid seeing him, but this wasn't the time." Harry made himself scarce. When Strutt asked in passing if he had submitted an article, Harry said he had not submitted anything, but his denial was disingenuous. Strutt said, "knowing his ability to discover a grievance, I realized he was giving a very bad version of the truth." Harry changed the subject, offering Strutt some material "in a sudden burst of generosity" by taking no cut for himself. Strutt saw through it and believed it was more than a little obvious that he had caught Harry in a lie.

The editor confirmed for Strutt that Harry submitted the article. Harry had told the editor that Strutt knew about it and that he would pay him his share. Tom Horner, the editor, knew right away he was in a bad spot, so he also informed Harry of Strutt's inquiry about his double-dealing. That infuriated Rieseberg and resulted in a letter to Strutt from his former friend, Harry Rieseberg, saying that both the NEA and his agent had told him about Strutt's inquiries. Harry observed, "maybe one doesn't trust one and has to run around checking up on them."

Strutt presented the situation to Gainfort "as one of the most interesting examples of double-dealing in which I have played the party of the second, and least lucrative, part." As a fellow tradesman, Strutt did not have to explain to Gainfort why this was troubling him as a freelance writer. The money was certainly a factor, but he also did not "enjoy the thought that I have been bilked in the past, that I am being bilked in the present, or that I may be put out on a limb in the future."[53]

A Guarded Response

Strutt asked Gainfort for an update on the book "on which he worked for so many weeks." He also requested that Gainfort provide a list of articles sold for Rieseberg to see if his partner owed him any money. Strutt was looking for an ally as much as information, but Gainfort could sense the dangerous ground on which he could find himself if he got involved in a discussion about money or rights. Gainfort opted out by telling Strutt, "practically all that you say is, of course, news to me and I don't really think that it calls for any comment on my part."[54] He did not pull punches with Strutt about his manuscript, however. "I can tell you, however, that the book manuscript submitted to us by Lieutenant Rieseberg was not in saleable form. Accordingly we had to have the entire manuscript re-written before it could be sold."[55] It is unclear what Harry told Strutt about the manuscript's status with the publisher or the subsequent parade of collaborators between their original submission and the printer. It does appear that Gainfort's acknowledgment of the condition of the manuscript was a surprise to Strutt and much more direct than the one Harry offered.

Even though the letter's tone put Gainfort squarely on the side of his contracted author, he was indeed beginning to wonder about his client. First, plagiarism, now the double-dealing with a friend—Gainfort had his hands full, and before long, he would be able to rattle off his own list of grievances with Lieutenant Harry E. Rieseberg.

Now He Is Gainfort's Problem

With the deadline for printing and publishing the book barely a month away, problems continued to mount. Even though Lanier thought he was finished, when his work was submitted to McBride in early March, Allen Churchill at McBride sent it back. Half of the pages had a green crayon mark in the upper right corner, indicating they must be retyped.[56]

Re-typing was not the only issue with Lanier. Gainfort learned that his latest ghostwriter had been corresponding directly with Harry about cooperating on future work together. Harry had cut out Strutt, and now he was trying to cut out his agent. Gainfort was becoming completely flabbergasted. It was understandable that someone new to the industry, like Harry, would need some education about how it all worked, but Lanier should have known better. Gainfort told Lanier, "I'm really rather at a loss how to make clear my previous requests that all correspondence should be directly with me."[57]

The Pot Boils Over

The lengthy letters of polite disagreement between Gainfort and Rieseberg made no progress in lowering the temperature on a heated discussion about the contract Harry signed a month prior. The two men were in a full confrontation in the letters and telegrams between Gainfort and Rieseberg about the contract terms and movie rights barely a month before the book was published. When men of words go after each other with typewritten postal letters, one would think there would be a natural temperance imposed by the mechanical limitations of the typewriter keys and the finality of each line as the carriage is shoved hard to the right. In today's communication, an email flame comes with words in ALL CAPS and the instant gratification of the "send" button. There is the immediate self-satisfaction and almost instantaneous reward of knowing that your subject is reading it at that very moment. The days it took to wait for a response only seemed to increase their anger and bluster. Harry's carefully contemplated words of attack simmered in his lingering discontent when Rieseberg thought his agent was bilking him.

Harry's attempt to claw back and modify the signed agreement was getting nowhere with Gainfort. Until his letter to Harry on March 2, Gainfort left some polite wiggle room to explain the contract to his newest client. At that point, Gainfort showed his personality under pressure; he retreated to a cold presentation of the in-your-face facts.

> Our agreement covers—I quote from the first paragraph—"The sale and/or other disposition of any and all rights to my literary compositions." This, of course, includes motion picture rights. It includes all rights of all kinds to all your literary work. This is the understanding as described in our correspondences, this is the standard agreement we make with all authors whom we undertake to represent, and this is the agreement we have made with you.[58]

With postal letters one cannot always tell with certainty when a letter arrived at its destination, but that is not the case with Gainfort's letter of March 2. Harry received that letter on March 6 and stormed his way to the telegraph office the same day to send a blunt reply to John Gainfort. "YOUR LETTER SECOND INSTANT NOT TO MY INTRESTS (*SIC*) AND UNSATISFACTORY THEREFORE STOP ALL FURTHER NEGOTIATIONS MY MATERAL (*SIC*) LETTER FOLLOW SHORTLY OUTLINING MY DECISION."[59] It took Harry only until the next day to compose a blistering three-page letter to Gainfort. In it, he unleashed what he had held back for over a few weeks. Harry worked hard to make several points in his letter. They were not necessarily based on facts since that was not his strong suit, but on making a case from his conspicuously self-centered perspective. His first point was not especially strong when he said, "only an incompetent would sign away 'any and all rights' to the disposition of everything one does."[60] Rieseberg had already done that with his agent in New York, so that argument was poorly thought out, and it was a standard agreement with authors.

His second point was not a home run, either. Harry said that he had been working in the movie studios for ten months, doing some writing of an unspecified nature and working in other capacities as well. Harry said the agreement if taken literally, would have required that he send Pauker their percentage based on his employment there. No agency agreement goes that far. Argument number three got nowhere despite Harry unleashing a verbal assault.

> I am not an alien refugee who doesn't understand such matters, and am not fool enough to now, after already having acquired a reputation in my field of endeavor, want to seek out someone, agent or otherwise, to share all my income with from all sources ... nor do I intend to sit on my fanny out here and wait for an agent some 3,000 miles away from pictures tell me that I cannot work unless I cut him in.[61]

Harry went on no less pointedly to explain why the book, in his view, was simply a way to promote his movie idea. He believed he had that part under control. Harry had done a lot of work, or at least a lot of dreaming and scheming, with his neighbors and relatives in the movie business. He told Gainfort he had "200,000 words" ready to promote. He was sure he could "place a series of short personal experience pictures with one of the largest studios at an early date" because he had been talking to "person contacts [sic]" for some time.[62] Harry said he did not "like to write this letter in this attitude," but the length and tone revealed that he relished it.

I Shall Expect an Apology for This Too

Gainfort used the first page of his two-page reply on March 11, 1942, to re-educate Harry about the contract and his misperceptions of the terms. In doing so, however, Gainfort exposed his mischaracterization of his angry client. Gainfort made a case for agency representation by explaining that "it is the writer's business to write," not to try to manage his business. To do so would detract from his focus on his core work. Gainfort said, "if he should determine to become an author's representative himself, then he would have no time to write."[63]

However, Harry was not a writer, even though his product was the written word. Gainfort's error was to see him as one. Lieutenant Harry E. Rieseberg was a tenacious, persistent, thorough, and unashamed self-promoter, casting his work and name in every direction, hoping that one of those seeds would find fertile ground in an investor. Any agent would be incapable of keeping up with the pace and volume of Harry's submissions. Harry constantly worked on finding any and every outlet he could and did not care what they were. The Pauker agency had difficulty understanding that Harry Rieseberg was not one of their regular authors.

After taking several paragraphs to try again to define their relationship, Gainfort made a gentlemanly accusation in response to Harry's telegram and letter. If they had been in the same room and another era, Gainfort might have picked up a pair of white gloves and slapped Harry with them on both cheeks. "Your telegram was dictatorial, unbusinesslike and to some extent offensive, and I look for an apology for the way it was worded."[64] Harry claimed he could not write books, but he knew how to type a withering letter. Gainfort was no less capable and probably much more experienced. Gainfort was blunt, but that was only his response to the telegram; Gainfort still had remaining comments about the letter.

> Your letter does not reveal a very much better state of mind. Please let me say at this point that your position is not and never had been one which would justify you in this premptory tone toward us. We do not encourage nor permit this attitude and I shall expect an apology for this too.[65]

Gainfort's letter was a three-page "no" to Harry's demands. If Gainfort thought that would be the end of it and Harry's heartfelt apology would be forthcoming, he would quickly be disappointed.

I Do Not Intend to Begin the Habit

Before Gainfort's letter asking for an apology could arrive in Los Angeles, Harry sent a follow-up to his request for a new contract in the form of an "amendatory agreement" he wanted Gainfort to sign. Harry said it had "never been my understanding that the agreement between us, dated the twelfth day of February 1942, covered your representing me in connection with the sale of motion picture rights to my works."[66] Harry drew up an amendment to the contract to clarify that point. He was certain Gainfort would "see (it) is reasonable and justifiable" and would, if signed, allow them to have a harmonious relationship. The agreement was simple. After the word "rights" in the contract, Harry wanted it to say, "excepting all motion picture rights." Simple.[67]

Gainfort acknowledged receipt of the agreement on March 16, but since there was no mention of an apology, Gainfort deferred his response until that matter was cleared up. Harry waited to write back for a full ten days. It was not a cooling-off period, however. Harry's verbose repetition of the previous events for recap led to a final, clear assertion. He had no "time or inclination to enter further into any discussion" about his dictatorial and offensive letter.[68] And if that did not register fully with Gainfort, Harry made it even more explicit. "I have never before had reason to make an apology to anyone; I do not intend at this late day to begin the habit." Rule number two of being Harry Rieseberg was that he did not apologize. Combined with rule number one, only doing what he is inclined to do, this statement gets to the core of Harry Rieseberg's personality. It was not that his life was devoid of occasions where an apology was called for; he was just not prone to accept responsibility.

He could have apologized to the Smithsonian for stealing two rare books. An apology was likely due to his first wife, Caroline, for his philandering and forcing her to live with his parents for too long. He could have apologized to Mr. Pauli for skipping out on his debt in Arizona. He could have apologized to the Postmaster about whom he lied in California. It would be hard even to describe whom the leader of a Ku Klux Klan chapter in the nation's capital should apologize to, but it seems that would be on the list. No apologies were apparently made to his second wife, Ellen, for losing his job and spending all their money on a crazy idea, or for leaving her and their children two times even after she had helped him recover from his severely broken leg. He owed Eric Strutt, a reported friend, an apology for stiffing him on his cut of the articles. One only needs to review Harry's life story to extend the list further. If he had not apologized in those situations, he certainly would not have made an apology for a few dictatorial and aggressive statements to someone three-thousand miles away. Gainfort's empathy for Rieseberg's personality flaw was thick with insult. "I am sorry to learn that you feel you can never make an apology; this attitude is hardly conducive to friendly relationships; nor does it recognize the almost universal fallibility of people."[69] Gainfort's four-page letter in response to Harry followed familiar patterns—a factual recap interspersed with blunt attacks. Gainfort again pointed out that Harry was trying to cut the agency out after realizing he could do some projects without them. Gainfort said, "I have no hesitation in saying that this is an attitude which is unbusiness-like, unfair, unreasonable and which we have no intention of concurring with."[70] In an earlier letter, Harry accused Gainfort of being evasive, so Gainfort sarcastically added at the end, "This, I trust, will not appear to you to be evasive."

Gainfort made his points, but by the end of the letter he tried offering an olive branch to Harry, saying he saw "no reason why this misunderstanding need cause any permanent friction between us," but with the subtext, *as long as you do what the contract says you will do.*[71]

Upon Further, Further Review

Harry was seething. As the days passed, he must have read the letter repeatedly so he would think of more objections. Harry fired off ten single-spaced typewritten pages in letters on March 25, March 26, and March 29 before Gainfort could even begin to catch up. Harry recognized that his legal standing was getting shakier with each reply, so he tried to appeal to Gainfort's sympathies instead. He reminded Gainfort of his mother's stroke and said that her "tragic sickness" caused him to "quickly sign the agreement, not paying much attention to its devious hidden intent."[72]

One of Harry's better arguments included the cold hard facts about the agency's lack of results on his behalf. Harry was a machine when it came to putting out work. Harry explained that since August 1941, he had earned $1,340 from the twenty-one manuscripts he submitted on his own while making absolutely nothing via his agreement with Pauker. He claimed to have sold ideas to the movies and done other work for the studios. It was simple for Harry when he said, "Had I waited to eat on the results in cash which you have so proudly boasted and feel that I should be highly honored in the results, I should still be sitting on my fanny waiting for a handout."[73]

Harry made a good point. His high energy and low standards resulted in hundreds of articles. He was tireless in promotion, especially in Hollywood, and there was no way an agent could keep up with him. Harry continued his demands, using the shift lock key on his typewriter.

> I ENCLOSE A NEW CONTRACT AGREEMENT IN DUPLICATE; IF YOU WISH TO SIGN THIS BY RETURN MAIL, THESE MUTUAL ARRANGEMENTS MAY BE ACCOMPLISHED, OTHERWISE, AND WITHOUT FURTHER LENGTHY DISCUSSIONS, I _____ ____ THAT YOU RETURN IMMEDIATELY ALL MATERIAL YOU POSSESS OF MINE AND MAKE NO FURTHER NEGOTIATIONS FOR SALES.[74]

Harry closed his letter with, "I have nothing more to say in the matter." Harry asserted that it was his final letter. It was, but only overnight. The following day, he fired off another three-page letter in which he said absolutely nothing new. After three more days of hearing nothing back from Gainfort, Harry followed up with a third letter on March 29.[75]

Gainfort could see this was not going well. Gainfort canceled a lecture tour for Harry to promote the book, using "a critical illness in his (Harry's) family" as the reason.

Considering Recent Long Letters

After receiving Harry's three lengthy epistles and amended agreement, Gainfort discovered his most effective response. His response by letter was one sentence: "I will give consideration to your recent long letters within the next few days and write to you finally on this matter about the first of next week."[76] Harry was not so disciplined—he wrote another letter on April 6—but at least he limited himself to only two pages to repeat the same arguments and demands.

It was an off-hand comment in Rieseberg's letter of April 6, 1942, which finally crystallized Gainfort's resolve. Harry mentioned he had "another deal which I have closed recently in Hollywood from which the Pauker agency would be eliminated because of their failure to come to a revised agreement."[77] Harry was making mistakes now, and Gainfort had the advantage of a signed agreement. Before his following letter went out, Gainfort prepared a boilerplate letter intended for the legal department of any Hollywood studio, magazine, or publishing house where Harry might try to cut a deal on his own. The letter politely made its point, saying, "we would like to place on record with you the fact that we have a contract with Lieutenant Rieseberg covering the sale or other disposition of any and all rights to all of his literary productions."[78] Harry Rieseberg had painted himself into a corner.

Amid the Argument, a Book

Gainfort waited almost a week to reply to Harry's furious communiques. Not only had he said all he could, but there was also a book to produce. When he finally replied to Harry on April 14, he had only two important messages. First, if Harry made a film sale, he should immediately send the particulars to Gainfort along with their ten percent commission. Secondly, and somewhat anti-climactically, Gainfort announced that *I Dive for Treasure* was now printed, and the first copies would arrive any day.[79] Given their bitter disagreements, it hardly seemed like a celebration by either party to the contract.

Despite Gainfort's brief requirement for information and royalties on any film, Harry expressed his position in no uncertain terms in a way that made clear his refusal to keep the contract terms.

> … I want to advise you plainly and for all time in these words—any idea created in my own mind for pictures or any accompanying film taken by myself and disposed of by myself is my own business, has no connection whatever with you or any other agency or individual in any manner.[80]

Neither man budged on their position. After castigating Gainfort for his "arbitrary, procrastinating and most unethical attitude," Rieseberg sent another letter pronouncing the contract as revoked.[81] Gainfort's response also made clear the agency's stance—they would continue to act as contracted and expected Harry to do the same.[82] Harry was expected to fully inform them of any movie deals he might make on his own and pay them their commission, which would be twenty percent instead of ten if the film had anything to do with the book's content. Harry was reminded to send his next book manuscript to them as well. Finally, there was the remaining threat of legal action, warning Harry that he would be accountable for "any damaging and false statements you may have made or that you may make, in correspondence or otherwise, to third parties, concerning your relations with us."[83] That was a direct reference to two letters Harry sent to Allen Churchill at Robert M. McBride & Co complaining about Gainfort and his treatment by the Pauker agency.[84]

At that point, the steady stream of communication between Harry and Gainfort abated. Despite their lack of focus on the project for the previous two months, *I Dive for Treasure* was finally on the bookshelves. Both men retreated to their corners, and *I Dive for Treasure* made its debut in the market without any support from Harry and begrudging interest by his agent.

Harry Rieseberg was hitting the big time, and it was making him miserable.

Chapter 9

The Business of Being Harry

*[Rieseberg] was such a fraud. All his wrecks were intact
and had treasure chests with an octopus on top and a skeleton
guarding the whole thing. It was junk, but I fell for it.*
—Robert Marx[1]

Despite Rieseberg's many claims about treasure recoveries of tens of thousands of dollars in gold or silver, his financial situation did not reflect access to great wealth. He explained that away differently over time, shuffling it off to taxes, gifts to others, or the deterioration of rusted relics. His business was not in salvage, diving, or even selling information from his early research on sunken vessels. Harry was a peddler of as many made-up stories as he could sell at any price. And he was good at it.

Rieseberg learned the hard way that writing was a financial challenge, so he often had an alternate second income. On the edge of Hollywood, just a few blocks north of Santa Monica Boulevard, Harry and his father lived in an eighteen-unit apartment complex with bungalows arranged around a courtyard. For seventy-five dollars a month, they enjoyed a nice neighborhood and maid service. They must have also had a bit of space where they could raise chickens. Barred Rocks and Jersey White Giants were available from Rieseberg's Canoga Park Hatchery at 21517 Saticoy Street. The war required many adjustments, and Harry had to make a living somehow.[2]

The public persona of the successful, adventurous treasure hunter and the private reality of Harry's struggle to make ends meet were in sharp contrast. Harry Rieseberg, the world's greatest treasure expert and perpetually broke writer, wanted readers to know there were billions of dollars out there just waiting for someone to come and get it from the bottom of the sea and to pay him for what he knew. His circumstances made one wonder why he did not go get some of it for himself. In a few of his articles, Harry used the war effort to explain away why he was not involved in any salvage. He crowed that the war's end would bring an explosion in recovery efforts.

Brave and Resourceful Men

The lead time for magazine articles could be several months. So, when Harry's article titled "Billions Waiting to be Taken" appeared in the May 1942 issue of

Popular Mechanics, it still touted Harry's first book with a completely different working title, *I Hunt Treasure*. In the article, Rieseberg did his best to build the premise he had suggested Gainfort consider for their marketing brochures for the book—that treasure is out there, just waiting to be recovered.[3]

During this period in the publishing world, authors writing science fiction, adventure, or true crime stories benefited from the work of many talented illustrators. In the *Popular Mechanics* article, Frank Beatty produced an illustration showing the long-lost Romano diving bell large enough for the operator to stand up and in action retrieving a treasure chest sitting exposed on the sea floor.[4] The art was exceptional, but the scene was hard to swallow. Harry opened the article with suspenseful invigoration appropriate to the artwork. "Someday when peace returns to the oceans, we'll start prying open Davy Jones's locker to wrest from it the fabulous treasure sealed there under shifting sands and barnacles, guarded by treacherous deep-sea fish and octopus and the enormous pressure of the depths."[5] The themes in this article were those he repeated hundreds of times: one-eighth of the world's gold is lost at sea, Harry in his robot and iron man suit had been there but brought home nothing, and centuries of salvage efforts have been attempted but were unsuccessful, so the treasure is still there. That was his formula.

Book Seller, Deal Maker

When *I Dive for Treasure* hit the bookstores in 1942, its cover price was $2.75. McBride promoted the book widely with advertisements in newspapers around the country.[6] Book reviews appeared nationally, speaking favorably about the book and repeating Harry's claims as if they were fact. One review even suggested Harry provided the "indisputable truth" for the many treasure wrecks to be found.[7]

Positive book reviews appeared in May 1942 in the *Indianapolis News*, the *New York Herald Tribune*, and the *Chicago Sun*. In June, the *New York Times*, the *Albany Times Union*, the *Atlanta Constitution*, the *El Paso Times*, the *San Francisco Chronicle*, and the *Los Angeles Times* followed with their own recommendations. The reviewer for the *Seattle Argos* said that Harry "writes well in a dramatically pulsating style. His tales are stirring, and so far as this reviewer is informed, entirely truthful."[8]

Despite Harry's earlier refusal to do anything to promote the book, he ultimately made some appearances and took advantage of the publicity to push out many more articles. His dour demeanor in a publicity photo for a book signing at a California bookstore shows that he did finally agree to some appearances but did not appear happy about it.[9] Gainfort was right about the market potential; the National Travel Club of New York picked up the book and published it for their book club readers. He was also right about Harry's intention to use the book as a vehicle for his real goal of making a movie. *Variety* magazine reported on May 25, 1942, that Harry was looking for a movie deal in Hollywood.[10]

Attention Getter

Rieseberg became well known on the west coast due to his magazine and newspaper articles about treasure hunting. After the book came out, even more attention was given to the life story he had created for himself. Kate Holliday of *Coronet* magazine did a biographical piece in June 1942 titled "He Dives for Doubloons."[11] The newspaper article that Strutt did for him, "He Walks With Davy Jones," continued to appear in full-page newspaper stories all across the country for several months. Over fifty published articles by and about Harry from 1942 to 1944 have been located, and it can be assumed there were many more. *Boys' Life*, *Popular Mechanics*, *Sea* magazine, *St. Joseph's* magazine, and *True* each published multiple articles during those years.

Fame dies quickly, however, and after hitting its peak when the book came out, the attention Harry received began to fade. He needed something new to keep himself before the public.

Giant Tongs Get Press

Harry's next big idea was based on an invention he discovered while he was looking for patents related to his underwater interests. In 1932 and 1933, Claude Byler applied for two patents that caught Harry's attention.[12] The first mention of Byler's inventions in the press was a short article in January 1934 when his patents were in process.[13] Byler was identified as the inventor of a "giant sea rake, working somewhat on the principle of a grappling hook." Simply by the description, one could determine this would have been a massive piece of equipment. Warren told a reporter he had worked on his design for the tongs for thirty years before getting the patents.[14] Harry Rieseberg waited almost ten years to promote the idea. In February 1943, one of Harry's wash drawings illustrated a story about the tongs in *Popular Mechanics*, with an image of the Romano robot dangling beneath its underwater tender.[15] As one might expect, the device was never built.

The article described a floating pontoon platform open in the middle, 715 feet long and 250 feet wide, which rose to 130 feet above the surface. It would carry enough lighting to produce 6,000,000 candlepower of illumination. Ten or more grappling hooks, which looked like gigantic ice tongs, were central to the invention. Their design was to lower the grapplers to the bottom, grip a ship up to 600 feet long, and hoist it to the surface.

Harry Was Desperate

In 1942, following a big splash with the release of his book, Rieseberg's articles generated some regular income as a writer but no book royalties. Even when royalties began to appear, the checks were small because he had to pay 50 percent to his ghostwriter, Lanier, and grudgingly pay Pauker their 10 percent agent's fee.

Chapter 9. The Business of Being Harry

A "floating drydock" Rieseberg claimed to have invented. Detailed drawing from *Popular Mechanics*, February 1943 (courtesy Hearst Magazine Media, Inc.)

Early in the year, Harry had been turned down for a job with the Veterans' Administration, but despite that, he wrote the personnel director a second time.[16] He pled his case for employment as if they had not understood their mistake in not hiring the famous Harry Rieseberg the first time. Harry went on for two pages in great detail, restating his background and proposing how he might be used to assist in the war effort. He also made sure the hiring administrator knew he was an important person. "You, no doubt," Harry told the hiring officer, "have at some time read of my activities in another field." He hoped the hiring manager would be star-struck.

A handwritten note on the letter pointed out that Harry was a "former civil service employee, not a veteran." Despite Harry calling attention to the fact that he was "49 years of age, white, Gentile, and exempt from military duty," the reply from the VA only a few weeks later made clear for a second time that Harry's services would not be needed.[17] The idea of meeting his growing financial needs by returning to jobs he had done years before would not happen.

Shortly after the publication of *I Dive for Treasure*, Rieseberg wrote to the Edmond Pauker agency in New York in September 1942 asking for a financial favor. Compared to the tone of his earlier letters, Harry was subdued and humble but unapologetic in his request to Pauker. This time, he needed something from them—Harry Rieseberg needed money.[18] Harry's spin this time was that he had "applied for overseas service, and may be called at any moment now," so he was trying to "straighten out and bring up to date as many of my financial matters as possible."[19] Harry asked Pauker to have McBride pay him any royalties due at that time, well before the December schedule. Along with his expressed understanding of why this was an unusual request outside the terms of the contract, he also built a case as to why he deserved it due to his extra effort on behalf of the book. His letter said there were three printings of the book by that time, so it had achieved a measure of success.

McBride declined to pay any early royalties since they were not obligated to do so. From Harry's perspective, one can understand his frustration. He had published a book, the publisher had sold his books, and yet Harry had not received one penny of royalties.

Have Tongs, Need Money

What is most interesting about Rieseberg's letter is what he claimed about a second reason Harry needed the money—that he was working on a big idea involving Claude Byler's giant tongs. "… at the moment, I am having prepared some most sensational drawings out here of the new invention which has already been pronounced most startling in its nature by engineers. The idea is so large that it would take pages to adequately describe it herein …"[20] Harry needed money to promote his next big idea. He offered up that when the world heard about the tongs the book "will take another flurry and go into its fourth, fifth, or more editions from the publicity."

Stories about Harry's undersea tongs idea began appearing in newspapers and magazines nationwide. The *Atlanta Constitution* published an Associated Press article making the rounds about "Plan Proposed to Salvage Sunken Freighters After War" on October 22, 1942.[21] Despite the rash of publicity, or perhaps because so many people could see the failings of such a massive undertaking, Harry's tongs idea gathered no steam. Within a year their mention disappeared in the press and in Harry's magazine articles. Giant tongs did not help Harry's bank account or his credibility. Unsurprisingly, the monstrosity was never more than a drawing.

Nothing but Letters and Bouquets

I Dive for Treasure was in a third printing by September 1942, but Harry Rieseberg had yet to receive a single cent in royalties. Such was the accounting craft of the publishing industry. Harry's life that fall was troubled by more than the lack of income from his book. His mother, Jennie Rieseberg, succumbed to the effects of her stroke and died on October 29, 1942, at age 73. If some of his bitterness toward his agent were to be explained away, it would be for the stresses of the past few years with his mother's health. As Harry would later prove, however, the source of his biting aggression came from within himself.

My Interests Absolutely Ignored

According to Harry's contractual agreement with Robert M. McBride & Company, his publisher was to report sales every year on the first day of May and November. On November 1, Harry was to get a report of sales from April 1 to September 30 of that year, along with a check for his share of the royalties. McBride's report to Pauker noted sales through September 30, 1942, as the first indication of the book's initial success. Domestic sales of the full-price edition for $2.75 had reached 2,891, and 266 copies of a cheaper edition had sold. The National Travel Club edition sold another 1,396 copies.[22] His first royalty check was a whopping $492.16, about the same as he could make on a couple of articles for *Popular Mechanics*.[23] Even that amount was overstated since McBride and Pauker forgot to pay Henry Lanier his half.

As frequently happened in the era when postal mail delivery was the primary communications medium for business, Pauker's letter to Rieseberg with his royalty and Harry's letter to his agent complaining about his lack of any accounting or payment crossed in the mail. Gainfort was no longer with the Pauker agency, a sign of some of the financial difficulties caused to the industry by the war, so Harry addressed his letter to Denis Plimmer. Rieseberg returned to his preferred communication, a four-page, single-spaced letter, but this time with legitimate complaints.

Harry Rieseberg was relentless, both in asserting his opinions and in executing his own business plans. He never backed down from a position or conceded a point. He was equally unyielding in perpetuating his version of the facts. His earlier letter asking for the advance made it appear that the government's call for Harry to enter overseas service was waiting for the right moment to send Harry in there to straighten things out. He claimed he would soon be "called into active commissioned service."[24] His ability to reinforce every façade, remarkable in its ceaselessness and pathology, was a constant throughout his life.

On the first page of the letter, Harry replayed the communications of the months prior while chastising McBride for not keeping their part of the agreement and missing his very first royalty report. To make it worse, McBride told him he would be paid in November, then changed it to December, then told him he would get it in early January. McBride got off to a bad start with Harry by not promptly reporting sales to him and not making the required payment until January 12, 1943. The check was in the mail finally, but it would only generate more questions.

McBride had repeatedly provided glowing reports of how well sales were doing but without numbers. To make matters worse, Harry was already getting letters from McBride reminding him that he had a legal obligation for a second book. The tone of those letters was, in fact, somewhat aggressive, and Harry's response showed he was still in form. "What the hell do they (McBride) think this is—a joke—and I am supposed to furnish them manuscripts that go into fourth and fifth editions and receive in return nothing but letters and bouquets about it?"[25] Even after Harry received the publisher's report and the check he had been expecting for months, his concerns were not reduced. He was sure it confirmed the fishiness of the whole arrangement. He took another four typewritten pages to itemize his questions and objections.[26]

Sales as High as the Rough Waves

Part of the problem with the accounting was that an overly enthusiastic salesperson had given Harry the idea that books were rushing off the shelves. As early as June 15, only two months after publication, someone at McBride wrote Harry to tell him, "The sale of the book is mounting as high as the rough waves you have to combat on your undersea adventures." Harry had been told in June that sales were more than 5,000 already, so when he got a report months later in January that fewer were sold, he questioned it. Harry was so suspicious of McBride's accounting that he even wondered why the publisher charged him $1.71 for a book. Though he called it "a small trick," he made sure they knew he was checking every number.[27]

Indications of the financial strains caused by the war were starting to mount. Gainfort and Plimmer were no longer with the Pauker agency, so Edmond Pauker himself wrote Harry in response to his letters. Pauker appeared not to know the whole history with Harry, so he may have been coming face to face with Harry's complaints for the first time. Pauker was just a few years older than Harry but responded with a much more mature, genteel approach saying, "there is no reason and no purpose to get excited … all problems can be better solved by calm and careful consideration."[28]

Pauker had to review the file from the beginning to examine what his employees had done to date. Unsurprisingly he found they had done all that an agent could be expected to do. He cautioned Harry, "if you write us again, please talk in the same calm, reasonable, and human vein as we talk to you."[29] By mid–February, Harry had finally begun to do just that and resolved that "in the future when I received letters from publishers who foam over like the froth on a glass of beer, I'll ignore their frothings—until I see the returns in the form of a check."[30]

Back to No Royalties

There were signs that both the Pauker agency and McBride publishing felt the financial strains of the war. Even Henry Lanier, the final ghostwriter of *I Dive for Treasure*, wondered if he would get paid for his work on Harry's book. Lanier sent a letter to the Pauker agency in January 1943, reminding them he was to receive his percentage of the royalties and politely presuming there must have been some payment in the months since the book's release.[31]

Even when royalty checks did arrive, there were questions about McBride's solvency. In June 1943, Harry used a McBride check for $232.78 to make a purchase at the Canoga Park Lumber Company. The check was refused because it was post-dated, a way of pushing out the use of a check so that funds would not be available until the date on the check. Pauker explained away the date as a mistake, but it was another sign of their financial troubles.

Regardless of the ups and downs of publishing, Harry kept up his efforts to generate publicity and produce articles and stories on his own. The newspaper insert, *American Weekly*, was a major outlet publishing stories for millions of readers. Their lushly illustrated two-page stories were the perfect venue for Harry's tales of adventures. In a story that was a take-off on the work of Eric Strutt, which again did not mention his name, Harry published "I Walked the Streets of a Sunken City" in August 1943.[32] It was the same Port Royal formula he would use for years, but the illustrations always made it more enticing.

By the end of 1943, book sales were starting to slow down. From October 1, 1943, to March 31, 1944, a little over 1,300 books were sold, with some foreign sales beginning to show. Harry typically gained less than five hundred dollars for each semi-annual royalty period. Harry's production of published articles also slowed down a bit as well. It was an excellent time to gather his work back together, so he wrote Pauker asking that any of his work in their files for the last two years be returned.[33] Other than placing his first book, there is no indication in the records that Pauker got any of his other work published. Pauker still had Harry's book manuscript, "Man of Destiny," that Harry begged them to publish. Instead, Pauker threw in the towel; they returned everything they had to Harry, acknowledging their relationship was ended.

Troubles at McBride continued to mount. An April 1944 letter to Pauker from the publisher explained that spring royalties would be late due to the death of McBride's auditor. Harry had to wonder if this entire venture was coming to an end. Whether he was making a living raising chickens or by some other means, it certainly was not his publishing royalties that paid the rent.

Big Changes

More than anything happening with his writing, two events in the fall of 1944 impacted Harry significantly and personally. Harry married for the third time in September 1944, and his father, Henry Rieseberg, died the following month.

Marrying Into a Social Circle

Valentine Curran Gore was at the center of social activity in Bakersfield, California. She led a life relatively free of complications and financial stress. Her family, the Currans, were well-off and well-connected. Her father, James Curran, had started a brick and building materials company in Bakersfield in 1918.[34] She was pictured on the front page of the *Bakersfield Californian* in August 1942 at a reception for Bakersfield native and California Attorney General, Earl Warren. Warren later served as Governor of California from 1943 to 1953 before becoming Chief Justice of the Supreme Court. Warren and Val were high school classmates.[35]

Her first husband, Jack Gore, died in May 1939 after twenty-six years of marriage. He was known as both an automobile dealer and an avid photographer. He had a weak heart and had even told friends his life would end abruptly, and that it did, with a heart attack. He was described as "a civilized man, with a nice wit, urbane manners, and a tactful, unaffected honesty."[36] What Valentine saw in Harry Rieseberg and how she ever connected with him is an interesting story we may never fully know.

In whatever manner they met, Harry and Val kept their relationship somewhat secret. A report at the time said that the wedding surprised local friends in Bakersfield. Since the newlyweds moved back to Harry's mobile home in Canoga Park near Los Angeles after their marriage, we might assume their relationship began in the city. When they were married, she was a secretary for a building materials company, presumably her father's. It is interesting to consider that they could have met in June 1943 at a lumber company in Canoga Park, where Harry tried to use a bad check from McBride to make a purchase.

The newspaper reported the groom as "Lieutenant Harry E. Rieseberg, United States Navy, retired," which was not true, and the "author of many well-known adventure books." One has to wonder if that was simply a slip-up by the newspaper or the story Harry was pitching to Val and her family. Harry and Val married on Sunday, September 18, 1944, in a private garden ceremony at the home of Val's sister in Canoga Park. The wedding news did not filter back to Val's Bakersfield friends and remaining family until a few days later. Notably, her parents were not in attendance.

A Somber Celebration

Any nuptial afterglow was suspended when Harry's father, Henry, died at age eighty only a few weeks later on October 7, 1944. Harry and his parents had a complex, co-dependent existence, particularly with his father. Harry was an only child who was intelligent, curious, engaging, and a bit precocious. Besides a few independent years during his previous two marriages, Harry lived with his parents well into adulthood.[37]

Somehow Harry needed them as anchors. He needed a wife, his parents, and someone who helped take care of the routine aspects of life so he could have his big ideas and his modicum of fame. With his father and mother gone, he had only had his new wife, Valentine, on whom to rely. He had no communication with his children from either of his previous marriages. With Val's family's position and her husband's struggling personal affairs, one might expect she had some financial support, but that is uncertain.

After allowing time for Henry Rieseberg's burial and mourning, Valentine's sister, Mrs. Bennett Nofziger, held a garden tea for Harry and Val, and for her son and daughter-in-law who had married a few months earlier. Sixty guests were there, including James Curran and his wife from Bakersfield. Tea was served to the Curran clan from the "lovely patio" of the Nofzigers on "lace-covered tables centered with low white bowls of bronze and gold dwarf zinnias." In what was perhaps polite deference to her marriage beneath her social milieu, that evening there was a separate barbecue dinner "in compliment to relatives of Lieutenant Rieseberg." With his father and mother gone, the only relatives ever mentioned were Martin relatives of his mother's, and the director and producer, Leo McCarey.[38]

An Author with a New Book

At least Harry had something to crow about at the big social event surrounding his hasty marriage—he had a new contract to publish a second book. Just a few days before the tea party, Rieseberg signed an agreement to publish *Treasure Hunter*, an alternate title for his "Man of Destiny" manuscript he had been promoting for years. Sir William Phipps and his recovery of treasure from a Spanish vessel in 1687 fascinated Rieseberg for many years, not just because of the story of treasure but because of its seeming potential for a movie script.

His unnamed ghostwriter this time was Frank Owen, a New York author of fiction and fantasy novels, some under the pseudonym Roswell Williams.[39] The original contract called for Owen to receive $500 as an advance against his one-third of the royalties. For some reason, however, Owen later relinquished any claim for royalties, stating that he had been fully paid already. One can assume there was more to that rather odd statement than what is stated in the letter.[40]

I Dive for Treasure continued to have a long shelf life. Between 1943 and 1946, over 1,300 pocket-sized books were published for distribution to the troops as armed services editions of already available works. The small books, less than five inches on the longest edge, were never intended to survive the war and were printed on very inexpensive papers. Publishers agreed to very low royalties in part because the books were not expected to come back into the market.[41] Harry Rieseberg's *I Dive for Treasure* was book N19 in the series, the 417th issued out of 1,322. Harry mentioned the agreement to allow the publication in a letter to Pauker in July of 1945, indicating it had been agreed to a few months earlier.[42] Sales of the full edition of his book were starting to pick back up as well, with Harry's royalty for October 1944 to March 1945 sales being $826.34.[43]

Treasure Hunter was finally published in January 1946. Rieseberg's second book was not only about Phipps' story, but it was also about other treasure hunters through the ages. Then, as usual, Harry threw in some of his data about wrecks and their possible wealth, always implying that he knew where to find them. He never missed a chance to try and hook intrepid adventurists with made-up stories of his exploits. In Harry's world, treasure was always sitting there for the taking if one used the knowledge and technology he claimed to possess.

More Trouble with Royalties

Beginning with yet another missed deadline for a royalty report and payment from McBride in June 1946, the correspondence between Rieseberg and his agent became almost exclusively about Harry not getting paid. Harry received no information about sales of *Treasure Hunter* for six full months after its release.[44]

McBride offered a new excuse for the delay in paying royalties. The war was over, and that excuse was not workable anymore. Instead, the publisher explained that they had moved to a new office, putting them behind. Even their letter about late payments was two months in coming.[45] Harry's royalty was only $107.74 for six months, so it seemed small enough to pay. However, by the end of the year, Pauker's patient support of the publisher's normal delays had changed tone. Edmond Pauker was not getting paid either, so his impatience also grew. Pauker had repeatedly written and called McBride on Rieseberg's, and his own, behalf but had gotten no reply. Pauker lamented, "We are at a loss to understand the delay." When McBride finally responded, it was a confirmation of what everyone already knew—the publisher was in financial trouble.[46]

A Soft Spot in Our Finances

E.C. Turner of the Robert M. McBride & Company finally stepped out of the silence to admit the publisher's difficulties meeting their obligations. Turner admitted that McBride's accountant had "referred all of your previous letters to me and I humbly apologize for the long delay in writing you."[47] The soft spot in their finances was their own making. They had indeed moved to a new location, likely because they were not paying their obligations there either. The new building required remodeling and cost several times what they expected. On top of that, two "extremely important books that were to be published in February have been held over for delivery until March 17th and 24th."[48] Though he regretted not writing and confessing the difficulties earlier, he still asked their patience to wait even longer.

Pauker and Rieseberg agreed they were getting the runaround. Rieseberg said he had become "so damn tired of writing letters to them that I am afraid I'll blow-up were I to do so." Harry told Pauker to handle it however he chose since Pauker knew "how to treat these cases better than I do." It should be noted, however, despite their months-long refusal to honor their contract, McBride's accountant dared to ask Harry to send them another manuscript, and Harry "flatly turned him down."[49]

Take Matters Into His Own Hands

Pauker did what he probably should have done months prior; he sent McBride a demand letter and threatened legal action. "Should you again fail to meet your obligations [before March 1, 1947] we will have to advise him [Rieseberg] to take matters into his own hands and start legal steps."[50] McBride seemed to lack the energy to resist, and their reply said they were "hoping you will refrain from referring this matter to your attorney for the present, believe me."[51]

A final promise was made to send Pauker a check for royalties due for *I Dive for Treasure* and, on the same date, send a check for *Treasure Hunter* directly to Rieseberg since Pauker was not his agent for that book.[52] McBride met that obligation with a check to Pauker for $146.48. *Treasure Hunter* had yet to earn enough to cover the advances already made. McBride was indeed in financial trouble, and it was carrying over to Harry Rieseberg.[53]

Men's Adventure

Tagging publications as "pulp" harkens back to the genre's earliest years at the turn of the 20th century. They were published for broad public consumption with specialized topics and spicy undertones. Printed on cheap, woody paper, the dime novels and nickel magazines were inexpensive and generally not enduring. Hundreds of magazines were published and read by tens of millions of avid followers. In the 1920s, after World War I ended, the audience for these publications increased in size and was ready for more. The pulps turned up the underlying sexuality, the passionate romance, and the bloody conflict. Detective stories, horror tales, and emotionally charged novels worked to outdo each other to attract readers and boost revenue.[54]

Although Rieseberg had one of his earliest stories, "Old Chinatown," appear in Will Carleton's *Every Where* magazine in 1912, one of the earliest notable pulps, all his other work during the twenties was limited to poems or travel stories about Arizona. It was during the 1930s that Rieseberg began to appear on the pages of some of the most iconic early magazines of this sort. The decade after the Great Depression demonstrated that stories of danger and excitement could entice readers despite challenging economic times.

Characters with exceptional strength or skill, worldwide villains, and over-the-top danger were ongoing themes along the shelves lined with over forty such magazines on the rack each month. *Adventure* magazine was one of the centerpieces of that group. One author said *Adventure* "stood head and shoulders above the field" in the general adventure mags.⁵⁵ Although Rieseberg did not publish an article in *Adventure*, he was prominent in the pages for many years as one of the "experts" whom readers could consult with their questions about lost ships.

After mid–1935 when Rieseberg broke his leg, there was a two-year gap in his writing while he recovered. After he emerged as Lieutenant Harry E. Rieseberg, the world's greatest underwater treasure hunter, his writing focus shifted and the magazine market was ready for him. One writer of the time estimated that there were around 150 pulp magazines in 1934.⁵⁶ Rieseberg's titles with "Man-Made Monsters," "Death Battles," and "Terror in the Deep" blared from the pages of *Focus*, *American Weekly*, and *Popular Mechanix*. His primary outlets were still newspapers then, but Rieseberg was finding his footing with adventure-laden tales of danger and near-death. Though they were fiction, he sold them as first-person adventures. If there were questions about his credibility, they never seemed to translate to a loss in sales. Pulp buyers were not interested in reality.

Pre-Playboy Adventure, Prime Rieseberg Outlets

Milton Moskowitz, an advertising executive in the 1950s, called the period from 1940 to 1953 the era of "pre–Playboy adventure" magazines.⁵⁷ Following the publication of Rieseberg's *I Dive for Treasure* in 1942, he amped up his earlier tales of treasure dives with even more terrifying, near-death adventures. Rieseberg's stories appeared in *Blue Book*, *True*, *Everybody's Weekly*, *Coronet*, *Stag*, *Men*, and *Fate*, each representative of their pulp ancestors. Pictorial publications like *PIC* and *Eye* were perfect outlets for Harry's faked photos of octopus attacks. "Cannibal Dinner Party" in *Male* and "Wooden God" in *Swagger* had Harry branching out to jungle stories of man-eating savages in places he had never visited.

Oddly, while Rieseberg was publishing articles in racy men's magazines, he placed an equal number of cleansed versions of his work in religiously oriented publications. These were sometimes collectively referred to as the "Sunday School" publishing houses in the trade. In the 1930s, they paid from a tenth of a cent to half a cent per word.⁵⁸ Harry placed multiple articles in *The Grail*, *St. Joseph Magazine*, *Catholic Digest*, and *Cor*, all for religious audiences. Youth magazines like *Boy Life* (not *Boy's Life*), *Classmate*, *American Girl*, and *Open Road for Boys* also put Rieseberg in front of youthful readers. The mix of publications reinforces his assertion that he would send his articles anywhere that would pay him, and he did not care how much.

He-Man Adventure

Moscowitz characterizes the period in which he was immersed in 1957 as one where "new magazines are being launched today at a feverish pace." What he observed made him wonder, "Has there ever been another three-year period in which seventy-five consumer magazines were born?"⁵⁹

The founding of *Playboy* in 1953 was a significant milestone in the magazine industry. After that debut, Moskowitz outlined three categories of magazines for similar audiences. "The Playkids" were offshoots of *Playboy*—magazines like *Cabaret*, *Dude*, and *Jem*, all featured "models in states of undress." Rieseberg published articles in a number of these during this period. Moskowitz called the gossip magazines and celebrity exposés the "Peeping Toms." It was his categorization of the third grouping into which much of Rieseberg's work would fall—the "He-Man Adventures." Moskowitz called them "offshoots of Jack London by way of *True*, *Argosy* and the old pulps" and included as examples titles like *Rugged*, *Real Action*, *Duel*, *True Men's Stories*, and *Man's Illustrated*.

Graphic magazines with bright covers had to compete with television in the 1950s. Resistance to the perceived rise of the power of women in American culture led to more stories in magazines like *Man's Magazine* and *Man's Illustrated*, which included "conflict where man was challenged and triumphed." Earle's illustration of a cover for *Man's Conquest* in 1956 showed a theme he called "shirtless men in peril."[60]

A Mechanical Lobster-Tractor-Tank

Harry Rieseberg's energy and persistence meant he always had more than one prospect going simultaneously. In addition to his hopes for a movie, Harry was promoting an incredible mechanical invention as if it were docked and ready to be towed into place above a wreck where its riches could be hauled to the surface.

Interest in Harry's idea to build giant tongs for salvage appears to have lasted only as long as the syndicated article with his impressive drawings was routed around the nation's newspapers. If anyone with actual technical knowledge gave it a second thought, it would have been only to dismiss it for its apparent limitations and faulty assumptions. One cannot help but wonder about Harry's purpose in pursuing or promoting such an idea. Was he only trying to spark interest and add to his reputation? Did he have an agreement that paid him some percentage if the inventor produced a marketable device? Or did he honestly think such a contraption would work, much like he seemed to have believed in the Romano diving bell? Nothing indicates which of those possibilities, or others, were dominant in his ongoing efforts to update his credibility with somewhat outlandish salvage technology.

One failed effort, however, was not reason enough for Harry Rieseberg to stop trying others. At the end of his second book, *Treasure Hunter*, he introduced yet another technological approach to salvage that the popular press tagged as the "mechanical lobster."[61]

An Assemblage of Leak Points

Rieseberg proposed an idea for an underwater tank equipped with five cranes that could work on salvage operations at any depth. Since there was no illustration in the book, readers had to wait a whole year until a November 1947 article in *Mechanix Illustrated* to get an artist's conception and to see a model built with the help of

Charles Warren, an engineer from South Gate, California. Rieseberg promoted the tank as his idea, assisted by Warren, but it appears that the design was entirely done by Warren.[62]

> The machine is similar to a huge Army tank on caterpillar treads and is operated by powerful electrically driven motors within sealed chambers, and will travel on the uneven, rocky sea floor at about five miles per hour. It is equipped with five gigantic cranes, four of them fold-back, each fifteen feet in length, but made in a way that they can be extended to almost any desired length for various, complicated undersea work. A fifth crane, for heavy duty, is mounted on the top of the control compartment and has a swing of 360 degrees, and a reach of thirty-five feet or more in any direction.[63]

Out of Stock?

In January 1948, Harry told his former agent that no one seemed to be able to find a copy of *I Dive for Treasure* in bookstores. Harry wondered why McBride

Photograph of Harry Rieseberg with model of "Mechanical Lobster." International News Photo, November 1947 (photograph courtesy Harry Ransom Center, University of Texas at Austin).

would have stopped printing it when there was some demand, even if they "put it into a $1.00 edition like so many others have done."[64] Pauker acknowledged that the reason was probably due to McBride's financial condition rather than a sense of the marketability remaining in the six-year-old book.[65] Pauker wrote McBride to inquire on Harry's behalf and got a positive response. He was told that a new edition was in the works, and plans were to continue selling it at the original price. However, McBride was making plans that would impact Harry more strongly than reviving a waning volume.

A New Publisher

A change in his publisher's business fortunes ultimately led to a revival of both of Harry's books. Dodd, Mead, and Company informed Harry in July 1948 that they had taken over the books previously published by Robert M. McBride.[66] "We are assuming all the obligations of the contracts between you and the McBride Company as of June 10, 1948," they wrote, "and royalties on sales made on and after that date will be our responsibility."[67]

Though McBride fizzled, they did help open up one new market for Harry's work by selling foreign publishing rights. In December 1947, with the help of Franz J. Horch, a well-established author's representative, they made arrangements to sell French serial rights.[68] Sales were minimal, however, and Harry's royalties were often under a hundred dollars. In April 1949, Dodd, Mead told Rieseberg they discovered McBride had arranged for a French edition of *I Dive for Treasure* and sent him four copies they had just received.[69]

Harry's new publisher also offered to pursue the sale of French rights to his second volume. Although Dodd, Mead owned the publishing rights to *Treasure Hunter*, they did not even have a copy of the book since it was rather quickly out of print. They asked Harry if he had a spare copy he could send them. Harry told them he had only his original and no extras, suggesting they "may secure copies at many of your larger New York second-hand book stores who specialize in back copies of books."[70]

Franz J. Horch was the one driving the foreign sales effort, and he continued to make headway. In May 1949, he reported that *I Dive for Treasure* was beginning French publication in serial form in a newspaper, and a Belgian newspaper was about to publish sections of the book in both French and Dutch.[71] The Belgian article netted about $120.00 for Harry. Over the next three years, Horch helped secure foreign editions of Harry's books and serialization in magazines and newspapers for Swiss, German, Spanish, Finnish, Norwegian, Danish, and Argentinian versions. At least part of Harry's false narrative was genuine—he really was becoming "internationally famous."

Staying in Business?

Harry's writing slowed to a trickle, with his two books taking on a renewed life and receiving interest for editions in other languages. The author has located only twenty-three magazine articles published from 1945 to 1949. Perhaps Harry's method of flooding the market with his articles had started to wear thin. Oddly, in 1951 he published an article under the pseudonym of Donald Wright Kelly.[72] Rather than establishing a separate identity, it was simply Harry's way to get two articles in the same issue of *Stag* magazine. Rieseberg later admitted it was a method he used when a "publisher owned several magazines to avoid the conflict of the same author having articles in all three mediums."[73]

Balboa Amusements

With his insufficient income from writing, Rieseberg had to find other ways to supplant his income. He no longer lived at the location where he had the chicken hatchery, so was likely out of that business. There is, however, evidence that Harry had ownership in an amusements and games concession at the famous and historic Balboa Pavilion in Newport Beach, California.[74]

The Balboa Pavilion was initially constructed in 1906 as part of an effort to attract land developers. It was built on wooden pilings on a very narrow sliver of land, essentially in the water. Over the years, it had become a focal point of visitors to the area with entertainment that at various times included a bathhouse, big bands like Count Basie and Benny Goodman, and even gambling. After World War II, sport fishing, bowling, and an amusement center developed in the space. Harry's ownership of the amusement concession at Balboa Pavilion came to light because of his classified ad trying to get out of that business. In June 1948, he ran an ad in the *Los Angeles Times* touting the income potential at an average of "$1000 to $1500 a week during season."[75] A second advertisement ran in the *San Bernardino Sun* on July 17, 1948, and Harry revised the low end of the income range in the ad.

> FOR IMMEDIATE SALE. Amusement concessions, best spot Balboa, returns $500 to $1500 per week. Roulette, poker roll, miniature bowling wheel, horse races, etc., fully stocked for season. ½ interest, $7500 handles. Terms. Owner called away this week. See Lieut. Rieseberg, Balboa Pavilion, Balboa.[76]

Harry did not mention in the advertisement that Balboa Pavilion was in disrepair and in danger of crumbling into the bay at that time. The wooden pilings supporting the structure had begun to rot and disintegrate. Art Gronsky bought the Pavilion in 1948 or 1949 with ideas about renovation, but there were rumors that it might be torn down. Gronsky reinforced the foundation with concrete pilings and re-opened it in 1949, but by then, the amusement center had been vacated and replaced by another tenant.

Owner Called Away?

A curious note in the ad is where Harry said, "owner called away this week." What exactly did he mean? There is no indication in any of the records found that he was *actually* called away on any business. Was it simply a ploy to try and get a quick sale before the Balboa Pavilion fell into the bay, or is something unknown to

Chapter 9. The Business of Being Harry

Balboa Pavilion, 1950s, location for Harry's amusements concession (photograph from Balboa Island Museum).

us these many years later? *Something* was pulling him away from attention to his side business, however. Events around him began to re-ignite the energy Harry once had about his work. As fishermen know, putting more bait in the water increases their chances of catching a fish. Harry's efforts to flood the market with stories and articles and to promote them endlessly appear to have led to something.

He was "called away" by an active interest in producing a film based on one of his stories. Harry Rieseberg was finally about to get into the movie business.

Chapter 10

Movie Time

> *Any man who can unselfconsciously refer to himself*
> *as the greatest living anything*
> *sounds like a good guy to stay away from.*
> —Reviewer for SEA OF TREASURE

Harry was right in the middle of Hollywood and had no success. Even with family and friends in the movie business he had trouble getting an inside track. Rieseberg's harangue of his agent in New York, John Gainfort, at the Pauker agency, about them being too far away from the movie business in Los Angeles to represent him seemed misguided. It was a contact from the East Coast who began to show a glimmer of interest in one of Harry's stories for movie production.

In November 1947, Harry Klinger, the New York story editor for Twentieth Century–Fox, called Edmond Pauker to say they would like to look at the "Man of Destiny" manuscript that became Rieseberg's most recent book, *Treasure Hunter*.[1] Pauker was no longer Harry's agent, but as the industry's last contact point for Rieseberg, he continued to hear from those interested in contacting his former client. After Pauker told Harry about the interest, Rieseberg quickly wrote to his publisher at Robert M. McBride asking that a copy of the book be sent to Pauker to share with the rep from the movie studio.

At the same time, Harry told Pauker that there might be some complications. Rieseberg explained he was also working on a movie deal. Rieseberg had signed an agreement in September 1947 with a man named Michael Baker. The deal gave Baker ninety days to sell a Hollywood movie idea. Harry went out of his way to make the point that Baker was not his agent, but precisely what Baker's connection to the movie industry might have been was not made clear.

Baker's initial interaction with Harry must have made a favorable impression. Harry told Pauker that "there happens to be some real interest in that story at the Fox studio for some particular actor. However, I just cannot gather who it happens to be."[2] Baker said he had contact with an actor who was "very much enthoused (*sic*) in the story, and he actually asked for it."[3] Rieseberg thought it might be actor John Payne who was coming off what would be his career-defining role as the attorney who helped Edmund Gwenn in the movie *Miracle on 34th Street*, produced by Twentieth-Century Fox.

When Pauker passed this rumor on to Klinger, he was told that Payne was no longer under contract with Fox, and besides, "he had word from the studio that the story didn't click with anybody else there."[4] Harry could not allow an opportunity for a movie deal to pass, so he suggested another option for Pauker to propose to his Fox contact in New York. He asked Pauker, "Do you think that there is a possibility of interesting them in price and accepting as low as $5,000 for this story and volume?"[5] Pauker brought him back to reality by explaining that if the studios had no interest in the story, it would not suddenly spring up because it was cheaper to acquire. Movie interest in *Treasure Hunter* fizzled—for a time.[6]

Tell Me Again, Who Has Rights?

By the end of 1949, Harry was fifty-seven years old and had to wonder if his shot at a movie deal had passed. After his marriage into a well-connected Bakersfield family in 1944, his single-mindedness about his treasure passions seemed to cool. Thoughts of the big screen re-energized his focus but also put him in a legal briar patch. Just as Harry had been warned by his agent years prior, by having multiple representatives promoting his work, Harry invited problems due to the competing and overlapping interests. By early 1949, Harry's double-dealing set him up for legal troubles.

In early January 1949, Rieseberg signed an agent's agreement with the Mark Herstein Agency in Los Angeles.[7] Mark Herstein and Harold Cornsweet were the two principals. When Harry signed his agreement, Herstein had only recently become a literary agency; six months prior, they had only represented performing talent.[8] Herstein and Cornsweet had big ideas about combining *I Dive for Treasure* and *Treasure Hunter* into one packaged publishing option and re-printing a mass run of 500,000 copies or more.[9] Herstein was to market the book content for radio, movies, television, dramatization, newspapers, and magazines, but they also had a financial interest in any treasure salvage expeditions that might ensue. These agents were new to the Harry Rieseberg formula for prevarication and appeared to have held some belief that Rieseberg might find treasure at some time.

Herstein was also appointed as the exclusive agent to hawk Harry's latest manuscript, "Cathedral of the Sea," a story about Port Royal, to the usual markets. Their arrangement said that in the event of a sale for a movie, Rieseberg and Herstein would split the proceeds fifty-fifty. For a book publication, the agents would receive only ten percent royalties.[10] With their agreement in place, Herstein and Cornsweet went to work.

After the agreement with Herstein was in place, a movie industry report in May 1949 said that Harry had also sold rights to all his published works to a company called Tele-Radio Inc. This was the same arrangement he had made with Herstein only four months prior. James Schwartz of Tele-Radio had recently acquired the movie rights to the story of Pancho Villa and had all the right connections in the industry. The article in *Variety* announcing the partnership with Rieseberg reported that Tele-Radio had already been in contact with Humphrey Bogart about starring in a radio dramatization based on a series of Harry's stories.[11] Harry had described his "radio idea programs" to Edmond Pauker eighteen months earlier. Harry had pitched his programs and gotten at least a minimal response, but he complained that "each (studio) seems to want to hold it until God or someone else comes along and they have me tied up for it."[12]

Could Harry Even Sell Movie Rights?

Rieseberg seemed to sense something big was about to break, even if he was unsure what it was, where it might be, or with whom. How he managed to entangle all the rights he was putting in the hands of multiple agents is a product of his aggressive promotion. The result of his actions was clear, however. He was inviting a lawsuit from one or more parties. Harry recognized he was getting into a tight situation and contacted his former agent, Edmond Pauker, for advice. He explained to Pauker that three movie studios were negotiating for rights to his book—a man named Edward Nassour with a new studio, General Service Studios, and Paramount Pictures were expressing interest.[13]

At what turned out to be the last minute in all the pending negotiations, Harry wrote Dodd, Mead asking for a copy of the contract he had signed to see what it may require of him should there be a sale of his work to produce a movie. He not only wanted to be reminded what obligations he had about film, radio, and television rights, he wanted to know if they could be waived by Dodd, Mead so he could make a new deal.[14] In the letter to Dodd, Mead, Harry went into a detailed, somewhat convoluted discussion about the reasons for his request, focusing on how any movie would boost sales of the two books now handled by Dodd, Mead. His publisher was more than happy to allow that waiver. Their reading of the contract made "no provision for the publisher's participation in dramatic or television rights, and it is therefore not necessary to formally relinquish such rights" to Rieseberg.[15]

A Movie Deal with Albert Cohen

After running script ideas in front of directors, producers, and actors since he arrived in Hollywood in 1937, Harry finally got a commitment. When the *Los Angeles Times* announced on December 6, 1949, that the rights to *I Dive for Treasure* had been purchased to produce a movie, it must have been a day of celebration for Harry. Several studios reportedly considered the option, but the well-known producer Albert J. Cohen purchased the rights. Though the article said the movie would be based on Harry's book, *I Dive for Treasure*, it was his tale about the lost city of Port Royal which became the focal point of the picture.[16] Within the prior year, Cohen had produced *Unknown Island*, a movie about dinosaurs, so he had some experience with sets based on exotic places no one had seen.

The agreement between Cohen and Rieseberg had several key provisions outlining the responsibilities and benefits to each party. In exchange for being named as a technical adviser during the writing of the screenplay, Harry gave Cohen the okay to have his own writer develop the script. In exchange, Cohen agreed to publicize that the book was based on a "true and factual report" of Harry's experiences as a deep-sea diver. Cohen eased back on that statement as he got to know Harry better.[17]

Mark Herstein claimed that he was the one who had shown the work to Cohen but that it was Rieseberg who engaged in double-dealing, bypassing the agent and selling the rights directly to Cohen. This was in direct violation of their agent's agreement.[18] Cohen had the deal done with Rieseberg, but he still had to promote the idea to the studios to get financing to make a movie. In correspondence between Cohen and Rieseberg immediately after the deal was announced, Cohen told him that "any and all information that you can keep me advised about that will in any way plug I DIVE FOR TREASURE is of interest; keep sending it in to me as fast as you can get it." Cohen wanted his portfolio as complete as possible, with anything demonstrating the level of public interest in Rieseberg's story.[19]

In late December 1949, Harry received an inquiry from a television producer about the Port Royal story he had sold to Cohen. They were producing a program to be emceed by Frank Buck, the famous hunter, focusing on treasure hunts. They asked Harry about using his story, about any film he may have, and even asked if he would like to play a part in the show.[20] Harry forwarded the letter to Cohen, who quickly informed the inquiring producer that he already had an agreement with Harry for those rights and would not allow anything to interfere with the movie's production.[21]

Cohen began actively working on the production of the movie in February 1950. He met with members of the British colonial government of Jamaica to see if they could make a beneficial deal to film there.[22] By May 1950, the *Los Angeles Times* said Cohen had the movie "on his schedule."[23] However, whether Twentieth Century or United Artists would make the film was still uncertain.[24]

While Cohen was working on the movie, James Schwartz of Tele-Radio Inc. acted on his part of the agreement with Harry by producing a radio play for the *Escape* radio series on CBS. CBS had reportedly bought the option on a series of Harry's tales, but only one ever aired.[25] The March 10, 1950, segment titled "Port Royale" followed the pattern of the times with a suspenseful premise opened with the booming voice of William Conrad asking: "Tired of the everyday grind? Ever dream of a life of romantic adventure? Want to get away from it all? We bring you—ESCAPE!"[26] Harry may have been the one who needed to escape. His history of using people for his own gain and double-dealing was about to get him dragged into court.

A Friendship, a Collaboration, a Lawsuit

Hearing some of his own words on the radio must have angered the patient and tolerant Eric Strutt enough to act. As Harry's first ghostwriter and collaborator on *I*

Dive for Treasure, Strutt was already aware of the book derived from his work with Rieseberg. Strutt still considered it *his* book. He was also likely cognizant of Rieseberg's deal with Cohen since Strutt was part of the Hollywood crowd and undoubtedly an active reader of *Variety*, where Rieseberg's deals were publicized. The radio broadcast took the lid off his boiling pot of resentment. One week after the *Escape* radio episode aired in 1950, Eric Strutt sued Harry Rieseberg and his publishers, Robert M. McBride and Dodd, Mead, for violating his rights as an author of Rieseberg's book.[27]

In his filing, Strutt said that he and Harry had entered a verbal agreement around July 1939 to "exploit commercially and profitably the subject of the search for and recovery of treasure from sunken ships, through the creation and marketing of literary products and entertainment vehicles, of every type and description." They agreed to share equally in any profits. Besides the one hundred dollars Harry paid him for his book manuscript, Strutt said he had received nothing from Harry from the *I Dive for Treasure* royalties. Strutt claimed the book was a work in which his words were "inextricably intermingled" and "cunningly and shrewdly" used without his knowledge or consent. Strutt asked for damages of $50,000. Rieseberg's attorney began his response by noting that Strutt had "neglected to avail himself of any rights he might have had under the alleged oral agreement" for an "undue and unreasonable length of time." Strutt's patience and tolerance for the situation for eight years may have hurt his case.[28]

The case was set for trial on August 30, 1950, in the Superior Court of California for Los Angeles, but Strutt and Rieseberg settled their disagreement six days before the hearing. Rieseberg convinced Strutt he had received less than $1,500 in royalties from *I Dive for Treasure*, despite Harry's claims of hundreds of thousands sold. He also claimed that he had received less than $5,000 cash for selling the movie rights and that any other value would only come as deferred income from the producer's profits.

Consequently, Harry agreed to pay Strutt two hundred dollars immediately, five hundred dollars by October 18, 1950, and two hundred fifty dollars every month until $2,800 was paid. Strutt finally got his due in court, and whether he collected or not was another story. An interview with Eric Strutt's son suggested that Harry may not have met his obligations.[29] Strutt also continued to pursue Albert J. Cohen in a lawsuit. Still, in January 1951, the Los Angeles County Sheriff said rather disingenuously that he could not find the offices of Cohen Productions to serve the garnishment order. It took a full year for the judge to issue another summons, but by then the movie was in full production.

Sealing the Deal

Harry Earl Rieseberg was made for this kind of Hollywood backstage drama. With the movie deal done, it was just a matter of time until production began and the whole process could roll toward a release in theaters. His articles found a renewed proliferation in magazines and newspapers across the country. Between 1949 and 1952, almost one hundred authored works have been found by the author. Dodd, Mead and their foreign agents continued to sell Rieseberg's work into Europe via translations and serial rights. Rights were sold in Sweden, Norway, and Finland from 1950 to 1952. Spanish and Argentinian rights were sold in 1951. German rights resulted in the publication of several articles about Port Royal in the magazine *Kristal*, a German publication like *Life* magazine. Harry's reach was growing to include a broad overseas audience.

Promotion, Promotion, Promotion

Harry also wasted no time taking advantage of his association with the movie producer, Albert J. Cohen, and the fact that there was now an actual movie deal. In March 1950, when Harry traveled to New York for the *Escape* radio program, Rieseberg hoped to finally meet his former agent, Edmond Pauker, something he had never done. Pauker was not available, so that opportunity was missed. In a letter following that visit, Harry told Pauker about all the publicity he was getting. Rieseberg was featured in a four-page spread in *FOTO Magazine*, six pages in *Stag*, and "WE THE PEOPLE aired a story with myself in person on the radio and at the same time televised it too."[30] Harry added a handwritten note letting Pauker know "there's a television series brewing there in NY, which was discussed with me while there." Harry was happy to share his sudden renewal of fame.

Newspaper articles about Harry released during the early 1950s focused on two primary subjects—the underwater tractor-tank and Port Royal. Dozens of versions of the same two articles were all over the publishing landscape. Sometimes the two stories melded together. One piece in his wife's hometown of Bakersfield suggested she might make the trip to Port Royal with him so they could film the movie there.[31] Rieseberg told Cohen that the heavily illustrated article "Sunken City of Port Royal" appeared in forty-three magazines and uncounted Sunday supplements.[32]

In one NEA article, Harry claimed he had driven the non-existent underwater tank *into* the sunken city of Port Royal thirty fathoms (180 feet) down.[33] Rieseberg later claimed that his make-believe underwater tank was not just a model but a 25-ton reality. Rieseberg said the Romano diving bell was no longer Romano's but was his now because of his $48,000 expense to build it. His explanation for that stiff-kneed limp noticed by the reporters? He consistently claimed it resulted from a horrible accident during a hurricane at sea, not from a fall on a berthed schooner. Sometimes, his exaggerated efforts to sell a story turned into outlandish lies. His star turn was bringing out the worst of him.

Success Brings Success

A rash of other movies about undersea adventures was in the works while Cohen worked on Harry's film about Port Royal. This new trend followed a period where outer space and science fiction seemed to be the rage. Charles H. Schneer, head of Esskay Productions, was also interested in Harry's stories for his own movie. Their discussions reached the point of an agreement proposed by Harry that would essentially give Schneer the same rights to his work as he had already sold to Cohen. Since the Cohen deal was already in place, Schneer would have had to wait until after July 15, 1952, for distribution. Harry had apparently cleared the offer with Cohen and communicated about it with him. No deal was made, and Schneer instead released *It Came from Beneath the Sea* in 1955 with a story about a giant octopus that attacked the Golden Gate Bridge. Octopi seemed to be everywhere.

Attracting wealthy investors had always been Harry's goal, but the reality of those efforts constantly fell short. Harry went to the opposite end of the financial spectrum to hedge his bets to offer an item for one dollar that anyone with the treasure bug could afford. Rumpus room walls were about the only place where Harry's maps were useful. Harry's partner and illustrator, Edwin A. Hird, Jr., would never know whether the letters he would open might contain a dollar bill or an offer from one of those moneyed investors Harry sought with nothing to lose.[34] It would take a lot of one-dollar maps to gain any rewards.

So Many Scripts

When Harry Rieseberg made his movie deal with Albert J. Cohen, Cohen was operating as an independent producer. Cohen had worked at Universal in the early 1930s and was an associate producer at Republic Pictures for eight years in the 1940s. When he connected with Harry, Cohen independently wrote and produced his own movies. With this project, Cohen began working more actively and directly for Universal Studios again.

It was the job of Cohen's scriptwriters to start with the primary setting of Harry's tale about Port Royal and create both the storylines and the drama needed for movie audiences, adding that "boy/girl interest" Rieseberg thought was needed. Before finally arriving at the finished product, multiple iterations of the script and more than a handful of writers were involved. Changes to the script continued even after the director started shooting.[35] In the end, other than the setting of the pirate city of Port Royal and the notion of treasure, there was little in the script that could be directly attributed to anything Rieseberg had written.

The first story work-up for Cohen on this project was done by Ray Buffum in April 1950, not long after Cohen signed the agreement with Rieseberg.[36] Buffum developed the initial story using the working title "I Dive for Treasure," and the script identified him as the writer of the original story. Curiously, below the title on the typed script, someone had crossed out the line where it said the screenplay was based on the published work of Harry Rieseberg.

Buffum wrote a twenty-three-page, first-person account that used scenes and phrases from Rieseberg's book woven into six primary characters who came together to look for the sunken city. Elements of Buffum's treatment remained in future scripts—a crusty ex–Navy diver, two women who received attention and gave off sexual energy, and a fight with an octopus.

The second version of the evolving movie script by Ray Buffum was titled "Sunken City, an original story and adaptation," with a fully developed screenplay by Jack Harvey.[37] The credit line, "Based Upon Best Selling Novel 'I Dive for Treasure' by Lt. Harry Rieseberg," was not typed on the cover but written in heavy pen as an afterthought at some point. The third script, dated June 11, 1951, was authored by Ramon Romero. Though Romero was involved in the earliest version of the screenplay, other writers moved to prominence as the project developed, leading Romero to file grievance against Universal Pictures to require they credit both him and Jack Harvey equally with the original story and screenplay. There was an undisclosed money payment, and Romero's name ultimately appeared in the movie credits.[38]

As the drafts and revisions continued, other names were added to the work, though not to the final credits in the movie. The remaining versions include a revised first draft dated September 13, 1951, and a second draft for continuity dated November 17, 1951, credited to Jack Harvey. A copy of the "Final Shooting Script" was provided to actress Peggy Dow in late December 1951. That version credited the screenplay to Jack Harvey with additional dialogue by Don McGuire.[39] Establishing credits for such a work are more complicated and critical than it might appear to those of us in the audience.

Legal Loose Ends

During Cohen's efforts to secure a studio partner, Harry realized that his earlier agreement with the Mark Herstein agency left him in a precarious legal position. On December 26, 1950, Rieseberg tried to extricate himself from that commitment to sharing his profits when he sent Herstein and Cornsweet a modification to their original agreement. This was the same approach he had so clumsily and vehemently tried with John Gainfort at the Pauker Agency. In the letter, he sought to terminate his agreement with them for "any and all" of his work other than *I Dive for Treasure*, leaving it the only work covered by their agreement going forward.[40] Harry took that further and completely terminated their contract on February 17, 1951. In the letter influenced by legal counsel, Rieseberg told them they had the rights for "more than a reasonable period of time without any sale or financial result" and that their agreement was void.[41] Herstein and Cornsweet were not happy about that.

While Rieseberg worked to get his legal entanglements cleared up, Cohen continued to pitch the movie to studio executives. The producer kept a steady stream of letters going to Universal, letting them know that this project already had a presence in the market with magazine stories and newspaper articles. In a letter to Edward Muhl at Universal on May 14, 1951, Cohen told him that Harry's Port Royal story had already appeared in forty-three magazines and Sunday supplements.[42] Harry was certainly doing his part to keep Cohen fully loaded with information about his work and his standing in the media. He reminded Cohen of the 120,000 copies of *I Dive for Treasure* that appeared as an Armed Forces Edition and the multiple foreign language printings arranged by Dodd, Mead.

Cohen applied all the leverage he could to Hollywood studio executives and continued to look for an investor to take on the project. In July 1951, Cohen pitched Rieseberg's movie to Henry (Hank) Spitz. Spitz had directed and produced dozens of films, most recently for RKO Pictures. Cohen wrote to Spitz in Mexico City to offer him the rights to the screenplay and the book for $20,000, telling Spitz that "the book has had tremendous publicity, as you well know, and the entire setup is an extremely commercial one, in my opinion."[43]

Securing a Movie Title

The first documented event indicating Universal Pictures' eventual acceptance of the project was in June 1951 when they registered the movie's name, *City Beneath the Sea*.[44] Only a few months later, however, a *Los Angeles Times* article mentioned that American Pictures Corporation was getting underway on a movie with the same name.[45] It was not until February 1952, when Cohen's production was getting closer, that the two companies seemed to discover the conflict. American Pictures planned to begin production in March, with Cohen not slated until late April or early May.[46]

It turned out that not only were the two movie titles the same, but their focus on Port Royal was as well. American Pictures first tried "Port Royal" as a title, but William Cagney Productions already took that, so they went to "City Beneath the Sea" and discovered Universal's claim. As a third attempt, they sought "Sunken City," but that was also under wraps by Universal.

Port Sinister was the name that finally stuck for the other production.[47] As it turned out, words like "sunken" and "beneath" were not entirely appropriate for the script treatment American Pictures had in mind. As the second movie about Port Royal to be released in 1953, *Port Sinister* had a bit of a twist. An explorer led an expedition to Port Royal, not for an underwater treasure hunt, but to wait for it to rise to the surface following a volcanic eruption. There was a hurricane, the hero parachuted from a plane, and there were giant crabs and lava-crusted quicksand—content that made for a fine Saturday afternoon matinee.

Casting and Filming

Albert Cohen's production for Universal-International began in earnest in February 1952. Oscar "Budd" Boetticher (pronounced bet'-i-ker) was essentially the next director available at Universal and was assigned to the project on February 26. Boetticher directed several "B" movies that became classics, to the point that his work is sometimes mentioned in the same sentence as the richly talented John Ford.[48]

After many script revisions, the writers finalized the adventure, the suspense, and, as Harry said, "the boy/girl interest" as part of the script. The movie's basic story is based on two divers who go to Port Royal on a contract salvage job for an insurance company. One million dollars of gold are under the surface, and they stand to make $25,000 if they successfully bring it up. The two manly men quickly meet an attractive female ship owner who agrees to take them to the dive site. On one night a song, a relationship, and a fight all break out at a bar, where a second female lead enters the story. One of the divers double-crosses the other and tries to recover all the gold for himself in a dirty deal with the insurance representative. When locals discover someone is diving near the sunken city they consider sacred, there are voodoo dances and drums. If that were not enough, an earthquake causes a tsunami, and the renegade diver is trapped below the surface, only to be rescued by his former partner. Both men ended up with a girl, but not the treasure. As the movie ended, they received an offer for one more attempt at the gold and joked about underwater honeymoons.

The Cast

After some indecision and rescheduling, Robert Ryan was cast in the lead role of Brad Carlton. Ryan would squeeze this film between *The Texas Man* and *The Naked Spur* for MGM.

The nineteen-year-old Suzan Ball was signed next to play a character who operates a local nightclub named The Rum Pot. The PR mythmakers in Hollywood liked to say she had been discovered when she won a cake-baking contest, but the actress said, "I can't even do it with those ready mixes."[49] She had only minor or uncredited roles before *City Beneath the Sea*. Her role as Venita (aka Mary Lou Beetle) included a vocal performance, "Handle with Care."

It took another two weeks to sign the second male lead for the film, Anthony Quinn. He had just finished filming *Against All Flags* and was appearing as Marlon Brando's brother in *Viva Zapata!* Quinn's characters tended toward the heavies, but in this movie, he played a character who got the girl … and not just in character.

The roles played by Quinn and Suzan Ball were love interests in the film, but that also played out in real life. During the shooting on Catalina Island, Suzan Ball fell in love with Quinn, and they had an affair that continued for almost a year even though Quinn was married at the time. Their co-starring roles continued with their next movie, *East of Sumatra*, directed again by Boetticher.[50]

Mala Powers was the final female lead cast in the role of Terry McBride, a character who operates a banana boat inherited from her father. The twenty-one-year-old Powers had received much acclaim for her role as Roxanne in the 1950 release of *Cyrano de Bergerac*. She had been working in radio since age sixteen, had a series of notable roles, and appeared in four movies in four months for Howard Hughes.

Czech actor Karel Stepanek, Hawaiian Hilo Hattie, and African American athlete and actor Woody Strode rounded out the key players. Boetticher had already directed three movies for Universal by March 1952, and once his directorial contract for another year at Universal was finalized, filming was ready to begin.

Filming Begins

Filming finally began on March 31, after Boetticher finished his eleventh-hour negotiations with Universal. He had been working non-stop, making nine movies in only two years. In a later interview, Boetticher said, "I'd finish a film on a Thursday or Friday and begin on another the next Tuesday or Wednesday." He would have only a weekend to read the next script and said, "That's how I made *City Beneath the Sea*."[51]

While studio executives crowed about the efficient and effective operation of the studio in turning out so many films, Director Boetticher spared little in his disdain toward their methods. Boetticher disliked Universal's mechanical approach to moviemaking and ridiculed the Rieseberg-sourced story Universal Pictures gave him to direct. Boetticher said he only took it on because he had been promised Anthony Quinn, his favorite actor. It did not take the director long to change the script. "Well, at page 102, I put down the manuscript and I went out with my secretary to have a cup of coffee and I said to her, "My God, it's terrible. At the rate things are going I'm prepared to bet that on page 125 there'll be a giant squid." I was wrong it was on page 127."[52] Boetticher had only a few days to get the squid out of the script. At the same time, he added some "gags" at the beginning and altered the ending. When reading the script, Boetticher also realized early on that

Movie Publicity Poster for *City Beneath the Sea* (1953), Universal-International Pictures (photograph used with permission, PhotofestNYC).

the earthquake scene where Port Royal was toppled was not depicted realistically and that buildings would not remain standing in a natural underwater earthquake. Boetticher called Cal Tech to ask what would be left of an underwater city in the event of an earthquake. They told him nothing would be left at all. Boetticher said that knowledge "kind of saved the picture."[53]

With a projected budget of $350,000, the movie got underway in early April, filming in Hollywood and on Catalina Island off the coast of California. A large water tank was built on the set for the ocean scenes, but many of the underwater sequences were not underwater at all. Filming the submerged sequences was more challenging for the special effects team than for the actors, who did not even get wet. The actors donned diving suits and walked on foam rubber in front of a studio set, giving the appearance of walking underwater. Using slow-motion filming, special effects artists added the appearance of water and hand-painted the bubbles from the diving gear.[54]

The movie's climax was an underwater earthquake where Anthony Quinn's character became trapped while diving in a hard-hat suit and was rescued by Robert Ryan. To simulate the slow movement of divers underwater, Boetticher shot the 90-second scene with three Technicolor cameras at two and one-half times the normal film speed. He cranked out 1,012 feet of film at 11.25 feet per second. At fifty-five cents a foot, Boetticher said he set a new cost record spending $556.87 on the segment for film negatives alone. That number would barely suffice for coffee and donuts in today's Hollywood.

The set for the underwater scenes was called the "world's first plastic city" when it was built for the set. The full-scale buildings filled a 20,000-square-foot sound stage. Set designers built it from blocks made of Pyrocel, a "porous chemical substance that rises like bread when mixed," to create stone-like blocks weighing only fifty to sixty pounds.[55] The nineteen-second shot took four days to prepare. Parts of the simulated sea floor appeared to fissure because of rollers mounted under the set. Steam jets and dry ice created a visual simulation of a pressure release. Helium-filled balloons held strands of seaweed aloft, and piano wires were used to topple the blocks during the simulated earthquake.[56]

The technical aspects of a scene where sets are destroyed like this were no small feat. It took a cadre of ninety-four craft and technical people to build the set, prepare the artwork, and ultimately destroy their work. The whole set would have to be rebuilt if things did not go well on the first take. On Boetticher's signal, hydraulic jacks shook the castle-like buildings, and movable sections of the set split apart. The final result has a rather amateurish effect, but the complexity of the shooting, given 1950s technology, was impressive.[57]

The actors still had somewhat strenuous roles to endure. Though never actually underwater, Ryan and Quinn had to don hard-hat diving gear for some of their scenes. Hedda Hopper, a gossip columnist of the time, noted that Ryan lost fifteen pounds during the movie's filming. Mala Powers had a different complication. Since she played the boat captain, she was wetted down occasionally to get her "in character." The sweater she wore kept shrinking, so to avoid possible censorship problems, the studio had her change to a pre-shrunk t-shirt.[58]

Filming Is Over in a Month

Filming was completed by May 1952, and the project went into post-production for editing and special effects. The technology of the movie industry was changing as competition with television for audiences began to increase. Technicolor movies were relatively new to the scene but widening in scope. Universal budgeted the release of thirty-six top-budget films for the fiscal year 1952–53, and a record twenty-six of them, including *City Beneath the Sea*, were in Technicolor.

All the studios, particularly the frugal Universal Pictures, tried to keep movie sets for use in subsequent productions. Whether by design or spite, Boetticher destroyed or rendered unusable four of the five primary sets used for *City Beneath the Sea*. Ryan and Quinn drove a British sports car into carts of bananas on a waterfront street scene. The Rum Pot nightclub, where Venita was the torch singer, was broken to pieces over four days of stunt performers duking it out with the two main characters. The earthquake scene crumpled 20,000 square feet of the underwater city.[59] Boetticher was done. Now it was time for the publicists and lawyers to get to work.

Movie Publicity Begins

With underwater bubbles added and music recorded, *City Beneath the Sea* was ready for release. The copyright was issued on January 2, 1953, so it was time for the publicity to begin. Universal had high hopes for the film and put significant effort into making a splash with its marketing. Not only was the movie expected to draw attention due to the big-name stars and the fact that it was in Technicolor, but it also generated press based on the advertising campaign. *Variety* magazine noted that Universal-International would, for the first time, "combine the use of television, radio, and newspapers for a three-way territorial saturation ad campaign," combining the ads simultaneously with movie openings and appearances by the stars. The world premiere was to be in Cleveland on February 5, followed by Detroit, Boston, and San Francisco.[60]

The publicity hounds found every opportunity to promote the film. Three of the principals, perhaps the most available ones unable to say no, were sent on a three-week promotional tour.[61] Suzan Ball, the statuesque young actress, was on hand and made multiple appearances leading up to the release. Frank Westmore, head of Universal's make-up department, also made department store appearances trading on his good looks and salesmanship.[62] Right there with them was Lieutenant Harry Rieseberg.

By Monday, February 16, the trio was in Boston for another round of local radio, newspaper, and television duties. Harry held a Boston audience of crusty reporters attentive for an event at the Ritz Hotel when he described his pretend adventures. Harry's presence and the prospect of his vast knowledge leading to instant riches drew "a steady stream of divers and other rovers who have hunted treasure themselves, or who want to share their dreams with a man who has stood on the deck of a sunken galleon and brought up bags of gold and silver." At least he convinced his audience of that.[63]

The Movie Premieres

When the movie finally premiered on February 5, 1953, Suzan Ball had endured a grueling schedule. A radio station held a treasure hunt, doling out clues during the week, and she appeared as a guest on local TV and radio to promote it. The ad for the premiere said she would "personally greet each and every one" who came to the movie that evening.[64] There would be no break for Ball, Westmore, and Rieseberg. On Tuesday, February 10, a photo in the *Detroit Free Press* showed them all in the lobby of the Palms Theater for a "star-author autograph party."[65] On Friday, February 13, Suzan Ball appeared at a department store in Lansing in advance of the movie showing at the Gladmer Theater on the 14th.[66] Rieseberg was alone in Saginaw on the 15th, displaying his "fame and fortune and a leg which does not bend at the knee" to convince the public of his stories.[67]

The movie openings shifted to the West Coast with a scheduled premiere in Los Angeles at the Four Star, Hawaii, and Lowe's State theaters on March 6.[68] In San Francisco, the studios used a young, attractive starlet to substitute for Suzan Ball. The *San Francisco News* promoted the movie with some staged photos of Harry in a watch cap and wool coat, with a man in a diving suit posing with a Miss USA runner-up, Ruth Hampton, aboard a barge.[69]

Harry was clearly not the center of attention in the movie tour, so he made efforts to talk about himself occasionally with reporters. When he arrived in Seattle in early March, Rieseberg increased the attention on himself to the point that his visit got as much coverage in the newspaper as Mickey Rooney's appearance during the same time. A photo on March 4 showed Harry displaying what he reported to be gold bars worth $60,000, which he carried with him "wherever he goes as though they were good-luck trinkets."[70] The sample of his treasure looked like movie props. The story Harry promoted this time was that he had found the gold bars and coins he displayed in 1936 in the wreck of the *Santa Paula*, a year when he was either in the hospital or in rehab for his broken leg. When asked the obvious question of why he had not turned the gold into cash in the last seventeen years, he told them he did not need the money because he had made enough money from his books, articles, and salvage that he could "keep the gold just as I found it."[71] It is unclear if that story worked for him, but he continued that version after the movie's promotion. He used the Universal Studios press photo of the same fake gold bars as illustrations in his later books and articles.[72]

When Harry returned home from the tour and was profiled by his wife's

Full house for Kansas City, Kansas premier of *City Beneath the Sea* at the Fox Granada Theater; June 19, 1953. The Granada was a "first run" theater (photograph by James E.E. Post, Theater Manager, courtesy his son, Jim Post).

hometown newspaper, the *Bakersfield Californian*, he engaged in some Rieseberg mathematical inflation. Harry said he had been on the road for six weeks. Given that the tour started in Cleveland on or around February 1, the duration was closer to four weeks. On March 2, Suzan Ball was reported as having "just returned from a three-week tour for City Beneath the Sea."[73] Harry's exaggeration of the duration was only the beginning. Harry claimed that during that reported six-week time frame, he visited 136 cities. That would be twenty-two cities a week or three to four different locations each day for seven days a week. This seems impossible, or at least wildly unlikely. He goes on to say that during his forty-two-day run, he did 169 radio broadcasts, 74 television appearances, and 80 press conferences.[74] No doubt Harry was busy and tired from the constant promotion, but the schedule he floated fails the tests of simple, mathematical truth.

The Reviews Are In

With the publicity tour over and the movie opening at theaters around the county, it was time for the studio to get feedback from the public about whether the movie was a success. *Variety* magazine previewed the movie before its release and published its review on February 4.

High romance of the pulp-fiction variety is niftily shaped in "City Beneath the Sea" to strike audience fancy in the action and general market. In addition to the excellently handled regular adventure ingredients, the film stages an undersea "earthquake" in Technicolor as a capper to the derring-do yarn laid in the West Indies.[75]

Other reviews followed, but with fewer nice things to say.

Its title has a more imaginative connotation than the film justifies [Los Angeles Times].[76]

… is about as banal and uninspired as they come. The entire enterprise, including a fairly ambitious finale, give the impression of having been slung together during lunch time [New York Times].[77]

Despite the reviews, audiences flocked to the theaters. Press reports of the movie's box office success had it in the top tier of releases during that time, regardless of the reviews. In San Francisco's opening at the Orpheum the first week of March, the movie sold $12,000 worth of tickets in a week.[78] The following week in Los Angeles at Loew's State theater, the box office take was $27,000.[79] With ticket prices in 1953 hovering around fifty cents, that is a lot of movie-goers. Despite bad weather impacting theatergoers, the movie sold $7,000 in the first two days and $21,000 in the first five days at the State Theater in New York, finishing the week with $27,000. By the end of April, *City Beneath the Sea* held its own at number twelve in the *Variety* "Golden Dozen" for that period.[80]

The Movie Opens; Call in the Lawyers

No sooner had filming finished than two different legal actions were initiated. One was to tidy up a bit, and the other was to ensure proper credit was given. Harry Rieseberg sold all rights to *I Dive for Treasure*, other than the right to publish the book, to Universal Pictures Company Inc. On July 31, 1952, Harry sent a legal document to Dodd, Mead to secure a quitclaim and to assign their rights to Universal.[81] Copyrights to the work had been reserved by McBride on May 8, 1942, and transferred to Dodd, Mead on June 29, 1948, when they acquired McBride's assets and liabilities. The agreement kept the publication rights with Dodd, Mead but assigned everything else to Universal.

The lawsuit filed by Harry's former agents, Herstein and Cornsweet, was not just about the rights to the story, but about the compensation. The legal action forced an accounting for money paid to Rieseberg for his story—a percentage they believed should go to them. The lawsuit also alleged that Cohen and Universal Pictures knew about the arrangement between Herstein and Rieseberg and that all the parties "conspired to defraud plaintiffs by failing to recognize the agreement between the plaintiffs and the defendants, Harry E. Rieseberg and Albert J. Cohen." The plaintiffs' claims about Harry's avoidance of paying some of his share of the proceeds to his able agents sounded precisely like the double-dealing he was accused of by Eric Strutt. To add insult to injury, Mark Herstein had loaned Harry four hundred dollars and was not repaid. Harry's methods were repeating themselves.[82]

When Rieseberg tried to cancel his relationship with Herstein and Cornsweet in February 1951, he had already done the deal with Cohen and was only trying to cover his tracks. Cohen said he discovered Harry's story about Port Royal in *Fate* magazine in the spring of 1951 after Harry unilaterally canceled his contract with Herstein, which was not the case.[83] A December 1949 article in the *Los Angeles Times* had already announced Cohen's deal with Rieseberg well before Harry canceled his contract.[84]

In an initial ruling, the judge dismissed the case against Universal Pictures on January 25, 1954. However, he also allowed time for the plaintiffs to make an amended complaint and they did so in March. Using financial information provided to the agents, they updated their allegation to claim that Rieseberg received $8,000 from Cohen for the rights to his work and that Herstein and Cornsweet were owed $4,000.

A bench trial with no jury was finally set for February 18, 1955, but the trial never happened. After two years and just a few days before the trial, Rieseberg settled with Herstein and Cornsweet. Harry agreed to pay them the amount of $1,081.75, starting with a deposit of $250 immediately and $50 per month after that until the total amount was paid. Only when the full amount was paid would the lawsuit be dismissed. It took Harry eighteen months to pay out the cost. The case was finally dismissed on July 30, 1956.

While still giddy with his success in the movie business, in 1953, Rieseberg began to somewhat prematurely boast that he was "busy preparing the script for my second treasure motion picture to be titled 'PORT ROYALE' which would be in 3-D. Regardless of his plans, Harry's first movie would be his last."[85]

Chapter 11

Paradise

> *Fiction writers have not been slow to seize upon such fragments of truth as there may have been in many of these tales [of treasure] to work them into a form of romance which will never lose its appeal to the public.*
> —Vaughn Greene[1]

Following the release of *City Beneath the Sea* in 1953, Harry Rieseberg's notoriety was at an all-time high. He had toured the country with a Hollywood starlet supporting the film, had his photo taken with Anthony Quinn, and achieved a long-sought goal to elevate one of his stories to the big screen. Rieseberg always looked for ways to extend his ability to make money from his well-polished reputation and his embellished narratives. After a climactic career accomplishment, he was poised to capitalize on his progress however he could.

In 1956, with the movie complete and his legal troubles behind him, Valentine and Harry moved far away from Los Angeles to a trailer park in Paradise, California, seven hours north of Los Angeles. Their new home was in the Acres of Paradise trailer park, a wooded development overlooking West Branch Canyon.[2] Harry was ready to retire to a life of prolific writing in a more relaxing setting.

Rieseberg's writing habits changed with the scenery. For years, his routine had been to write late at night, typing until dawn to benefit from uninterrupted quiet. The trailer park where he last lived in Los Angeles was crammed with mobile homes too close for much privacy. With the move to Paradise, he took up a daytime spot in front of the trailer's picture window where peace and quiet were more readily available. In a letter to one of his agents, Harry said he was happy to be "away from smog, traffic, make-believe and the breeding of defense worker's brats!"[3] Harry minced no words in his disdain for the big city, including continuing his racial slurs and derogatory comments, particularly toward African Americans. Harry's correspondence with another friend was more unfettered about why he moved to Paradise. Harry said there were no "demonstrations, rapes, property take-over, agitators and other like menaces." Using a racially derogatory label, he also added there were no black people because "we have none and take none among the 20,000 inhabitants that make up this community."[4] His former role in the Ku Klux Klan was more than just being a paid recruiter. It was better for everyone that Harry Rieseberg was away from other people.

Harry and Val's home in Paradise, California (photograph provided to author by Al Mikalow).

With Harry, There Was Always More

Several aspects of Harry Rieseberg's personality and career stand out clearly throughout his life. He was a relentless self-promoter, a prodigious writer, and an unapologetic defender of his narratives. He was also a man who never stopped looking ahead. After his initial book in 1942, *I Dive for Treasure*, and the follow-on, *Treasure Hunter*, was released in 1945, it was another ten years before Harry sought to publish more books. He found that publishing short articles was more lucrative and had a quicker payoff. He could also use them repeatedly, relatively unchanged, in many different publications. In the interim, *I Dive for Treasure* was translated into French, German, Swedish, Finnish, Italian, Norwegian, Spanish, and Dutch between 1948 and 1957. On more than one occasion, Harry accepted a lump sum payment of $300 as a royalty for printing 1,500 additional copies of the work.[5]

In 1955 a small book for an audience of nine to fourteen-year-old boys, *Diving for Sunken Treasure,* appeared with Harry's name as the author, but he probably had little direct involvement. A second youth volume the same year for readers twelve and up, *My Compass Points to Treasure*, was also tossed into the mix, and both were filled with a retelling of his familiar stories and faux adventures. The next round of books Rieseberg published was a compilation of magazine articles reusing material from *I Dive for Treasure*. A manuscript he submitted to his publishers in 1956 had already seen the light of day in a series of nine articles in *Rudder* magazine beginning in July 1954. The articles were titled "Sea of Treasure," just like a book he submitted to Bobbs-Merrill publishing ten years later.[6]

Rieseberg repeated and reinforced the same series of exaggerations and false claims that had gotten him through his writing career. Article one had an underwater photo clearly from the recent movie, but Harry said it was of himself wearing diving gear. He declared he had just taken his twelfth expedition in search of the wreck of *El Capitan* when there is no evidence a sixty-two-year-old Harry *ever* went to sea in search of treasure, and certainly not after breaking his leg. A photo of the *Constellation,* which Harry claimed was used for that venture, added credibility unless the reader knew it was at the bottom of a Bahamian lagoon. Harry tried to avoid questions by labeling photos of the *Constellation* as the *Cholita* but continued using the same 1933 photo for years after its sinking. In the fourth article, Harry repeated his claims of being attacked by a giant octopus and visiting Port Royal. Harry of the He-Man Adventures escaped cannibals in Trinidad, was kidnapped by murderous thieves, and went shark fishing. He did not relent from the narrative he began in 1937 when he left the hospital in Galveston. And he never would.

Harry tried to publish more books during the 1950s, but at least one publisher turned away a submission based on brutal comments by reviewers. A commentator for the Bobbs-Merrill Company, publishers of a wide variety of books, wrote some scathing remarks about two of Harry's submissions. Whether Harry was privy to the details of their comments is unknown, but the reviewer had his own unique way of expressing his displeasure with the work. When this work was submitted to Bobbs-Merrill in 1956, it was tentatively titled *Sea of Treasure*, a book title which later saw print in 1966. The reviewer went on for two pages about the problems with Harry's work.

> Lieutenant Rieseberg, thrilled to death to be in the know, catalogs various cargoes of treasure which he believes to be lying at the bottom of American coastal waters. He has made no move to furnish documentation for his statements, and I have a feeling he would be offended to be asked for it.[7]

The reviewer could not know how correct he was about Rieseberg's being offended if questioned, never giving in to the fact that his adventures were untrue. A second reviewer called Harry's work "a gaspy little narrative" in which "the author fairly gurgles as he describes the sunken ships and their vast treasures." His summary was that Harry's work was "Adventure stuff, very badly written."[8]

During Harry's promotional stops for the movie in Detroit and Cleveland in May 1953, he told reporters that in addition to *City Beneath the Sea*, Universal-International had also bought two other stories of his to turn into movies. One of those was to be titled "Seascape." The "Seascape" manuscript was a fictional work Harry thought could be a movie with comedians playing the lead acting roles.[9] The difference in this work was that it was not his. The story belonged to Pauline Smith of

Sunland, California. Based on the tone of two 1953 letters between Smith and Rieseberg, she and Harry had been on familiar terms for some time. Smith authored an article about Harry for *PIC* magazine, "He Walks with Davey Jones," which appeared in June 1954.[10] In a letter to Rieseberg in August 1953, Smith told Harry that "Seascape" had not been accepted by a publisher, and she chalked it up to the nature of the business.[11] A second letter to Harry in December 1953 alluded to the fact that Harry had asked for the "Seascape" manuscript. Smith told Harry she had abandoned the project after her agent, Jacques Chambrun, told her it was poorly written, and that Harry could do anything he liked with it.[12] Harry tried out the story idea with an agent but got nowhere with it either.

Always Another Agent

Jacques Chambrun, whom Pauline Smith said rejected "Seascape," was a literary agent Smith and Rieseberg shared. Chambrun was most often characterized as a fraud who charged excessive fees and reportedly stole money from his clients. At one time, he had several famous clients but gradually lost them due to his unscrupulous methods. Harry stuck with him through at least 1960.[13]

Dr. Edmond Pauker had stopped being Harry's agent many years prior but was still Harry's connection to Dodd, Mead publishing. Dodd, Mead wrote Pauker to request permission to print another edition of *I Dive for Treasure*, offering three hundred dollars' royalty for 1,500 copies.[14] When there was no reply after six weeks, Dodd, Mead repeated their request by letter on November 16, 1959.[15] A December 12 letter from Harry to Pauker asking about royalties he was expecting in November also went unanswered. A note explained the reason. Pauker became so gravely ill in 1959 that he could not return to his long-held business and died three years later. When Edmond Pauker realized his illness was so severe that he would not recover, he had the foresight to assign power of attorney to manage the business to his attorney, David N. Fields, and hired Elisabeth Marton of the Martonplay Agency to manage the remaining company business.

Marton's letters to Dodd, Mead, and to Rieseberg in December 1959 demonstrated her active engagement in resolving Harry's question about missed royalties. She asked the demanding author for "a little patience now, as I have to try and disentangle matters, in great part unknown to me."[16] By the following month, she got Harry his three-hundred dollars for the 1,500-volume print run. Marton also learned from Dodd, Mead that the $104.31 due Harry for the previous six months' royalties had already been paid to Pauker but not passed on to Harry. Both Fields and Marton contacted Pauker's wife about the money.[17] Perhaps because they did not know Harry Rieseberg well, they also told him that Mrs. Pauker had received the money he was due. That did not sit well with Rieseberg. His response was another example of self-centeredness and lack of empathy, which had been Rieseberg's *modus operandi* for many years.

The record does not retain Harry's letter to the widowed Mrs. Pauker. All that remains is her desperate request that Harry be paid to avoid any problems. Whether there were any pleasantries or condolences for Mrs. Pauker in Harry's letter is not known but highly unlikely. Harry apparently made clear to Mrs. Pauker that he would sue her if she did not pay him the $104.31 due. She asked for a check from the agency so she could "transfer it immediately to Mr. Rieseberg to avoid unnecessary and unpleasant actions."[18] Harry seemed to have few qualms about threatening to sue a woman who had just lost her husband.

Harry's first letter back to Marton, topped by his usual **IMMEDIATE ATTENTION** heading, gave her a quick summary of his current business and pending work. Harry recognized he had a fresh opportunity to impress. His offerings to Marton were a review of projects for which he had already tried and failed to find outlets.[19] Harry's disclosures gave her new facts about her inherited client. Marton let Harry know about Dodd, Mead's inquiry as to whether he had any new work that might interest him. The publisher had already turned down some recent submissions, so Harry was not enthusiastic about giving them another shot. Since Dodd, Mead's prior interest, Harry had published three books for a youthful audience with Henry Holt & Co. and with Samuel Gabriel and Sons. His favorite topic, Sir William Phipps, was again the subject of a 65,000-word biography. Harry sent that manuscript to another publisher, Duell, Sloane, & Pearce. He told Marton hid he did not know if they would pick it up … they did not … but expressed his confidence that "it will finally be accepted by someone."[20]

During that back-and-forth correspondence, Marton must have found time to review Harry's previous correspondence with the Pauker agency. When she read the angry and aggressive missives between Harry and John Gainfort, she better understood whom she was dealing with in Harry Rieseberg. She set the tone early in her reply to one of his letters by telling him, "Please be sure that your letters get immediate attention anyway, even without your especially calling for it from now on."[21]

Harry's letter also provided an update on how he managed his business. He told Marton that Jacques Chambrun was his present agent and that Chambrun had just been provided with the manuscript for a book titled "Treasure of the Bahama Sea." Harry sent Marton a 3,000-word condensed version so she could evaluate the basic story.[22] When Harry told the volatile Chambrun about his communication with Marton and suggested that they perhaps share a commission, Chambrun angrily returned the manuscript to Rieseberg with his chippy response of "fine, let her have it all."[23]

Always Another Business

One of Harry's long-held ideas for income generation and publicity was the concept of a floating treasure museum. While in Seattle during his movie tour, the *Seattle Times* reported that Harry was looking at an old merchant vessel as one of his money-making ideas. Harry toured the steamship *Victoria*, owned by the Alaska Steamship Co. The *Victoria* was 82 years old and converted for freight but was once a popular passenger ship. Harry said the vessel might be used for a salvage effort but could also become a floating marine museum traveling from port to port.[24] The seed of the museum idea was a carryover from the attention gained by the *Constellation* docked in Washington, D.C. The romance of a venture of that nature endured, but there was virtually no money to be made selling tickets to tour a treasure ship, even with the attention-getting Romano diving bell on deck. Built in 1870, the *Victoria* had an illustrious tenure as both a passenger ship and a cargo vessel, partly due to a solid hull. At the time of Harry's perusal, its primary advantage was its availability. By the following year it was headed toward the scrap yard.

Indications that Rieseberg was again promoting a similar idea showed up before the movie premiere, as early as 1952. For this idea, Rieseberg printed up letterhead with bold letters at the top touting "The Treasure of the Silver Fleet," saying his next expedition was potentially worth $19,000,000. The address just below was Harry's residence at the time, a mobile home and RV park. Harry pulled out all the stops in touting the alleged experience of his collaborators. At the top of the letterhead were the names of Arthur H. Trevor and Captain Charles W. Huckins, both Seattle-based divers. Huckins had worked on the recovery of the *Islander* with Carl Wiley back in 1934. When a British freighter stuck a dock near Seattle in 1939, Trevor and Huckins were consulted on possibly re-floating the vessel.[25] One of the accounts of that Alaskan salvage effort was Huckins' description of an attack by *two* giant octopi, one of which he said had fifteen-foot tentacles.[26]

Rieseberg later had to explain that Trevor was no longer part of the project. Trevor was caught siphoning off the money he raised from investors in a scheme of his own.[27] His replacement was suspect as well. The U.S. Government had indicted James E. Zoes for conspiring to violate the Defense Production Act by buying and selling oil well drilling pipe on the black market and was involved in selling securities.[28] Another member of Rieseberg's letterhead team was Charles G. Warren, the engineer who had built the model of the underwater tank Harry was promoting. The letterhead said Warren was "now constructing a submarine tractor-tank robot." Whether Mr. Warren even knew he was listed, along with his model tank, is uncertain.

Harry stuck with the romantic hook of having an incredibly beautiful four-master to lure people who needed "comfort [for] expedition personnel and the wives and friends of heavy investors in the venture." For that part of the pitch, he claimed he would use the 257-foot *Fantome*, a four-master built in 1927 for the Duke of Westminster.[29] It began life with "luxurious fittings" but had been laid up in Seattle unused for a few years, so its condition was far from ocean-ready.[30] The seaworthiness and location of the proposed vessel did not deter Harry from seeking investors by advertising in *Rudder* magazine. Harry Rieseberg made sure readers knew he was an experienced salvor, a best-selling author, and an internationally known authority. It was touted to be the first of many postwar expeditions, but there is no indication that any such excursion ever took place. In fact, while Harry was saying he would use the *Fantome* for fantastic adventures in the Caribbean, it was being sold for scrap.[31]

Harry Rieseberg and Frank Fish

In the 1940s or early 1950s, Harry formed a friendship with Frank Fish, a land-based treasure hunter from Amador City, California. Fish operated the Gold Rush Museum in a former Wells Fargo depot, where he displayed relics and artifacts found digging around old mines. Their connection probably emerged from a shared interest in magazines of Western tales and the growth in sales of metal detecting equipment for amateurs.[32] Rieseberg and Fish were kindred souls, shoring each other's tall tales. Rieseberg was certainly more business savvy, but Fish was more of a real treasure hunter. Perhaps inspired by Frank Fish and his Gold Rush Museum, Harry held on to the idea of a floating treasure museum for many years. Harry's letter to Elisabeth Marton at the Pauker agency in March of 1960 told her about the revival of his planning "for a $500,000 corporation to finance my TREASURAMA floating treasure museum to tour the United States."[33] Harry's statement sounded dramatic and immediate, but all that was happening was that a newly incorporated entity was being discussed.

Rieseberg engaged Frank Fish in the venture by getting his help as an illustrator

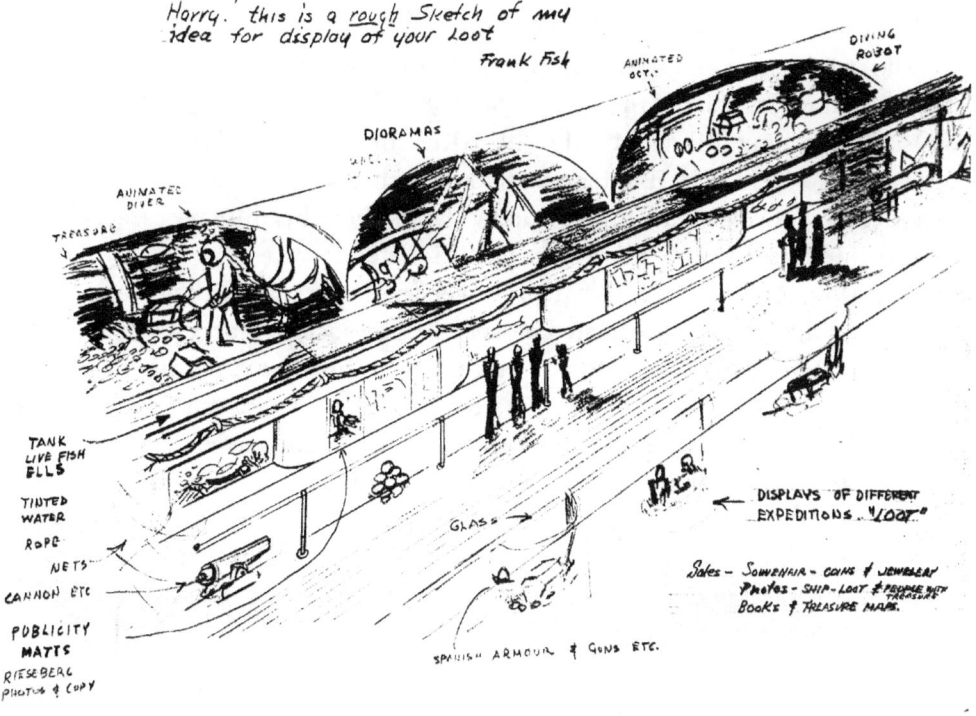

Frank Fish sketch of ideas for Treasurama museum, undated (~1960) (photograph provided to author by Al Mikalow).

for the concept. Harry's grand scheme was to have museum-like displays aboard a vessel of some significance and finance it by selling space for advertising. Harry's business plan was that the ship and the treasure museum would attract large numbers of visitors who would then see as many as fifty businesses represented on this "trade ship," which would sail from port to port. He said it would become the "first floating industrial exposition of treasure, diving, boating, and other displays ever to sail the seas as a museum."[34] This word blizzard of a description seemed an attempt to cover every possible angle for his idea.

> An idea-project for a new, different, thrilling, adventurous, and public-appealing merchandising sales promotion for TV and personal contact advertising media, for regional or otherwise promotion heretofore never available or produced in any manner.[35]

Writing business proposals was not Harry Rieseberg's forte, but he nonetheless held on to the project for over twenty years. The essence of the concept was right up his alley. One thing that Harry could be counted on to deliver was big ideas. Harry's pro forma budgets called for the sale of 1,000,000 shares of stock at one dollar per share, with 350,000 going to Rieseberg himself and 300,000 for sale to the public, with the balance in reserve. First-year capital requirements were expected to be almost $300,000. Rieseberg pitched the idea to advertising and public relations firms in San Francisco. The idea languished and lacked attention to the details it would take to start up and manage such a project.

AL MIKALOW AND THE *RIO DE JANEIRO*

Harry Rieseberg and Al Mikalow were an interesting pair. In 1950, Alfred Alexander Mikalow, Jr., started the Coastal School of Deep-Sea Diving in Oakland and ran that operation until he retired in 1985. Rieseberg said he learned to dive in the Navy during World War II but appears to have shared résumé exaggeration skills with Rieseberg. Even Mikalow made many claims about his military careers and his treasure interests that were more than a little inflated.[36]

Mikalow was thirty-five years younger than Harry, but they were brother Masons and shared racially oriented perspectives on society. Harry needed relationships with men like Mikalow to add credibility to his ideas and mine for details about their trade for his books. Even before he met Harry Rieseberg, Al Mikalow caught the treasure bug and tried for years to locate a famous wreck near the Golden Gate bridge. The National Park Service controlled access to all shipwrecks within the Golden Gate National Recreation Area. One of those is the *City of Rio de Janeiro* which sank in 1901. The vessel was a 344-foot-long iron-clad steamship initially servicing Brazil and Panama but later put into trans–Pacific service to Asia. On February 22, 1901, it sank in a dense fog as it entered San Francisco Bay, killing 128 passengers.[37]

By 1968, Mikalow and Rieseberg were upping the ante by trying to raise money from others to recover the *Rio de Janeiro*. They formed a Nevada corporation in May 1968 named Treasure Recovery Inc. and planned to sell $200,000 in stock to go after what they claimed was $2,000,000 in gold, silver, and jewels. After that recovery, they would then work offshore of Ecuador and Peru for five galleons sunk in the 1750s, information contributed by the expertise of Harry Rieseberg. According to their charter, their focus was to "engage in research, recovery, salvage, and sale of sunken cargoes and buried treasures, and to mine the bottoms of the oceans and seas and other bodies of water." Despite the permits and the prospects for selling stock to raise funds, that effort went nowhere, but it generated much press for Rieseberg and Mikalow when they were selling books.[38]

Nature Fakery and Giant Octopi

In the years between the release of the *City Beneath the Sea* in 1953 until his passing in 1970, Harry Rieseberg was a productive reseller of his work, placing articles at double the output of prior years. Harry's lifelong assertion that he was not a writer was true, up to a point. His body of work comprised about a dozen core themes that he repeatedly placed in hundreds of different publications over the years. His underwater battle with a giant octopus, and his filming of a death duel between a shark and an octopus, were propagated repeatedly. Stories about the diving robot and the underwater tank found many outlets. His focus on the treasure of the *Merida* and the sunken city of Port Royal was tried and true for decades, published in dozens of publications in essentially the same form. No matter how many times Harry trotted out the same stories and the same themes, he continued to find outlets where he could make a living.[39]

I Battled an Octopus for Treasure

One of the themes Harry relied on throughout his career was his claim to have engaged in hand-to-tentacle combat with a giant octopus on more than one occasion. He began his claims not long after he left the hospital in Galveston in 1937 and moved to Hollywood. In a 1939 *Mechanix Illustrated* magazine article, readers learned how Harry survived an encounter with a giant octopus that was guarding a chest full of gold and silver coins.[40]

The same story found its way into *I Dive for Treasure*, and various versions appeared over the years in many of his articles. One of the later versions of the story in a 1965 issue of *True Comics* magazine was the pinnacle of the romantic retelling. Harry claimed he slashed at the tentacles with his knife and resisted the need to pull on his lifeline and be brought to the surface until just before losing consciousness—again.[41] He was revived only by the shot of brandy poured down his throat, the same cure he said he gave a crew member in an earlier retelling where the crewman was the one caught in the monster's death grip. Harry relied on the octopus encounters to spice up his work from time to time, and the enthusiasm of his telling seemed enough for his readers. The facts clearly mattered less.

The creature was squeezing him to death! He gave a last, weak tug on the life-line.

Illustration from Rieseberg article in *True Comics & Adventure Stories*, Issue #1, January 1965.

Never Anger an Ichthyologist

In 1949, the world's preeminent ichthyologist had it in for Harry Rieseberg. He was passionately intent on defending octopi from the "nature faker" Rieseberg, who turned them into man-killing undersea monsters.[42] Carl Leavitt Hubbs was a Professor of Biology at the Scripps Institution of Oceanography of the University of California at La Jolla, teaching and conducting research at Scripps between 1944 and 1969. His name was assigned to "five genus and twenty-two species of fish, a genus of lichen, a species of birds, two species of mollusk, a species of crabs, three species of cave arthropods, two species of insects, three species of algae, a species of lichen, a whale, and a dried-up (Ice Age era) lake in Nevada."[43] Hubbs's credentials were unmatched in his field.

Hubbs's characterization of Rieseberg as a nature faker was not an idle use of the expression. President Theodore Roosevelt is most often attributed with popularizing the phrase in the early twentieth century by calling out writers like Jack London who misrepresented the true nature of animals, romanticizing or humanizing their behavior, turning them into something they are not. The derision of the phrase was typically directed toward people who intentionally made-up stories about the world of nature.[44]

Since the 1942 publication of *I Dive for Treasure*, the popularity of the book and Rieseberg's articles with multiple tales of giant octopi had led reporters and fellow scientists to consult Hubbs, the nation's expert on octopi. After reading the book, Hubbs concluded that it "is either pure fiction, inexcusably presented in such a way as to lead many to regard it as a documented account, or it is unmitigated fakery."[45] In November 1949, Hubbs had enough. The scholar composed a five-page, single-spaced letter he distributed to other researchers, government officials, and museum directors. He defended the octopus and excoriated Rieseberg in a zealous campaign to expose his misrepresentations.

Hubbs's critique began with a defense of the octopi. In the experience of the scientific world, they were non-aggressive creatures with a tendency toward fright and escape when challenged. He believed that any descriptions of dangerous encounters with giant octopi were a myth of the sea. Beyond a rebuttal of the aggressive behaviors Rieseberg described, Hubbs called attention to the fakery of the photos of octopi found in the book. These photos, he said, were clearly not real. One photo Rieseberg said was a 24-foot octopus appeared to be taken in an aquarium with freshwater plants and brook trout swimming nearby. The lighting and the perspective on another exaggerated the eyes in a way that made clear they were not from a living specimen. Hubbs was convinced these were photos of preserved specimens, pickled and placed in a tank to purposely deceive the reader.

Long before the photographic wizardry that can be conducted with Photoshop, Hubbs pointed out photos with double exposures, putting a diver in a place where they were not. He noted that an image of a sunken vessel had a chain draped over the edge that showed no corrosion. Plants in a photo said to be from Jamaica were of giant kelp found only on the coast of California. He discounted Rieseberg's assertions about an octopus propelling itself with water from its lungs, octopi chasing fish in open water, and many octopi hidden in the same recess in a sunken vessel. Added to the debunked dangers were the dangers of seafloor quicksand, moray eels that could break a leg with their tail, and three-foot clams from the Caribbean that could clamp a diver's foot. Hubbs noted that such clamping clams are only found in the Indo-Pacific region.

Rieseberg's relentless multiple claims were "piling improbabilities on improbabilities." Hubbs found Harry's assertion that he could see the "triangular cutting teeth with their saw edges" on a twenty-foot shark at 170 feet below the surface before killing it with one stroke of his knife, particularly unbelievable. Hubbs's sarcastic summation was that "the author's bravery was a match for his vision."

Hubbs's critique continued with questions and disbelief around almost every aspect of Rieseberg's claims. His depiction of algae growth at 170 feet below the surface, the impact of dynamite on the bottom bubble-lifting a huge schooner, the curse on treasure hoards, and Harry's accuracy in locating wrecks on the first attempt were each the target of Hubbs's refutations. Hubbs made the case that the harm Harry did by "rendering terrifying one of the most entrancingly beautiful parts of nature" should lead to a public warning of his misleading and false assertions.

In the interest of scientific accountability, Hubbs sought input on his assertions and support for a public calling-out of Rieseberg's grand fakery from a who's who of marine scientists. In November and December of 1949, Hubbs polled several colleagues and experts for their feedback: S. Stillman Berry, a marine biologist, and independent researcher who focused on cephalopods and had worked at Scripps early in his career; Charles M. Breder, Jr., who had been director of the New York Aquarium and became curator and chair of the American Museum of Natural History's department of ichthyology; and Waldo L. Schmitt worked at the United States National Museum, the Smithsonian, as the head curator of Zoology. As an affiliate of the institution where Rieseberg had once worked, Hubbs thought that the Schmitt and the Smithsonian should be actively discrediting Rieseberg's "fantastic statements."

Going to the Source

Hubbs also wrote a letter of complaint to the publisher of Harry's book, Robert M. McBride, and Company. He wanted to know if they considered the work to be fiction or not. Hubbs pushed the publisher to "give some indications in future printings as to its (the book's) real nature." If it was indeed fiction, Hubbs wanted them to declare that truth.

Dodd, Mead & Company had taken over the rights to the book by that time, and Hubbs received a reply from R.T. Bond on December 9, 1949. Bond was the secretary of Dodd, Mead at the time and was later president of the publishing house. The polite and deferential letter to Hubbs pointed out that Dodd, Mead had acquired the rights from McBride but had yet to reprint the book. They were still selling inventory from the McBride transfer. Bond was deferential in explaining that whatever McBride had done or not done, in scrutinizing the book that it was not Dodd, Mead's practice to ignore the facts. He cited multiple examples of books they had sent through editorial review, including one they had rejected based on its "questionable authenticity."

After considering Hubbs' challenges, Dodd, Mead added a disclaimer on the copyright page of *I Dive for Treasure* saying that although the book was based on Rieseberg's experiences, "certain liberties have been taken both in the text and the illustrations" to add more drama. They admitted that the words and the images diverged from the truth for the story's benefit.[46]

Reigniting His Ire

After Hubbs's initial thoughts of a direct campaign in opposition to Rieseberg's falsehoods, his polling of colleagues for support confirmed his opinions but subdued his passion. However, two separate events in the following two years fanned the flames.

Unrelated to Hubbs's criticisms, Rieseberg wrote a letter to the Scripps Institution on another matter. It is unlikely that Rieseberg ever knew anything about the discussion of him in academic circles. Evidence of Rieseberg's contact is found in a letter of reply by the acting director, Roger Revelle, that Hubbs received as a blind copy. In response to Rieseberg's unspecified request, Revelle sent a brochure about the Scripps Institution and told Rieseberg that Scripps could not "participate in any commercial venture from which an individual or company may make a private profit." Revelle, no doubt privy to Hubbs's concerns, told Harry that they would support publicity only "through the medium of legitimate news stories based entirely on factual accounts of the activities of the Institution."

An irksome mention of Rieseberg in a credible journal also appeared two years after Hubbs's original round of letters, and it rekindled Hubbs's strong feelings toward Rieseberg. Robert C. Miller was managing editor of the California Academy of Sciences, which published the journal *Pacific Discovery*. In the issue published at the end of 1951, the journal included a lengthy article by Rieseberg titled "The Story Behind Cocos Island and the 'Loot of Lima.'" This decision to publish Rieseberg in a journal for an association with which Hubbs was affiliated did not set well with him.[47]

Hubbs wrote a pointed letter to Miller about the journal's commitment to check their author's submissions for facts. Hubbs reserved additional criticism for the editor, Don Greame Kelley, in giving an outlet for Rieseberg not only with the article but in a blurb to "watch for the movie *City Beneath the Sea.*" Hubbs said the journal's treatment of Rieseberg was "a major disservice to truth." Being a man of science, Hubbs was disappointed that the journal had provided an outlet for Rieseberg.

> This sort of tommytrot is bad enough in an adventure book or a movie but surely has no place in a journal that purports to be authentic. I am amazed that it got by. You owe it to science to make some sort of correction.[48]

Miller replied with some apologies in late December 1951, but not without qualifiers. He pointed out that the Academy did not have Hubbs's background information at the time of the publication. Upon checking, Miller said they found a few minor errors of detail but that the article was interesting and held no apparent inaccuracies. He offered Hubbs an outlet for his indignation as a Letter to the Editor but was cautious in suggesting his complaints deal only with the *Pacific Discovery* article and not with Rieseberg's other work.

Hubbs waited only through the end of the holiday season in January 1952 to send a terse reply to Miller. When Hubbs's ire was struck, his letters got longer, and this two-page response showed his passion. Hubbs downplayed the impact of a letter to the editor and pressed Miller to help "squelch the complete faked nonsense that Rieseberg has perpetrated." He blasted Miller and the journal, saying that the publication "prostituted itself" through any association with Rieseberg but particularly in mentioning his movie. On a broader scale, Hubbs suggested a "rational discussion of the distinction between science and fiction in writing."

Minor Satisfaction

Around the time of Hubbs's communication with the editor of *Pacific Discovery*, preparations were underway for *City Beneath the Sea*. In his letters with Miller, Hubbs recounted a story of getting a call from a Hollywood movie producer asking about the availability of "whale pictures" (moving images) for use in the movie. Hubbs said, "I opened up a bit on Rieseberg. The phone call was soon terminated, and I have not been contacted again."

One of Hubbs' more intriguing contacts regarding Harry Rieseberg was with Commander Henry J. White, a decorated naval aviator. White was fluent in German and had been a translator for two books by Dr. Wernher von Braun. White was retired to West Virginia when Hubbs spoke with him by phone in July 1953 but was in California visiting a friend who took him to meet Harry Rieseberg in person. Harry Rieseberg, a man who pretended to be retired from the U.S. Navy, met face-to-face with a decorated naval aviator.

The circumstances of this encounter with Rieseberg are not known. White was taken to Harry's home by a friend, an actor known as Jonathan Hale, who lived only about seven miles away. Hale appeared in many TV and movie productions, so he may have known Rieseberg from other studio work. The timing of the visit was not long after the release of *City Beneath the Sea*, but Hale was not in the credits for the movie based on Port Royal.

The military man, who probably had many situations where he honed his perceptions of others, "sized him (Rieseberg) up as a crook." Harry told his two visitors about his qualifications as a former employee of the Bureau of Navigation. Before their meeting, Hale appears to have shared *I Dive for Treasure* with White, who noted many "linguistic errors indicating fakery." White judged Harry's language not to be that of a "seafaring man" and "doubts if he has been to sea."[49]

What Would Be the Use?

One of the more widely known experts that Hubbs consulted was William Beebe. Hubbs's questions for the deep-sea depth record holder were more about whether he should publicly debunk Rieseberg's disinformation. During their communication, Beebe was the director of the Department of Tropical Research at the New York Zoological Society and was on the cusp of opening a research station in Trinidad and Tobago.

Beebe's reply came quickly after receiving Hubbs's letter and was both wise and disappointing to the fomenting Hubbs. Beebe agreed with Hubbs's factual disputes and suggested he could have used rougher language but followed that support with, "but what would be the use?" Beebe's "old age" left him without the energy to push back against such outrageous claims. He explained that "People (damn'em) love to be fooled and to hug fears to their breasts, and I am almost tired of debunking." Beebe reminded Hubbs of another similar matter where an author's falsehoods were exposed but told Hubbs most people said of that, "Yes, I suppose he is not truthful, but he is such good reading."[50]

A Certain Amount of Literary Exaggeration

Despite producing questionable work filled with fantastic tales of treasure recovery in the face of death, Rieseberg's romantically vivid descriptions of an undersea world few could visit attracted young men to the profession. At the peak period of Harry's writing, the physical and logistical challenges of hard hat diving prevented most from undertaking a complicated dive. However, with the invention of the Aqua Lung by Jacques Cousteau and Emile Gagnan in 1943, scuba diving could be taught as a recreational hobby at YMCAs beginning in 1959. More and more people could see first-hand what the undersea world was like. Scuba diving pioneers were younger when Harry Rieseberg published his books, and several credited Rieseberg for inspiring their interest and adventure.

Gilbert Doukan

Dr. Gilbert Doukan was a French physician with notable credentials and experience in underwater exploration. In one of Doukan's numerous books, *World Beneath the Waves (1957)*, he reviewed "the reasons why the sea reveals its secrets so reluctantly." He also exposed how Harry Rieseberg could slide past the expectation that facts should be a consideration. When it came to treasure, said Doukan, men tend to be wrapped up in the possibilities more than the realities. Doukan politely described Harry Rieseberg's work as containing "a certain amount of literary exaggeration." The very tactful summation was brilliantly simple in its critique, leaving readers to decide on their own how much of what they read was fact and how much was a fable. He said, "As soon as the topic of sunken treasure arises, man reverts to a child's mentality."[51]

Doukan found Rieseberg's books and articles filled with tales that would "'do nothing to cool the ardor' of anyone inclined toward treasure."[52] Even while calling out Rieseberg's fabrications, Doukan offered him props for stimulating those you-too-can-get-rich thoughts found in businessmen, daredevils, and everyday people. Doukan's take on Harry Rieseberg was of a writer whose primary skill was stirring the souls of adventurers while using "literary exaggeration" as his tool of choice.

Robert Marx

Harry Rieseberg's book fell into Robert Marx's hands when he was nine, growing up in Pittsburgh. The descriptions of the dangers and adventure captured the young boy's interests. The only problem was that Marx could not swim. That summer at Lake Clair, just across the Canadian border from Detroit, an older cousin, one of the first U.S. Navy divers, decided the best way for Marx to learn was to throw him into the lake. The cousin's wife saw young Bob struggle and gave him some swim goggles. Once Marx could see beneath the clear water's surface, he said he "forgot that I could not swim."[53] After making a fish spear from a broom handle and a nail, he spent the rest of the summer swimming underwater during the day and reading Rieseberg's tales at night. The goggled boy acted out every Rieseberg adventure in Lake Clair that summer. Looking back at that time, an older Marx said Harry's books were the "biggest load of crap you ever read. Every one of his galleons were intact, skeletons at the wheel, fish nets caught in the rigging. But I really believed this bullshit, because everybody else did."[54] Even though Marx later saw through all of Rieseberg's tales, reading them had a lasting impact on his career.

Bob Marx went on to become one of the earliest treasure salvors to make use of scuba equipment. He was a contemporary of Mel Fisher, the famous treasure hunter who salvaged the $450 million riches of the *Atocha*, a wreck lost in 1622. When television turned entertainment into broadcasting in the early and mid–1950s, Marx and Fisher started making underwater films together. Marx said that he and Fisher "got a whole bunch of 16mm cameras surplus ... the first cases were made out of pressure cookers. Anything we shot we got on television. We made a lot of money in those days."[55]

When Fisher and Marx got hooked on the idea of making millions by looking for treasure, they gathered "all these phony charts and books" from Rieseberg's writing. Harry had written about wrecks along California's coast, so Fisher and Marx often headed out on treasure hunts. In the Caribbean, Rieseberg listed almost one hundred wrecks in his charts; Marx found only two. Marx learned the hard way that seventy-four of those one hundred "existed only in the fertile imaginations of the authors." As Marx gained actual experience, he and his fellow treasure divers became convinced that "all the books on treasure hunting at the time by the Harry Reisberg [Rieseberg] type were all complete bullshit. They never even went in the water."[56]

Robert Sténuit

Robert Sténuit was three years older than Bob Marx but did not discover Harry Rieseberg's romanticized work until he was twenty. Sténuit's introduction was the French translation of *I Dive for Treasure,* titled *600 Milliards Sous les Mers.* After reading Harry's book, Sténuit dropped out of the Université Libre in Brussels to begin hunting for treasure. Like Marx, he eventually migrated to underwater archaeology and research and had a distinguished career as an early pioneer in the diving world.[57]

John S. Potter, Jr.

In looking back toward treasure hunters with the resources and equipment to undertake credible searches, one will encounter John S. Potter, Jr. In many ways, Potter did the things Rieseberg only claimed to have done. Potter was a successful businessman with connections all over the world. In 1955, Potter was on holiday in Mallorca, Spain, where he spent some free time snorkeling and spearfishing. He met a fellow sportsman Potter called "a supercharged American from Cuba," and who had an aqualung that he allowed Potter to try.[58]

The wealthy vacationer was instantly hooked on diving further into the underwater world. One thing led to another, and Potter became part of a diving club that included professional divers. On one of Potter's earliest dives with them, he was mesmerized by the marine life, the colors, and the energy of being in another world. Potter said he "never dreamed anything could be so exciting." After several fishing dives with the group, the discussion turned to treasure, aided by what Potter called "heady punches" from the Bar Bellver. At one of their after-hours recaps, someone pulled out a treasure map of the Caribbean. Potter noted that the group "laughingly glanced over the elaborately designed treasure chests and Jolly Rogers printed on the artificially aged parchment." Potter didn't say it was Harry Rieseberg's 1951 map, but it seems likely it was after what happened to him a few weeks later. On a trip to Madrid, Potter noticed a pocketbook in a kiosk that caught his eye. It was Harry Rieseberg's 1942 book, *I Dive for Treasure*. Reading Rieseberg's descriptions of treasure galleons, particularly about Vigo Bay in Spain, where Potter was at the time, had his head spinning. After reading Harry's tales of the wealth beneath the waves, Potter focused heavily on recovery.

After World War II, an author reviewing the "great treasure hunts" listed Potter's attempts to find the Vigo Bay treasure that he detailed in his book as one of the best-funded and most technically capable. Though Potter's 180,000-word book extensively describes their adventures, Potter failed to find the treasure "due to the unpalatable fact that it does not exist."[59]

E. Lee Spence

Dr. E. Lee Spence, a notable diver and marine archaeologist, recalled how in the year just before Harry died in 1970, Spence called Rieseberg on the phone. Spence was another of those divers who discovered Rieseberg's romantic adventures as a young man and credited them with sparking his interest in diving.[60]

Spence said he basically told Harry that he knew his stories were bullshit, but that it did not matter because they were still key influences on his pursuit of diving as a career. Spence reported Harry would have no part of that discussion, got testy and irate, and ended the conversation abruptly. Harry never admitted his stories were concocted or apologized for stretching his tall tales into a semblance of believable truth. In a work discussing both the legend and the science of giant octopi, a French author added his own commentary on Harry's assertions.

> Captain Harry Rieseberg, great salvager of sunken treasures and smiter of colossal octopus in front of the Almighty, claims this (a confrontation with a giant octopus) happened to him and that he is indeed the only one to whom it ever happened. We shall leave to him the entire responsibility of his declaration.[61]

Harry's Final Years

By the mid–1960s going underwater had progressed from the difficulties of hard hat diving with a crew on deck manning the air pumps to recreational scuba diving.

Advances in dive technology changed diving from an unattainable adventure to a weekend hobby. When Harry's descriptions of undersea adventure moved from dramatic thrillers to blasé flashbacks to another era, perceptions of the author went from celebrity to huckster.

If anything, Harry Rieseberg was resilient, and the last five years of Harry Rieseberg's life were as productive as any he ever had. In 1965, he turned seventy-three years of age, and his correspondence and publications showed no sign of slowing. His words continued to have a sharp edge when expressing his complaints. The pace at which he kept making the same claims he had for thirty years, and the intensity with which he defended them, were unchanged.

Between 1956, when he moved to Paradise, and 1970, over five hundred publications have been located and identified by the author, and there is no doubt there were hundreds more published.[62] Rieseberg claimed he was writing from four to ten magazine articles each month. Always fond of touting the scope of his publications, by 1969, he credited himself with 4,000 articles in 180 magazines and newspapers, with appearances on 167 television programs and fifty-seven radio programs.[63] In a letter to a friend, Harry bragged about how well he had done during only two months in 1970, making $3,455. Harry said he could "manage to eat a few x-tra hamburgers these days since this sudden outburst of acceptances seems to be going so good." Given the amount of detail he provided, this is likely an accurate assessment of a good run that Harry had at seventy-eight years of age. There were plenty of outlets for his type of material then, and Harry kept feeding them repeatedly.[64]

Adding to His Legend

Toward the end of his life, Harry Rieseberg embellished his personal narrative at every opportunity. He claimed that since 1931 he "had no other business than treasure salvaging, and I have no regrets."[65] Harry Rieseberg's rule number three was found within that simple statement—have no regrets. The statement about having no other business but salvaging is partially true since he probably began his research around that time. Still, he was no salvor, only a researcher and writer. Harry had no regrets about pretending he was something other than that for his entire writing career.

Despite his fabrications, his stories continued to find readers willing to believe. In 1964, Harry Rieseberg was named "Mr. Treasure Hunter" by the Treasure Trove Club of New York. This organization was formed in the 1930s along the lines of the Adventurer's Clubs. Initially, it was exclusive and included only vetted world travelers, but it struggled for relevancy at the time of the award. In the early 1950s, previous recipients included Lowell Thomas and historian J. Frank Dobie. By the time they got to Rieseberg in 1964, their standards had changed, and the membership was not quite as credible. They had also awarded a man who falsely claimed to be the nephew of Kit Carson, so it was not a stretch to add Rieseberg to the list of honorees.

In a press release by the Treasure Trove Club, they repeated all the supposed accomplishments Harry promoted for himself. Harry's narrative remained unchanged, beginning with his falsehood about accompanying Teddy Roosevelt on safari and ending with promises of projects yet to come.

Protecting His Turf

During this period of Harry's most prolific writing, he took legal action to defend his self-identified role as the world's greatest treasure expert. Between 1955 and 1959, one of Harry's targets was F.L. Coffman. Ferris LaVerne Coffman was a Michigan man who, like Harry, had become interested in the contents of sunken vessels. In Coffman's case, his initial focus was the Great Lakes, but after years of research, his domain expanded. After going to Florida on fishing vacations for a few seasons, he became interested in sunken treasure. The business-minded Coffman partnered with a man in Palm Beach, and the two of them began selling treasure-locating devices for both land and water with offices in Michigan and Florida. In Michigan, the business name was Algomah Instruments, and in Florida, they used Caribbean Instruments. One of their devices was advertised as able to locate metal underwater.[66]

In 1951 Coffman began actively trying to partner with the owner of a ship to conduct treasure salvage in the Caribbean. A display ad of almost a quarter page appeared in *Motor Boating* magazine in November 1951.[67] The ad got right to the point that Coffman, a "male, married Gentile, formerly a Druggist, now a resort hotel owner," had information about where wrecks were located and had instruments to help find them. What he did not have was the money for such an expedition or a vessel capable of carrying it out. By 1955, Coffman had built his own 18-foot, two-person submarine out of plastic and steel that could reportedly dive to 600 feet for up to 30 hours.[68]

Coffman repeatedly used Harry's phrasing in articles about his ventures by saying, "one-eighth of the world's wealth is at the bottom of the ocean." Coffman's publication of an atlas-sized volume with treasure maps seemed to have peeved Harry the most. The treasure map business was good enough in December 1955 for Coffman and his partner to hire a salesman who could contact "drug, sundry, gift, sporting goods, bookstores, magazine stands, with new multicolor TREASURE MAP set." They told the truly industrious they could make fifty dollars a day selling these "Red Hot!" seven-map sets for $10.00.[69]

Coffman wrote about wrecks in much the same way Rieseberg had done—telling stories and touting locations that others had largely covered. He may have tried to make nice with Harry and pay homage to his tales in a 1957 book. In Coffman's book *1,001 Lost, Buried or Sunken Treasures-Facts for Treasure Hunters*, his chapter titled "Ace Treasure Hunter" called Rieseberg "the greatest authority on treasures and the methods of the successful recovery of these hoards that there is today."[70] Coffman called attention to Rieseberg's "voluminous files of information regarding undersea treasure hoards and praised his 'thoroughness in preparation for any venture.'"

The praise did not matter to Rieseberg when he discovered Coffman's methods involved misappropriating some of his own material. When Coffman lifted six pages of data from one of Rieseberg's books, Harry sued both Coffman and his publisher. The lawsuit was filed after Coffman died in 1961, so Harry sued the estate, and they paid a settlement rather than going to court. Harry got crafty over the years. He later told a fellow treasure hunter that he would frequently insert a "few improvised ringers" among his "true tales" so he could tell who was lifting information from his compiled lists of wrecks. That way, Harry knew they would only see mention of his fabrications if they copied his texts.[71]

Eleven years after Coffman's *Atlas of Treasure Maps*, Harry was still angry in describing Coffman to a government bureaucrat. When Coffman's book was listed as a treasure resource in a 1968 government publication, Rieseberg was not pleased and wrote the civil servant that Coffman's book of treasure maps was a "phoney" and that "only God himself could locate any wreck from the data therein." Harry complained that Coffman essentially did exactly what he had done in becoming an "expert."

> (Coffman) was what one might call a "culler" of newspaper reports, and the data is most vague and useless to a salvor…. Too, he never made a successful expedition himself, but lived on the income of such reports.[72]

It takes a culler to know a culler, and Rieseberg's name could easily be substituted in that complaint.

Not Afraid to Dispute Clear Facts

With the popularization of scuba diving around 1959, Rieseberg recognized he had to alter his approach to writing. That was the year he began directing articles toward recreational scuba divers, trying to convince them that there was Spanish gold in almost any waterway. One of those articles found its way to *Virginia Wildlife* magazine, and Harry's false expertise was the subject of a letter of complaint to the editor.[73]

In a story about a man finding gold bars from a Spanish wreck at the mouth of Chesapeake Bay, Harry strayed out of bounds on a safety and technical concern. Rieseberg suggested that 200 feet was a safe working depth for scuba divers and drew the rebuke of an expert diver. L. David Horner, III, was an expert commercial diver and one of the first Nationally Certified Scuba Instructors in the United States. Mr. Horner pointed out that a diver can only stay at 200 feet for about six minutes. After that, there are concerns about the bends. He found Harry's article to be both unsafe and foolish.

The magazine also published Rieseberg's reply beneath Horner's letter. Rather than acknowledging his error, Harry raised the stakes with a vacuous deception, saying he had "explored to depths of 220 feet in such gear" when he had done no such thing.[74]

Defending his Depth Record

Rieseberg did not pass up an opportunity to defend his claims from questions raised at any level. He was so upset by a 1964 newspaper article suggesting that his stories might be suspect that he wrote a letter to the newspaper disputing the report. A page one article led with the headline "Deep Sea Divers Set for Adventure."[75] The story was about Robert A. James, who built a "sea tractor" that he proposed for use in deep oil fields and for mining manganese. The self-propelled diving bell could hold one or two divers and had long arms that could accomplish much of a diver's work but at a greater depth. It looked remarkably like the Charles Warren "underwater tank" that Rieseberg promoted. When James called treasure hunting "the biggest farce there is," it raised Rieseberg's ire and sent his fingers to the typewriter keys. Rieseberg was even more upset by James's claim about what the tractor had done. James said, "this is the first underwater working bell that has ever made a 1,000-foot dive."

The same newspaper published an article about Harry's response two weeks later titled, "Adventurer Takes Issue Over Dive."[76] Rieseberg said he had exceeded that depth in 1936, a patently false claim he had continued for thirty-five years.. "This statement is entirely erroneous," said Rieseberg, "as the writer of this letter happened to be the first man to ever penetrate an underwater depth of 1,404 feet in a working bell!" The paper gave "the colorful treasure hunter" a few column inches but was careful not to take sides.

Harry's Descent

Harry Rieseberg was not expecting to die, but he was planning for it. In a small, three-ring binder, Rieseberg kept track of article submissions, rejections, and the payments for the articles he placed. Each page was a different publisher or magazine with his handwritten list of dates, article names, and royalty amounts. One of the pages in the notebook stood out for its difference in tone and content. The page began with Harry writing to his wife, Val, "should anything happen to me."[77]

The page was a listing of three sources for ongoing book royalties to be notified in the event of his death so that royalties could be sent to Val. He listed The Naylor Company of San Antonio for his book, *Treasure of the Buccaneer Sea*, and Frederick Fell, Inc. for three other books: *Guide to the Sunken Ships of the World*, *Sea of Treasure*, and *Adventures in Underwater Treasure Hunting*. Six years of royalties for *Treasure of the Buccaneer Sea* had paid $564.61, and the three Fell books paid $765.00, $1,045.43, and $1,432.87, respectively. Dodd, Mead was also listed for *I Dive for Treasure*, with a handwritten notation that they were "out" of books. Rieseberg made sure she also understood that half of the royalties for *Guide to Sunken Treasure Ships* went to Al Mikalow.

It was Harry's instruction at the bottom of the page that had the most impact. That is where Rieseberg left a note for his wife on what to do when he died. His simple direction was that when he died "all my materials go to Mikalow." Harry Rieseberg passed all his collected manuscripts, letters, and files to his friend, Al Mikalow. Judging from the author's visit to Mikalow's home in Lake Havasu, Arizona, to talk about Rieseberg and see those materials, Val did as Harry wished.[78]

The Death of His Son

By 1964, at age seventy-two, Harry Rieseberg was beginning to sense his mortality. Not only was he beginning to feel more physically limited, but the unexpected passing of one of the few people with whom he felt a warm connection gave him an emotional jolt and triggered a harsh recognition of his own limitations. On August 14, 1964, Rieseberg's son, Henry, died at age thirty-seven due to a rapidly developed brain tumor while serving as a missionary for the Adventist Church.

Since Harry left his family to move to Los Angeles in 1937, Henry had little contact with his father. After Rieseberg moved to Paradise, Henry and his wife, Marilyn, and their four children, visited Harry and Val on only one occasion in 1959 or 1960 when they were back in the United States on furlough from a mission assignment in Africa. They found him at home in his new relaxing environment in Paradise, where he sat in an easy chair with his legs up. His broken leg would still bother him. He was talkative and self-confident when discussing himself but seemed a bit indifferent to their visit. Henry and Marilyn never questioned whether Harry had accomplished the diving he said he had and accepted his stories. It was notable, however, that there were no visible artifacts or treasures.[79]

The news of Henry's sudden death arrived via telegram while Harry was away from home. He did not immediately reach out to his daughter-in-law or attend the funeral. In a letter he wrote two weeks after his son's passing, Harry Rieseberg exposed himself emotionally in a way he had perhaps never done before. He apologized for his behavior during the last visit that Henry and Marilyn made and acknowledged his "attitude and quietness." Rieseberg explained that it was a poorly executed front necessary because he was not feeling physically well. He added a reminder that being an "unexpressive individual" often led to the perception that he was "cold of attitude."[80]

When he received the news of Henry's death, Harry said, "tears came to my eyes, it was the first time in my life." After making that confession, Harry deflected from it by suggesting that "in his field," he had seen death many times "both above and under the sea and little attention did I give to it." Even at this emotional moment, he was unrelenting in perpetuating his self-ascribed myth as a hard hat diver and salvor.

It was telling that he admitted to crying upon learning of his son's death when he had never cried in his life. The life of a narcissist can be sad indeed. Rieseberg said that the memory which triggered his sadness was shaking Henry's hand the night of his final visit with his father in Paradise. Harry told his son it would probably be the last time they met due to his age and failing health. Little did he know it would be Henry who would die before him.

On an evening when Henry last visited his father without his wife and children present, on the last night they would see each other, Harry Rieseberg was moved to have a "discussion of things I wanted him to know and which we had never before talked about plainly." Harry admitted to Henry that he had a half-brother, Robert Rieseberg, from a first marriage. Harry was led to believe that Robert had died during World War II and had only recently been told by a friend from Washington, D.C., that he was still alive. Harry asked Henry to try to find Robert, but since Henry was returning shortly to West Africa, he could not pursue the request. He also spoke with Henry about his German heritage and his grandfather and namesake, Harry's father, also named Henry.

Harry also wanted to clear the air about the financial support of his abandoned family. Harry showed his son some receipts for monthly payments made to support him and his sister, Shirley, financially.[81] The remainder of their discussion has died with them.

Unfinished Last Wishes

Harry promised to send some unspecified financial help to Henry's wife and children but reminded her that "things are not like they were some years ago when money came quite easily, from motion pictures, books, articles, etc." Notably, that was money from activities other than diving for billions in gold. With Henry's death creating a sense of mortality, in 1965, Harry Rieseberg typed up a will. It is unknown whether it was ever signed or executed; no proof of a will has been found. Harry bequeathed all his estate to his wife, Valentine, "in the confidence that she will make a fair distribution at her death of my property between her daughter and my four grandchildren." Harry's will mentioned his daughter but did not leave her any of his estate. It did not name his oldest son, Robert.[82]

Harry sent a draft of that unsigned will to Henry's wife, Marilyn, but that was the end of the communication. Marilyn did not know when Harry died. Shortly after Henry's death, Marilyn asked Val if she would send some mementos of their grandfather for her children and was shipped very impersonal items like a pen and a key chain. Harry's grandchildren do not have any relics or artifacts from his reported deep-sea diving expeditions. It perhaps helps to take that less personally to know there was none to give.

A French Visitor (1967)

The French seemed to have a particular fascination with Harry Rieseberg and his treasure stories. With some of his books translated into French, his publications reached an international audience. One of the most notable people who latched on to Harry's Cocos Island tales was Michel Bagnaud. Bagnaud was a French treasure aficionado and adventurist who later wrote books about treasure seeking. He had also visited Cocos Island in search of the treasure that may or may not exist there. A brief bio said he was "driven by his penchant for adventure." In 1967 he visited Paradise, California, to visit Harry Rieseberg.

Bagnaud learned about Rieseberg from Robert Charroux, who founded the International Club of Treasure Seekers. Charroux himself had given Bagnaud Harry's address, and Bagnaud could not wait to meet "this great man to whom we owed the greatest books on sunken treasures." Rieseberg's books had made Bagnaud dream about treasure, so when he came to the U.S. in search of the Lost Dutchman Mine, he visited Harry. Bagnaud found Harry eager to tell stories to a willing subject, a trait the Frenchman attributed to an American "desire to pass on advice or knowledge so that after their death, the adventure can continue."[83]

Harry played off the fact that he lived in a mobile home by saying he could pick up and leave anytime and did not want to be trapped or tied down. Bagnaud found the interior to reflect that of a writer focused on tales of treasure. One living room wall held books from across the world, with details of locations that he used for his descriptive narratives. A copy of a letter from Harry's files showed his requests for travel brochures from numerous countries. Rieseberg showed his French visitor shoeboxes that Val used to file letters from readers or "solicitations from amateur divers who hoped Harry would put them on to something good." His certificate recognizing him as Mr. Treasure Hunter of 1964 was also paraded out for his guest.

Rieseberg relied on a collection of what Bagnaud called "treasure location cards" to keep up with the legends of wealth on land and in the sea. These note cards had been boiled down to "an eloquent, inflated value estimate" of the riches to be found and a small map with an "X" marking the spot. Bagnaud said he was new to treasure hunting but knew a cross on a map like that could represent a few hundred square miles of searching.

It would be interesting to know what Bagnaud expected when he drove up to the Paradise home of the "great man" of underwater treasure hunting. Harry had a few gold coins to show him and displayed some fine china of unknown origin, not the sort of thing one would recover from a wreck. There were no millions, artifacts, or objective evidence of Harry's recorded adventures. Rieseberg had even said he usually destroyed his book manuscripts as soon as a book was published. When Harry pulled out "ingots piled up in a chest topped by skull and crossbones," it was the same set of fake gold bars seen so often in photo illustrations for Harry's work, the same ones he carried with him on the movie tour. Bagnaud even said it looked fake, "like a movie set, I didn't mind, it was the American way."[84]

Busy 'till the End

Harry was a driven man. He was unyielding in his efforts to publish magazine articles using stories he had already told for many years. During the six months before his death in late 1970 at age seventy-eight, he placed at least thirty-one magazine articles that were accepted for publication. Using *Writer's Market* and *The Writer* to find outlets, Rieseberg sent queries to a wide variety of outlets.

Marine-related magazines like *Seaports & Shipping, Ocean Industry,* and *Pennsylvania Angler*; lifestyle publications like *Peninsula Living, Northeast Outdoors, and Minnesota AAA Motorist*; and the usual adventure and men's titles such as *SAGA, Police Gazette, Frontier,* and *Old West* were all among his targets.[85]

Several editors called him out for sending them articles and photos that had already been published. In responding to a submission of an article titled "The Ship in the Rockbound Cavern," one editor called it "very interesting, and I remember reading the article in one of the men's magazines several years back."[86] Harry claimed it was probably an article by someone who knew little about treasure hunting. But the editor remembered Harry's trademark use of a green typewriter ribbon as much as he did the story.

The volume and pace of his submissions sometimes made it difficult to keep track. In May 1970, Harry submitted an article titled "The Old West's Lost Spanish Mines" to *Real West* magazine. The editor had paid him for the same article in April for a sister magazine titled "The Old West's Lost Jesuit Mines." Instead of asking Harry to return the $80 he was paid for the second article, they accepted the second article without payment.[87]

Loose Ends

The final, personal letter written by Harry Rieseberg was not very personal at all. In May 1970, he penned another letter to his son's widow.[88] He began the letter by explaining that he did not write personal letters and acknowledged what he expected would be her "extreme surprise" at hearing from him again. The letter was their only communication since the one he sent when Henry died six years prior.

Harry's purpose in communicating again was to provide Henry's wife with items that would allow her to tell her children more about their famous grandfather. What made it seem so impersonal and self-serving was that the material he sent was not much more than what he would send to an editor needing some background information for a magazine article. The photo of himself he enclosed was from 1953, where he stood before his treasure map, pointing at places he said he had been.

The most difficult bit of unfinished business that Rieseberg would never be able to repair was his relationship with his daughter, Shirley. In his letter to Henry's widow, Harry asked that she send his articles and a photo to Shirley. Rieseberg did not know her married name, where she lived, or any other information about her at all. Harry said he would like to have some color photographs of her and her family since he had never seen them since he left the family in 1937. However, he would accept them only if Shirley would "grant the favor." He said he would not dare to ask her himself since "she wrote me many letters condemning me for breaking up with her mother years ago." Shirley's doggedness in rejecting her father and occasionally excoriating him by mail was likely a trait she inherited from her father.

Harry's Death

Harry Earl Rieseberg died of a cerebral hemorrhage on the afternoon of Tuesday, October 27, 1970, in Paradise, California, at the age of seventy-eight. He had been admitted to the hospital a week earlier. Harry's remains were sent to Union Cemetery in Bakersfield for cremation and a private ceremony. His ashes were interred beneath a small granite memorial in the plot for his wife's family. Only his name, birth, and death dates are inscribed on the plain, flat marker.[89]

Rieseberg had been having physical problems for some time. Only two months earlier, he complained to a friend that he had "been under quite a siege of x-rays, enemas, blood counts, and other experiments" to discover what was causing his unnamed symptoms.[90] Mentally, however, there was no slow, downhill path toward senility for Harry. Only two months before he died, Harry sent three derisive two-page, single-spaced letters to his publisher, Frederick Fell, chastising him because Harry was "fed-up with promises as I remember once I worked-out agreements with various outlets for large scale exploitation and sales set-up, each of which was promised and then forgotten."[91]

In Rieseberg's final book, a 1970 rewrite of *I Dive for Treasure*, the last chapter reads like a farewell. Even though he was almost seventy-eight years old when he wrote it, Harry still wanted readers to believe he was just about to make that next big find of the *Brother Jonathan*. He acknowledged that "such an ambitious achievement no longer is within my sphere of opportunity, and I must leave the search and salvage to all of these underwater treasure targets to this younger generation of seekers."[92] Until the end, Harry Rieseberg never let anyone know his secrets.

What Kind of Legacy?

There is something ironic about the fact that the last known photograph of Harry Rieseberg shows him with a smile. The polaroid image shows him sitting in front of a stack of books, some of which were his own, at a table in front of the picture window in his mobile home. From there, he looked into the forest surrounding the trailer park, toward the canyon and river. His view was quite a change from the Birmingham Trailer Village on Balboa Avenue in Van Nuys, a "deluxe" facility of 500 families with only a view of each other.

A Closing Rejection

The final rejection letter for one of Rieseberg's article submissions arrived very near the date of his passing. That it was noted in his ledger indicates that it received attention from Rieseberg himself. The letter is dated October 17, 1970, and was from Margaret E. Dougherty, the editor of *Maryland Magazine*. Harry had only recently submitted, and Dougherty said she did not want to keep him waiting "since the photographs you sent … are destined for your upcoming book." Dougherty's feedback to

Photograph of Harry Rieseberg at his home in Paradise, California, November 1968 (photograph provided to author by Al Mikalow).

Harry on this article summed up his entire career as a writer and his persona as an "international expert."[93]

> I have read the GREEN GHOST OF THE MERIDA and find that again the basic information is of considerable interest; however, its presentation needs strengthening. To begin with, the story of greatest interest is the one about your experiences in the salvage efforts for the MERIDA. Three and a half pages of the seven-page article are devoted to an editorialized history of the Hapsburg family, its treasures and ill fate. The possible presence of that treasure aboard the MERIDA does not warrant that much background information in a treasure-search story.[94]

Had Harry avoided using his routinely applied literary mechanisms to sidestep the truth, the ones Dougherty so carefully identified, he might never have had a career as a writer. The methods she called out were the *foundation* of Rieseberg's stories. That his last recorded rejection points that out so tidily helps bring understanding to those of us looking back on his work.

An Absent Father and a Confidant

Harry's children were not a part of his life at all. Robert was a decorated naval officer stationed at the Command Center for the Northeast Atlantic fleet and later worked as an executive for an international shipping company. Henry graduated high school as an honor roll student in Galveston in 1944. He was a distinguished and accomplished young man, active as an officer in the ROTC unit at Ball High School and later in the military. Like his mother, he was an active Adventist, a *colporteur evangelist* who went door to door with religious tracts. Shirley was perhaps not the student that Henry was, but she was active and involved in the Girl Scouts, earning merit badges for first aid and cycling. She ran on the track team and won a pantomime contest. They no doubt missed their father at some level or at least having a father to count on. Harry Rieseberg never filled that role.

Harry's wife, Ellen, became a faithful and committed Seventh-Day Adventist church member. She married a second time to a man in a stable job this time. Charles Sucich was an Army veteran and a member of the Galveston Fire Department. She continued to be regarded by her supervisor as competent, cooperative, agreeable, and dependable nurse. Her performance evaluations were as reliably positive as she was for her children.

A Close Friend

Harry Rieseberg and Al Mikalow collaborated on a couple of books late in Rieseberg's life, and Rieseberg would occasionally visit Mikalow at his diving school in Oakland. Only a month before Mikalow died in September 2014, the author visited Al at his home in Lake Havasu, Arizona, to speak with him about Rieseberg and his own adventurous life.[95] Mikalow had indeed received Rieseberg's "material," his personal collection and writing.

When the author asked whether his brother Mason, Harry Rieseberg, had done any of the things he claimed, Mikalow paused and remained silent, then pointed to the Masonic ring on his gnarled hands ... a signal that

Alfred Alexander Mikalow, Lake Havasu, Arizona (photograph by author, August 11, 2014).

secrets would be kept, and a tacit confession that Harry had not always done what he claimed. Both men were skilled bullshitters, but they were also fellow Masons.[96]

No Way to Get Rich

As technology progressed, the drama and romanticism of diving moved from exotic and inaccessible to a weekend hobby. The prospect of becoming wealthy from treasure hunting also became more wishful. Carl Clausen, the first marine archaeologist for the State of Texas, expressed the odds for striking it rich in a 1973 article for the *Los Angeles Times*.

> Take all the money you can get—$200,000 would be a nice round number—get in a boat and run out in the ocean a ways. Then pile the money up on the deck and drink a beer while the wind blows it away. That way you can waste your money without all the miserable, hard work involved in a treasure hunt, and the return to you should be about the same as if you'd actually gone treasure hunting—zilch.[97]

As a marine archaeologist, Clausen decried the treasure hunters who would dynamite a wreck and destroy any artifacts in hopes of finding a few gold coins. Robert Marx acknowledged that "there's something about sunken treasure that literally can drive sane men crazy." Harry Rieseberg built his entire career on feeding that human trait and the innate desire for adventure. That archetype continues to find expression in the modern era. At the entrance to the Miss Adventure Falls attraction in Disney's Typhoon Lagoon waterpark attraction in Lake Buena Vista, Florida, visitors file past a mockup of a diving bell. The Mary Oceaneer diving bell looks exactly like the Romano diving bell.

When the concept for the attraction was being formulated ahead of the 2017 opening, the art director looked for inspiration from diving bells of the past and found that "the navy had some with this general shape and robot arms for underwater salvage and recovery."[98] Given Brad Matsen's good fortune in discovering William Beebe's diving sphere in Coney Island, which he described in *Descent*, this author could not help but hope Disney engineers had worked their magic yet again and located the lost Romano bell. It was only a reproduction, but the feeling of adventure was real.

On Lying

In an email conversation with one of Rieseberg's descendants, I was questioned about my characterization of Harry as a liar. It was a valid question and one which has been carefully considered. The question prompted a deeper dive into the meaning of a four-letter word that can elicit such emotion. The descendant's suggestion was that there is a difference between a liar, someone who purposefully tells lies, and a storyteller or fiction writer who may stretch the truth. In any language when there are many words to describe a gradation or continuum of meaning, one can be certain there are reasons for that. The alternative expressions for liars are many.

Cheat. Con artist. Deceiver. Fabricator. Fibber. Imposter. Mythomaniac. Perjurer. Phony. Prevaricator. Storyteller. Trickster. Fraud. Fibber. Deluder. Dissembler.

Words suggested by a thesaurus only offer options from a list without assigning levels of severity or purpose. Degrees of lying must be understood to make the best designation. Intent and motivation are also factors. Was the teller exaggerating facts or telling fibs to protect someone? Some people lie about almost anything and for no apparent reason or gain. Lying to protect one's identity or diverting facts into the realm of lies are also methods that must be evaluated.

It is not altogether surprising that there is a broad range of research, books, articles, and anecdotal information related to lying.[99] Philosophers especially enjoy this dissection of meaning and have word formulas to help diagram the intent and motivation. An entry in the *Stanford Encyclopedia of Philosophy* examines the difference between a "liar" and a "deceiver" saying, "A liar is someone who intentionally tells a falsehood, while a deceiver is someone who uses trickery or guile to mislead someone." Intention, means, and motivation are characterized by a conclusion that "a liar is typically motivated by self-interest, while a deceiver may be motivated by a variety of factors, including self-interest, altruism, or a desire to protect someone else."

Perhaps the most helpful continuum is provided by Zee Kadih in his presentation of a continuum of truth and lies.[100] He uses fourteen characterizations of lying to provide meaning to the sometimes-subtle differences. Emergency Lies and White Lies are on the lowest end, causing the least harm, with Big Lies and Elaborate Lies at the worse end of the continuum. In considering Harry Rieseberg's lifelong commitment to his representation of himself as a treasure diver, the lower end of the continuum quickly fades. It took little effort to omit Bad Faith, Exaggeration, and Bluffing from consideration.

A pause at Half-Truth, number ten on the scale, to think about whether Rieseberg was simply "telling the truth in a way that could be easily misinterpreted" also failed to match his apparent intent. Harry's stories left no room for the reader's interpretation when he said he was attacked by cannibals or killed a giant octopus. At number eleven on the list of fourteen, a description of Rieseberg's writing method was ably expressed. A Haystack Lie, "telling a small truth, coupled with a ridiculous amount of lies," reflected the way Harry retold the history of a sunken ship, often accurately describing what is known, but then inserting himself into an underwater exploration for which there was no evidence to support its existence.

Based on this research and Harry Rieseberg's own words, it was at level thirteen, the second of the worst kind of lies, where the author found a distinction that matched Rieseberg's lifelong behaviors. Kadih called this level the Big Lie. That name has many connotations in today's political environment, but the characterization was completely on target in describing Rieseberg's stories. The author's definition of the Big Lie is an "absurd lie that most knowledgeable people could easily disprove." Knowledgeable experts during his lifetime, like real treasure divers and a Professor of Biology at the Scripps Institution of Oceanography, disproved his stories about intact two-hundred-year-old wrecks and giant killer octopi. Both ultimately decided it was not worth the energy to push back. Others simply bought the stories, for whatever reason, as good adventure reading and accepted them as true.

Harry Rieseberg made it all up. Even with repeated evidence that his tales were false accounts of underwater adventures, he never once relented in his affirmation that he did all the things he claimed. His failure to admit his thirty-five-year campaign to promote himself as the world's greatest underwater treasure hunter was built on stories that were not true, even up to the last months before his death, is a compelling verdict. The reader assigned to one of his submitted manuscripts may have summed it up best in saying "(Rieseberg) has made no move to furnish documentation for his statements, and I have a feeling he would be offended to be asked for it."[101]

An Epilogue

The old Meeting Hall in Jaffrey, New Hampshire, had a long history. It had once been a school and a Masonic Temple, but in 1991 was abandoned and filled with rubble, some of it a foot deep. The renovation was just getting underway when workers operating a front-end loader heard a thud. The bucket hit something hard and metallic. When they dug into the pile, they discovered a safe—locked and buried for years inside the old building.

The Town Manager was notified, and there was some discussion about how to proceed. Everyone wanted to know what treasures might be hidden inside. Then, just as the safe was being taken off the front-end loader, it was jarred, and the door sprung open!

But the safe was empty.[102]

Hunter Rieseberg, the Town Manager, had hoped for more, just as his grandfather had decades before. "We were looking for a bit more intrigue, a bit more mystery." As Harry Rieseberg understood, people love to be fooled.

Chapter Notes

Preface

1. Harry E. Rieseberg, *I Dive for Treasure* (New York: Robert M. McBride and Co., 1942). Reading Rieseberg's book will provide the reader with a full understanding of the stories he told. The 1942 edition of the book is long out of print and only occasionally available from booksellers. The 1970 reissue of the book using the same title is somewhat different than the original but still provides a sense of Rieseberg's style and content. The 1970 edition of *I Dive for Treasure* and *The Sea of Treasure* (1966) are available from the Independent Publishers Group in Chicago.

Chapter 1

1. "Schooner Revives Memories of Old Days," *Washington Evening Star*, October 2, 1934, p. A-3.
2. *Robot Sous-Marin* (Underwater Robot), Reference No: PJ 1935 291 7 (Gaumont-Pathé Archives, 1935). See also: *Une Nouvelle Cloche a Plongeurs* (A New Diving Bell), Reference No: 3523GJ00008 (Gaumont-Pathé Archives, 1935).

Chapter 2

1. An online obituary posted shortly after Robert Rieseberg's death on January 25, 2011, misstated this information about his father. Robert Rieseberg was buried at sea.
2. *Emigration and Immigration: Reports of the Consular Officers of the United States* (Washington, D.C.: Government Printing Office, 1887), p. 146. During the 1880's, almost 1.5 million Germans immigrated to the United States. Many of them were young men like Harry's father who left to escape compulsory service in the German (Prussian) military.
3. Stan Hoig, *Fort Reno and the Indian Territory Frontier* (Fayetteville, AR: University of Arkansas Press, 2000), p. 154. An October 1887 inspection report noted that Fort Reno had "an offensive cesspool in back of the quarters (and) the worst bathing facilities of any post in the department." Wind-blown dust seeped into all the buildings. Even the post cemetery needed repair. See also http://fortreno.org/history.html.
4. In a photo of Troop C of the 5th Cavalry, which arrested boomers and squatters, the soldier who stands third from the right bears a striking resemblance to Harry Rieseberg.
5. Register of Enlistments in the United States Army, 1798–1914 (Washington, D.C.: National Archives and Records Administration, 1956). Henry Rieseberg enlisted on January 28, 1886.
6. "The Courts, District Court," *Leavenworth Times*, March 3, 1891, p. 4.
7. Year: 1900; Census Place: Washington, Washington, District of Columbia; Roll: 162; Page: 20A; Enumeration District: 0109; FHL microfilm: 1240162.
8. Annual Report of the Public Printer: For the Fiscal Year Ended June 30, 1894. Submitted to the Congress of the United States on January 3, 1940 (Washington, D.C.: Government Printing Office, 1894). Henry worked 2,305 hours that year for the annual pay of $604.65.
9. "Personal," *Topeka Daily Capital*, December 7, 1881, p. 8. In 1868, at the age of eight, Curtis moved from the Kaw Reservation to his paternal grandparents in Topeka. His grandfather built a race track, and in 1869 Charles Curtis rode in his first race. He continued to ride until 1876 in Kansas, Indian Territory, and in Texas.
10. Memo to Rieseberg regarding probational appointment as a Messenger, May 13, 1909; Harry Earl Rieseberg employment records; Smithsonian Institution, Official Personnel Folders; National Personnel Records Center, St. Louis, MO. Harry became a permanent employee in November 1909. Subsequent citations for this source will note the agency of employment and OPF. See the bibliography head note for more information.
11. Correspondence regarding an order for stamps by Harry Rieseberg, December 16, 1909; Record Unit 45, Box 48, Folder 1: Office of the Secretary of Records 1890–1929, Smithsonian Institution, Washington, D.C.
12. Application for Consular Service, Harry Rieseberg; Record Group 59; Applications and Recommendations for Appointment to the Consular and Diplomatic Services, 1901–1924, General Records of the Department of State, 1756–1979; Civilian Records LICON, National Archives at College Park, Maryland.

13. "Wants Legal Residence Here, Washington Boy Makes a Strange Request of the County Clerk's Office," *Leavenworth Times*, March 27, 1909, p. 5. Contact with the county clerk found no record of this request.

14. Letter to Crescent City (CA) Chamber of Commerce from Harry Rieseberg, September 21, 1970. Rieseberg/Mikalow Collection. See also *I Dive for Treasure*, 1970 edition, p. 36.

15. "Society," *Washington Post*, August 6, 1911, Sunday edition, p. 3.

16. "Society," *The Washington Star*, August 6, 1911, Sunday edition, sec. 7, p. 2.

17. "Deep Sea Gold Taker Here to Pay Off 'Old Debt,'" *San Francisco Chronicle*, September 3, 1937, sec. Second, p. 17.

18. Rieseberg, *I Dive for Treasure*, 1970, p. 46.

19. In Harry's 1970 revision of *I Dive*, he removed Capt. Dorpen's name from the narrative, and simply mentioned the names of the ships. A search of ships log found no captain named Dorpen. The *Roanoke*'s captain at the time was named Jensen or Jessen.

20. Regarding some of the facts of this possible activity, there was at least the possibility that Harry worked on the *Roanoke* out of San Francisco for part of the time he was in California. Shipping news detailed in the *San Francisco News* provided the comings and goings of the *Roanoke* during the time Harry was in California. Based on the published schedules of ship traffic through the port there is at least the possibility that Harry worked on the *Roanoke* for a couple of coastwise runs. Not so with the *Admiral Farragut*. The ship was nowhere near there at the time. Curiously, however, the *Farragut* was involved in a shipwreck that Harry later touted as seeking. The Los Angeles part of Harry's trip was not documented, but his mother had Martin relatives there whom Harry would return to in a few years. "Searches for 'Stmr Roanoke' and 'Steamer Roanoke,' 1911," California Digital Newspaper Collection, accessed February 8, 2023, http://cdnc.ucr.edu/. See also: "Admiral Farragut," Guide to the Pacific Coast Steamship Company Records MS 72, 1879–1938 (San Diego History Center), accessed February 8, 2023, https://sandiegohistory.org/findaid/ms72.html.

21. "Deep Sea Gold," *San Francisco Chronicle*, September 3, 1937.

22. Rieseberg, *I Dive for Treasure* (1942), p. 24. Though Rieseberg first told his story about going to Africa with former President Theodore Roosevelt in his initial book, *I Dive for Treasure*, published in 1942, he repeated it in 1958 in a magazine published by the Methodist Church. See also: Harry E. Rieseberg, "Boy Meets Teddy," *Together*, May 1958, p. 17.

23. Rieseberg, *I Dive for Treasure* (1942), p. 28.

24. Letter from Rieseberg to Bureau of Indian Affairs, December 12, 1910. Department of the Interior, OPF.

25. Letter from Anthony to Bureau of Indian Affairs, January 23, 1911. Department of the Interior, OPF. See also, Letter from Charles Curtis to Bureau of Indian Affairs, February 20, 1911, OPF.

26. Letter to Rieseberg re: Opening at Sac and Fox Reservation, March 22, 1912. Department of the Interior, OPF.

27. Letter to Rieseberg with Directions to Sac & Fox, April 29, 1912. Department of the Interior, OPF. The letter stated the "route to the Sac and Fox Agency, is as follows: Railroad Station: Stroud, Okla., on St. Louis and San Francisco Rwy.; thence hired team, 6 miles. Or Davenport, on Santa Fe Rwy. And St. Louis and San Francisco Rwy.; thence hired team, 9 miles."

28. Letter of Resignation from Rieseberg, May 16, 1912. Department of the Interior, OPF.

29. Telegrams from Sac & Fox School re: Rieseberg, May 17, 1912. Department of the Interior, OPF.

30. Postal Savings Banks were a means by which less affluent citizens without access to banks could save money.

31. Letter from Rieseberg asking about a position, August 24, 1912. Post Office Department, OPF.

32. "Museum Books Disappear, Charges Are Preferred Against a Former Employee," *The Washington Evening Star*, October 26, 1912, p. 2. Richard Magoon Barnes was an expert in the exchange price for North American birds, as well as their nests and eggs. His collection was donated to the Field Museum in Chicago. He was also an attorney and judge in Illinois. Barnes returned them but should have known better than to acquire them in that manner.

33. "Sad," *The Oologist* XXIX, no. 12 (December 15, 1912): p. 390.

34. Note from Rieseberg to Secretary of the Smithsonian, December 27, 1912; Smithsonian Institution, OPF.

35. Letter of Reference on Rieseberg from Southern Railway Company, August 12, 1918; War Risk Insurance Department, OPF.

36. Rieseberg, *I Dive for Treasure* (1942), p. 24.

37. Rieseberg lived with the Martins at 620 Stevens Place in Los Angeles. Harry was listed with them at that address in the 1914 Los Angeles City Directory.

38. Letter of Reference re: Rieseberg from Barker Brothers, July 7, 1915, Rieseberg-Mikalow Collection. Further references to this source will use RMC. See the bibliography head notes for more information.

39. "For Sale, Trade and Exchange," *The Philatelic West* 59, no. 3 (July 31, 1913). https://archive.org/details/philatelicwest1913nebr.

40. "Want Ads," *Weekly Eagle* (Wichita, KS), October 10, 1913, p. 7.

41. "Classified Ads," *Los Angeles Daily Times*, October 14, 1913, Sec 1, p. 7.

42. This information is found in Rieseberg's federal employment records containing personal information forms completed for job applications

at the War Risk Bureau, on July 26, 1918, and at the Rural Mails System of the Post office on July 26, 1918. A letter of reference dated August 5, 1918, from the United Verde mine is found in his War Risk employment folder. All from OPF.

43. Harry E. Rieseberg, "Old Chinatown," *Every Where*, no. 6 (August 1912): pp. 329–332.

44. Harry E. Rieseberg, "Arizona, The Land of Mystery," Arizona, July 1913, pp. 7–18.

45. Harry E. Rieseberg, "In Cattle Land, The Old Santa Fe Trail (Among Our Poets)," *The Santa Fe Magazine*, December 1915, pp. 51–52.

46. Harry E. Rieseberg, "Coconino Jim, Lumberjack," *The Coconino Sun*, September 15, 1915, p. 2.

47. Earle Spamer (https://earlespamer.acade mia.edu/) called attention to Rieseberg's plagiarism in an article for the Grand Canyon Historical Society titled "Harry Rieseberg Takes the Santa Fe Railway for a Ride (A Plagiarist Exposed," The Ol' Pioneer" (Grand Canyon Historical Society), Vol. 35, no. 2 (Spring 2024). Spamer noted that Rieseberg illicitly used the words of Fannie Isabel Sherrick, William Lawrence Chittenden, and Emily Pauline Johson as his own. The article was unpublished at the time of this writing.

48. "A World Brotherhood of Boys, Over-Land and Over-Seas Correspondence Club," *Boys' Life— The Boy Scouts' Magazine*, March 1916, p. 37.

49. His July 1916 petition to join the Mount Pleasant Lodge No 33 of the Masonic order states that he had been back in Washington D.C. for one year. Additionally, his poem published in *Santa Fe* magazine in December 1915 states he was again a resident of the district.

50. "Ancient and Honorable Fraternity of Free and Accepted Masons, Membership Application for Harry Rieseberg, Mount Pleasant Masonic Lodge #33." Washington, D.C., July 12, 1916. Many thanks to Bilal M. Raschid for his help with these records.

51. "Society," *The Washington (D.C.) Sunday Star*, March 18, 1917, part 7, p. 2. Christ Church was an Episcopal congregation, founded in 1765.

52. Eric F. Rieseberg, *Heroes Alongside Us* (Naples, FL: Salt Island Publishing, 2014), pp. 9–10.

53. "United States World War I Draft Registration Cards, 1917–1918", database with images, FamilySearch (https://www.familysearch.org/ ark:/61903/1:1:KZVJ-NT3: 24 December 2021), Harry Earl Rieseberg, 1917–1918. His registration card was stamped by the City Clerk's Office in Washington. Instructions for registration directed anyone unable to reach home in time to register to get a card from the county clerk where they are at the time and mail it to their home Sheriff or Mayor. Based on later events it appears that Harry was in the process of moving to Los Angeles and gave his new address for the draft. In an application for a federal position in 1921, Rieseberg claimed he had been "rejected in Navy, Marine Corps, and draft." No records have been located to support that assertion.

54. Letter of Reference to War Risk Insurance from Collins, September 10, 1918. War Risk Insurance Bureau, OPF.

55. "New P.O. Clerk Here," August 4, 1917, Imperial Valley Press (El Centro, CA).

56. Letter from John H. Kettner to Veterans' Bureau regarding Rieseberg's character, August 22, 1921; Veterans Administration, OPF.

57. *Ibid*. Letter of Reference to War Risk Insurance from Collins, September 10, 1918, OPF.

58. Letter to 1st Ass't Postmaster General from Bureau of War Risk Insurance, October 23, 1918; War Risk Insurance Bureau, OPF.

59. Letters from members of Congress supporting Rieseberg, May 13, 1909; War Risk Insurance Bureau, OPF. Letters were received from Sen Hiram Johnson (December 13, 1917), Sen. James D. Phelan (December 13, 1917, Rep. Julius Kahn (December 15, 1917), and Rep Charles Randall (December 20, 1917).

60. Temporary Appointment job as Clerk, January 2, 1918; Bureau of Markets, OPF.

61. Rieseberg, *I Dive for Treasure* (1942), p. 35.

62. 1918/04/29, Food Surveys newsletters.

63. Hollerith's company became IBM.

64. Letter to Thompson McIlhenny listing Rieseberg's qualifications, March 13, 1918; Department of Agriculture, OPF.

65. Application for Position at Bureau of War Risk Insurance, June 17, 1918; War Risk, OPF.

66. *Ibid.*

67. Resignation from Bureau of Markets, June 23, Department of Agriculture, OPF. Rieseberg resigned only a week after accepting the job.

68. Letter from Macfarlane to Batchelder regarding Rieseberg's appointment, July 19, 1918; War Risk, OPF. There was also a bit of civil service maneuvering going on while waiting for his appointment. Harry took the examination for "Clerk, qualified in Statistics or Accounting" and passed with a 72.8 percent rating. As a result, Macfarlane tried to get Harry on board at $1,500 per year, but his pay remained at $1,100 and his classification stayed as Assistant Tabulating Expert.

69. A note in Harry's personal journal seems to indicate that he had an older sister, Joyce.

70. Note initiating investigation of Rieseberg, July 25, 1918; War Risk, OPF.

71. Personal History form, July 26, 1918; War Risk, OPF.

72. Letter from King to Rep. Randall requesting a reference, July 26, 1918; War Risk, OPF

73. *Ibid.*

74. Letters of reference, War Risk, OPF. Letters were received from William Lowe (July 30, 1918), Colin T. Martin (August 2, 1918), A.A. Ormsby (August 5, 1018), and C.W. Thompson (August 5, 1918).

75. Letter of Reference from United Verde Copper Co, August 5, 1918; War Risk, OPF.

76. Letter of Reference from Southern Railway, August 12, 1918; War Risk, OPF.

77. Internal memo from A.S.H. to McKenzie, August 6, 1918; War Risk, OPF.

78. Letter of Reference from Cain to King, August 20, 1918; War Risk, OPF. Cain, Assistant Cashier for the Franklin National Bank, said he had known Harry for two years, but did not say how. He also was the first to note that Harry's father was originally from Germany.

79. Letter of Reference from Barker Bros., August 26, 1918; War Risk, OPF.

80. Follow up from King to Barker Bros., September 13, 1918; War Risk, OPF

81. Letter from Collins at El Centro to King, September 10, 1918; War Risk, OPF.

82. Letter from War Risk to Post Office Inspector, September 17, 1918; War Risk, OPF. Reply from Post Office Inspector to King, September 23, 1918; War Risk, OPF.

83. Letter to War Risk from Post Office Department, November 1, 1918; War Risk, OPF.

84. Letter from King to Batchelder, November 14, 1918; War Risk, OPF.

85. Internal memo from King to Macfarlane, September 16, 1918; War Risk, OPF.

86. *Ibid.* Kettner letter, August 22, 1921; Veterans' Bureau, OPF.

87. Divorce proceedings, Harry Rieseberg vs. Caroline Lowe Rieseberg, October 29, 1920; Superior Court of Yavapai County, State of Arizona.

88. *Ibid.* Deposition by Henry R. Rieseberg.

89. "Cruelty Is Charged," Local Briefs, May 7, 1920, Arizona Republican, Phoenix, AZ, p. 6.

90. Coler to Civil Service, December 26, 1919; War Risk, OPF.

91. Letter of Reference to Rieseberg from Macfarlane, January 3, 1920; War Risk, OPF.

92. Letter from Col to Veterans' Bureau, January 23, 1920; Veterans' Bureau, OPF.

93. Confirmation of Telegram to Rieseberg from Federal Board of Vocational Education, January 27, 1920; War Risk, OPF.

94. Internal Memo from New Orleans Federal Board of Trade, January 28, 1920; Federal Board for Vocational Education, OPF.

95. Surgeon General to U.S. Public Health Hospital in Prescott, AZ, Letter of appointment, February 6, 1920; War Risk, OPF.

96. Rieseberg Expense Report Voucher, February 17, 1920; War Risk, OPF. Harry was notified that his expenses getting to Prescott would be reimbursed by the department. His travel from Washington by rail through St. Louis and Kansas City cost the department $101.50, and Harry spent another $20.30 on meals and tips. Harry tried to charge the department $1.00 for a hotel stay and $1.50 for dinner on the day he arrived, but those were not reimbursed ... an act of incredible scrutiny by the government employee reviewing his expenses.

97. Ralph C. Williams, The United States Public Health Service, 1798–1950 (Washington, D.C.: Commissioned Officers Association of the United States Public Health Service, 1951), p. 602.

98. *Ibid.*, p. 605. Both the War Risk Insurance Bureau and the Public Health Service, as well as the Federal Board of Vocational Education, were part of the Department of Treasury.

99. Letter from Rieseberg to Surgeon General requesting transfer, March 31, 1920; Veterans' Bureau, OPF.

100. Letter from Surgeon General to Rieseberg, April 7, 1920; Veterans' Bureau, OPF.

101. Letter from Rep. Osborne to Surgeon General, April 5, 1920; Veterans' Bureau, OPF.

102. Application for Graduate Nurse Examination, Ellen Carver Rieseberg Employment files, September 29, 1922; Public Health Service, OPF.

103. "Camp Lee, 1918–1925," Email to author from Karl Rubis, Command Historian, CASCOM History Office, U.S. Army Combined Arms Support Command, September 21, 2022.

104. Sheet music with lyrics and score found in Rieseberg ephemera discarded at estate sale following the death of Al Mikalow. The author identifies this collection as the Christensen Portfolio (CP). See bibliography head notes for more information.

105. "Grand Jury Indicts Girl War Workers," *Washington Evening Star*, June 11, 1920, p. 2.

106. "Proceedings of the Board of Supervisors of Yavapai County, Arizona," *Weekly Journal-Miner* (Prescott, AZ), May 19, 1920, p. 2.

107. Letter from Saks to Chief Clerk, War Department, August 27, 1920; Department of Treasury, OPF.

108. Request for Transfer, Rieseberg to Surgeon General, August 1, 1920; Veterans' Bureau, OPF.

109. *Ibid.*

110. Letter from Sen. Smith to Surgeon General, August 30, 1920; Veterans' Bureau, OPF.

111. Letter requesting transfer, Rieseberg to Surgeon General, August 26, 1920; Veterans' Bureau, OPF.

112. Letter re Report on Rieseberg from Surgeon General to Medical Officer in Charge, Whipple Barracks, August 27, 1920; Veterans' Bureau, OPF.

113. *Ibid.*

114. Letter from Rieseberg to Ijams, requesting return to War Risk Insurance Bureau, August 30, 1920; War Risk, OPF.

115. Rieseberg to Lt. Col. Shepard denying charges by his wife, September 10, 1920; War Risk, OPF.

116. Memo from Shepard to Surgeon General, September 9, 1920/09/09; War Risk, OPF.

117. Letter to Rieseberg from Surgeon General withdrawing charges, September 25, 1920; Veterans' Bureau, OPF.

118. Letter to Sheriff of Yavapai Country from Chief of Military Police, Whipple barracks, canceling indictment, September 25, 1920; Veteran Bureau, OPF.

119. Telegram from Stanley to Surgeon General, requesting transfer of Rieseberg, October 5, 1920; Veterans' Bureau, OPF.

120. Letter to Rieseberg from Surgeon General, October 20, 1920; Veterans' Bureau, OPF. Oteen is Asheville, NC.

121. Ancestry.com. *Texas, Select County Marriage Index, 1837-1977* [database on-line]. Provo, UT, USA. Original data: *Texas County Marriage Index, 1837-1977*. Salt Lake City, Utah; Family Search, 2013.
122. Robert Rieseberg had a distinguished military and business career. Even though he grew up in Washington he never knew his father. Robert had a Harvard MBA and spent twenty-two years in the Navy, retiring as a Captain. He later worked for W.R. Grace & Co. as vice-president of steamship operations.
123. Letter from Rieseberg to Maj. Hedding, October 30, 1910; War Risk, OPF.
124. Letter to Medical Officer in Charge from Surgeon General, November 18, 1920; Veterans' Bureau, OPF.
125. Letter to Rieseberg from Surgeon General, November 25, 1920/11/25; War Risk, OPF. See also, Senior Surgeon, Oteen, to Surgeon General, December 11, 1920; Veterans' Bureau, OPF.
126. Rieseberg Application for Position at Bureau of Markets, December 4, 1920; Agriculture Department, OPF. See also, Richardson to Department of Agriculture, December 8, 1920, Agriculture Department, OPF.
127. Chief Personnel Officer to Rieseberg, December 16, 1920; Agriculture Department, OPF. See also, Certified for position with IRS, February 16, 1921; Treasury Department, OPF.
128. Kettner letter to Veterans' Bureau, August 22, 1921; Veterans' Bureau, OPF.
129. Classification Sheet, Description of job duties, May 15, 1923; Treasury Department, OPF.
130. Ibid.
131. Harry E. Rieseberg, "Ask Adventure," *Adventure*, June 10, 1923, p. 184.
132. Letter from Rieseberg to John Gainfort, January 29, 1942; PP-NYPL.
133. Harry E. Rieseberg, "Ask Adventure," *Adventure*, February 20, 1924, p. 185.
134. Ibid.
135. Personnel Classification Sheet, job duties, July 5, 1928, Department of Treasury, OPF.
136. "Appointing Army Field Clerks and Field Clerks, Quartermaster Corps, Warrant Officers, U.S. Army: Hearing before the Committees on Military Affairs, Congress of the United States," Appointing army field clerks and field clerks, Quartermaster Corps, warrant officers, U.S. Army: hearing before the Committees on Military Affairs, Congress of the United States, § (1926).
137. Rieseberg to Carson, Bureau of Navigation, June 19, 1925; Bureau of Navigation, OPF.
138. Letter to War Risk Department from Aetna Casualty and Surety Company, October 20, 1925; Veterans' Bureau, OPF. Aetna, Cayuse. Aetna sought a reference to support a bond attesting to Harry's honesty.
139. Harry E. Rieseberg, "The Lights of Clarkdale (Poem), Into the Land of Yavapai (Article)," *Progressive Arizona*, May 1926, pp. 4–26. See also, Harry E Rieseberg, "To the Highest Peaks in Arizona," *Progressive Arizona*, September 1926, pp. 13–15.
140. Letter of Separation, June 30, 1927; Ellen C. Rieseberg, Treasury Department (Public Health Service), OPF.
141. George D. Riley, "The Federal Diary," *The Washington Post*, January 9, 1933, p. 4.
142. Ibid.
143. "Fraternal Organizations, Tall Cedars of Lebanon," *The Washington Post*, July 10, 1927, p. F-5.
144. "Colorful Charity Ball Scheduled for Tonight," *The Washington Evening Star*, December 5, 1928, p. 6; "Tall Cedars Honor New York Leader," *The Washington Evening Star*, October 30, 1928, p. 25; "Fraternal Organizations, Tall Cedars," *The Washington Post*, July 31, 1932, p. S-7.
145. "Fraternal Organizations, Tall Cedars," *The Washington Post*, December 25, 1932, p. A-6.
146. Nancy MacLean, *Behind the Mask of Chivalry: The Making of the Ku Klux Klan* (New York, NY: Oxford University Press, 1994), pp. xii, xi.
147. Anonymous letter to the Secretary of Commerce, May 9, 1929; Notes on the investigation of claims, May 21, 1929; Bureau of Navigation, National Archives and Records Administration, Washington, D.C. This source will be referred to in the future as NARA. See the bibliographic head not for more information.
148. Ibid.
149. Robert A. Goldberg, "The Ku Klux Klan in Madison, 1922–1927," *Wisconsin Magazine of History* 58, no. 1 (1974): pp. 31–44.
150. CP. Author's collection.
151. Harry E. Rieseberg, "Are There Slackers in the Ku Klux Klan," *The Kourier: The Magazine of Americanism*, January 1929, p. 8.
152. "Ku Klux Membership Falls from 8,904,871 in 1925 to 34,964 Now," *The Washington Post*, November 30, 1930, pp. M-1, M-4.
153. "DePriest Incident Hit by Klan Ruler: Imperial Wizard Is Speaker at Big Mass Meeting Held in Forestville, MD," *The Washington Post*, July 7, 1929, pp. M-1, M-2.
154. "Club and Society Activity of Nearby Towns, Forrestville," *The Washington Post*, July 14, 1929, p. M-16.
155. "National Order of Protestant Clubs," National Republic Collection, Box 227, Folder 6 (Reel 233) Hoover Institution Archives, Stanford University. This record holds undated articles from April 1931 in the *Washington Post* and *Washington Evening Star*.
156. Ibid.
157. Charles H Joseph, "Random Thoughts, Another Era of Hate," *The Sentinel*, May 22, 1931, p. 10.
158. "Fraternal Organizations, Tall Cedars," *The Washington Post*, July 31, 1932, p. S-7.
159. "Tall Cedars 4-Day Assembly Nearing, 100 Bands Will Attend Gala National Gathering of Masons in May," *The Washington Post*, March 19, 1933, p. 5.

160. "Fraternal Organizations, Tall Cedars," *The Washington Post*, August 14, 1932, p. S-7.
161. "Arizona Scores in Big Parade," *The Prescott Courier*, June 23, 1932, p. 3.

Chapter 3

1. Charles Morrow Wilson, "Now Comes a New Day of Treasure Hunting," *The New York Times*, May 29, 1932, sec. SM, p. 13.
2. "Liner Egypt Yields £45,000 More Gold," *The New York Times*, July 13, 1935, sec. Social News, p. 15. The exchange rate in 1935 was .2 pounds to the dollar, so £45,000 equaled about $9,000.
3. Arthur Warner, "Sunken Gold, Now as Ever, Lures Man; Science, Adventure and the Gambling Instinct All Play a Role in an Endless Search for Treasure-Laden Hulks," *The New York Times, New York Times Magazine*, August 9, 1931, p. 68.
4. "Spring Treasure-Hunting," *The New York Times*, March 27, 1939, p. 11.
5. A.J. Tyrer, "Navigation Bureau Arm of Commerce; Enforcement of Difficult Maritime Laws Supervised by Officials," *The Washington Post*, December 31, 1931, p. DC-13.
6. "Ships Scrapped," *Tipton Tribune*, January 28, 1930, p. 5.
7. Rieseberg, *I Dive for Treasure* (1942), pp. 36–40.
8. Harry E. Rieseberg, "Last Voyages of American Clipper Ships Are Writing Finis to Glorious Era of Adventure," The *Washington Post*, October 29, 1933, p. SM-8, 9. One of the formerly gloried ships he mentioned, the *Star of India* owned by the Zoological Society of San Diego, was moored at Balboa Park for use as an aquarium and marine museum at that time of the article. Harry would be pleased to know that the *Star of India* is still the centerpiece of the San Diego Maritime Museum.
9. Harry E. Rieseberg, "Treasures at the Bottom of the Sea," *The Sunday Oregonian*, Magazine Section, November 19, 1933, pp. 1–2.
10. *Ibid.*
11. *Ibid.*
12. *Ibid.*
13. *Ibid.*
14. Harry E. Rieseberg, "Hidden Treasure Waters of the Americas," *Cleveland Plain Dealer*, Magazine Section, November 26, 1933, p. 1.
15. Harry E. Rieseberg, "Go Down to the Sea ... for Gold!," *Los Angeles Times*, Sunday Magazine, January 7, 1934, pp. 8, 14. Harry E Rieseberg, "Mystery Ships Add Exiting Chapter to Lore of the Sea," *The Washington Post*, January 7, 1934, pp. SM-8, SM-15.
16. "The Treasure Hunters," *Popular Mechanics*, August 1934, pp. 212–215, 122A.
17. John D. Craig, *Danger Is My Business* (United Kingdom: Simon & Shuster, 1938), p. 235.
18. *Ibid.*
19. Morgan Baker, "The Federal Diary, Here's to Arizona," *The Washington Post*, June 15, 1934, p. 11.
20. Don Block, "Diving Robot Capable of Greatest Depth Coming to Washington Soon," *The Washington Evening Star*, March 7, 1935, p. A-10.
21. Navy diving school—outtakes. (Fox Movietone News Story 3-138.) Fox Movietone News Collection. Moving Image Research Collections. University of South Carolina. https://digital.tcl.sc.edu/digital/collection/MVTN/id/1336/rec/1.
22. Rieseberg, *I Dive for Treasure* (1942), p. 47. Thompson was also a member of the Order of Red Men and may have known Harry through that fraternity.
23. *Ibid.*
24. Rieseberg's claim of taking leave from his federal position makes the story far less credible. Harry's federal personnel file had paperwork for single days off and the newspaper had items when federal employees were on vacation or out for illness. If he had taken months of leave, it would have been recorded in some way or mentioned in a contemporaneous employment record.
25. "Young Adventurer to Be on Lusitania Job," *The Oshkosh Northwestern*, February 28, 1936, p. 17.
26. Rieseberg, *I Dive for Treasure* (1942), p. 47.
27. *Ibid.*, p 52. Rieseberg claimed he spent seven years learning his craft.

Chapter 4

1. "Navy Diving Bell Tests Take Officer 400 Feet Undersea," *Washington Evening Star*, November 4, 1933, p. 1.
2. Romano's patent no. 1,975,333 for salvage buoys had been approved on October 2, 1934, and patent no. 1,940,326 for salvage apparatus using those buoys to lift intact ships from the bottom of the sea filed in October 1931.
3. Leonard H. Delano, *Sunken Klondike Gold: How A Lost Fortune Inspired an Ambitious Effort to Raise the S.S. Islander* (Newberg, OR: Delano Pub., 2011).
4. "He Exhibited the Machine, Defendant in Slot-Machine Case Found Guilty," *Seattle Times*, November 17, 1903, p. 4.
5. "Monoplane Dives in Lake Waters, Aviator Sticks by Machine to Shut Off Engine," *Los Angeles Times*, July 5, 1911, p. 5.
6. Articles about the Romanoplane appeared in multiple issues of *Aero* magazine, titled "American's Aviation Weekly," during late 1911 and early 1912. Romano ran an ad looking for "one or two second-hand Gnome motors. With a workshop and hangar on Harbor Island, by the summer of 1912 Romano had two "big" planes and was working on a third, burning through his funding quickly. One plane was equipped with pontoons for a water landing and another as an instructional vehicle. Romano sought investors following his experimental flights on the island but could find no one willing to take the risk.
7. "Seattle-Built and Invented Aeroplane to Fly at Potlatch," *Seattle Times*, June 8, 1912, pp. 1, 5.

8. "Application to Sell Securities," October 29, 1931. Romano Marine Salvage Co, Securities Division, Washington State Archives, Washington Secretary of State, Olympia, WA. Future footnotes will refer to this source as WA-SOS.
9. "Lure of Gold Is Inventors' Call Below the Sea," *Seattle Times*, March 14, 1932, p. 15.
10. Patent for Wiley mechanical arm and hand, diving bell. Patent # 1,979,782.
11. Letterhead, March 26, 1932; WA-SOS.
12. "Off in April to Hunt Sunken Ship's Gold," *New York Times*, February 14, 1932, sec. Financial, p. N-1.
13. Letter from Romano Marine, March 26, 1932. Case #13331 and Case #13266 were lawsuits among the parties involved in the dredging and impoundment of the Romano diving bell. Record Group 21, Admiralty Case Files, 1929–1942, National Archives and Records Administration, Seattle, WA. This source will be cited at NARA-Seattle. See the bibliographic head notes for more information.
14. Lawsuit pleadings, January 12, 1933; NARA-Seattle.
15. Letter to Larson from Romano Marine, October 11, 1932; NARA-Seattle.
16. Affidavit of publication, October 12, 1933; NARA-Seattle.
17. Fleming affidavit, October 14, 1932; NARA-Seattle.
18. Patterson Affidavit, October 18, 1932; NARA-Seattle.
19. Romano Marine business plan, October 30,1931. WA-SOS.
20. "Crew of Nine Missing After Tug Sinks; Blast Rocks Ship, Debris Only Remains," San Bernardino Daily Sun, November 22, 1926, p. 1.
21. "Salvage Firm to Raise Tug Sunk Seven Years Ago," *Seattle Times*, July 23, 1933, p. 15.
22. The American Society of Naval Engineers presents the annual Harold E. Saunders award in his honor. He is still cited as an authority on the resistance and propulsion of naval ships. The loss of forty lives aboard the S-4 was a tragic event in Naval history. Salvage of the S-4 took three months, forty-four winter working days, and 566 separate dives. It was finally completed on March 17, 1928. See: Joseph A. Williams, *Seventeen Fathoms Deep: The Saga of the Submarine S-4 Disaster* (Chicago, IL: Chicago Review Press Incorporated, 2015).
23. Quinault Canyon is the nearest underwater feature of that depth, and it is two hundred miles off shore.
24. D. Adams Frost, Letter to Commandant, Thirteenth Naval District, "Description of Salvage Work being undertaken on Tug BAHADA by Romano Marine Salvage Company of Seattle," October 4, 1933; Department of the Navy.
25. Ralph W. Andrews, "Bahada Came to a Tragic End," in *Photographers of the Frontier West: Their Lives and Works, 1875 to 1915* (New York, NY: Bonanza Books, 1967).
26. Frank Kester, "Barkentine Is to Fit Out for Treasure Hunt," *Oakland Tribune*, May 20, 1933, p. 16.
27. Financial report for Romano Marine, February 28, 1934; WA-SOS.
28. Naval Commander C.W. King to Romano Marine, December 5, 1933; SOS-WA.
29. "Bell to Light Bay Depths, Plead for Diving Sphere Bridge Use," *San Francisco Call-Bulletin*, January 27, 1934.
30. Johanna Loesche Whicker, "The Four-Masted Schooner 'Constellation' (Es Sally Persis Noyes)," *Nautical Research Journal* 7, no. 7–8 (1955): pp. 108–112. Johanna Loesche's first-hand accounts of the *Constellation's* history are used throughout this section.
31. James W. Hunt, "Changing Tacks," *Changing Tacks* (1993), p. 41. Jim Hunt produced a complete history of the *Constellation*.
32. Mark W. Hennessy, "Mysterious Rejuvenation Famous Windjammer at Boothbay Harbor Reveals New Life for Craft," *Portland Press-Herald*, September 18, 1932, pp. D-1, D-3.
33. Hunt, p. 47. Harry Rieseberg may have had an administrative duty related to the *Constellation* while he was still working at the Bureau of Navigation. Late in 1933 or early 1934, Royall was corresponding with the Bureau to get the vessel's name formally changed. After the requisite red tape, the notice was posted four times in the *Boston Daily Globe* and the task was complete.
34. Hunt, p. 48.
35. Hunt, p. 49.
36. Hunt, p. 53.
37. "Mrs. Alwyn Inness-Brown," *Washington Post*, October 13, 1934, p. 11.
38. Evelyn Peyton Gordon, "Guests Dine on Schooner Docked Here," *Washington Post*, October 16, 1934, p. 15.
39. Albert C Wagner, "Washington Club Notes," *Hobbies, The Magazine for Collectors*, March 1935, p. 109. See also, Scrimshaw, "The Shipmodeler, Treasure Hunter," *Hobbies, The Magazine for Collectors*, September 1935, p. 13.
40. Hunt, p. 78. The ad appeared in *Yachting* magazine, Vol 57, pp. 23–24.
41. Letter from Director to Secretary of Commerce, October 18, 1934; Treasury Department, OPF.
42. Letter acknowledging Rieseberg's resignation, November 23, 1934; Treasury Department, OPF.
43. Letter of reference for Rieseberg, December 18, 1934; Bureau of Navigation, NARA.
44. "Divorce Petition," Rieseberg vs. Rieseberg (Galveston County District Clerk September 4, 1940).
45. Rieseberg, *I Dive for Treasure* (1942), p. 103.
46. Letter from Carpenter to Romano Marine, December 5, 1934; SOS-WA.
47. Rieseberg, *I Dive for Treasure* (1942), p. 104.
48. Ray Coll. Jr., "Shoreside Shorts," *Honolulu Advertiser*, January 22, 1935, p. 9.

49. Rieseberg, *I Dive for Treasure* (1942), p. 104.
50. "Ingenious Inventor Dies of Operation," *Spokane Press*, February 12, 1935, p. 3.
51. "Diving Bell to Seek Sea's Gold," *Seattle Daily Times*, May 1, 1935, p. 9.
52. Rieseberg, *I Dive for Treasure* (1942), p. 107.
53. Agreement between Rieseberg and Romano Marine, April 15, 1935. Rieseberg-Mikalow papers, images during visit. Images of some documents were made during an author's visit and interview in August 2014 with Al Mikalow before his death. Future references to this material will be cited as RMV. See the bibliographic head notes for more information.
54. Rieseberg, *I Dive for Treasure* (1942), p. 107.
55. Letter from Carpenter to Romano Marine, December 5, 1934; SOS-WA.
56. Romano Patent for Submarine Salvage Apparatus, Patent No. 2,061,256; Filed January 16, 1935, Approved November 17, 1936.
57. Bloch, *Washington Evening Star*, March 7, 1935. The book manuscript mentioned is likely an early version of his first book in 1942, *I Dive for Treasure*.
58. *Ibid.*
59. "Schooner to Leave in Quest for Gold, Lieut. Rieseberg to Pilot Vessel Down Potomac to Spot Off Haiti," *The Washington Evening Star*, Sunday Edition, April 28, 1935, p. A-16.
60. Press Release with markup, *Science News Digest*, May 7, 1935; Smithsonian Institution Archives. Record Unit 7091, Box 373, Folder 37. From http://siarchives.si.edu/findingaids/FARU7091.htm.
61. "Diving Bell Will Seek Treasure," *Seattle Daily Times*, March 16, 1935, p. 3.
62. Letter from Fleming to Sisson, March 23, 1935; SOS-WA.
63. *Ibid.*
64. Romano Submarine Engineering & Salvage, Articles of Incorporation, April 9, 1935; SOS-WA.
65. Hunt, *Changing Tacks*, pp. 89–91. The first-hand information from Carey was communicated in letters to Fred Kaiser and to Jim Hunt in 1992.
66. Rieseberg, *I Dive for Treasure* (1942), p. 171.
67. Items view in visit by author with Jim Hunt.
68. Hunt, *Changing Tacks*, p. 65.
69. Hunt, *Changing Tacks*, p. 68.
70. Letter from Fleming to Lawler, May 31, 1935; Jim Hunt Collection. A person named J. Howard Lawler was present at a psychic reading by Edgar Cayce in 1931. See: http://radialappliance.teslabox.com/radial-appliance-readings/gallbladder/.
71. The author's research has found no information to confirm this.
72. "Two More Are Held in Salvage Swindle," *Daily Boston Globe*, November 23, 1934, p. 40.
73. "Two More Are Held in Salvage Swindle," *Daily Boston Globe*, November 23, 1934, p. 40. He had additional similar scams in October 1935, see "Two Held as Swindlers by 'Treasure Hunt,' Boston Brokers Are Accused of Taking Woman's $38,000 to Finance Undersea Search," *New York Times*, October 13, 1935.
74. "Diving Bell Will Seek Treasure," *Seattle Daily Times*, March 16, 1935, p. 3.
75. Rieseberg, *I Dive for Treasure* (1942), p. 169.
76. *Ibid.* Interestingly, Mr. Carl Estes, publisher of the author's hometown paper, *The Longview (TX) News-Journal*, was among those present.
77. "Treasure Hunt Trap Displayed, Diving Sphere with Claws Shown," *Pittsburgh Post-Gazette*, May 18, 1935, p. 29.
78. Letter from Fleming to O'Neal, May 21, 1935/05/21; Jim Hunt Personal Collection.
79. *Ibid.*
80. Letter from Fleming to Lawler, May 31, 1935; HUNT.
81. *Ibid.*
82. The image appeared in the *Washington Times*, on May 17, 1935. Other than staged publicity photos, this is the only photographic evidence of Harry's presence at the demonstration.
83. Rieseberg, *I Dive for Treasure* (1942), pp. 248–249.
84. C.L. Douglas, "Visitor Here Is Planning Hunt for Sunken Treasure, Lieut. Rieseberg Knows Locations of Gold-Laden Wrecks; Will Take Texans Along," *Fort Worth Press*, November 6, 1935, p. 13. See also, Sam Weiner, "'Thar's Gold in Them Thar Seas,' Is Belief of Man Who Plans Lost Treasure Expedition," *Galveston Tribune*, January 6, 1936.
85. Rieseberg, *I Dive for Treasure* (1942), p. 249.

Chapter 5

1. Hunt, *Changing Tacks*, pp. 89–91. Harry's repeated return to the *Constellation* is described in the first-hand account by Bill Carey, one of the crewmen.
2. "Internationally Known Authority, Public Notices," *New York Times*, June 16, 1935, p. N-2. Harry says in *I Dive for Treasure* (1942), p. 167, that he also ran an ad in the *Washington Post*.
3. Rieseberg, *I Dive for Treasure* (1942), p. 167.
4. Hunt, *Changing Tacks*, p. 70.
5. Hunt, *Changing Tacks*, p. 73. There was a similar effort made in printing up "membership" certificates for the Undersea Explorers & Engineers Syndicate. The fee was $100, and bearers would receive 1/1000 share of 25 percent of any profits.
6. "Queens Sea Scouts to Visit Four-Masted Schooner," *Brooklyn Daily Eagle*, October 31, 1935, p. 8.
7. Madelene Ferguson Allen and Ken Scadden, *The General Grant's Gold: Shipwreck and Greed in the Southern Ocean* (New Zealand: Exisle Publishing Limited, 2010), p. 122.
8. "Schooner as Cruise Ship, Motorless Windjammer to Take Passengers on West Indies Trip," *New York Times*, January 19, 1936, p. 36.
9. Hunt, *Changing Tacks*, p. 79c.
10. Hunt, *Changing Tacks*, pp. 80–82.
11. Frederick F. Kaiser, *Built on Honor, Sailed*

with Skill: *The American Coasting Schooner* (Ann Arbor, MI: Sarah Jennings Press, 1989), p. 243.

12. Dan Rogers, "Four-Master Constellation Sails to See Sunken Treasure with Two Robot Divers," *Portland Press Herald*, August 21, 1936, p. 3.

13. Hunt, *Changing Tacks*, p. 83.

14. Hunt, *Changing Tacks*, p. 85. Hunt cites a letter from Royall to his parents, August 13, 1936.

15. See: "Clipper Ship Sails to See Bullion Treasure Lost When Merida Sank Off Virginia Capes," *Washington Post*, August 21, 1936, p. X-1.

16. Hunt, *Changing Tacks*, p. 88. Hunt cites a letter from Royall to his parents on August 21, 1936.

17. "Ocean Gold Quest Halted by Weather," *Washington Post*, September 4, 1936, p. X-7.

18. Hunt, *Changing Tacks*, p. 89.

19. Hunt, *Changing Tacks*, p. 90. Hunt cites a letter from Royall to his parents on September 9, 1936.

20. "Treasure Hunt," *Mansfield News-Journal*, September 1, 1936, p. 12.

21. Hunt, *Changing Tacks*, p. 90.

22. Frank Reil, "Moses Not Only Build Belt Parkway but He Gave Us Brand New Shoreline," *Brooklyn Daily Eagle*, July 12, 1940, p. 12.

23. Kaiser, p. 247.

24. R.J. Peterson, "Early Sailors Did Not Have Such Easy Berths (Letter to the Editor)," *New York Times*, April 26, 1943.

25. Hunt, *Changing Tacks*, pp. 98–99.

26. The *Constellation* is now a diver's tourist destination. The storied vessel was featured in Peter Benchley's 1977 movie, *The Deep*. The *Constellation* remains as an easily accessible dive site in Bermuda and was memorialized on a Bermudan postage stamp.

27. Huse to Romano Marine, December 27, 1935; SOS-WA.

28. Fleming to Huse, January 3, 1936; SOS-WA.

29. Letter from Dave Grant, Inspector, October 30, 1936; SOS-WA.

30. Conover to Huse, May 25, 1938; SOS-WA.

31. Robert L. Royall vs. The Romano Submarine Engineering & Salvage Corporation (City Court, Queens County, New York, June 4, 1936).

32. Letter from J. William Karbe to Romano Stockholder, September 26, 1943; Eugene Romano Scrapbook, Rockwell Hammond, Jr. Collection. Future references to this collection will be Romano-Hammond. See the bibliographic head note for more information.

33. Letter from Fleming to Karbe, January 27, 1943; Romano-Hammond.

34. Simon Lake to Harry Rieseberg, October 11, 1935/10/11, RMV.

35. "Bay Beach Sites Show Sales Gain," *Washington Herald*, October 16, 1921, p. 2.

36. Simon Lake to Harry Rieseberg, October 11, 1935/10/11, RMV.

37. Rieseberg, *I Dive for Treasure* (1942), Chapter XX, pp. 251–260.

38. C.L. Douglas, "Visitor Here Is Planning Hunt for Sunken Treasure," *Fort Worth Press*, November 6, 1935, p. 13.

39. The author's research on Trammel's Trace resulted in a book by Texas A&M University Press titled *Trammel's Trace: The First Road to Texas from the North (2016)*. That research is where he first discovered Harry Rieseberg. The story of the Hendricks Lake treasure, and Rieseberg's role in it, is in the author's work *True Believers-Treasure Hunters at Hendricks Lake (2019)*. www.trammelstrace.com and www.hendrickslake.com.

40. "All Trace Now Lost of Pirate Jean Lafitte's Mightiest Treasure Haul," *Washington Post*, October 6, 1935.

41. "Harry Rieseberg Papers," deGrummond Children's Literature Collection, The University of Southern Mississippi; https://www.lib.usm.edu/legacy/degrum/public_html/html/research/findaids/DG0816.html.

42. Weiner, *Galveston Tribune*, January 6, 1936.

43. This hospital was built in 1931 and became part of the University of Texas Medical Branch (UTMB).

44. Confidential Efficiency Report for Ellen Rieseberg, Galveston, January 1, 1936; Federal Security Agency, OPF-Ellen Rieseberg.

45. Confidential Efficiency Report for Ellen Rieseberg, Galveston, June 30, 1936; Federal Security Agency, OPF-Ellen Rieseberg.

46. Ellen Rieseberg, Efficiency Report, January 1, 1936; OPF-Ellen Rieseberg.

47. Galveston (TX) City Directory, 1936–1937, p. 306. The styling of the entry in the city directory had Ellen as the head of household.

48. Weiner, *Galveston Tribune*, January 6, 1936.

49. Rieseberg, *I Dive for Treasure* (1942), Chapter XX.

50. What remained of Harry Rieseberg's medical records from his stay at John Sealy Hospital were provided by a member of the family.

51. Rieseberg, *I Dive for Treasure* (1942), p. 257.

52. Letter from Hanni to Mrs. Royall, March 20, 1936; HUNT-PRC.

53. Rieseberg, *I Dive for Treasure* (1942), p. 259.

54. "The Camp Fire, A Meeting Place for All," *Adventure Magazine*, July 15, 1935, p. 118.

55. "Ask Adventure," *Adventure Magazine*, March 1, 1943, p. 116.

56. Rieseberg, *I Dive for Treasure* (1942), p. 258.

57. Letter from Rieseberg to U.S. Department of Commerce, Coast and Geodetic Survey, June 7, 1968; RMC.

Chapter 6

1. Rieseberg, *I Dive for Treasure* (1942), p. 259.

2. *Ibid.*, p. 265.

3. *Ibid.*, pp. 261–262.

4. *Ibid.*

5. "Yarns of Fabulous Riches on Ocean Floor Fill Treasury Files, but 100% Record of Salvage Failures Dims U.S. Reward Hope," *Washington Post*, October 11, 1936, p. M-10.

6. I.G. Stafford, "Texas City, Town Talk," *Galveston Daily News*, November 22, 9136, p. 4.

7. "Treasure!, Business Opportunities," *San Antonio Light*, December 12, 1936, sec. 7, p. 4.

8. Information about Rieseberg's mailing addresses comes from a variety of sources including correspondence, classified ads, and other research material. The author has identified almost 200 documented references to a home address.

9. Breevort Apartment-Hollywood (sic) (blog) (L.A. Kompany, Driving Around the Desert by the Sea, January 4, 2010), http://lakompany.blogspot.com/2010/01/breevort-apartments-hollywood.html. The correct spelling is Brevoort.

10. "Sunken Treasure Lures Salvager," *Oakland Tribune*, May 18, 1937.

11. Letter from Hancock Pacific Expeditions to Rieseberg, June 9, 1937; RMV.

12. "Deep Sea Gold Taker Here to Pay 'Old Debt,'" *San Francisco Chronicle*, September 3, 1937, p. 17.

13. *Ibid*.

14. *Ibid*.

15. "Narcissistic Personality Disorder," Diseases & Conditions, Patient Care & Health Information, Mayo Clinic, Accessed April 18, 2023. https://www.mayoclinic.org/diseases-conditions/narcissistic-personality-disorder/symptoms-causes/syc-20366662.

16. Letter from Rieseberg to *Variety*, September 15, 1937; Variety Protected Materials Department Collection, MSS 017. Emerson College Archives and Special Collections. http://public.archspace-prod.emerson.edu/repositories/2/resources/61. Accessed April 18, 2023. The mail to *Variety* had a return address to Harry but in care of Arthur Van Slyke.

17. Letter from Rieseberg to Variety, December 2, 1937; Variety Protected Materials Department Collection.

18. William Phipps and the treasure of the *Golden Hind* were lifelong interests of Harry's, and he would later write a short book about Phipps titled *Treasure Hunter*.

19. "Robots Will Aid Search for Lost Sea Treasures," *Los Angeles Times*, October 31, 1937, sec. 2, p. 6.

20. *Ibid*.

21. Fan-Fare, "Cecil B. DeMille Is Organizing Treasure Hunt, Director Seeks Loot in Depths of Ocean," *Windsor Daily Star*, November 25, 1937, sec. 2, p. 2.

22. Taylor to Vaughn, February 9, 1938; SOS-WA.

23. *Ibid*.

24. Taylor to Securities Division, February 9, 1938; SOS-WA.

25. "A Proven Success, Big Money for All. Business Opportunities," *The Sun and the New York Herald*, August 8, 1920, p. 65.

26. "To Raise the Lusitania, Divers to Attempt Recovery of Six Millions in Gold on Sunken Vessel," *Wellsboro Gazette*, July 5, 1922, p. 2.

27. Earl L. Shaub, "Firms to Get Coal Sunk in Ships at Sea," *San Antonio Evening News*, January 16, 1923, p. 3.

28. "No Coal Delivered, Two Are Indicted," *Brooklyn Daily Eagle*, February 28, 1934, p. 10. See also, "Coal Salvaging Charges Dismissed," *Brooklyn Daily Eagle*, June 26, 1924, p. 124.

29. Karbe to Latta, May 25, 1939; Romano-Hammond.

30. Brad Matsen, *Descent: The Heroic Discovery of the Abyss* (New York, NY: Pantheon Books, 2005), p. xii.

31. Karbe to Rieseberg, June 16, 1938; Rieseberg-Mikalow Collection.

32. *Ibid*.

33. Karbe to Latta, May 25, 1939; Romano-Hammond.

34. *Ibid*.

35. Lawrence Wright, *Going Clear: Scientology, Hollywood, and the Prison of Belief* (New York, NY: A.A. Knopf, 2013).

36. "Four-Masted Schooner Doris Hamlin," *Baltimore Sun*, January 1, 1938, p. 17.

37. Rieseberg Deposition for Karbe, June 25, 1935; O'Neal Deposition for Karbe, April 17, 1939; Rieseberg-Mikalow Collection.

38. *Ibid*.

39. *Ibid*.

40. Karbe to Romano stockholder, September 26, 1943; Romano-Hammond.

41. Taylor to Karbe, January 27, 1943; Romano-Hammond.

42. *Ibid*.

43. "Captain Loesche, 64, in Seven Shipwrecks; Sailing Master Who Search for Gold on Last Voyage Dies," *New York Times*, April 18, 1939.

44. Harry E. Rieseberg, "City Beneath the Sea," *Los Angeles Times*, October 13, 1940, sec. Sunday Magazine, pp. 6–8.

45. Comment on Henry Rieseberg's Letter of Resignation Public Printer, GPO, June 2, 1930; Henry Rieseberg employment record, Government Printing Office, OPF-Henry Rieseberg.

46. Confidential Efficiency Report, July 1, 1938. and July 1, 1940, Ellen Rieseberg OPF.

47. "Student Arriving for Christmas Holidays Complete Family Circles," *Galveston Daily News*, December 19, 1937, p. 10. See also, Barbara Friston, "High Schools, Lovenberg," *Galveston Daily News*, February 16, 1942, p. 3.

48. "Boy Scout Activities, Troop No. 5," *Galveston Daily News*, October 26, 1941, p. 21.

49. Ellen Rieseberg vs. Harry Rieseberg (Galveston County District Clerk September 4, 1940).

50. Ellen Rieseberg vs. Harry Rieseberg (Galveston County District Clerk October 10, 1940).

51. The foundation for these descriptions of equipment are largely from a *New York Times* article of June 11, 1939, about the diving profession of the time titled "Handy Man of the Sea Bottom." Also helpful was U.S. Navy Standard Deep Sea Diving Outfit Training Film, 43424 NA. Periscope Film | YouTube, 1950. https://youtu.

be/1cwYe9gga9k; "Deep Sea Diving, the Diving Dress," United States Navy Training Film, 1943.

52. "Diving Manual, 1943," United States Navy Department. Bureau of Ships. Washington: U.S. Government Printing Office. A pseudopsychological theory common at the time described four basic personality types. A phlegmatic disposition meant the person was relaxed and peaceful.

53. *Ibid.*

54. "Fathoming the Sea," *Focus Magazine*, October 1938, pp. 16–17.

55. Rieseberg, *I Dive for Treasure* (1942), p. 47.

Chapter 7

1. Lawrence Barber, "Ocean Treasure Object of Urgent Sea Quest, Divers to Hunt for Sunken Gold," *Portland Oregonian*, November 9, 1937, p. 18.

2. "Henry R. Rieseberg Dies; Former District Resident," *Washington Evening Star*, October 24, 1944, sec. A, p. 6. Henry Rieseberg's obituary substantiated the 1937 date for their move to California.

3. Research on print publications from the late 1930s' is difficult, but the author has located about fifty Rieseberg articles between 1937 and 1940, far fewer than Harry suggested. The more obscure, fleeting, and minor publications Harry found to accept his articles are less likely to survive either in print or as digital archives, so it is likely there were more.

4. F. MacDonald Bryan, "Old Diver Relates Tale of Sea Gangsters, Liquor and $100,000 on Hijacked Ship," *Washington Post*, January 23, 1938, p. TS-7.

5. "Helium Method Raises Sunken Treasure," *Modern Mechanix*, March 1938, pp. 35–124.

6. "News of the Radio World," *Fresno Bee Republican*, March 23, 1938, p. 3. Beebe had indeed set a verified depth record of 3,028 feet in August 1934 in his massively constructed bathysphere. Max Gene Nohl set the record for a free dive of 420 feet in Lake Michigan in December 1937. Capt. C.B. Mayo set a Navy record by going down to 485 feet in the Romano bell in Puget Sound.

7. "Trio Wrongly Imprisoned to Talk Tuesday," *Harrisburg Telegraph*, December 14, 1940, p. 24.

8. "Giant Octopus in Attack on Deep Sea Diving Bell," *St. Louis Post-Dispatch*, August 14, 1938, pp. 10–11. See also: "Giant Octopus Loses Death Battle with Deep Sea Divers," *Kansas City Star*, August 28, 1938, p. 2.

9. Perry Windham, Jr., "Speak Up (Letters to the Editor), Rieseberg Weapon," *PIC Magazine*, November 12, 1940, p. 3. The article the reader cites is: "Death in the Deep," *PIC Magazine*, August 20, 1940, pp. 26–28.

10. "Giant Octopus Loses Fight to Repulse Invaders of Deep Sea Treasure Lair," *Cleveland Plain Dealer*, November 27, 1938, p. 8. The same story got an even broader audience in the February 1939 edition of *Mechanix Illustrated* and was then upgraded and largely repeated in the November 1939 issue. See: Harry E. Rieseberg, "Octopus! Terror of the Deep," *Mechanix Illustrated*, February 1939, pp. 42–44; and Harry E. Rieseberg, "I Battled an Octopus for Treasure," *Mechanix Illustrated*, November 1939, pp. 36–120.

11. Rieseberg, *I Dive for Treasure* (1942), pp. 261–272.

12. "Drama of the Deep: Octopus vs. Diving Robot," *Newsweek*, October 31, 1938, pp. 24–26.

13. Eric Strutt, "He Walks with Davy Jones," *Arizona Republic*, December 28, 1941, p. 40. If the reader has not yet read, *I Dive for Treasure*, this article is a brief summation.

14. "Cocos Island: A Place of Fabled Treasure," *New York Times*, January 31, 1932.

15. Malcolm Campbell, Searching for Pirate Treasure in Cocos Island (New York, NY: Frederick A. Stokes Co., 1932).

16. Harry E. Rieseberg, "'X' Marks Nothing on Cocos," *Los Angeles Times*, February 11, 1940, sec. Sunday Magazine.

17. *Ibid.*

18. Bloch, *Washington Evening Star*, March 7, 1935.

19. "Obituaries, Eric Strutt," *Newport Beach Daily Pilot*, September 5, 1997, p. 3.

20. Eric Strutt to John Gainfort, February 27, 1942; NYPL-BRT.

21. "I Walk with Davy Jones," Preface, draft of manuscript; STRUTT.

22. Eric P. Strutt vs. Harry E. Rieseberg, Robert W. McBride & Co., a corporation, Dodd Mead and Co., a corporation, Doe One, Doe Two, Doe Third, and Doe Fourth (Superior Court of the State of California, County of Los Angeles March 17, 1950).

23. Harry E. Rieseberg and Eric P. Strutt, "Neptune's Treasure, A New, Different, and Original Radio Program for Sponsorship," Neptune's Treasure, A New, Different, and Original Radio Program for Sponsorship (1939); Personal Papers of Eric P. Strutt. In future references, this collection will be referred to as STRUTT. See the bibliographic head notes for more information.

24. *Ibid.*

25. The author has documented almost 1,800 published works by Harry Rieseberg.

26. Letters of rejection are found in the Strutt Collection.

27. Rieseberg to Edmond Pauker, July 3, 1941; NYPL-M&A.

28. *Ibid.*

29. Rieseberg to Gainfort, July 8, 1941; NYPL-M&A

30. Rieseberg to Gainfort, July 14, 1941; NYPL-M&A. The two-thirds of the manuscript that was finished was submitted on August 5, 1941.

31. Rieseberg to Gainfort, July 29, 1941; NYPL-M&A.

32. Letter of agreement, Rieseberg to Gainfort, August 8, 1941; YALE-Pauker.

33. Rieseberg to Gainfort, October 28, 1941; NYPL-M&A.

34. Gainfort to Rieseberg, November 15, 1941; NYPL-BRT.
35. *Ibid.*
36. Rieseberg to Gainfort, November 15, 1941; NYPL-BRT.
37. *Ibid.*
38. 1941/12/19, Rieseberg to Gainfort, NYPL. The letter is dated 1941/12/29, but the sequence of the letters makes clear that is a typographical error and it was sent on December 19 instead.
39. Obituary, Eric Strutt, *Newport Beach Daily Pilot.*
40. Gainfort to Rieseberg, November 24, 1941; NYPL-BRT.
41. Rieseberg to Gainfort, November 24, 1941; NYPL-BRT.
42. McCarey was married to Stella Martin, a relative of Harry's mother who was also a Martin.
43. Rieseberg to Gainfort, December 6, 1941; NYPL-BRT.
44. Gainfort to Rieseberg, November 27, 1941; NYPL-BRT.
45. *Ibid.*
46. Gainfort to Rieseberg, December 1, 1941; NYPL-BRT.
47. Plimmer to Churchill, December 1, 1941; NYPL-BRT.
48. Churchill to Plimmer; December 6, 1941; NYPL-BRT.
49. *Ibid.*
50. Rieseberg to Gainfort, December 16, 1941; NYPL-BRT.
51. "I Walk with Davy Jones" manuscript, STRUTT.
52. Strutt to Gainfort, February 27, 1942; NYPL-BRT.
53. Rieseberg to Director, Veterans Administration, December 18, 1941; Veterans' Bureau, OPF.
54. *Ibid.*
55. Veterans Administration to Rieseberg, January 15, 1941; Veterans' Bureau, OPF.
56. Gainfort to Rieseberg, December 18, 1941; NYPL-BRT.
57. Gainfort to Rieseberg, December 22, 1941; NYPL-BRT; and, Gainfort to Rieseberg, December 20, 1941; NYPL-BRT.
58. Pauker to Rieseberg, December 20, 1941; NYPL-BRT.
59. Rieseberg to Gainfort, December 26, 1941; NYPL-BRT.
60. Gainfort to Rieseberg, December 31, 1941; NYPL-BRT.
61. Rieseberg to Gainfort, January 15, 1942; NYPL-BRT.
62. Gainfort to Rieseberg, January 16, 1942; NYPL-BRT.
63. Gainfort to Rieseberg, January 21, 1942; NYPL-BRT.
64. Rieseberg to Gainfort, January 27, 1942; NYPL-BRT.
65. *Ibid.*
66. Rieseberg to Gainfort, January 26, 1942; NYPL-BRT.
67. Gainfort to Rieseberg, January 28, 1942; NYPL-BRT.
68. Churchill to Gainfort, February 2, 1942; NYPL-BRT.
69. Rieseberg to Gainfort, December 26, 1941; NYPL-BRT.
70. Rieseberg, *I Dive for Treasure* (1942), pp. 24–25. The name of the church did not get included until Rieseberg raised the story many years later in a magazine article. See, Harry E Rieseberg, "Boy Meets Teddy," *Together Magazine*, May 15, 1958, p. 17.
71. "Only Its First Story, Church of the Good Shepherd Awaits Completion," *Washington Post*, May 23, 1903, sec. A, p. 1. The church was located on Sixth Street NE and I Street in Washington D.C., and Harry's home with his parents was on Q Street NW.
72. "Theodore Roosevelt, Jr., Teaches in Sunday School," *Washington Evening Star*, April 2, 1905, sec. 2, p. 7.
73. Rieseberg, *I Dive for Treasure* (1942), pp. 24–25.
74. "President's Son as a Sunday School Teacher," *New York Times*, July 18, 1904, p. 7.
75. Frontispiece from Theodore Roosevelt, Jr., via Harry Rieseberg, July 29, 1941; NYPL BRT. The letter is undated, so this date is the same as the outline mentioning it to his agent.
76. Letter from U.S. Department of State to author, October 15, 2015.
77. Rieseberg to Gainfort; January 4, 1942; NYPL-BRT. The author would offer up several digits on his left hand in exchange for the contents of those boxes.
78. Rieseberg to Gainfort, February 22, 1942; NYPL-BRT.
79. Rieseberg to Gainfort, February 26, 1942; NYPL-BRT.
80. *Ibid.*
81. Rieseberg to Gainfort, January 29, 1942; NYPL-BRT.

Chapter 8

1. Correspondence between Vaughn Greene and Rieseberg, March 14, 1969; Rieseberg-Mikalow Collection.
2. Gainfort to Rieseberg, January 30, 1942; NYPL-BRT.
3. Harry E Rieseberg, "City Beneath the Sea," *Los Angeles Times*, October 13, 1940, sec. Sunday Magazine, pp. 6–8.
4. Rieseberg to Plimmer, December 2, 1941; NYPL-BRT.
5. *Ibid.*
6. Robert F. Marx, *Port Royal Rediscovered* (Garden City, NY: Doubleday & Company, 1973). The book was reissued in 2003, see Robert F. Marx, *Port Royal—The Sunken City* (Southend-on-Sea, Essex: Aquapress, 2003). Marx's publications about his work at Port Royal began in 1967, part of his commitment to the Institute of Jamaica.

7. Marx, *Port Royal*, p. 125.
8. Marx, *Port Royal*, p. 97.
9. Jean-Yves Blot, *Les Chasseurs de trésors du Gulf Stream* (Grenoble, France: Glénat, 1986), p. 51.
10. Gainfort to Jaquette, January 8, 1942; NYPL-BRT.
11. 1942/01/19, Jaquette to Gainfort, NYPL.
12. Gainfort to Rieseberg, March 10, 1942; NYPL-BRT.
13. Frank Gruber, *The Pulp Jungle* (Los Angeles, CA: Sherbourne Press, Inc., 1967), pp. 79–81.
14. Rieseberg to Director, Veterans' Bureau, December 18, 1941; Veterans' Bureau, OPF.
15. Gruber, p. 80.
16. Gainfort to Rieseberg, January 8, 1942; NYPL-BRT.
17. Robert Kurson, *Pirate Hunters: Treasure, Obsession, and the Search for a Legendary Pirate Ship* (New York, NY: Random House, 2016).
18. Rieseberg to Gainfort, January 10, 1942; NYPL-BRT.
19. Gainfort to Rieseberg, January 30, 1942; NYPL-BRT.
20. *Ibid.*
21. Rieseberg to Gainfort, February 2, 1942; NYPL-BRT.
22. Gainfort to Rieseberg, February 4, 1942; NYPL-BRT.
23. In prefacing his description of the shark and octopus fight in *Pearl Diver*, Berge said he had learned to maneuver the creatures into shallow, clear pools for observation and filming. Once there, he would force the encounter by pumping air bubbles from a perforated air, forcing an octopus out of hiding beneath the rocks.
24. *Samarang* (United Artists Corp., 1933).
25. "Shark-Octopus Undersea Battle Filmed," *Modern Mechanix*, July 1933.
26. "Flash Gordon: Space Soldiers, Captured by Shark Men" (Universal Productions, 1936), https://www.youtube.com/watch?v=RA9Ubx30rK0.
27. *The Incredible Petrified World* (G.B.M. Productions, 1957), https://archive.org/details/TheIncrediblePetrifiedWorld. This film was directed by Jerry Warren, famous for inventing stories that could glue together a movie from stock scenes.
28. Harry E. Rieseberg, "Octopus Battles Shark to Death in Undersea Duel," *SPORT Magazine*, November 1941.
29. Similar articles and claims were found in *Popular Mechanics*, September 1942; *U.S. Camera*, March 1943; *Argosy*, July 1947; PIC, June 1951; *National Enquirer*, January 1959.
30. Rieseberg to Gainfort, December 6, 1941; NYPL-BRT.
31. Gainfort to Rieseberg, January 12, 1942; NYPL-BRT.
32. Churchill to Plimmer, February 6, 1942; NYPL-BRT.
33. *Ibid.*
34. Gainfort to Rieseberg, February 26, 1942; NYPL-BRT.
35. Gainfort to Rieseberg, February 9, 1942; NYPL-BRT.
36. Lanier to Gainfort, February 23, 1942; NYPL-BRT.
37. Rieseberg to Gainfort, February 22, 1942; NYPL-BRT.
38. Rieseberg to Gainfort, February 10, 1942; NYPL-BRT.
39. Rieseberg to Gainfort, February 23, 1942; NYPL-BRT.1
40. *Ibid.*
41. Rieseberg to Gainfort, January 27, 1942; NYPL-BRT.
42. Rieseberg to Gainfort, February 12, 1942; YALE-Pauker.
43. Rieseberg to Gainfort, February 24, 1942; NYPL-BRT.
44. Rieseberg to Gainfort, February 24, 1942; NYPL-BRT.
45. Rieseberg to Gainfort, February 26, 1942; NYPL-BRT.
46. *Ibid.*
47. Rieseberg to Gainfort, February 27, 1942; NYPL-BRT.
48. *Ibid.*
49. Strutt to Gainfort, February 27, 1942; NYPL-BRT.
50. *Ibid.*
51. Harry E. Rieseberg, "'X' Marks Nothing on Cocos," *Los Angeles Times*, February 11, 1940, sec. Sunday Magazine.
52. Strutt to Gainfort, February 27, 1942; NYPL-BRT.
53. *Ibid.*
54. Gainfort to Strutt, March 3, 1942/03/03; NYPL-BRT.
55. *Ibid.*
56. Churchill to Gainfort, March 2, 1942; NYPL-BRT.
57. Gainfort to Lanier, March 5, 1942; NYPL-BRT.
58. Gainfort to Rieseberg, March 2, 1942; NYPL-BRT.
59. Rieseberg to Gainfort, telegraph, March 6, 1942; NYPL-BRT.
60. Gainfort to Rieseberg, March 2, 1942; NYPL-BRT.
61. *Ibid.*
62. *Ibid.*
63. Gainfort to Rieseberg, March 11, 1942; NYPL-BRT.
64. *Ibid.*
65. *Ibid.*
66. Rieseberg to Gainfort, March 12, 1942; NYPL-BRT.
67. *Ibid.*
68. Rieseberg to Gainfort, March 21, 1942; NYPL-BRT
69. Gainfort to Rieseberg, March 24, 1942; NYPL-BRT.
70. *Ibid.*

71. *Ibid.*
72. Rieseberg to Gainfort, March 25, 1942/03/25; NYPL-BRT.
73. *Ibid.*
74. *Ibid.*
75. Rieseberg to Gainfort, March 29, 1942; NYPL-BRT.
76. Gainfort to Rieseberg, April 2, 1942; NYPL-BRT.
77. Rieseberg to Gainfort, April 6, 1942; NYPL-BRT.
78. Gainfort, Draft of Letter to "Legal Department," Undated; NYPL-BRT. The letter was written in early April, around the 8th of the month.
79. Gainfort to Rieseberg, April 14, 1942; NYPL-BRT.
80. Rieseberg to Gainfort, April 15, 1942; NYPL-BRT.
81. Rieseberg to Gainfort, April 18, 1942; NYPL-BRT.
82. Gainfort to Rieseberg, April 23, 1942; NYPL-BRT.
83. *Ibid.*
84. Churchill to Rieseberg, April 18, 1942; NPL-BRT.

Chapter 9

1. Daryl Carson, "The Hard Way (a Profile of Robert F. Marx)," *Skin Diver Online* (Skin Diver Magazine, October 2000), http://www.skin-diver.com/departments/Personalities/oct00_marx.asp?theID=1337.
2. "Classified Ad; Poultry and Supplies; Baby Chicks! Jersey White Giants-the Largest Chicken," *Van Nuys News*, January 31, 1946, p. 22. The vocational sideline was also mentioned in a résumé written by Rieseberg in September 1952 that was noted in the author's visit to Mikalow, RMV. There was also a photo of chickens noted in Rieseberg's files, June 1943, RMV.
3. Harry E. Rieseberg, "Billions Waiting to Be Taken," *Popular Mechanics*, May 1942, pp. 50–179.
4. Frank Beatty joined *Popular Mechanics* in 1931 as a staff artist and went on to lead that group as Art Director in a thirty-one-year career.
5. *Ibid.*, p. 50.
6. "Display Ad, *I Dive for Treasure*," *Los Angeles Times*, May 17, 1942, p. C-7.
7. *I Dive for Treasure*. Envelope of press and magazine clippings, Sub-2, Box: 8. Albert J. Cohen Papers, msc0126. University of Iowa Special Collections.
8. *Ibid.* Book review by *Seattle Argos* on May 30, 1942.
9. *Ibid.*
10. "Chatter," *Variety*, May 25, 1942, p. 2.
11. Kate Holliday, "He Dives for Doubloons," *Coronet*, June 1942, p. 50.
12. Patent Nos. #1998607 and # 1983215.
13. "Science News," *Pottstown Mercury*, January 11, 1934, p. 4.
14. "West Texas Oil Man Plans $10,000,000 Salvage Craft," *El Paso Herald-Post*, February 15, 1937, p. 5.
15. "Floating Drydock Would Hoist Sunken Vessels," *Popular Mechanics*, February 1943, p. 89.
16. Rieseberg to Veteran's Administration, September 17, 1942; Veterans Administration, OPF.
17. Veterans Administration to Rieseberg, October 7, 1941; Veterans Administration, OPF.
18. Rieseberg to Pauker, September 15, 1942; NYPL-BRT.
19. Rieseberg to Pauker, January 12, 1943; NYPL-BRT.
20. *Ibid.*
21. "Plan Proposed to Salvage Sunken Freighters After War," *Atlanta Constitution*, October 12, 1942, p. 2.
22. McBride to Pauker, September 30, 1942/09/30; NYPL-BRT.
23. Pauker to Rieseberg, January 12, 1943; NYPL-BRT.
24. Rieseberg to Pauker, January 12, 1943; NYPL-BRT.
25. *Ibid.*
26. Rieseberg to Pauker, January 18, 1943; NYPL-BRT.
27. *Ibid.*
28. Pauker to Rieseberg, January 25, 1943; NYPL-BRT.
29. *Ibid.*
30. Rieseberg to Pauker, February 11, 1943; NYPL-BRT.
31. Lanier to Pauker, January 30, 1943; NYPL-BRT.
32. Harry E. Rieseberg, "I Walked the Streets of a Sunken City," *Portland Oregonian*, August 1, 1943, American Weekly Insert edition, pp. 58–64.
33. Rieseberg to Pauker, December 26, 1943; NYPL-BRT.
34. "Company to Dedicate New Office Saturday Evening," *Bakersfield Californian*, May 19, 1939, p. 9.
35. "Kern Friends Greet Warren," *Bakersfield Californian*, August 18, 1942, p. 1.
36. Jim Day, "Pipefuls," *Bakersfield Californian*, May 9, 1939, p. 17.
37. There is an unverified reference in one of Rieseberg's personal notebooks to an older sister named Joyce, but no other birth or death information has been found.
38. "Garden Tea Fetes Mrs. H.E. Rieseberg," *Bakersfield Californian*, October 23, 1944, p. 6. James Curran Nofziger was an older brother to Lyn Nofziger, a well-known conservative columnist and press secretary to Richard Nixon.
39. Agreement to publish *Treasure Hunter*, Dodd, Mead and Harry Rieseberg, October 20, 1944. Dodd, Mead mss., 1855–1992, Authors, Publishers, and Other Correspondents; Manuscripts Department, Lilly Library, Indiana University, Bloomington, Indiana. Future references for this collection will be styled DODD MEAD. See the bibliographic head notes for more information.

40. Owen to McBride Publishing, February 1, 1945; DODD MEAD.
41. For more about the Armed Services Editions see, Brianna Labuskes, "How the Armed Services Editions Created a Nation of Readers," *Literary Hub* (Grove Atlantic and Electric Literature, February 23, 2023), https://lithub.com/how-the-armed-services-editions-created-a-nation-of-readers/.
42. Rieseberg to Pauker, July 20, 1945; NYPL-BRT.
43. Pauker to Rieseberg, August 2, 1945; NYPL-BRT.
44. Rieseberg to Pauker, July 16, 1946; NYPL-BRT.
45. McBride to Pauker, September 12, 1946; NYPL-BRT.
46. Pauker to McBride, December 31, 1946; NYPL-BRT.
47. McBride to Rieseberg, February 8, 1947; NYPL-BRT.
48. McBride to Pauker, March 3, 1947; NYPL-BRT.
49. Rieseberg to Pauker, February 14, 1947; NYPL-BRT.
50. Pauker to Rieseberg, February 19, 1947; NYPL-BRT.
51. McBride to Pauker, March 3, 1947; NYPL-BRT.
52. McBride to Rieseberg, March 17, 1947; NYPL-BRT.
53. McBride to Pauker, April 10, 1947; NYPL-BRT.
54. Philip Athans, "A Brief History of Pulp Fiction," Fantasy Author's Handbook, February 23, 2021, https://fantasyhandbook.wordpress.com/2021/02/23/a-brief-history-of-pulp-fiction/. See also, Frank M. Robinson and Lawrence Davidson, *Pulp Culture: The Art of Fiction Magazines* (Portland, OR: Collectors Press, 1998).
55. Frank Gruber, *The Pulp Jungle* (Los Angeles, CA: Sherbourne Press, Inc., 1967), pp. 23, 153.
56. Gruber, p. 20.
57. Milton Moskowitz, "Newsstand Strip-Tease," in *A View of the Nation: An Anthology, 1955–1959*, ed. Henry M. Christman (Freeport, NY: Books for Libraries Press, 1970), pp. 76–79.
58. Gruber, p. 9.
59. *Ibid.* See also, David M. Earle, *All Man!: Hemingway, 1950s Men's Magazines, and the Masculine Persona* (Kent, OH: Kent State University Press, 2009), p. 2. Earle suggests that Moskowitz underestimated that number.
60. Earle, pp. 61, 84, 95.
61. Harry E. Rieseberg, "Mechanical 'Lobster'," *Mechanix Illustrated*, November 1947, pp. 58–169.
62. The author has been unable to locate additional information about this engineer.
63. Harry E. Rieseberg, *Treasure Hunter* (New York, NY: Robert M. McBride & Company, 1945), pp. 246–249.
64. Rieseberg to Pauker, January 10, 1948; NYPL-BRT.
65. Pauker to Rieseberg, January 15, 1948; NYPL-BRT.
66. Dodd, Mead to Rieseberg, July 22, 1948; DODD MEAD.
67. *Ibid.*
68. Memorandum of Agreement between Robert M. McBride and Les Editions Phidias, December 19, 1947; DODD MEAD.
69. Dodd, Mead to Rieseberg, April 7, 1949; DODD MEAD.
70. Rieseberg to Dodd Mead, April 8, 1949; DODD MEAD.
71. Horch to Winfield, May 14, 1949; DODD MEAD.
72. Donald Wright Kelly (pen name) and Harry E Rieseberg, "The Mad Cabbie of Cartagena," *Stag*, June 1951, pp. 40–41. Harry himself wrote "pen name" under the byline for the article. In the same issue was an article under his own name. No other instances have been identified. RMC.
73. "Deep Sea Treasure Hunter Keeps Busy on Books in Ridge Studio," *Chico Enterprise-Record*, August 20, 1964, p. 22.
74. "Author of '*I Dive for Treasure*' Now in Harbor Area 'To Live'," *Southern California Beachcomber*, 1948, pp. 3–8.
75. "Classified Ads, Business Opportunities," *Los Angeles Times*, June 13, 1948, p. B-3.
76. "Classified Ads, Financial, Business Opportunities," *San Bernardino County Sun*, July 27, 1948, p. A-16.

Chapter 10

1. Pauker to Rieseberg, November 12, 1947; NYPL-BRT.
2. Rieseberg to Pauker, November 24, 1947; NYPL-BRT.
3. Rieseberg to Pauker, January 24, 1948; NYPL-BRT.
4. Pauker to Rieseberg, January 28, 1948; NYPL-BRT.
5. Rieseberg to Pauker, January 24, 1948. NYPL-BRT.
6. Pauker to Rieseberg, January 28, 1948; NYPL-BRT.
7. Mark Herstein, Mark Herstein Agency, and Harold Conswuet vs. Harry E. Rieseberg, Albert J. Cohen, Universal Pictures Company, a corporation, Doe One, Doe Two, and Doe Three, No 616825 (Clerk of the Superior Court June 29, 1953).
8. "Herstein Goes Literary," *Variety*, July 26, 1948, p. 3.
9. Rieseberg to Pauker, March 25, 1950; NYPL-BRT.
10. Herstein vs. Rieseberg lawsuit, June 29, 1953.
11. "Schwartz Snags Rights to Treasure-Trove Tale," *Variety*, May 18, 1949, p. 9.
12. Rieseberg to Pauker, November 24, 1947; NYPL-BRT.
13. Rieseberg to Pauker, November 5, 1949; NYPL-BRT.

14. Rieseberg to Dodd, Mead, November 17, 1949; DODD MEAD.
15. Dodd, Mead to Rieseberg, November 22, 1949; DODD MEAD.
16. Edwin Schallert, "'I Dived for Treasure' Unusual Film Project; Adele Jergens in 'Doom,'" *Los Angeles Times*, December 6, 1949, p. B-7.
17. Ibid.
18. Herstein vs. Rieseberg lawsuit, June 29, 1953
19. Cohen to Rieseberg, December 7, 1949; COHEN.
20. Woodruff Associates to Rieseberg; December 27, 1949; COHEN.
21. Cohen to Woodruff Associates, January 6, 1950; COHEN.
22. "'Dive' for Dollars," *Variety*, February 2, 1950, p. 11.
23. Edwin Schallert, "Dvorak Makes Transit from Model to Moll; 'Bulldog' Beckons Brando," *Los Angeles Times*, May 13, 1950, p. 13.
24. "Ghost Sea-City Treasure, Old-Home-Week, in News Today; Brides, Babes Dominate," *Bakersfield Californian*, May 22, 1950, p. 12.
25. "CBS Has Taken an Option," *Variety*, March 10, 1950, p. 9.
26. "Radio Programs for Friday," *San Diego Union*, March 10, 1950, p. A-8.
27. Strutt vs. Rieseberg lawsuit; March 17, 1950.
28. Ibid.
29. Author's interview with Kim Strutt, May 30, 2014. Kim is the son of Eric P. Strutt.
30. Rieseberg to Pauker, March 25, 1950; NYPL-BRT.
31. *Bakersfield Californian*, May 22, 1950, p. 12.
32. Cohen to Edward Muhl, May 14, 1951; COHEN.
33. "He's Bound for Undersea Treasure," *Chillicothe Constitution*, April 27, 1950, p. 12.
34. "Legal Notices, Certificate of Business Fictitious Firm Name," *Van Nuys News*, April 24, 1952, p. 15-D.
35. Two collections have documents that illustrate a complete sequence of script revisions by various screenwriters. See, African American Film Script Collection, Manuscripts Department, Lilly Library, Indiana University, Bloomington, Indiana, and Albert J. Cohen Papers, The University of Iowa Libraries, Special Collections, Iowa City, Iowa.
36. "*I Dive for Treasure*, Original Story by Ray Buffum," April 11, 1950. COHEN.
37. "Sunken City, Original Story and Adaptation by Ray Buffum, Screenplay by Jack Harvey," Undated (est. January 1951); COHEN.
38. "City Beneath the Sea (1953)." AFI Catalog of Feature Films, 1893–1993. American Film Institute. Accessed April 21, 2023. AFI cites an article in the Hollywood Reporter on August 25, 1952, p. 4.
39. "City Beneath the Sea: [film script]/by Jack Harvey, Final Shooting Script." December 21, 1951, Universal-International Pictures; McFarlin Library Special Collections, University of Tulsa. http://library.utulsa.edu//record=b2178502.
40. Letter from Rieseberg to Herstein and Cornsweet, December 26, 1950, presented as evidence in Herstein vs. Rieseberg lawsuit, June 29, 1953.
41. Letter from Rieseberg to Herstein and Cornsweet, February 17, 1951, presented as evidence in Herstein vs. Rieseberg lawsuit, June 29, 1953.
42. Cohen to Muhl, May 14, 1951; COHEN. Edward Muhl was the vice president and general manager of studio operations for Universal at the time. In 1953, he led all production, rising quickly to the top post.
43. Cohen to Spitz, July 16, 1951; COHEN.
44. "Into Reverse Gear," *Variety*, June 22, 1951, p. 2.
45. Edwin Schallert, "McGuire, Keel Hinted for 'Leopold's Crown,'; Holloway Gets Break," *Los Angeles Times*, October 15, 1951, p. B-11.
46. "Hollywood Insider," *Variety*, February 12, 1952, p. 4.
47. "Title Tribulation," *Variety*, February 21, 1952, p. 1.
48. "Boetticher Directs 'City Beneath the Sea'," *Variety*, February 26, 1952, p. 1.
49. "A Publicity Gimmick Spoiled by Actress," *Kansas City Star*, February 8, 1953, D-1.
50. Ball died of cancer only six months after her 21st birthday and her last word reportedly was "Tony," referring to Quinn. She was married to actor Richard (Dick) Long at the time of her death. Marlon Brando is credited with saying that if Ball had lived, Marilyn Monroe would not have been the only eternal sex symbol.
51. Demetrius John Kitses, *Budd Boetticher: The Western* (London, England: British Film Institute Education, 1969).
52. Ibid.
53. Budd Boetticher and Drake Stutesman, "Interview with Budd Boetticher, with Drake Stutesman," *The Journal of Cinema and Media* 43, no. 1 (2002): p. 26.
54. Thomas M. Pryor, "Multi-Hued Hollywood, Industry to Make 128 Tinted Films Over Nex Six Months—Man Made Temblor," *New York Times*, May 25, 1952, p. X-5.
55. "Build Plastic City, Then Destroy It," *Akron Beacon-Journal*, May 18, 1952, p. 90.
56. Harrison Carroll, "Behind the Scenes in Hollywood," *Las Vegas Daily Optic*, May 20, 1952, p. 2.
57. Pryor, *New York Times*, May 25, 1952.
58. "Fitted to a T," *Variety*, April 17, 1952, p. 2. Though unrelated to the conditions on the set, Mala Powers' health changed not only plans for the movie, but largely ended her rising career as an actress. In late December 1951, the twenty-year-old went to Korea to entertain troops involved in the war. While there she became ill with flu-like symptoms. She had been in bed or at home ill during much of the time between her return from Korea and the start of filming. Early on in her hospitalization, she was treated for a recurrence of what was diagnosed as mononucleosis contracted in Korea,

but actually had a rare blood disease aggravated by antibiotics that were destroying her bone marrow. When she was discharged from the hospital in early June 1952, Powers had finished all but one of her scenes for the movie. Before filming ended, Boetticher and his crew concocted a rewrite where Powers could appear via a phone call to explain her absence. In the movie, Powers was to be in a scene where her love interest of Ryan's character gets in a fight in a bar. Instead, the sound crew came to her home and recorded a telephone conversation where she called Ryan to say she was drunk and that he should come to get her. It would take her eighteen months to fully recover, but Mala Powers never quite regained her stature in the business. Following the illness, studios told her they would have difficulty obtaining production insurance and this kept her from getting A-list movie roles. She doubted that information. See "Mala Powers Improves," *Variety*, June 4, 1952, p. 8.

59. "Only Love Survives 'Sea' Havoc at UI," *Variety*, May 19, 1952, p. 5.

60. "UI Will Tie in TV on 3-Way Ballyhoo Binge for 'City'," *Variety*, January 28, 1953, p. 11.

61. "Frank Westmore Explains Mask-Making Technique," *Cleveland Plain Dealer*, February 2, 1953, p. 16.

62. W. Ward Marsh, "Premiere of 'City Beneath Sea' for Palace on Thursday," *Cleveland Plain Dealer*, February 1, 1953, p. 32-D.

63. John Bunker, "Sunken-Treasure Talk Bobs to Surface in Hub," *Christian Science Monitor*, February 21, 1953, p. 7.

64. "In Person Tonight Only!," *Cleveland Plain Dealer*, February 5, 1953, p. 20. Ad for movie premiere at the RKO Theater.

65. "Three Hollywood Visitors (Photo)," *Detroit Free Press*, February 20, 1953, p. 22.

66. "Hosiery Special for Susan Ball Personal Appearance Day," *Lansing State Journal*, February 12, 1953, p. 19.

67. "'Soldier of Fortune' Tells His Story Here," *Saginaw News*, February 15, 1953.

68. "Melodrama Scheduled," *Los Angeles Times*, February 26, 1953, p. B-9.

69. Ted Smith, "Beauty Joins Treasure Hunt, Figureheads of Old Clippers South Off Golden Gate," *San Francisco News*, February 27, 1953, p. 17.

70. Louis R. Guzzo, "Exit Hutton; Enter Treasure Hunter and Rooney," *The Seattle Times*, March 4, 1953, p. 28.

71. *Ibid*.

72. The same photo appears in Rieseberg's *Treasure of the Buccaneer Sea* (1962) and again in his book, *Fell's Guide to Sunken Treasure Ships of the World* (1965).

73. Edwin Schallert, "Vittoria Gassman Will Costar with Stanwyck," *Los Angeles Times*, March 2, 1953, sec. III, p. 9.

74. "'City Beneath the Sea' Opens Run at California," *Bakersfield Californian*, March 11, 1953.

75. "City Beneath the Sea (Review)," *Variety*, February 4, 1953, p. 6.

76. Philip K Scheuer, "Divers in Caribbean Tale Lusty," *Los Angeles Times*, March 7, 1953, p. 9.

77. H.H.T., "The Screen: Four Films Make Debuts Here; 'City Beneath the Sea' Show by State and 'Thunderbirds' Lands at Holiday Theatre," *New York Times*, March 12, 1953, sec. Amusements, p. 24-L.

78. "'Beneath Sea' Trim 12G, Frisco," *Variety*, March 4, 1953, p. 8.

79. "'Madam' Sights Solid 13G Week Tho Most 1st Runs' Biz Spotty," *Variety*, March 10, 1953, p. 3.

80. "National Box Office Survey," *Variety*, April 29, 1953, p. 3.

81. Rieseberg to Dodd, Mead, July 31, 1952; DODD MEAD.

82. Herstein vs. Rieseberg lawsuit, June 29, 1953. Lawsuit.

83. Brief Pictorial History of the Birth, Growth, & Development of the Motion Picture "CITY BENEATH THE SEA," Personal copy of Albert J. Cohen, February 9, 1953; COHEN.

84. Schallert, *I Dived*, December 6, 1949.

85. Rieseberg to Tom Ferris, May 5, 1953; Edwin A. Link and Marion Clayton Link Collections, University Libraries, Special Collections; Binghamton University, State University of New York, Binghamton, NY.

Chapter 11

1. Vaughn Green to Rieseberg, March 14, 1959; RMC.

2. Deep Sea Treasure Hunter, August 20, 1964. Rieseberg gained some local fame when an article in the *Chico Enterprise-Record* updated the community on the famous man in their midst. In November 2018 Paradise was decimated by a devastating wildfire that destroyed 153,000 acres and 14,000 homes, including the mobile home park where Harry and Val once lived.

3. Rieseberg to Marton, January 16, 1960; YALE-Pauker.

4. Rieseberg to Raymond Dow, Treasure Trove Club, October 9, 1970; RMC.

5. Dodd, Mead to Rieseberg, January 15, 1960; YALE-Pauker.

6. Rieseberg, Harry E. "Sea of Treasure (Series of 9)." *The Rudder*, 1954. Articles for *The Rudder* appeared in nine issues from July 1954 to March 1955. Although the introductory material for the first article said it would appear in sixteen parts, nine was the final number of articles in the series.

7. Reader Review of Rieseberg's 'Sea of Treasure' by C.B., March 10, 1956; Bobbs-Merrill mss., 1885–1957; Lilly Library, Indiana University, Bloomington, IN. This collection will be noted as BOBBS for future citations.

8. *Ibid*.

9. Rieseberg to Marton, January 22, 1960; YALE-Pauker.

10. Pauline Smith, "He Walks with Davey (sic) Jones," *PIC Magazine*, January 1956, pp. 33–70.

11. Pauline Smith to Rieseberg, August 15, 1953; RMC.
12. Pauline Smith to Rieseberg, December 3, 1953; RMC.
13. Rieseberg to Marton, January 11, 1960; YALE-Pauker.
14. Dodd, Mead to Pauker, October 5, 1959; YALE-Pauker.
15. Dodd, Mead to Pauker, November 16, 1959; YALE-Pauker.
16. Marton to Dodd, Mead, December 18, 1959; YALE-Pauker. See also, Marton to Rieseberg, December 21, 1959; YALE-Pauker.
17. Fields to Marton, December 23, 1959; YALE-Pauker.
18. Mrs. Edmond Pauker to Jolan, January 13, 1960; YALE-Pauker.
19. Rieseberg to Marton, January 26, 1959; YALE-Pauker.
20. *Ibid.*
21. Marton to Rieseberg, January 15, 1960; YALE-Pauker.
22. Rieseberg to Marton, January 11, 1960; YALE-Pauker.
23. Rieseberg to Marton, February 2, 1960; YALE-Pauker.
24. "Rieseberg May Buy Victoria," *Seattle Times*, March 6, 1953, p. 33.
25. "Will Not Re-Float British Freighter," *Lansing State Journal*, April 10, 1939, p. 2.
26. "Divers Describe Furious Battles with Devilfish, Find Octopi Lurking About Sunken Treasure Ship," *Chicago Tribune*, August 5, 1934, p. 17.
27. Rieseberg to Ferris re Trevor, Undated (1953); LINK.
28. "Report of Special Study of Securities Markets, Chapter IV," Securities and Exchange Commission (1962), pp. 521–522.
29. Rieseberg to Ferris, March 12, 1953; LINK.
30. "To Be Used on Treasure Hunt," *Motor Boating*, August 1953, p. 110.
31. Jay Wells, ed., "Yacht Fantome Doomed to Sail to Scrap Heap," *Seattle Times*, March 14, 1953, p. 7. See also, J.W., "Chartroom Chatter: High Costs Let Fantome Go," *Seattle Times*, June 14, 1953, p. 42.
32. Rieseberg to Vaughn Greene, March 7, 1969; RMC. Harry claimed to have gotten Fish into treasure hunting in the late 1940s. He said he visited Fish nearly every month until the time of his murder and "advised him in his every operation."
33. Rieseberg to Marton, March 19, 1960; YALE-Pauker.
34. *Ibid.*
35. Rieseberg, Project Proposal for "Treasurama! Cargoes of Treasure," undated (~1964); RMC.
36. *Who's Who in the World, 2000: Millennium Edition* (New Providence, NJ: Marquis Who's Who, 1999). In his self-submitted bio, Mikalow claimed he was a Lieutenant Commander in the Navy, first as a torpedo bomber pilot and then as an underwater demolition frogman. None of that can be corroborated. He was discharged from the Navy as a Seaman First Class in 1946. It appears he learned to dive at the Almeda Naval Air Station.
37. James P. Delgado and Stephen A. Haller, "Submerged Cultural Resource Assessment: Golden Gate National Recreation Area, Gulf of the Farallones National Marine Sanctuary, and Point Reyes National Seashore," (1989), p. 179.
38. Articles of Incorporation, Treasure Recovery Inc., May 16, 1968; Secretary of State, State of Nevada.
39. The author has logged hundreds of magazine and newspaper articles that can be located and verified. There is no way to know how complete it is. However, the output of articles more than doubled beginning in 1954 to as many as fifty articles a year.
40. Harry E. Rieseberg, "I Battled an Octopus for Treasure," *Mechanix Illustrated*, November 1939, pp. 36–120.
41. Harry E. Rieseberg, "I Battled the Deadly Octopus," *True Comics and Adventure Stories*, January 1965.
42. Unless otherwise noted, the material for this section comes from the Carl L. Hubbs papers. SMC 5, Box 75, Folder 14, Special Collections & Archives, University of California at San Diego Library. Future citations will be styled as HUBBS. See the bibliographic head notes for more information.
43. "Hubbs, Carl Leavitt (Prof. Dr. PhD)," Shellers from the Past and Present (Conchology), accessed April 23, 2023, https://conchology.be/index.php?t=9001&id=21175.
44. For more on this topic see, Ralph H. Lutts, *The Nature Fakers: Wildlife, Science, and Sentiment* (Charlottesville, VA: University Press of Virginia, 2011).
45. "Interpretation of Authenticity of the Book by Harry E. Rieseberg, '*I Dive for Treasure*,' with a Special Reference to Claims of Encounters with Giant Octopi." November 10, 1949; HUBBS.
46. Rieseberg, *I Dive for Treasure* (1942), 11th printing (June 1954).
47. Harry E. Rieseberg, "The Story Behind Cocos Island and the 'Loot of Lima,'" *Pacific Discovery IV*, no. 6 (1951): pp. 4–15.
48. Hubbs to Robert C. Miller, California Academy of Sciences, November 28, 1951; HUBBS.
49. Henry J. White to Hubbs, July 16, 1953; HUBBS.
50. William Beebe to Hubbs, November 28, 1949; Hubbs.
51. Gilbert Doukan, *The World Beneath the Waves* (Les découvertes Sous-Marines Modernes). Translated by A. and R.M. Case, trans. Adrienne Case and R M Case (New York, NY: John de Graff, Inc., 1957), p. 211.
52. *Ibid.*
53. Peter Stone, "Interview with Robert Marx," Classic Dive Books (Oceans Enterprises, September 1977), http://classicdivebooks.customer.netspace.net.au/oeclassics-a-marx-interview.html.
54. *Ibid.*

55. Peter Stone, Marx Interview.

56. Robert F. Marx and Jenifer Marx, *The World's Richest Wrecks: A Wreck Diver's Guide to Gold and Silver Treasures of the Seas* (Garland, TX: RAM Books, 2009), pp. vii–xii.

57. Sean Holland, "Salvor, Archeologist Robert Sténuit," *Immersed: The International Technical Diving Magazine*, 1999, pp. 10–16. See also Megan Garber, "Robert Sténuit: The Original Aquanaut," *The Atlantic*, June 12, 2012, https://www.theatlantic.com/technology/archive/2012/06/robert-st-nuit-the-original-aquanaut/258407/.

58. John S. Potter, Jr., *The Treasure Divers of Vigo Bay* (New York, NY: Doubleday & Co., 1958), pp. 70–75.

59. Rupert Furneaux, *The Great Treasure Hunts* (New York, NY: Taplinger Publishing Company, 1969), p. 195.

60. Author's telephone interview with Spence. Spence is credited with the discovery of the H.L. Hunley submarine from the Civil War.

61. Bernard Heuvelmans, *Dans Le Sillage Des Monstres Marins, Le Kraken Et Le Poulpe Colossal (In the Wake of Sea-Monsters: The Kraken and the Colossal Octopus)* (Paris: Librarie Plon, 1958), pp. 49–52, fn 451.

62. Author's bibliography of works by Harry Rieseberg.

63. Barbara Harte and Carolyn Riley, eds., *Contemporary Authors, A Bio-Bibliographical Guide to Current Authors and Their Works*, vol. 5–8 (Gale Research Co, 1964), pp. 956–957.

64. Rieseberg to Lester U. Beitz; June 12, 1970; RMC.

65. Harry Rieseberg, as told to Eric Strutt, "I Walk with Davy Jones," undated (~1939), STRUTT.

66. "Classified Ads: Treasure Locaters (Sic)," *Palm Beach Post*, March 6, 1949, p. 33.

67. "Classified Ads: Treasure Hunt," *Motor Boating*, November 1951, p. 125.

68. "Michigan Man to Have Own Submarine, Tiny Craft Dives to 600 Feet, Can Stay 30 Hours," *Lansing State Journal*, February 28, 1955, p. 4.

69. "Classified Ads: Salesman," *Palm Beach Post*, December 15, 1955, p. 41.

70. F.L. Coffman, *1001 Lost, Buried or Sunken Treasures* (New York, NY: Thomas Nelson & Sons, 1957), p. 117.

71. Frank Fish to Rieseberg, March 7, 1962; RMC.

72. Rieseberg to John O. Boyer, Coast & Geodetic Survey Office, June 7, 1968; RMC.

73. Harry E. Rieseberg, "Safety on the Bottom," *Virginia Wildlife*, October 1963, pp. 18–22.

74. L. David Horner III, "'Disagrees' (Letter to the Editor)," *Virginia Wildlife*, January 1964, p. 26.

75. Bruce Coleman, "Deep Sea Divers Set for Adventure," *Daily Independent Journal*, December 15, 1964, p. 1.

76. "Adventurer Takes Issue Over Dive," *Daily Independent*, December 29, 1964, p. 12.

77. Note to Valentine Rieseberg from Harry Rieseberg's "black" notebook; RMC.

78. While meeting with Al Mikalow at his home over two full days, the author was able to take photographs of letters, Rieseberg's "black" and "green" notebooks, along with various other material. There was also a four-drawer file cabinet of Rieseberg's typescripts and some correspondence. The author is certain that there was also much more material from Rieseberg that was not seen at that time. When Mikalow died about a month later, an estate sale described by one attendee as chaotic and largely unmanaged unfortunately disposed of all that remained except for the contents of the file cabinet.

79. Marilyn Rieseberg Morgan, widow of Harry's son, Henry, has been helpful with first-person accounts and email communication.

80. Letter from Rieseberg to Marilyn Rieseberg Morgan, August 28, 1964.

81. *Ibid*.

82. Unsigned Last Will & Testament, Harry Rieseberg, sent to Marilyn Rieseberg Morgan, February 16, 1965.

83. Michel Bagnaud, *Profession, Inventeur De Trésors* (Paris: FeniXX reedition numérique, 1991), pp. 17–23. Translations from French by DeepL.

84. Rieseberg to Lens Young de Grummond, April 18, 1966; Harry Rieseberg Papers, de Grummond Collection.

85. Other submissions during this period included *National Informer, Argosy, Canadian Boy, Points, Camping Guide, Texas Metro, Newscene, Country Club News, Probe, Collector's World, Treasure World, Woodsman, Hawaii, Real Frontier, Southern New Jersey Living, Northeast Outdoors, CBS Playhouse, Truck Driver, Conoco 70, Grit Weekly, Compass, Move, New Mexico, Popular Mechanics, Northeast Outdoors, Smithsonian, Omen, Birmingham, Oklahoma Limited*.

86. Perrin at Explorer's Trade Mart to Rieseberg, April 21, RMC.

87. Krantz at Major Magazines Inc. to Rieseberg, May 14, 1970; RMC.

88. Rieseberg to Marilyn Rieseberg Morgan, May 9, 1970.

89. Certificate of Death, Harry E. Rieseberg, October 28, 1970; Butte County Health Department, Oroville, California.

90. Rieseberg to Bob Goodwin, August 31, 1970; RMC.

91. Rieseberg wrote letters to Frederick fell on May 1, 1970; July 1, 1970; August 6, 1970; and August 17, 1970. All from RMV.

92. Rieseberg, *I Dive for Treasure* (1970), p. 236.

93. Margaret Dougherty to Rieseberg, October 17, RMV. A page in Harry's black notebook has a page for Maryland Magazine, and it shows he sent the article on Sept 11, 1970.

94. Dougherty, October 17, 1970; RMV.

95. Letter to Author from Avis Mikalow, November 14, 2014.

96. Author interview at home of Al Mikalow in Lake Havasu, AZ; August 2014.

97. "Hunt for Sunken Gold? It's No Way to Get

Rich," *Los Angeles Times*, September 3, 1973, p. B-2.

98. Email to the author from Disney Archivist, March 21, 2023.

99. For an excellent scholarly overview see James Edwin Mahone, "The Definition of Lying and Deception," *Stanford Encyclopedia of Philosophy*, December 25, 2015, https://plato.stanford.edu/entries/lying-definition/#Aca. For an anecdotal model see, Dawson McAllister, 8 different types of lies people tell, February 4, 2023, https://www.thehopeline.com/different-kinds-of-lies-you-tell/.

100. Zee Kadih, Truth and Lies Continuum, November 9, 2015, https://prezi.com/t4reydcnfapo/truth-and-lies-continuum/.

101. Reader Review of Rieseberg's 'Sea of Treasure' by C.B., March 10, 1956; Bobbs-Merrill mss., 1885–1957; Lilly Library, Indiana University, Bloomington, IN. This collection will be noted as BOBBS for future citations.

102. "Discovery of Secret Safe Spurs Hopes of More Intrigue," *Sun-Journal*, May 16, 1991.

Bibliography

Abbreviations of sources cited in the endnotes are fully described here. Each of these sources contributed significant archival resources to this work. The author greatly appreciates the support and assistance of the archivists involved.

AF AMER FILM African American Film Script Collection, Manuscripts Department, Lilly Library, Indiana University, Bloomington, Indiana. The collection consists of typescripts of films written by, directed by, or starring African Americans.

COHEN Albert J. Cohen Papers, The University of Iowa Libraries, Special Collections, Iowa City, Iowa.

CP Christensen Portfolio. The author's collection of Rieseberg ephemera was sold or discarded at an estate sale following the death of Al Mikalow. It is named for the Lake Havasu resident who helped gather it.

DODD MEAD Dodd, Mead mss., 1855–1992; Manuscripts Department, Lilly Library, Indiana University, Bloomington, Indiana.

HUBBS Carl L. Hubbs papers. SMC 5, Box 75, Folder 14, Special Collections & Archives, University of California at San Diego Library.

HUNT-PRC Jim Hunt Personal Research Collection. Jim Hunt was an engineer, model builder, and skilled researcher who lived in Boothbay Harbor, Maine. He shared documents and images with me in a personal visit to his home, and his manuscript about the *Constellation* is cited with his widow's permission.

LINK Edwin A. Link and Marion Clayton Link Collections, University Libraries, Special Collections; Binghamton University, State University of New York, Binghamton, NY.

NARA National Archives and Records Administration, Washington, D.C.

NARA-SEATTLE Lawsuits involving Romano Marine Salvage, Record Group 21, Admiralty Case Files, 1929–1942, National Archives and Records Administration, Seattle, WA.

NYPL-BRT Edmond Pauker Papers, Billy Rose Theatre Division, The New York Public Library for the Performing Arts. *T-Mss 1960-001. Edmond Pauker Papers, *T-Mss 1960-001, Rieseberg, Harry, 1941–1947, Box 63, Folders 4 and 5. Billy Rose Theatre Division, The New York Public Library for the Performing Arts.

NYPL-M&A Edmond Pauker papers (MssCol 2354). Manuscripts and Archives Division. The New York Public Library. Astor, Lenox, and Tilden Foundations.

OPF Official Personnel Folders, National Personnel Records Center, St. Louis, MO. Personnel records for Harry Rieseberg, his father, Henry, and his wife, Ellen, are found in the files of many different departments. Unless otherwise stated, all of these citations are for Harry Earl Rieseberg's federal employment records.

RMC Rieseberg-Mikalow Collection. Rieseberg's personal files were transferred to Al Mikalow upon his death. Mikalow and a Rieseberg descendant transferred them to the author.

RMV Rieseberg-Mikalow Visit. In a visit by the author to Mikalow's home in August 2014, Mikalow gave permission to review documents and take images.

ROMANO-HAMMOND Several family scrapbooks regarding Eugene Romano are held by Rockwell Hammond, Jr., and have been freely shared with the author.

STRUTT Personal papers of Eric P. Strutt, provided to the author by a descendant.

WA-SOS Securities Division, Washington State Archives, Washington Secretary of State, Olympia, WA.

YALE-PAUKER Edmond Pauker Papers, 1898–1960, Beinecke Library, Yale University.

"Admiral Farragut." *Guide to the Pacific Coast Steamship Company Records MS 72, 1879–1938* Accessed February 8, 2023. https://sandiegohistory.org/findaid/ms72.html.

"Adventurer Takes Issue Over Dive." *Daily Independent* December 29, 1964.

Albert J. Cohen Papers, The University of Iowa Libraries, Special Collections, Iowa City, Iowa.

"All Trace Now Lost of Pirate Jean Lafitte's Mightiest Treasure Haul." *The Washington Post*, October 6, 1935.

Allen, Madelene Ferguson, and Ken Scadden. *The General Grant's Gold: Shipwreck and Greed in the Southern Ocean* New Zealand: Exisle Publishing Limited, 2010.

"American Tests Device for Submarine Rescues." British Movietone, 1935. https://www.youtube.com/watch?v=dbedtxDaKvk.

"Ancient and Honorable Fraternity of Free and Accepted Masons, Membership Application for Harry Rieseberg, Mount Pleasant Masonic Lodge #33." Washington, D.C., July 12, 1916.

Andrews, Ralph W. "Bahada Came to a Tragic End." Essay. In *Photographers of the Frontier West: Their Lives and Works, 1875 to 1915* New York: Bonanza Books, 1967.

"Annual report of the public printer: For the fiscal year ended June 30, 1894, submitted to the congress of the United States on January 3, 1940." Washington, D.C.: Government Printing Office, 1894.

"Arizona Scores in Big Parade." *The Prescott Courier* June 23, 1932.

Articles of Incorporation, Treasure Recovery Inc, May 16, 1968; Secretary of State, State of Nevada.

"Ask Adventure." *Adventure Magazine* 108, no. 5, March 1, 1943.

Athans, Philip. "A Brief History of Pulp Fiction." *Fantasy Author's Handbook*, February 23, 2021. https://fantasyhandbook.wordpress.com/2021/02/23/a-brief-history-of-pulp-fiction/.

"Author of 'I Dive for Treasure' Now in Harbor Area 'To Live.'" *Southern California Beachcomber*, 1948.

Bagnaud, Michel. *Profession, Inventeur de Treìsors* Paris: FeniXX reedition numérique, 1991.

Baker, Morgan. "The Federal Diary, Here's to Arizona." *The Washington Post* June 15, 1934.

Barber, Lawrence. "Ocean Treasure Object of Urgent Sea Quest, Divers to Hunt for Sunken Gold." *Portland Oregonian* November 9, 1937.

"Bay Beach Sites Show Sales Gain." *Washington Herald* October 16, 1921.

"Bell to Light Bay Depths, Plead for Diving Sphere Bridge Use." *San Francisco Call-Bulletin* January 27, 1934.

"'Beneath Sea' Trim 12G, Frisco." *Variety*, March 4, 1953.

Bloch, Don. "Diving Robot Capable of Greatest Depth Coming to Washington Soon." *The Washington Evening Star* March 7, 1935.

Blot, Jean-Yves. *Les Chasseurs de treìsors du Gulf Stream* Grenoble, France: Gleìnat, 1986.

Blot, Jean-Yves. *Les Chasseurs de Treìsors du Gulf Stream* Grenoble, France: Gleìnat, 1986.

Bobbs-Merrill mss., 1885–1957; Lilly Library, Indiana University, Bloomington, IN.

Boetticher, Budd, and Drake Stutesman. "Interview with Budd Boetticher, with Drake Stutesman." *The Journal of Cinema and Media* 43, no. 1 (Spring 2002): 18–39.

"Boetticher Directs 'City Beneath the Sea.'" *Variety*, February 26, 1952.

"Boy Scout Activities, Troop No. 5." *Galveston Daily News*, October 26, 1941.

Breevort Apartment-Hollywood (*sic*) (blog). L.A. Kompany, Driving Around the Desert by the Sea, January 4, 2010. http://lakompany.blogspot.com/2010/01/breevort-apartments-hollywood.html.

Bryan, F. MacDonald. "Old Diver Relates Tale of Sea Gangsters, Liquor and $100,000 on Hijacked Ship." *The Washington Post*, January 23, 1938.

"Build Plastic City, Then Destroy It." *Akron Beacon-Journal* May 18, 1952.

Bunker, John. "Sunken-Treasure Talk Bobs to Surface in Hub." *Christian Science Monitor*, February 21, 1953.

"The Camp Fire, A Meeting Place for All." *Adventure Magazine* 92, no. 6, July 15, 1935.

Campbell, Malcolm. *Searching for Pirate Treasure in Cocos Island* New York: Frederick A. Stokes Co., 1932.

"Captain Loesche, 64, in Seven Shipwrecks; Sailing Master Who Search for Gold on Last Voyage Dies." *New York Times*, April 18, 1939.

Carl L. Hubbs papers. SMC 5, Box 75, Folder 14, Special Collections & Archives, University of California at San Diego Library.

Carroll, Harrison. "Behind the Scenes in Hollywood." *Las Vegas Daily Optic* May 20, 1952.

Carson, Daryl. "The Hard Way (a Profile of Robert F. Marx)." Skin Diver Online. *Skin Diver Magazine*, October 2000. http://www.skin-diver.com/departments/Personalities/oct00_marx.asp?theID=1337.

"CBS Has Taken an Option." *Variety*, March 10, 1950.

"Chatter." *Variety*, May 25, 1942.

"City Beneath the Sea (1953)." AFI Catalog of Feature Films, 1893–1993. Accessed April 21, 2023. https://catalog.afi.com/Film/50786-CITY-BENEATHTHESEA?sid=6fb3f2d1-7b98-48e5-8e63-3f2705aa5074&sr=10.472799&cp=1&pos=0&cxt=Filmography2.

"City Beneath the Sea (Review)." *Variety*, February 4, 1953.

"'City Beneath the Sea' Opens Run at California." *Bakersfield Californian*, March 11, 1953.

"Classified Ad; Poultry and Supplies; Baby Chicks! Jersey White Giants-the Largest Chicken." *Van Nuys News* January 31, 1946.

"Classified Ads, Business Opportunities." *Los Angeles Times*, June 13, 1948.

"Classified Ads, Financial, Business Opportunities." *San Bernardino County Sun* July 27, 1948.

"Classified Ads: Salesman." *Palm Beach Post* December 15, 1955.

"Classified Ads: Treasure Hunt." *Motor Boating*, November 1951.

"Classified Ads: Treasure Locaters (*sic*)." *Palm Beach Post* March 6, 1949.

"Clipper Ship Sails to See Bullion Treasure Lost When Merida Sank Off Virginia Capes." *The Washington Post* August 21, 1936.

"Club and Society Activity of Nearby Towns, Forrestville." *The Washington Post* July 14, 1929.

"Coal Salvaging Charges Dismissed." *Brooklyn Daily Eagle* June 26, 1924.

"Cocos Island: A Place of Fabled Treasure." *New York Times*, January 31, 1932.

Coffman, F.L. *1001 Lost, Buried or Sunken Treasures* New York: Thomas Nelson & Sons, 1957.

Coleman, Bruce. "Deep Sea Divers Set for Adventure." *Daily Independent Journal* December 15, 1964.

Coll, Ray, Jr. "Shoreside Shorts." *Honolulu Advertiser*, January 22, 1935.

"Colorful Charity Ball Scheduled for Tonight." *The Washington Evening Star* December 5, 1928.

Committee on Military Affairs, U.S. Senate. Bill, Appointing army field clerks and field clerks, Quartermaster Corps, warrant officers, U.S. Army: hearing before the Committees on Military Affairs, Congress of the United States, §. H.R. 9512 (1926).

"Company to Dedicate New Office Saturday Evening." *Bakersfield Californian*, May 19, 1939.

"'Constellation,' Largest Sailing Ship to Dock Here in Many Years, Prepares for Another Expedition." *The Wave* August 15, 1935.

"The Courts." *Leavenworth Times* March 3, 1891.

"The Courts, District Court." *Leavenworth Times* March 3, 1891.

Craig, John D. *Danger Is My Business*. New York: Simon and Schuster, 1938.

"Crew of Nine Missing After Tug Sinks; Blast Rocks Ship, Debris Only Remains." *San Bernardino Daily Sun* November 22, 1926.

Day, Jim. "Pipefuls." *Bakersfield Californian*, May 9, 1939.

"Death in the Deep." *PIC Magazine* VIII, no. 4, August 20, 1940.

"Deep Sea Gold Taker Here to Pay 'Old Debt.'" *San Francisco Chronicle*, September 3, 1937.

"Deep Sea Gold Taker Here to Pay Off 'Old Debt.'" *San Francisco Chronicle* September 3, 1937, sec. Second.

"Deep Sea Treasure Hunter Keeps Busy on Books in Ridge Studio." *Chico Enterprise-Record* August 20, 1964.

Delano, Leonard H. *Sunken Klondike Gold: How A Lost Fortune Inspired an Ambitious Effort to Raise the S.S.* Islander Newberg, OR: Delano Pub., 2011.

Delgado, James P., and Stephen A. Haller. "Submerged Cultural Resource Assessment: Golden Gate National Recreation Area, Gulf of the Farallones National Marine Sanctuary, and Point Reyes National Seashore §" (1989).

"DePriest Incident Hit by Klan Ruler: Imperial Wizard Is Speaker at Big Mass Meeting Held in Forestville, MD." *The Washington Post* July 7, 1929.

"Discovery of Secret Safe Spurs Hopes of More Intrigue." *Sun-Journal* May 16, 1991.

"Display Ad, I Dive for Treasure." *Los Angeles Times*, May 17, 1942.

"'Dive' for Dollars." *Variety*, February 2, 1950.

"Divers Describe Furious Battles with Devilfish, Find Octopi Lurking About Sunken Treasure Ship." *Chicago Tribune*, August 5, 1934.

"Diving Bell to Seek Sea's Gold." *Seattle Daily Times*, May 1, 1935.

"Diving Bell Will Seek Treasure." *Seattle Daily Times*, March 16, 1935.

"Diving Manual, 1943," United States Navy Department. Bureau of Ships. Washington: U.S. Government Printing Office.

"Diving 'Tank' to Roam the Ocean Bottom." *Popular Science Monthly*, December 1949.

Dodd, Mead mss., 1855–1992, Authors, Publishers, and Other Correspondents; Manuscripts Department, Lilly Library, Indiana University, Bloomington, Indiana.

Douglas, C.L. "Visitor Here Is Planning Hunt for Sunken Treasure, Lieut. Rieseberg Knows Locations of Gold-Laden Wrecks; Will Take Texans Along." *Fort Worth Press* November 6, 1935.

Doukan, Gilbert. *The world beneath the waves (Les deícouvertes sous-Marines Modernes)* Translated by Adrienne Case and R.M. Case. New York: John de Graff, Inc., 1957.

"Drama of the Deep: Octopus vs. Diving Robot." *Newsweek*, October 31, 1938.

Earle, David M. *All Man!: Hemingway, 1950s Men's Magazines, and the Masculine Persona*. Kent, OH: Kent State University Press, 2009.

Edwin A. Link, and Marion Clayton Link Collections, University Libraries, Special Collections; Binghamton University, State University of New York, Binghamton, NY.

Ellen Rieseberg vs. Harry Rieseberg (Galveston County District Clerk October 10, 1940).

Ellen Rieseberg vs. Harry Rieseberg (Galveston County District Clerk September 4, 1940).

Emigration and Immigration: Reports of the Consular Officers of the United States. Washington, D.C.: Government Printing Office, 1887.

Eric P. Strutt vs. Harry E. Rieseberg, Robert W. McBride & Co., a corporation, Dodd Mead and Co, a corporation, Doe One, Doe Two, Doe Third, and Doe Fourth, Case #571352 (Superior Court of the State of California, County of Los Angeles March 17, 1950).

Fan-Fare. "Cecil B. DeMille Is Organizing Treasure Hunt, Director Seeks Loot in Depths of Ocean." *Windsor Daily Star* November 25, 1937, sec. 2.

"Fathoming the Sea." *Focus Magazine* 1, no. 5, October 1938.

"Fitted to a T." *Variety*, April 17, 1952.

"Flash Gordon: Space Soldiers, Captured by Shark Men." United States: Universal Productions, 1936. https://www.youtube.com/watch?v=RA9Ubx30rK0.

"Floating Drydock Would Hoist Sunken Vessels." *Popular Mechanics* 77, no. 2, February 1943.

"For Sale, Trade and Exchange." *The Philatelic West* 59, no. 3 (July 31, 1913).

"Four-Masted Schooner Doris Hamlin." *Baltimore Sun* January 1, 1938.

"Frank Westmore Explains Mask-Making Technique." *Cleveland Plain Dealer*, February 2, 1953.

"Fraternal Organizations, Tall Cedars." *The Washington Post* August 14, 1932.

"Fraternal Organizations, Tall Cedars." *The Washington Post* December 25, 1932.

"Fraternal Organizations, Tall Cedars." *The Washington Post* July 31, 1932.

"Fraternal Organizations, Tall Cedars of Lebanon." *The Washington Post* July 10, 1927.

Friston, Barbara. "High Schools, Lovenberg." *Galveston Daily News*, February 16, 1942.

Furneaux, Rupert. *The Great Treasure Hunts* New York: Taplinger Publishing Company, 1969.

Galveston (TX) City Directory, 1936–1937, p. 306.

Garber, Megan. "Robert Sténuit: The Original Aquanaut." *The Atlantic*, June 12, 2012. https://www.theatlantic.com/technology/archive/2012/06/robert-st-nuit-the-original-aquanaut/258407/.

"Garden Tea Fetes Mrs. H.E. Rieseberg." *Bakersfield Californian*, October 23, 1944.

"Ghost Sea-City Treasure, Old-Home-Week, in News Today; Brides, Babes Dominate." *Bakersfield Californian*, May 22, 1950.

"Giant Octopus in Attack on Deep Sea Diving Bell." *St. Louis Post-Dispatch*, August 14, 1938.

"Giant Octopus Loses Death Battle with Deep Sea Divers." *Kansas City Star* August 28, 1938.

"Giant Octopus Loses Fight to Repulse Invaders of Deep Sea Treasure Lair." *Cleveland Plain Dealer* November 27, 1938.

Goldberg, Robert A. "The Ku Klux Klan in Madison, 1922–1927." *Wisconsin Magazine of History* 58, no. 1 (Autumn 1974): 31–44.

Gordon, Evelyn Peyton. "Guests Dine on Schooner Docked Here." *The Washington Post* October 16, 1934.

Gray, Donald. "Millions in Gold Free for the Taking!" *Modern Mechanics and Inventions*, September 1931.

Gruber, Frank. *The Pulp Jungle*. Los Angeles: Sherbourne Press, Inc., 1967.

Guzzo, Louis R. "Exit Hutton; Enter Treasure Hunter and Rooney." *The Seattle Times*, March 4, 1953.

"Harry Rieseberg Papers," deGrummond Children's Literature Collection, The University of Southern Mississippi; https://www.lib.usm.edu/legacy/degrum/public_html/html/research/findaids/DG0816.html.

Harte, Barbara, and Carolyn Riley, eds. *Contemporary Authors, A Bio-Bibliographical Guide to Current Authors and Their Works*. Vol. 5–8 Gale Research Co, 1964.

Harvey, J., Rieseberg, H.E., Romero, R., & Boetticher, B. "City Beneath the Sea: [film script]/ by Jack Harvey, Final Shooting Script." December 21, 1951, Universal-International Pictures; McFarlin Library Special Collections, University of Tulsa. http://library.utulsa.edu//record=b2178502.

"He Exhibited the Machine, Defendant in Slot-Machine Case Found Guilty." *Seattle Times*, November 17, 1903.

"Helium Method Raises Sunken Treasure." *Modern Mechanix* XIX, no. 5, March 1938.

Hennessy, Mark W. "Mysterious Rejuvenation Famous Windjammer at Boothbay Harbor Reveals New Life for Craft." *Portland Press-Herald* September 18, 1932.

"Henry R. Rieseberg Dies; Former District Resident." *Washington Evening Star* October 24, 1944, sec. A.

"Herstein Goes Literary." *Variety*, July 26, 1948.

"He's Bound for Undersea Treasure." *Chillicothe Constitution* April 27, 1950.

Heuvelmans, Bernard. *Dans le sillage des monstres marins, Le Kraken et le poulpe colossal (In the Wake of Sea-Monsters: The Kraken and the Colossal Octopus)*. Paris: Librarie Plon, 1958.

H.H.T. "The Screen: Four Films Make Debuts Here; 'City Beneath the Sea' Show by State and 'Thunderbirds' Lands at Holiday Theatre." *New York Times*, March 12, 1953, sec. Amusements.

Hoig, Stan. *Fort Reno and the Indian Territory Frontier*. Fayetteville: University of Arkansas Press, 2000.

Holland, Sean. "Salvor, Archeologist Robert Sténuit." *Immersed: The International Technical Diving Magazine*, Spring 1999.

Holliday, Kate. "He Dives for Doubloons." *Coronet* 12, no. 2, June 1942.

"Hollywood Insider." *Variety*, February 12, 1952.

Horner, David L., III. "'Disagrees' (Letter to the Editor)." *Virginia Wildlife*, January 1964.

"Hosiery Special for Susan Ball Personal Appearance Day." *Lansing State Journal* February 12, 1953.

Hubbs, Carl Leavitt (Prof. Dr. PhD). "Shellers from the Past and Present." Accessed April 23, 2023. https://conchology.be/index.php?t=9001&id=21175.

Hunt, Charles J., John C. Cook, Stacy Woodard, W.C. Smith, Lincoln Lions, Tom J. Geraghty, Tom J. Geraghty, Abe Meyer, and Sam K. Wineland. *Samarang*. United States: United Artists Corp., 1933.

Hunt, James W., Personal Research Collection, Boothbay Harbor, ME.

Hunt, James W. Ms. *Changing Tacks* Boothbay Harbor, ME, 1993.

"Hunt for Sunken Gold? It's No Way to Get Rich." *Los Angeles Times*, September 3, 1973.

"In Person Tonight Only!" *Cleveland Plain Dealer*, February 5, 1953.

"The Incredible Petrified World." United States: G.B.M. Productions, 1957. https://archive.org/details/TheIncrediblePetrifiedWorld.

"Ingenious Inventor Dies of Operation." *Spokane Press*, February 12, 1935.

"Internationally Known Authority, Public Notices." *New York Times*, June 16, 1935.

"Into Reverse Gear." *Variety*, June 22, 1951.

Jamieson, Alan G. "A Brief History of Shipwrecks in Literature." *Literary Hub*, November 11, 2022. https://lithub.com/a-brief-history-of-shipwrecks-in-literature/.

Joseph, Charles H. "Random Thoughts, Another

Era of Hate." The Sentinel LXXXII, no. 8, May 22, 1931.

J.W. "Chartroom Chatter: High Costs Let Fantome Go." *Seattle Times*, June 14, 1953.

Kadih, Zee. "Truth and lies Continuum," November 9, 2015. https://prezi.com/t4reydcnfapo/truth-and-lies-continuum/.

Kaiser, Frederick F. *Built on Honor, Sailed with Skill: The American Coasting Schooner* Ann Arbor, MI: Sarah Jennings Press, 1989.

Kelly (pen name), Donald Wright, and Harry E. Rieseberg. "The Mad Cabbie of Cartagena." *Stag*, June 1951.

"Kern Friends Greet Warren." *Bakersfield Californian*, August 18, 1942.

Kester, Frank. "Barkentine Is to Fit Out for Treasure Hunt." *Oakland Tribune* May 20, 1933.

Kitses, Demetrius John. *Budd Boetticher: The Western*. London, England: British Film Institute Education, 1969.

"Ku Klux Membership Falls from 8,904,871 in 1925 to 34,964 Now." *The Washington Post* November 30, 1930.

Kurson, Robert. *Pirate Hunters: Treasure, Obsession, and the Search for a Legendary Pirate Ship*. New York: Random House, 2016.

Labuskes, Brianna. "How the Armed Services Editions Created a Nation of Readers." *Literary Hub* Grove Atlantic and Electric Literature, February 23, 2023. https://lithub.com/how-the-armed-services-editions-created-a-nation-of-readers/.

"Lawsuits Involving Romano Marine Salvage, Record Group 21." Admiralty Case Files, 1929–1942, National Archives and Records Administration, Seattle, WA.

"The Leading Paper in Kansas." *Leavenworth Times* March 17, 1870.

"Legal Notices, Certificate of Business Fictitious Firm Name." *Van Nuys News* April 24, 1952.

Letter from Rieseberg to *Variety*, September 15, 1937; Variety Protected Materials Department Collection, MSS 017. Emerson College Archives and Special Collections. http://public.archspace-prod.emerson.edu/repositories/2/resources/61. Accessed April 18, 2023.

"Liner Egypt Yields £45,000 More Gold." *The New York Times*, July 13, 1935, sec. Social News.

"Lure of Gold Is Inventors' Call Below the Sea." *Seattle Times*, March 14, 1932.

Lutts, Ralph H. *The Nature Fakers: Wildlife, Science, and Sentiment*. Charlottesville: University Press of Virginia, 2011.

MacLean, Nancy. *Behind the Mask of Chivalry: The Making of the Ku Klux Klan*. New York: Oxford University Press, 1994.

"'Madam' Sights Solid 13G Week Tho Most 1st Runs' Biz Spotty." *Variety*, March 10, 1953.

Mahone, James Edwin. "The Definition of Lying and Deception." *Stanford Encyclopedia of Philosophy*, December 25, 2015. https://plato.stanford.edu/entries/lying-definition/#Aca.

"Mala Powers Improves." *Variety*, June 4, 1952.

Mark Herstein, Mark Herstein Agency, and Harold Consweet vs. Harry E. Rieseberg, Albert J. Cohen, Universal Pictures Company, a corporation, Doe One, Doe Two, and Doe Three, No 616825 (Clerk of the Superior Court June 29, 1953).

Marsh, W. Ward. "Premiere of 'City Beneath Sea' for Palace on Thursday." *Cleveland Plain Dealer*, February 1, 1953.

Marx, Robert F., and Jenifer Marx. *The World's Richest Wrecks: A Wreck Diver's Guide to Gold and Silver Treasures of the Seas* Garland, TX: RAM Books, 2009.

Marx, Robert F. *Port Royal Rediscovered* Garden City, NY: Doubleday & Company, 1973.

Marx, Robert F. *Port Royal—The Sunken City* Southend-on-Sea, Essex: Aquapress, 2003.

Matsen, Brad. *Descent: The Heroic Discovery of the Abyss*. New York: Pantheon Books, 2005.

McAllister, Dawson. "8 Different Types of Lies People Tell." February 4, 2023. https://www.thehopeline.com/different-kinds-of-lies-you-tell/.

"Melodrama Scheduled." *Los Angeles Times*, February 26, 1953.

"Michigan Man to Have Own Submarine, Tiny Craft Dives to 600 Feet, Can Stay 30 Hours." *Lansing State Journal* February 28, 1955.

"Monoplane Dives in Lake Waters, Aviator Sticks by Machine to Shut Off Engine." *Los Angeles Times*, July 5, 1911.

Moskowitz, Milton. "Newsstand Strip-Tease." Essay. In *A View of the Nation: An Anthology, 1955–1959*, edited by Henry M. Christman, 76–79. Freeport, NY: Books for Libraries Press, 1970.

"Mrs Alwyn Inness-Brown." *Washington Post* October 13, 1934.

"Narcissistic Personality Disorder," Diseases & Conditions, Patient Care & Health Information, Mayo Clinic. Accessed April 18, 2023. https://www.mayoclinic.org/diseases-conditions/narcissistic-personality-disorder/symptoms-causes/syc-20366662.

"National Boxoffice Survey." *Variety*, April 29, 1953.

"National Order of Protestant Clubs," National Republic Collection, Box 227, Folder 6 (Reel 233) Hoover Institution Archives, Stanford University.

"Navy Diving Bell Tests Take Officer 400 Feet Undersea." *Washington Evening Star* November 4, 1933.

Navy diving school—outtakes. (Fox Movietone News Story 3–138.) Fox Movietone News Collection. Moving Image Research Collections. University of South Carolina. https://digital.tcl.sc.edu/digital/collection/MVTN/id/1336/rec/1.

"News of the Radio World." *Fresno Bee Republican* March 23, 1938.

"No Coal Delivered, Two Are Indicted." *Brooklyn Daily Eagle* February 28, 1934.

"Obituaries, Eric Strutt." *Newport Beach Daily Pilot* September 5, 1997.

"Ocean Gold Quest Halted by Weather." *The Washington Post*, September 4, 1936.

"Off in April to Hunt Sunken Ship's Gold." *New York Times*, February 14, 1932, sec. Financial.

"Only Its First Story, Church of the Good Shepherd Awaits Completion." *The Washington Post*, May 23, 1903, sec. A.

"Only Love Survives 'Sea' Havoc at UI." *Variety*, May 19, 1952.

"Personal." *Topeka Daily Capital* December 7, 1881.

Peterson, R.J. "Early Sailors Did Not Have Such Easy Berths (Letter to the Editor)." *New York Times*, April 26, 1943.

"Plan Proposed to Salvage Sunken Freighters After War." *Atlanta Constitution* October 12, 1942.

Potter, John S., Jr. *The Treasure Divers of Vigo Bay* New York: Doubleday & Co., 1958.

"President's Son as a Sunday School Teacher." *New York Times*, July 18, 1904.

"A Proven Success, Big Money for All. Business Opportunities." *The Sun and the New York Herald* August 8, 1920.

Pryor, Thomas M. "Multi-Hued Hollywood, Industry to Make 128 Tinted Films Over Next Six Months—Man Made Temblor." *New York Times*, May 25, 1952.

"A Publicity Gimmick Spoiled by Actress." *Kansas City Star* February 8, 1953.

"Queens Sea Scouts to Visit Four-Masted Schooner." *Brooklyn Daily Eagle* October 31, 1935.

"Radio Programs for Friday." *San Diego Union* March 10, 1950.

Register of enlistments in the United States Army, 1798–1914. Washington, D.C.: National Archives and Records Administration, 1956.

Reil, Frank. "Moses Not Only Built Belt Parkway but He Gave Us Brand New Shoreline." *Brooklyn Daily Eagle* July 12, 1940.

Report of Special Study of Securities Markets, Chapter IV § (1962).

Rieseberg, Eric F. *Heroes Alongside Us*. Naples, FL: Salt Island Publishing, 2014.

Rieseberg, Harry E. "Are There Slackers in the Ku Klux Klan." *The Kourier: The Magazine of Americanism* 5, no. 2, January 1929.

Rieseberg, Harry E. "Arizona, The Land of Mystery." *Arizona* 3, no. 9, July 1913.

Rieseberg, Harry E. "Ask Adventure." *Adventure* 41, no. 1, June 10, 1923.

Rieseberg, Harry E. "Ask Adventure." *Adventure* 45, no. 2, February 20, 1924.

Rieseberg, Harry E. "Billions Waiting to Be Taken." *Popular Mechanics* 77, no. 5, May 1942.

Rieseberg, Harry E. "Boy Meets Teddy." *Together Magazine* 2, no. 5, May 15, 1958.

Rieseberg, Harry E. "City Beneath the Sea." *Los Angeles Times*, October 13, 1940, sec. Sunday Magazine.

Rieseberg, Harry E. "Coconino Jim, Lumberjack." *The Coconino Sun* September 15, 1915.

Rieseberg, Harry E. "Go Down to the Sea … for Gold!" *Los Angeles Times*, Sunday Magazine, January 7, 1934.

Rieseberg, Harry E. "Hidden Treasure Waters of the Americas." *Cleveland Plain Dealer*, Magazine Section. November 26, 1933.

Rieseberg, Harry E. "I Battled an Octopus for Treasure." *Mechanix Illustrated* XXIII, no. 1, November 1939.

Rieseberg, Harry E. "*I Battled the Deadly Octopus.*" *True Comics and Adventure Stories*, January 1965.

Rieseberg, Harry E. "I Walked the Streets of a Sunken City." *Portland Oregonian*, August 1, 1943, American Weekly Insert edition.

Rieseberg, Harry E. "In Cattle Land, The Old Santa Fe Trail (Among Our Poets)." *The Santa Fe Magazine*, December 1915.

Rieseberg, Harry E. "Last Voyages of American Clipper Ships Are Writing Finis to Glorious Era of Adventure." *The Washington Post*, October 29, 1933.

Rieseberg, Harry E. "The Lights of Clarkdale (Poem), Into the Land of Yavapai (Article)." *Progressive Arizona* 2, no. 5, May 1926.

Rieseberg, Harry E. "Los Tesoros Del Fondo Del Mar!" *Prensa*, February 18, 1934.

Rieseberg, Harry E. "Mechanical 'Lobster.'" *Mechanix Illustrated* XXXIX, no. 1, November 1947.

Rieseberg, Harry E. "Mystery Ships Add Exciting Chapter to Lore of the Sea." *The Washington Post* January 7, 1934.

Rieseberg, Harry E. "Octopus Battles Shark to Death in Undersea Duel." *SPORT Magazine*, November 1941.

Rieseberg, Harry E. "Octopus! Terror of the Deep." *Mechanix Illustrated*, February 1939.

Rieseberg, Harry E. "Old Chinatown." *Every Where* XXX, no. 6 (August 1912): 329–32.

Rieseberg, Harry E. "Safety on the Bottom." *Virginia Wildlife* XXIV, no. 10, October 1963.

Rieseberg, Harry E. "Sea of Treasure (Series of 9)." *The Rudder*, 1954.

Rieseberg, Harry E. "The Story Behind Cocos Island and the 'Loot of Lima.'" *Pacific Discovery* IV, no. 6 (1951): 4–15.

Rieseberg, Harry E. "To the Highest Peaks in Arizona." *Progressive Arizona* 3, September 1926.

Rieseberg, Harry E. "Treasures at the Bottom of the Sea." *The Sunday Oregonian*, Magazine Section. November 19, 1933.

Rieseberg, Harry E. "'X' Marks Nothing on Cocos." *Los Angeles Times*, February 11, 1940, sec. Sunday Magazine.

Rieseberg, Harry E. *I Dive for Treasure* New York: Frederick Fell, 1970.

Rieseberg, Harry E. *I Dive for Treasure* New York: Robert M. McBride and Co., 1942.

Rieseberg, Harry E. Map. *A Treasure Hunter's Map of the West Indies* Van Nuys, CA: Scale approx. 1:8,000,000, 1951. University of Illinois at Urbana-Champaign.

Rieseberg, Harry E. *Treasure Hunter* New York: Robert M. McBride & Company, 1945.

Rieseberg, Harry E, and Eric P. Strutt. *Ms. Neptune's Treasure, A New, Different, and Original Radio Program for Sponsorship* Hollywood, CA, 1939.

"Rieseberg May Buy Victoria." *Seattle Times*, March 6, 1953.

Riley, George D. "The Federal Diary." *The Washington Post* January 9, 1933.

Robert L. Royall vs. The Romano Submarine Engineering & Salvage Corporation (City Court, Queens County, New York June 4, 1936).

Robinson, Frank M., and Lawrence Davidson. *Pulp Culture: The Art of Fiction Magazines* Portland, OR: Collectors Press, 1998.

Robot Sous-Marin (Underwater Robot), Reference No: PJ 1935 291 7. GP Archives, 1935. https://gparchives.com/index.php?urlaction=doc&tab=showStory&id_doc=10559&rang=7.

"Robots Will Aid Search for Lost Sea Treasures." *Los Angeles Times*, October 31, 1937, sec. 2.

Rogers, Dan. "Four-Master Constellation Sails to See Sunken Treasure with Two Robot Divers." *Portland Press Herald* August 21, 1936.

"Romano Marine Salvage Co," Securities Division, Washington State Archives, Washington Secretary of State, Olympia, WA.

"Sad." *The Oologist*, 305, XXIX, no. 12 (December 15, 1912): 390.

"Salvage Firm to Raise Tug Sunk Seven Years Ago." *Seattle Times*, July 23, 1933.

Schallert, Edwin. "Dvorak Makes Transit from Model to Moll; 'Bulldog' Beckons Brando." *Los Angeles Times*, May 13, 1950.

Schallert, Edwin. "'I Dived for Treasure' Unusual Film Project; Adele Jergens in 'Doom.'" *Los Angeles Times*, December 6, 1949.

Schallert, Edwin. "McGuire, Keel Hinted for 'Leopold's Crown,' Holloway Gets Break." *Los Angeles Times*, October 15, 1951.

Schallert, Edwin. "Vittoria Gassman Will Costar with Stanwyck." *Los Angeles Times*, March 2, 1953, sec. III.

Scheuer, Philip K. "Divers in Caribbean Tale Lusty." *Los Angeles Times*, March 7, 1953.

Schneider, Stephen. *Iced: The Story of Organized Crime in Canada*. Mississauga, Ontario: Wiley, 2009.

"Schooner as Cruise Ship, Motorless Windjammer to Take Passengers on West Indies Trip." *New York Times*, January 19, 1936.

"Schooner Revives Memories of Old Days." *Washington Evening Star* October 2, 1934.

"Schooner to Leave in Quest for Gold, Lieut. Rieseberg to Pilot Vessel Down Potomac to Spot Off Haiti." *Washington Evening Star*, Sunday Edition, April 28, 1935.

"Schwartz Snags Rights to Treasure-Trove Tale." *Variety*, May 18, 1949.

"Science News." *Pottstown Mercury* January 11, 1934.

Science News Digest, May 7, 1935; Smithsonian Institution Archives. Record Unit 7091, Box 373, Folder 37.

Scrimshaw. "The Shipmodeler, Treasure Hunter." *Hobbies, The Magazine for Collectors* 40, no. 1, September 1935.

"Searches for 'stmr Roanoke' and "steamer Roanoke,' 1911." California Digital Newspaper Collection. Accessed February 8, 2023. http://cdnc.ucr.edu/.

"Seattle-Built and Invented Aeroplane to Fly at Potlatch." *Seattle Times*, June 8, 1912.

"Seattle-Built and Invented Aeroplane to Fly at Potlatch." *Seattle Times* June 8, 1912.

"Shark-Octopus Undersea Battle Filmed." *Modern Mechanix*, July 1933.

Shaub, Earl L. "Firms to Get Coal Sunk in Ships at Sea." *San Antonio Evening News* January 16, 1923.

"Ships Scrapped." *Tipton Tribune* January 28, 1930.

Smith, Pauline. "He Walks with Davey Jones." *PIC Magazine*, January 1956.

Smith, Ted. "Beauty Joins Treasure Hunt, Figureheads of Old Clippers South Off Golden Gate." *San Francisco News*, February 27, 1953.

"Society." *The Washington Post* August 6, 1911, Sunday edition.

"Society." *The Washington Star* August 6, 1911, Sunday edition, sec. 7.

"'Soldier of Fortune' Tells His Story Here." *Saginaw News* February 15, 1953.

"Spring Treasure-Hunting." *The New York Times*, March 27, 1939.

Stafford, I.G. "Texas City, Town Talk." Galveston Daily News. November 22, 9136.

Stone, Peter. "Interview with Robert Marx." *Classic Dive Books*, September 1977. http://classicdivebooks.customer.netspace.net.au/oeclassics-a-marx-interview.html.

Strutt, Eric. "He Walks with Davy Jones." *Arizona Republic* December 28, 1941.

"Student Arriving for Christmas Holidays Complete Family Circles." *Galveston Daily News*, December 19, 1937.

"Sunken Treasure Lures Salvager." *Oakland Tribune* May 18, 1937.

"Tall Cedars 4-Day Assembly Nearing, 100 Bands Will Attend Gala National Gathering of Masons in May." *The Washington Post* March 19, 1933.

"Tall Cedars Honor New York Leader." *The Washington Evening Star* October 30, 1928.

"Theodore Roosevelt, Jr., Teaches in Sunday School." *The Washington Evening Star*, April 2, 1905, sec. 2.

"Three Hollywood Visitors (Photo)." *Detroit Free Press*, February 20, 1953.

"Title Tribulation." *Variety*, February 21, 1952.

"To Be Used on Treasure Hunt." *Motor Boating* 92, no. 2, August 1953.

"To Raise the Lusitania, Divers to Attempt Recovery of Six Millions in Gold on Sunken Vessel." *Wellsboro Gazette* July 5, 1922.

"Treasure!, Business Opportunities." *San Antonio Light* December 12, 1936, sec. 7.

"Treasure Hunt." *Mansfield News-Journal* September 1, 1936.

"Treasure Hunt Trap Displayed, Diving Sphere with Claws Shown." *Pittsburgh Post-Gazette*, May 18, 1935.

"The Treasure Hunters." *Popular Mechanics*, August 1934.

"Trio Wrongly Imprisoned to Talk Tuesday." *Harrisburg Telegraph* December 14, 1940.

"Two Held as Swindlers by 'Treasure Hunt,' Boston Brokers Are Accused of Taking Woman's $38,000 to Finance Undersea Search." *New York Times*, October 13, 1935.

"Two More Are Held in Salvage Swindle." *Daily Boston Globe*, November 23, 1934.

Tyrer, A.J. "Navigation Bureau Arm of Commerce; Enforcement of Difficult Maritime Laws Supervised by Officials." *The Washington Post* December 31, 1931.

"UI Will Tie in TV on 3-Way Ballyhoo Binge for 'City.'" *Variety*, January 28, 1953.

Underwater Salvage Device, United States. Patent number US2040956, filed (March 27, 1933) and issued (May 19, 1936).

Une Nouvelle Cloche a Plongeurs (A New Diving Bell), Reference No. 3523GJ00008. GP Archives, 1935. https://gparchives.com/index.php?urlaction=doc&tab=showStory&id_doc=201785&rang=8&langue=EN.

"United States World War II Draft Registration Cards, 1942." Provo, UT, n.d. Accessed April 8, 2016.

U.S. Navy Standard Deep Sea Diving Outfit Training Film, 43424 NA. Periscope Film | YouTube, 1950. https://youtu.be/1cwYe9gga9k.

Wagner, Albert C. "Washington Club Notes." *Hobbies, The Magazine for Collectors* 40, no. 1, March 1935.

"Wants Legal Residence Here, Washington Boy Makes a Strange Request of the County Clerk's Office." *Leavenworth Times* March 27, 1909.

Warner, Arthur. "Sunken Gold, Now as Ever, Lures Man; Science, Adventure and the Gambling Instinct All Play a Role in an Endless Search for Treasure-Laden Hulks." *The New York Times, New York Times Magazine*, August 9, 1931.

Weiner, Sam. "'Thar's Gold in Them Thar Seas,' Is Belief of Man Who Plans Lost Treasure Expedition." *Galveston Tribune* January 6, 1936.

Wells, Jay, ed. "Yacht Fantome Doomed to Sail to Scrap Heap." *Seattle Times*, March 14, 1953.

"West Texas Oil Man Plans $10,000,000 Salvage Craft." *El Paso Herald-Post* February 15, 1937.

Whicker, Johanna Loesche. "The Four-Masted Schooner 'Constellation' (Es Sally Persis Noyes)." Nautical Research Journal 7, no. 7–8 (1955): 108–12.

Who's Who in the World, 2000: Millennium Edition New Providence, NJ: Marquis Who's Who, 1999.

"Wido File Action in Alleged Swindle, Names Boston Pair in Deal to Salvage Sunken Ship." *Daily Boston Globe*, January 25, 1933.

"Will Not Re-Float British Freighter." *Lansing State Journal* April 10, 1939.

Williams, Joseph A. *Seventeen Fathoms Deep: The Saga of the Submarine S-4 Disaster* Chicago, IL: Chicago Review Press Incorporated, 2015.

Williams, Ralph C. *The United States Public Health Service, 1798–1950.* Washington, D.C.: Commissioned Officers Association of the United States Public Health Service, 1951.

Wilson, Charles Morrow. "Now Comes a New Day of Treasure Hunting." *The New York Times*, May 29, 1932, sec. SM.

Windham, Perry, Jr. "Speak Up (Letters to the Editor), Rieseberg Weapon." *PIC Magazine* VIII, no. 10, November 12, 1940.

"A World Brotherhood of Boys, Over-Land and Over-Seas Correspondence Club." *Boys' Life—The Boy Scouts' Magazine* VI, no. 1, March 1916.

Wright, Lawrence. *Going Clear: Scientology, Hollywood, and the Prison of Belief* New York: A.A. Knopf, 2013.

"Yarns of Fabulous Riches on Ocean Floor Fill Treasury Files, but 100% Record of Salvage Failures Dims U.S. Reward Hope." *The Washington Post*, October 11, 1936.

"Young Adventurer to Be on Lusitania Job." *The Oshkosh Northwestern* February 28, 1936.

Index

Admiral Farragut 17
Adventures in Underwater Treasure Hunting (1965) 213
Arizona 22–23, 28, 32–36, 40–41, 47, 111, 214, 220

Bagnaud, Michel 215–216
Bahada 66–67
Baker, Michael 176
Balboa Pavilion 174–175
Ball, Suzan 185, 188–190
Beebe, William 50, 106, 117, 206, 221
Below the Sea (1933) 117–119
Berge, Victor 133, 143–145
Berry, S. Stillman 204
Big Lie 222
Bobbs-Merrill Co. 195
Boetticher, Oscar "Budd" 184–188
Bogart, Humphrey 178
Bond, R.T. 204
Boothbay Harbor, Maine 9, 70, 87, 89
Bowdoin, Harry 65
De Braak 52, 99, 115
Breder, Charles M., Jr. 204
Broiled Sea Cow 71
Brother Jonathan 52, 99, 115, 218
Buffalo Bill (William F. Cody) 5, 14
Buffum, Ray 182–183

Camp Lee 33
Campbell, Sir Malcolm 121
Carey, Bill 78–79
El Capitan 195
Carleton, Will 169
Carpenter, J.W. 74–77
Carver, Bernard Ralph 94
Carver, Ellen (wife) *see* Rieseberg, Ellen Carver
Chambrun, Jacques 196–197
Charroux, Robert 216
chickens 158, 165, 174
Church of the Good Shepherd 134–135
Churchill, Allen 128, 133, 147, 152, 157
City Beneath the Sea (1953) *see* Rieseberg, Harry Earl, movies
City of Rio de Janeiro 200
Clausen, Carl 221

Coastal School of Deep-Sea Diving *see* Mikalow, Alfred Alexander, Jr.
Cocos Island 120–121, 123, 124, 150, 205, 215
Coffman, F.L. (Ferris LaVerne) 211–212
Cohen, Albert J. 178–184, 191–192
Coler, Wendell P. 28–29, 31
Coll, Ray, Jr. 74
Collins, C.W. 25, 29
Coney Island 106, 221
Connelly, Thomas P. 87–88, 99, 104
Conqueror 68, 89
Conrad, William 179
Constellation 9–13, 69–104, 108–110, 114, 195, 198
Cornsweet, Harold 177, 183, 191–192
Craig, John 54–55, 117–118
Cumming, Hugh S. 35
Curran, James 166–167
Curtis, Charles 15, 21

DeMille, Cecil B. 7, 104, 117
diving: hard hat 2, 6, 56–57, 60, 76, 83, 99, 106, 112–115, 119, 141, 187, 207, 209, 214; scuba 140, 207–209, 212
diving bells: Nohl (Hell Below) 58; Romano 3, 9–11, 60–61, 64–69, 73–87, 89–91, 95, 102, 104–106, 108–110, 114, 117–120, 129, 136, 140–141, 145, 159, 171, 181, 195, 201, 221; Wiley 61, 65
Diving for Sunken Treasure (1955) 194
diving robot *see* diving bells
Dodd, Mead & Co. 173, 178, 180–181, 184, 191, 196–197, 204, 213
Doris Hamlin 108
Dougherty, Margaret E. 218
Doukan, Gilbert 207
Dow, Peggy 183

Earl of Abergavenny 92
Eggers, George 94–96
Egypt 49, 61
Empire Marine Salvage and Engineering 87–90, 103
Escape Radio series *see* Rieseberg, Harry Earl, radio

Fantome 198–199
Fell, Frederick 213, 218
Fish, Frank 199–200
Fleming, Mrs. R.S. 109
Fleming, Ralph 4, 9–11, 65–68, 73–75, 78–87, 90–91, 108
Fort Reno 14, 19
Fort Whipple 32–36, 129

Gainfort, John 124–159, 163–164, 176, 183, 197
Galveston 7, 94–96, 98–100, 111–112, 115–116, 195, 201, 220
General Service Studios 178
Golden Hind 77
Gore, Jack 166
Government Printing Office 14, 111
Great Depression 2, 7, 48–49, 58, 69, 169
Gruber, Frank 141–142
Guide to Sunken Treasure Ships of the World (1965) 213

Hale, Jonathan 206
Hammond, Mickey Ann *see* wife, wonderful
Hammond, Rockwell, Jr. 10, 62, 63, 64, 107
Hampton, Ruth 189
Hancock, G. Allan 101
Harborside Warehouse Company 91, 106, 110
hard hat diving *see* diving, hard hat
Harvey, Jack 183
Hattie, Hilo 185
Hayes, Grace 127
Heller, Edmond 18
Hendricks Lake 93
Herstein, Mark 177, 179, 183, 191–192
Hird, Edwin A., Jr. 182
Horch, Franz J. 173
Horner, L. David, III 212
Hubbard, L. Ron 108
Hubbs, Carl Leavitt 202–207, 222
Huckins, Charles W. 198
Huse, Harry 90
Hussar 52, 99

I Dive for Treasure 12–13, 17, 18, 19, 26, 58, 80, 84, 86, 94, 95, 98,

253

99, 101, 114, 120, 123, 124, 126–127, 134, 135, 140, 143–146, 157, 159, 162, 163, 165, 167, 169–170, 172–173, 177–178–180, 182–184, 191, 194–196, 201, 203–204, 206–209, 213, 218
Inness-Brown, Alwyn 70
Islander 52, 61, 65, 198

Jaquette, Arabel 136
John Dwight 117
John Sealy Hospital 94, 111

Karbe, J. William 97, 104–110
Kelley, Don Greame 205
Kelly, Donald Wright *see* Rieseberg, Harry Earl, pseudonym
Kettner, John H. 25, 30–31, 38
Kieran, James M., Jr. 130, 133, 148
King, C.W. 27, 29
King, Ernest J. 68
King Kong (1933) 119
Klinger, Harry 176

Lake, Simon 92, 99
Lanier, Henry Wysham 133, 143–145, 148, 152, 160, 163, 165
Larson, Olaf 65
Lawler, J. Howard 79, 82
Leavenworth, Kansas 14–16, 73, 94
Leavitt, Benjamin Frankin 105
lobster, mechanical *see* tank, underwater
Loesche, Alvin and Johanna (Hanni) 4, 70–71, 78, 82–89, 96, 103–104, 110–111
Lowe, Caroline (wife) *see* Rieseberg, Caroline Lowe
Lowe, William 28
Lundt, Earnest G. 110
Lusitania 105

Macfarlane, William 27–31
Magruder, Fred 31, 92, 97
Martin, Colin T. 21
Marton, Elizabeth 196–197, 199
Marx, Robert 139–140, 207–208, 221
Masonic order 24–25, 28, 42–44, 46, 72, 97, 109, 111, 200, 220–221, 223
Matsen, Brad 106, 221
McBride, Robert M., and Company 125, 128, 130, 133, 136–138, 142, 144, 147, 150, 152, 157, 159, 162–166, 168–169, 173–173, 176, 180, 191, 204
McCarey, Leo 127, 147, 167
Meeker, Kenneth 136
Merida 52, 65, 69, 88, 99, 110, 115, 123, 201, 219
Mikalow, Alfred Alexander, Jr. 194, 199, 200–201, 213–214, 219–220
Miller, Gerrit S. 16–17
Miller, Robert C. 205–206

Miner, E. J. 90
Miss Adventure Falls (Mary Oceaneer, Disneyworld) 221
Moskowitz, Milton 170
movies *see* Rieseberg, Harry Earl, movies
Muhl, Edward 183
museum, floating *see* Treasurama
My Compass Points to Treasure (1955) 194

narcissism 1, 12, 102–103, 214
Nassour, Edward 178
nature fakery *see* Hubbs, Carl Leavitt
Nohl, Max Eugene (Gene) 58–59, 114, 117–118

octopus 1, 3, 6–7, 54, 99, 104, 112, 117–120, 124, 142–145, 158–159, 170, 182–183, 195, 198, 201–207, 209, 222–223
O'Neal, John 108–109
Ormsby, A.A. 28
Owen, Frank 167

patents 6, 8–9, 60–65, 74, 77, 82, 90, 105, 110, 160
Pauker, Edmond (Pauker Agency) 124–125, 127–128, 130–133, 143, 147–150, 153–157, 160, 164–170, 173, 176–178, 181, 183, 196–197, 199
Pearl Diver 133, 143–145
Pearl Harbor 128
Peterson, R. J. 89
Phipps, William 4, 103, 127, 131, 146–147, 167–168, 197
Plimmer, Denis 128–130, 133, 139–140, 148, 163–164
Port Royal 6–7, 120, 123, 124, 138–140, 165, 177–179, 181–187, 192, 195, 201, 206
Port Sinister 184
Potter, John S., Jr. 208–209
Powers, Mala 185, 187–188
pulp magazines 169–171
Pyne, Leo C. 79–80

Quinn, Anthony 185–187, 193

Randall, Charles 27–28
Revelle, Roger 205
Rieseberg, Caroline Lowe 24–25, 27, 29–36, 41, 71, 155
Rieseberg, Ellen Carver 33–37, 41–42, 71–73, 91, 94–95, 100, 111–112, 155, 220
Rieseberg, Harry Earl: arrest 20; death 218; divorces 34, 36, 73, 112; education 15; employment 8, 13, 15–16, 19, 20–27, 31, 32, 36–37, 116–117, 129, 135, 158, 174–175; fraternal organizations 13, 24, 42–43, 46, 72; ghostwriters 125–128, 130; 133, 150–152, 167; investigations 25, 27–28, 35, 44, 71–72; Ku Klux Klan 43–45, 193; lawsuits 179–180, 191–192; marriages 24, 36, 166; movies 130, 148–149, 175–192, 195, 205–206; passport 135; photos 6, 141; plagiarism 23, 122, 143–145, 151; poetry 2, 7, 22–23, 28, 32–34, 41, 122, 169; pseudonym 174; radio 31, 179, 181; reserve duty 41, 53, 141
Rieseberg, Henry Earl (son) 41–42, 71, 94–95, 100, 111, 214–217
Rieseberg, Henry Robert (father) 14–15, 21, 32, 92, 100, 111, 166–167
Rieseberg, Hunter (grandson) 223
Rieseberg, Jennie Martin (mother) 14–15, 32, 92, 100, 131, 163
Rieseberg, Marilyn 42, 214–217
Rieseberg, Robert W. (son) 12, 27, 30, 32, 35–36, 41–42, 71, 215, 270
Rieseberg, Shirley Ellen (daughter) 41, 71, 94, 100, 111, 215, 220
Rieseberg, Valentine Curran Gore 166–167, 193–194, 213–216
Roanoke 17
Romano, Eugene 9–10, 61–64, 68, 73–75
Romano diving robot *see* diving bells
Romano Marine Salvage 64–69, 76, 78, 104–106, 109
Romano Special 63–64
Romano Submarine Engineering and Salvage Corporation 10–11, 74–79, 83, 85–86, 90, 104, 108–109
Romanoplane 62–63
Romero, Ramon 183
Roosevelt, Theodore 5, 18–19, 133, 135, 202, 211
Roosevelt, Theodore, Jr. 133–135
Royall, Robert 9–10, 69–71, 73–79, 82, 85–90, 96, 108
Ryan, Robert 185, 187

Sagamore 79
Sally Persis Noyes 69
San Miguel 102
Sanders, H.E "Savvy" 67
Santa Paula 189
Santa Rosa 93
Schmidt, Waldo L. 204
Schneer, Charles H. 182
Scott, Charles F. 16
Scripps Institution of Oceanography *see* Hubbs, Carl Leavitt
scuba *see* diving, scuba
Seth Parker 114
Silver Shoals 6, 80, 118, 123, 124
Sisson, Eugene 78, 80
Smith, Paula 196

Index

Smithsonian Institution 5, 13, 15–20, 109, 135, 155, 204
Spence, E. Lee 209
Spitz, Henry (Hank) 184
Sténuit, Robert 208
Stepanek, Karel 185
Strode, Woody 185
Strutt, Eric 121–130, 133, 138–139, 144, 150–152, 155, 160, 165, 179–180, 191
Sucich, Charles 220

Tall Cedars of Lebanon 43, 46–47
tank, underwater 6, 171–173, 181, 198, 201, 213
Taylor, Edward R. 104
Tele-Radio Inc. 177, 179
tongs, giant 6, 160–163, 171
Treasurama 197–200
treasure hunting 49–53, 56, 85, 88, 93, 98, 99, 100, 107, 121
Treasure of the Buccaneer Sea (1962) 213
Treasure Trove Club of New York 210
Trevor, Arthur H. 189

Undersea Explorers Legion 107
U.S. Navy Diving School 56–57, 113–114
U.S. Patent Office *see* patents

Van Slyke, Arthur 103
Victoria 197

Warren, Charles 160, 166, 172, 198, 213
Westmore, Frank 188–189
White, Henry J. 206
wife, wonderful *see* Hammond, Mickey Ann
Wiley, Carl 61, 65–66, 198
Wiley, Elbert 65
Wolcott, Charles D. 18
Wray, Fay 119
Wright, George 58, 98

Zoes, James E. 198

www.ingramcontent.com/pod-product-compliance
Lightning Source LLC
Chambersburg PA
CBHW060339010526
44117CB00017B/2884